# Bobby Fischer: A Study
# of His Approach to Chess

*Chess is a matter of delicate judgement;
knowing when to punch and how to duck.*

Bobby Fischer, *Boys' Life*, June 1968

## Cadogan Chess Books

*Executive Editor:* PAUL LAMFORD
*Adviser:* MALCOLM PEIN, IM
*Russian Series Editor:* KEN NEAT

Some other general titles for the keen student:

**The Application of Chess Theory**
Geller

**Dynamic Chess Strategy**
Suba

**From the Middlegame into the Endgame**
Mednis

**From the Opening into the Endgame**
Mednis

**The Games of Tigran Petrosian, Volumes 1 & 2**
Shekhtman

**New World Chess Champion**
Kasparov

**Test and Improve Your Chess**
Alburt

**The Test of Time**
Kasparov

**Three Steps to Chess Mastery**
Suetin

For a complete catalogue of Cadogan Chess Books (which includes the former Pergamon and Maxwell Macmillan chess lists), please write to:

**Cadogan Books, 38 Warren Street, London W1P 5PD**
**Tel: 071 388 2410     Fax: 071 388 2407**

# Bobby Fischer: A Study of His Approach to Chess

by
**Elie Agur**

with a foreword by
**Garry Kasparov**

CADOGAN
**CHESS**
KNIGHTSBRIDGE, LONDON

# CADOGAN BOOKS
# DISTRIBUTION

**UK/EUROPE/AUSTRALASIA/ASIA/AFRICA**
**Distribution:** Grantham Book Services Ltd, Isaac Newton Way, Alma Park Industrial Estate, Grantham, Lincs NG31 9SD. Tel: 0476 67421; Fax: 0476 590223.

**USA/CANADA/LATIN AMERICA/JAPAN**
**Distribution:** Macmillan Distribution Center, Front & Brown Streets, Riverside, New Jersey 08075, USA. Tel: (609) 461 6500; Fax: (609) 764 9122.

---

First published 1992


**Library of Congress Cataloging-in-Publication Data**
(applied for)


**British Library Cataloguing in Publication Data**
A CIP catalogue record for this book is available from the British Library


ISBN  1 85744 013


Cover by Pintail Design
Printed in Great Britain by BPCC Wheatons Ltd, Exeter

# Contents

What's in a Style?   1

Pawn Structure   8
  The G-Pawn   21
  The Pawn Chain I   24
  The Pawn Chain II   28
  The Pawn Triangle   31
  The King's Indian Centre   35

Piece Placement   40
  Exceptional Set-Ups   49

Material Considerations   52

Timing   58

Strategy   64
  Strategic Plans   64
  Seizing the Initiative   70
  Typical Manoeuvres   76
  The Art and Craft of Liquidation   84
  Maintaining the Positional Tension   96
  Switching Advantages   105
  Playing for Space   111
  The Role of Aesthetics   114
  The Poetry of Empty Squares   120

Clarity   128

Straightforwardness   136

Alertness   144

Reducing the Opponent's Options   150

Playing to Win   157
  The Will to Win   157
  Active Defence and Counterplay   161
  Taking Risks   176

Practical Chances                                                185
   Exploiting Practical Chances                  185
   Traps                                         187

Tactics                                                         192
   Tactical Insight                              192
   Double-Edged and Speculative Chess            197
   Missing Tactical Tricks                       207

Technical Aspects                                               214
   Technique                                     214
   The Bishop Pair                               223
   Rook Endgames with Bishops of Opposite Colours  228

Superficiality                                                  233

Misplaying Won Positions                                        237

Typical Blunders and Oversights                                 241

Towards a Comprehensive Vision                                  249
   The Grand Lines                               249
   The Unified Vision                            253

Epilogue                                                        259

References                                                      261

# Foreword

I still remember the days of the World Championship match between Spassky and Fischer in 1972.

I was a nine-year-old boy making the first steps in his chess career, back in peaceful Baku.

I knew of course that Spassky, the reigning World Champion, was a very strong player, but I had the idea that Fischer, my chess idol then, was a player of another calibre, someone in a class of his own.

The chess scene has changed a lot since then, and I, too, have made some progress in those twenty years ...

When I compare my own career with that of Fischer, I have to admit that I enjoyed a certain advantage over him. He had no-one besides himself to draw him up to the heights he reached, whereas I have been privileged in having a high-class player like Karpov, who forced me to exert myself and advance ever higher.

If one may judge a player's strength by comparing him with his contemporaries, it seems to me that Fischer's achievement is unsurpassed – the gap between him and his closest rivals was the widest there ever was between a World Champion and the other top-ranking players of his time. He was some 10-15 years ahead of his time in his preparation and understanding. This could be attributed in part to his dedication to the game, which was unequalled by any other player before or since.

I regard him as a mythological combination of sorts, a centaur if you will, a synthesis between man and chess.

It isn't this or that game of his which impresses me, though he played many remarkable games. It is his out and out professional attitude to the game and his fighting qualities that appeal to me so much.

Fischer was the first real professional player to emerge on the chess stage, and as far as this is concerned, I hope to be considered his follower.

Studying Fischer's games is important, I think, for any player of any playing strength. Above all, it will give you a good idea how to approach the game, or, to put it another way, it will change your attitude to the game in a way that is bound to improve your own play.

GARRY KASPAROV

# Introduction

Another book on Bobby Fischer – what for? More books have been written about him than any other chess player, so why yet another one?

I could answer this question by pointing out that no serious book has been written about him in more than a decade and a half, or say that he, nonentheless, remains enigmatic as both chess player and person.

Whereas the first is true, the second part is not, or at least not wholly so. Many interesting and revealing things have been written about Fischer, and as a matter of fact one of the objectives of this book was to give a panoramic impression of the player and the views held about his play by other players and critics.

As the title indicates, there was a second aim in writing this book: 'Study' and 'Approach to Chess' – the terminology discloses that this is (a) a research work (probably the most extensive of its kind done so far), and (b) that the subject matter is not Fischer's games as such; rather they are considered in so far as they allow us insight into his thought patterns and style of play. And this, in turn, brings us to the two broader undertakings of the book.

Besides being a study on Fischer, it is a treatise on the middlegame at large. What I have attempted was to analyse the elements of the middlegame as they find their expression in the approach of an eminent universal chess player.

This combination is quite instructive, I believe, in that it gives us the opportunity to learn not only about Fischer but to deduce from his games everything of relevance for any player of universal chess aspirations. I certainly hope, at the same time, that this multi-faceted mosaic does indeed give a reliable picture of the integrated chess personality of Bobby Fischer himself.

The three years I have dedicated to the research and writing of this book were for me a time of great intellectual adventure and aesthetic pleasure. And while I strove to maintain the utmost objectivity in this study, I am afraid the reader might well detect the author's fascination with his material throughout.

It has been my good luck that I happen to live a couple of minutes' ride from the Royal Dutch Library in The Hague, a place which contains one of the largest collections of chess literature in the world. I could not have written the book as it is in its present form without regularly consulting the sources found in this huge treasury of chess books and magazines, and without having the assistance of its two librarians, Christiaan Bijl and Rob Verhoeven. Bijl, himself an expert on Fischer, directed my attention to a number of important sources (not least of which was his own magnificently edited collection of Fischer's games in German). Rob Verhoeven's constant guidance, advice and encouragement were invaluable to me.

I have indicated every source I used in the text, including those places in the analyses where I borrowed from existing published material (unless the lines were too obvious or too trivial to make a mention worthwhile).

One technical point. A cross-reference system refers the reader to all other places where the game under discussion has been handled. These references are introduced by the words 'see also'. This, I hope, will make the reading of the book more satisfying and complete.

And two other small points. In order to make a clear distinction between a question and a questionable move, I have used a dash in those cases in which a question mark appears after a move that is not questionable. And the initials *MSMG* refer to Fischer's book *My 60 Memorable Games.*


P.S.

This book goes to press while Fischer is staging his comeback match with Spassky in Yugoslavia.

The material handled in this book goes up to 1972, and no changes have been made in the 'past tense' which permeates the text.

It is certainly to be hoped that retrospectively we will be able to regard that period as 'the first part of Fischer's career', and that the 'second part' will provide an equally fascinating source of material for many future books.

# What's in a Style?

The primary objective of every player is to impose his own style on the game. The more the development of a game chimes in with the temperament and chess vision of one of the players, the greater the likelihood the battle will end in his favour.

A case in point were the two World Championship matches played between Botvinnik and Tal in 1960 and 1961. In the first, it was Tal who was able to impose his chess vision on the games: sharp, tactical tussles, and complicated positions which required, besides combinative intuition, a good deal of calculating work. Tal proved far superior to Botvinnik there. The task Botvinnik set himself in the second match was to steer the games into positions where the specific qualities of Tal's style would find the most limited outlet possible. This he did, right from the initial stages of the games. In the simplified and technically-oriented positions that ensued, Tal's fantasy could find nothing to nourish itself upon.

His interest in the games gradually diminished, and he played like a shadow of the player of the year before.

What typifies Fischer's style? In 1963 Fischer wrote a series of articles for the American magazine *Chess Life*. In the September issue of that year he analysed his game against Hans Berliner from the Western Open 1963, which he concluded with these words: "It is difficult to find one particular game that is typical of my 'style'. This comes close." I should like to examine the critical phase of that game (Pos. 1), which displays much that is typically 'Fischerian'.

Fischer's (Black's) slight advantage consists of a two to one pawn majority on the queenside, and White's doubled and vulnerable e-pawns. We realise that Black hasn't so far undertaken any action that would compromise his pawn structure. He would soon do so – with a move that is a typical Fischer device. Black's pieces are quite actively placed. His position

1

**1**                                    **B**

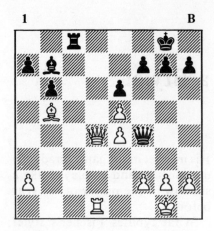

would have looked rather innocuous, though, had it not been for
the queen at f4. A queen at, say,
e7 or c7 would have been a more
common sight for this type of
position. How much is the queen
'in the game' at f4? Fischer is most
sensitive to questions of piece
placement. As we shall soon see,
the queen would play a decisive
role there in the outcome of the
game. What concrete threats does
Black have? The most obvious
and immediate is of course ...
♕xe4. But White's pawn on e5
can come under attack as well by
... ♖c5. Black has only to see to it
that his king gets some 'air', after
which the above threats, plus two
other rook moves along the c-file,
namely ... ♖c2 and ... ♖c1, are to
be reckoned with. The unassuming
20 ... h6 is good enough a move to
keep all the threats and secure

some advantage, e.g. 21 ♕d7
♖c1! (certainly not 21 ... ♕xe4?
22 ♕xc8+! ♗xc8 23 ♖d8+ ♔h7 24
♗d3, winning), and Black wins
one of the e-pawns. Or 21 f3 ♖c5
22 ♕d7 ♗c8 23 ♕e8+ ♔h7, and
again White faces some difficulties.
Fischer notices, however, that by
playing

**20 ... g5!**

he will make White face greater
problems. White can't avoid playing f3 as he must protect e4, but
this will then be answered by ...
g4, rendering his king's position
dangerously exposed.

Apart from these objective
considerations, the advance of
the g-pawn whether as White or
as Black, is a move Fischer was
partial to. This will be extensively
dealt with in the next chapter (see
Pos. 33-40).

**21 f3 g4!!**

Extremely alert! (There is a
chapter dedicated to this – the
reader is referred to pp.144-9.)
On the face of it, he just carries
out his above-mentioned plan.
Yet wasn't 21 ... ♖c5, apparently
winning the pawn on e5, better?
Not when one observes White's
subtle resource 22 ♗e8!. White,
all of a sudden, threatens to win
by 23 ♗xf7+!!; and after 22 ...
♖c1 (best, since 22 ... ♗c8 is met
by 23 g3! ♕xf3 24 ♗xf7+!! ♕xf7

25 ♕d8+ ♕f8 – 25 ... ♔g7 26 ♖f1 – 26 ♕xg5+ ♕g7 27 ♖d8+ ♔f7 28 ♕h5+ ♕g6 29 ♕f3+ mating) 23 ♗xf7+! ♔xf7 24 ♕d7+ draws.

**22 ♗e2**

22 ♕d7 would have been answered by 22 ... gxf3! 23 ♕xb7 ♕e3+ 24 ♔h1 fxg2+ 25 ♔xg2 ♖c2+ and wins.

**22 ... gxf3?**

And this, too, is typical of Fischer! After having reached a winning position he might, at times, fail to find the most direct win. 22 ... ♖c2! 23 g3 ♕h6 24 ♕d3 ♖xa2 25 fxg4 (25 f4 ♕g6) 25 ... ♔g7! 26 ♕f3 ♕g6 27 ♗d3 ♖a4 leaves White completely helpless.

For similar examples see 'Misplaying Won Positions', pp.237-40.

**23 gxf3**

23 ♗xf3 ♔g7!, and White can't prevent 24 ... ♖c5 (24 ♕d7 ♕e3+ 25 ♔h1 ♖c1!), with a won position for Black.

**23 ... ♔h8!**

23 ... ♖c2 is a grave mistake now, as Fischer pointed out in *Chess Life*, in view of 24 ♔h1 ♖xe2 25 ♖g1+, and White wins.

**24 ♔h1 ♗a6!**

The point of all the previous operations. Typically, Fischer li-quidates to a technically superior endgame, as 25 ♗xa6? ♕xf3+ 26 ♔g1 ♖g8 is mate. It is worth paying attention to the fact that the road to a 'technically superior endgame' has been paved by tactical means. Fischer usually kept a keen eye on both the positional and tactical implications of his moves, the combination of which shall be the subject matter of the last chapter of this book.

**25 ♕f2 ♗xe2 26 ♕xe2 ♕xe5**

And in the ensuing endgame, Black's material plus, and his pawn majority on the queenside, decide the game.

So within a short space of seven moves we have witnessed a number of themes that were recurrent in Fischer's games.

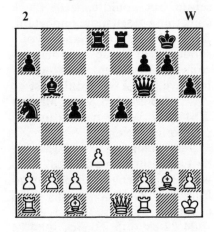

2        W

Yet sometimes it might be a single move that would combine a couple of characteristic elements of a player's style. One such move was **20 ♕c3!** in Fischer's game against Bisguier, New York State Open Championship 1963 (Pos. 2). Like many of Fischer's moves this, too, looks so unremarkable that one would hardly stop to consider it attentively, let alone ascribe to it any profundity.

A promising strategic plan for White seems to consist of the following moves: ♕e2 (against ... c4), c3 (preventing ... ♘c6-d4), ♗e3, ♖g1, ♗e4, with play on the g-file. Fischer's move evinces, among other things, his awareness of the explosive potential of the advance ... c5-c4. A queen at e2 would be directed against it all the same, and would co-operate better with the other pieces in the above set-up, but would concede Black something much more important: 20 ... c4! 21 dxc4 e4! and all of a sudden White's position has become badly cramped. Now, for instance, 22 ♗xe4 would lose to 22 ... ♕e5 23 f3 f5, while after 21 ♖b1 ♗c7 White has an uneasy position to defend.

Very tempting also was the development move 20 ♗d2, and after 20 ... ♘c6 the queen centralisation – 21 ♕e4 – looks quite attractive. The sequence 21 ... ♘d4 22 c3 ♘f5 23 ♕c4 ♘h4 24 ♗e4 confirms this to some extent, though Black may hold his own

with 24 ... g5!?. Greater doubt is cast on this continuation, however, by 23 ... ♘d6, when again Black gets a dangerous initiative after 24 ♕g4 c4! (better than 24 ... e4 25 dxe4 ♘xe4 26 ♗e3!) 25 dxc4 e4! 26 ♗e3 ♘xc4 27 ♗xb6 (or 27 ♖ab1 ♗xe3 28 fxe3 ♕g5!) 27 ... axb6 etc.

Fischer's move (20 ♕c3), achieves a number of aims at the same time – the essence of economy in chess. The queen is switched from the e-file, where it faces the black rook, to the a1-h8 diagonal, placed vis-à-vis its opposite number – the black queen. In addition, a clear positional objective has been created – pushing f2-f4, when White's dark-squared bishop would gain more scope, and his rook would become operative on the f-file. Moreover, the advance ... c5-c4 has lost all its effectiveness now since it can't be followed up by ... e4.

The next two moves were **20 ... ♘c6 21 f4 ♘d4 22 ♕c4!**. As compared with the above variation, the queen has reached c4 before the knight has reached f5, and instead of playing ♗d2, White has carried out the positionally more significant advance f2-f4. At c4 the queen eyes f7, and precludes ... c4 for many moves to come, thus rendering Black's bishop a valueless piece.

Fischer has displayed great agility and precision in countering his opponent's threats and creating his own counterplay. This will be discussed at length in the chapter 'Active Defence and Counterplay', pp.161-76. (see also Pos. 89)

We shall also deal in this book with subjects like 'Materialism', 'Alertness' (mentioned before), 'Liquidation', 'Straightforwardness' and 'Clarity', among others. These were well embodied in the following example (Pos. 3), which serves perfectly as our introductory exposition. The game is Addison-Fischer, US Championship 1963-64, after White's 21st move.

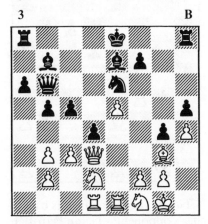

3                                         B

It looks as though Black's most natural move in this position is 21 ... 0-0-0, securing his presence in the centre. Actually, the move would thwart Black's own intentions, since White has 22 c4!, establishing a strong knight at e4 after 23 ♘e4 and 24 ♘fd2. Fischer

was alert to this possibility, and his next move is directed towards its prevention, while heading for an advantageous endgame: **21 ... ♛c6!**. Now 22 ♘e4 is out of the question, in view of 22 ... c4, when Black increases his domination.

The next phase of the game is highly instructive for its combination of optimal piece placement, timely liquidation and material gains:

**22 ♕e4 0-0-0 23 ♕xc6+ ♗xc6 24 c4 ♔d7! 25 ♖a1 ♖a8 26 ♘e4 ♗xe4!**

The point. White doesn't get the chance to reinforce this knight's position by ♘fd2. **27 ♖xe4 ♘g7!**. Straightforward and very effective. The knight goes to f5, after which the pawn on h4 falls, leaving White with not a shadow of compensation. At the same time e6 is freed for the centralisation of the king. **28 ♘d2 ♘f5 29 ♖f4 ♔e6**. Black has achieved all his objectives, and soon won the game. (see also Pos. 108)

The formation of conceptions in chess is a complex process. I have confined myself in this book to a factual analysis of the various aspects of Fischer's way of playing. Here I should like to dedicate a couple of words only to the rapidity and apparent ease with which this complexity was unravelled in Fischer's mind.

Calculating concrete variations and forming abstract conceptions are two different processes in chess. Yet they do sustain each other to a large extent, since any concept has to be checked against the harsh reality of the factual elements of a position, and the reverse is true, too: making a choice between a number of concrete variations can be done only with regard to an abstract evaluation of the positions to which they lead.

The following two instances are rather unintricate as far as variations are concerned, and for that reason they offer us a good insight into the abstract side of Fischer's way of thinking.

The first (Pos. 4) is from his game (as White) against Barcza, Stockholm 1962. The observation is Alexander Kotov's:

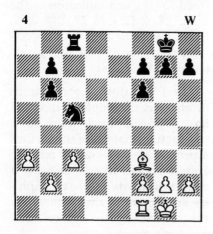

4                              W

"I was sitting next to the table on which the game was played. In a matter of seconds Fischer found the right way to win. He played 27 ♖d1! ♔f8 28 ♖d4 ♖c7 29 h3 f5 30 ♖b4 ♘d7 31 ♔f1 ♔e7 32 ♔e2 ♔d8 33 ♖b5!. Here the rook stands the best. After 33 ... g6 34 ♔e3 ♔c8 35 ♔d4 ♔b8 36 ♔d5 an obvious winning position was reached. Every chess master knows how difficult it is to find such plans in the endgame."[1] (see also Pos. 167)

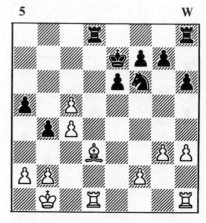

5                              W

The next observation is by Fischer's opponent – Tigran Petrosian. Played a year earlier, at Bled 1961, they reached Pos. 5 after Petrosian's (Black's) 23rd move, when Fischer played 24 c6!. Petrosian related:

"Quick as a flash came Fischer's move. At first glance I was inclined to regard it as meaningless. What difference does it make on which square the c-pawn would be captured? As will soon become apparent, the move has a profound side to it." **24 ... ♖d6 25 ♖he1!**. "That is it! The white rook gets through to the fifth rank and forces Black to defend his pawns there."[2]

The manifestation of the various qualities of Fischer's chess playing, abstract and concrete, is the matter to which we shall apply our attention throughout the book.

The opening chapter of this exposition covers the most fundamental element of the game – pawn structure.

# Pawn Structure

*Dime con quien andas y te diré quien eres*, say the Spaniards, and this means, in plain English, "Tell me with whom you associate and I will tell you who you are". In the same inferential vein one could paraphrase and say, "Tell me what pawn formations you favour, and I'll tell you what player you are".

No single element of the game reflects the whole player as faithfully as does pawn structure. Fischer is no exception to this. His attitude to questions of pawn structure reflects his overall approach to the game, and especially so in the way it mirrors the tension between well-balanced features and dynamic ones.

Fischer was always very well aware of the outcome of his and his opponent's actions, in terms of both sides' pawn formations. His 7th match game against Petrosian, Candidates 1971, saw the following position (Pos. 6), after Petrosian's (Black's) 12th move.

Fischer played here **13 ♖e1**, a decision which has, in the main, to be understood with regard to

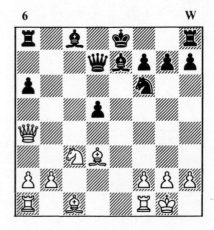

6                          W

the position's pawn structure. He is willing to enter a queenless middlegame, since the two-to-one pawn majority on the queenside, plus an isolated black d-pawn, would favour White sufficiently to offer him a concrete advantage in many possible endgames. He envisages moreover that White will be able to play b4 in the very near future to check the advance ... a5, thus subjecting the pawn on a6 to long-term pressure (see Pos. 158). This, as a matter of fact, turned out to be the factor which caused Black's position to crumble (see also Pos. 285). One interesting and important point is the fact that White's pawn structure is intact, while the opponent's shows intrinsic weaknesses, around which Fischer would develop his play. The following pair of examples illustrates this principle in Fischer's approach and indicates his basic inclination towards clear and static structures, where defects in his opponent's position offer him something definite to play for.

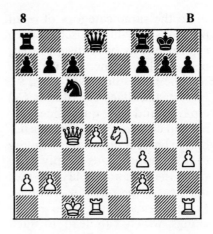

8            B

Against Mednis (who had the white pieces) at the US Championship 1963-64, Pos. 8 was reached after White's 14th move. White's pawns are scattered in four 'islands', and are evidently weak. Fischer set out to attack them with **14 ... ♛h4** and **15 ... ♛f4** (see Pos. 227).

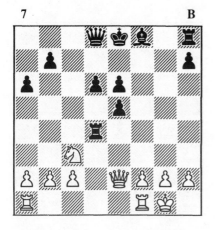

7            B

Pos. 7 occurred after Fischer's 18th move, as White, in the 6th match game against Taimanov, Candidates 1971. The favourability of White's pawn structure consists in the greater vulnerability of Black's central pawn mass and the isolated h-pawn.

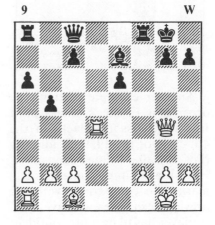

9            W

To the same category of open positions in which Fischer's two central pawns have disappeared, belongs his game against Trifunović from Bled 1961 (Pos. 9). Here again, Black's (Trifunović's) e-pawn and his queenside formation constitute an obvious liability. There is no point in arguing that these positions simply arise from the openings played, since it's clearly the other way round: Fischer consciously chooses openings which can lead to such structures.

that his technique will enable him to make use of such structural advantages as White has here.

The same held good for a couple of other cases. In March of the same year in which the above game was played, Fischer took part in the annual event at Mar del Plata, where he had to win his game with the white pieces against Jacopo Bolbochan in the penultimate round to remain in the race for first place. Remarkably enough, he steered for a technical game (see also p.224).

| 10 | B |
|---|---|

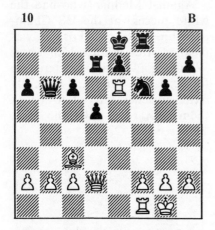

| 11 | W |
|---|---|

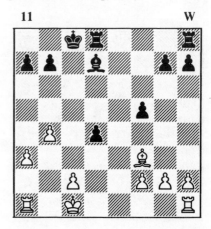

Another example of this type occurred in Fischer's game against Fridrik Olafsson (Black) in the 4th cycle of the 1959 Candidates (Pos. 10), after White's 22nd move. Here Black's predicament is less marked in comparison with the previous examples we have seen. A player has to be quite confident

In the first position (Pos. 11, after Black's 17th move), he had already obtained some advantage in the shape of Black's isolated pawn at d4, and the slightly weak pawn at f5. Yet, after exchanging a pair of rooks he saw no way of taking advantage of the d-pawn, and exchanged his c-pawn for it, thus reaching Pos. 12 on move 28. Here the superiority of White's pawn structure is reduced to a minimum, offering no more than a slight spatial plus.

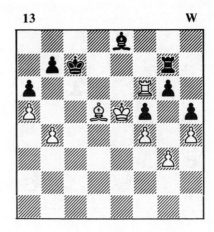

13                                    W

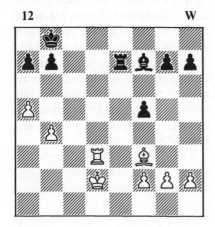

12                                    W

The most important factor remains of course Black's pawn at f5. In the long run it will have to be defended by ... g6. In this way all the black pawns on that wing would stand on light squares, which is precisely what White would like to see, given the presence of the two light-squared bishops. The transformation of this position into Pos. 13 within thirteen moves (we have it here after Black's 40th move), more than justified Fischer's positional expectations.

All Black's pawns are stationed on light squares, and White's spatial advantage, owing to the present pawn formation, bears the signs of a truly critical advantage. White's king and bishop are ideally centralised, and the rook rules happily on the 6th rank. Of special importance are both sides' pawn configurations on the kingside. Later on in this chapter (Pos. 53-58), we shall observe how Fischer's opponents are forced, time and again, into creating such structural 'triangles', and how Fischer exploits them. The conspicuous difference between the two 'triangles' here stands in direct relation to the colour of the bishops, as mentioned before.

Another very instructive (and curious) case related to our present topic was Fischer's 2nd match game against Taimanov, Candidates 1971 (see Pos. 154 in 'Maintaining the Positional Tension').

**14**                                                          **W**

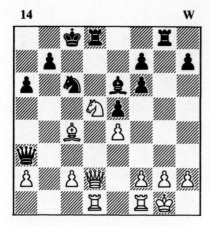

Questions of pawn structure cannot of course be separated from the position as a whole. Thus, against Rossetto at Buenos Aires 1960, Fischer (White) would offer a queen exchange (Pos. 14) by **16 ♕e3 ♕xe3 17 fxe3!**, in order to limit the scope of the knight (d4 was too good a spot for it), and open the f-file for the rook, while preventing 16 ... ♖xg2+!.

And against Panov, for instance, at Skopje 1967, Fischer (White, Pos. 15) would recapture after **14 ... ♗xc3** with the pawn – **15 bxc3** – so as not to let the position get too simplified after 15 ♕xc3 c5 (16 ♖ad1 ♖ad8 etc). Though a queen recapture would have conformed with the conventional approach of leaving the pawn structure in such positions unaltered, Fischer wished to introduce some slight measure of tension into the position by this dynamic twist. (see also Pos. 126).

These two examples show Fischer's readiness to compromise his pawn structure to a certain extent. In the one case it was for completely objective reasons, in the other for more subjective ones. Yet both were in agreement with the positions' dynamic demands. The same principle directed Fischer in the next instance, taken from his

**15**                                                          **B**

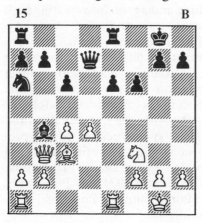

**16**                                                          **B**

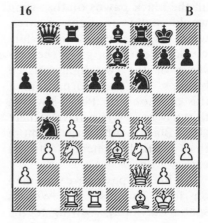

game (as White) against Najdorf at the 1970 Siegen Olympiad (Pos. 16).

After Najdorf's **22 ... bxc4** a routine 23 ♗xc4 could have been satisfactorily answered by 23 ... ♘xe4 24 ♘xe4 d5 25 ♘ed2 dxc4 26 ♘xc4, with approximate equality. In this line White has no clear positional objectives to play for in the next phase of the game, whereas after Fischer's **23 bxc4!** he managed to create before long a passed c-pawn, with the help of an e5 push: **23 ... a5 24 ♘d4 ♕a8 25 ♕f3 ♘a6 26 ♘4b5 ♘c5 27 e5!** **dxe5 28 ♕xa8 ♖xa8 29 fxe5 ♘fe4** **30 ♘d6 ♗c6 31 ♘cxe4 ♘xe4 32 c5** with a very favourable endgame in sight.

So besides his normal inclination to play for clear structures, concrete considerations relating to the positions's other factors naturally play a major part in Fischer's decisions. It is only very rarely that he makes a mistake in evaluating these other factors and puts too great an emphasis on considerations of pawn structure alone.

One such case was his game against the Romanian Victor Ciocaltea from the Varna Olympiad 1962 (Pos. 17). Fischer (Black) played here **12 ... fxe4**, and there followed **13 dxe4 d5 14 exd5 ♕xd5** **15 ♕xd5 ♘xd5**. He certainly evaluated his position as better in view

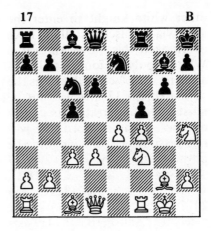

17                    B

of the sounder pawn formation, taking into account mainly White's weak pawn on f4 (and his misplaced knight on h4). If he were to be given a free hand for another couple of moves, Black could play ... ♗e6-g8 and ... ♖ae8, with ideal placement of his pieces and indeed the better pawn structure, which would then play a most significant role. Ciocaltea shows, however, that Fischer made the mistake of evaluating the position in static terms, while ignoring the dynamic possibilities. By a very timely regrouping he proves that f4 is not an irreparable weakness in White's camp, as Fischer must have taken it to be: **16 ♘g5!**. Fulfilling four tasks: A) defending the pawn on f4, B) attacking Black's knight on d5, C) preventing the manoeuvre ... ♗e6-g8, D) making it possible for the other white knight to enter the game via f3. Fischer couldn't have overlooked this move, since it is White's only serious resource – after 16 ♘e5 ♘ce7! Black has the strong threat 17 ... g5! – but he must have underrated its consequences. In other words, he was not dissuaded from judging the position statically. **16 ... ♘b6 17 ♗e3 ♘a4 18 ♖ae1! ♗d7** 18 ... ♘xb2? 19 ♗xc5 wins. **19 ♗c1 ♗f6 20 ♘hf3 ♗f5 21 ♘e5.** Look how nicely the "anti-hero" on f4 assists the manoeuvring of the knights! **21 ... ♘e7 22 ♘e4 ♗h4 23 ♖d1 ♖ac8 24 ♘d6.** In order to cope with all the problems White has set him, Black has had to misplace his pieces. This disharmony leads now to the loss of a pawn – **24 ... ♖c7 25 ♘b5 ♖cc8 26 ♘xa7** – and eventually it led to White's win (see Pos. 283 and the remark in Pos. 236).

That Fischer was usually very well aware of the dynamic features of a position when taking decisions pertaining to pawn structure was borne out by the many seminal decisions he took. Here are three cases.

Position 18 arose after White's 12th move in Fischer's well-known game against Robert Byrne, US Championship 1963-64. Fischer (Black) played here **12 ... e5.** "I was amazed at this advance, which seems to leave Black's

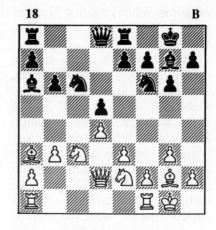

18                                        B

queen's pawn a hopelessly weak isolani", confessed Byrne in *Chess Life*[1]. Fischer, in *MSMG*, admits he was indeed worried about the pawn at d5, but relied on the great activity of his minor pieces. He thought that 12 ... e6 would probably have led to a draw.[2] As in Pos. 15 we see Fischer refraining from a more conventional treatment of the pawn formation for the sake of a sharper battle, in which the opponent would find it difficult to fall back on a standard equalising line.

Two years after this game, Robert Byrne, in one of his articles,[3] named Fischer "an expert pawn surgeon". Was it under the influence of the above?

Donner's **14 cxb5** in Donner-Fischer, Santa Monica 1966 (Pos. 19), had been answered earlier in that tournament in a similar posi-

**19** **W**

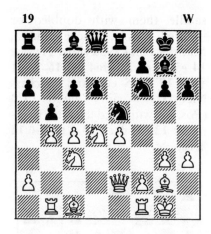

tion by ... axb5 (Donner-Najdorf), a move that maintains an elastic pawn formation on the queenside. Fischer's **14 ... cxb5!?** was anything but conventional. (It might have inspired Garry Kasparov's similar capture many years later – in his first match game against Karpov, New York 1990.) The pawn on d6 remained now a poor isolani, and the square d5 a badly weakened spot. Instead of explaining what were its positive sides, we allow the game's continuation to speak for itself: **15 ☐d1 ♗b7 16 f4 ♘c4 17 ♕d3 ☐c8 18 ♔h2 ♕c7 19 ☐b3 ☐e7 20 ☐e1 ☐ce8 21 ♘c2 ♕c8 22 ♘e3 ♘xe3 23 ☐xe3 ♘xe4 24 ♗xe4 ♗xe4 25 ♕xd6 ☐d7 26 ♕c5 ☐c7 27 ♘xe4 ☐xc5 28 ♘xc5 ♗d4 0-1**. This is it then: great Black activity on the open c- and e-files and an open diagonal for his light-squared bishop. This proved

to be much more than White could handle, or put up any resistance against.

More critical than these two was the position Fischer reached (as White) in his game against Max Euwe at the Leipzig Olympiad 1960, after Black's 14th move (Pos. 20).

**20** **W**

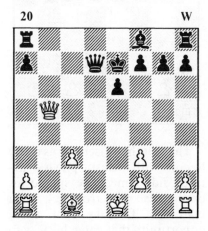

From Fischer's description in *MSMG* following his **15 ☐b1!**, one learns that this position had been on his 'agenda' long before the game was played, and only after thorough analysis and deliberation did he come to the conclusion that "horrible as White's pawn structure may be, Black can't exploit it because he'll be unable to develop his kingside normally".[4] Again we see how the intrinsic weakness of White's pawn structure is weighed up against other factors, and Fischer's final verdict is given only with regard to a comprehensive view of the position.

**21**                **W**

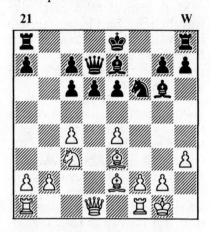

The fact that Fischer was ready to cope with inelastic pawn structures didn't mean he spared his opponents this trouble. As a matter of fact, he took every opportunity that came his way to

**22**                **W**

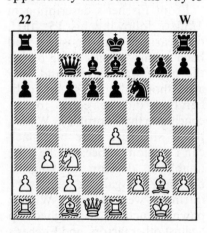

saddle them with doubled or isolated pawns. Fischer-Emma, Mar del Plata 1959 (Pos. 21) saw **14 e5! dxe5 15 ♕a4 0-0 16 ♖ad1 ♕e8 17 ♕a5** etc, and Fischer-Ničevski, Rovinj Zagreb 1970 (Pos. 22) witnessed the same treatment: **12 e5! dxe5 13 ♗b2 0-0 14 ♕e2**, etc.

**23**                **W**

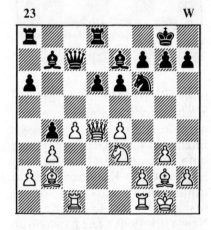

Fischer's **16 c5!** in Pos. 23 (Fischer-Petrosian, 4th cycle Curaçao 1962), besides shattering Black's pawn formation, also had the double purpose of taking c5 away from Black's knight, while freeing c4 for White's knight. And after **16 ... dxc5 17 ♕xb4** Black couldn't play 17 ... cxb4, in view of 18 ♖xc7 ♖d7 19 ♖xb7!.

The same pawn advanced to the same square in Fischer-Najdorf, Santa Monica 1966 (Pos. 24) and had devastating effect:

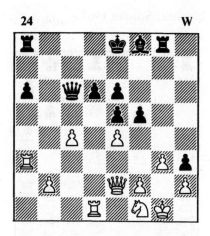

**24** **W**

**26 c5! ♕xe4 27 ♕xe4 fxe4 28 cxd6.** (see also Pos. 264)

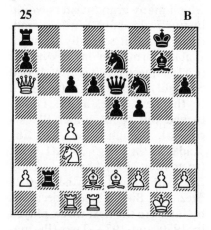

**25** **B**

Very interesting is our next case (Pos. 25). It is the position after White's 20th move in Taimanov-Fischer, 1st match game, Candidates 1971. Black's central pawn mass is still quite elastic. The elasticity of a particular pawn formation is measured by its possibility to change form, that is, its potential mobility. In the present case it consists of the potential moves ... c5, ... d5, ... e4, or ... f4. Yet the position remains at its maximum elasticity when *none* of these moves has been carried out.

Here the elastic structure is of great importance, since it checks the activity of the white pieces – he can't play ♗e3 in view of ... f4, nor can he play ♗f3 in view of ... e4. Should one of these pawns advance, then the pawn configuration would be doomed to stay static for the rest of the game, or at least a good deal of it. ... f4 would minimise Black's control of e4 and g4, whereas ... e4 would do so for f4 and d4. Thus, after ... f4 a White bishop at f3 could hardly be chased away by ... f4 or ... d4. In both these cases, White would gain important space for his pieces' activity, and we could rightly speak of Black losing his control of the *three* squares of opposite colour around the advanced pawn.

Fischer played **20 ... e4?!** nonetheless! Taimanov was quick to make use of the three weakened dark squares – f4, e3, d4: **21 ♕a3 ♖b7 22 ♗f4 d5 23 cxd5 cxd5 24 ♘b5 ♘g6 25 ♘d4 ♕d7 26 ♕e3.** Tal's comment was a good account of Fischer's 20th move: "An urge to set in motion the pawn group as soon as possible. However, by activating his forces, Black also activates the forces of his opponent."[5]

Balashov suggested instead 20 ... ♘d7 21 ♕a3 ♖b7 22 ♗e3 ♘c8 23 ♘a4, and "White has good play on the open lines".[6] But why should Black place his pieces so disharmoniously, and lose his grip on d5? Much better seems 20 ... ♔h8, removing the king from the diagonal a2-g8, and making room for a possible ... ♖g8. For instance: 21 ♕a3 ♖b7 22 ♗e3 ♖d7 23 f3 ♖g8, and Black now has much the better piece play, besides his pawn plus. (see also Pos. 181)

Was Fischer overconfident in his belief he could successfully handle positions of inelastic pawn structures? If so, he wasn't too seriously wrong! His masterful management of such positions was, to be sure, second to none. Besides the last couple of examples, he was quite an exception among top grandmasters in his readiness to play for broken pawn structures as, for instance, in his 3rd match game against Spassky, Reykjavik 1972 (11 ... ♘h5 12 ♗xh5 gxh5), or, years before that, at the 1963 New York Open against Bisguier (9 ♘h3 – see the result in Pos. 89), or in taking decisions such as 23 ... gxh5! in Pos. 26 (Portisch-

Fischer, Sousse 1967).

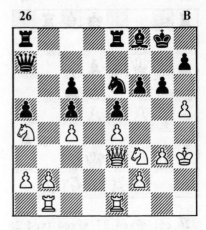

26                                    B

This last move was something which many grandmasters would instinctively have shrunk from doing, since it so badly damages Black's formation on the kingside (on the queenside it is already bad enough!), especially with regard to the new 'hole' at f5. Things turned out to be under Black's control though after **24 ♖h1 ♖ad8 25 ♔g2 ♕g7 26 ♔f1 ♕g4!** (to answer 27 ♘h4 by 27 ... ♗h6!! 28 ♕xh6 ♕xe4) **27 ♖h4 ♕g6 28 ♕e2 ♗h6.** But his boldest decisions by far were the next three, played in 1970 and 1972. Two (Parma-Fischer, Rovinj-Zagreb 1970, Pos. 27, and Spassky-Fischer, 7th match game, World Championship Reykjavik 1972. Pos. 28), were the direct result of Fischer's exceptionally profound acquaintance with, and understanding of, structures related to the Poisoned Pawn Variation of the Sicilian. The third (Reshevsky-Fischer, Palma de Mallorca 1970, Pos. 29), might well have been influenced by it.

**27** **W**

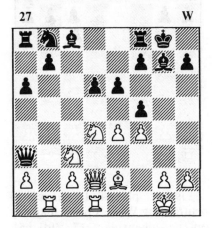

Parma's **14 exf5**, Spassky's

**28** **W**

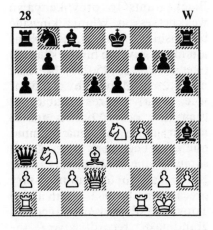

**14 f5** and Reshevsky's **12 f5** were all answered by ... **exf5**. It should be noted that in all three cases the

**29** **W**

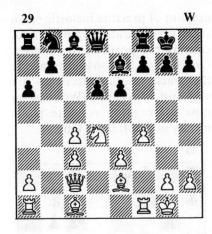

pawn on d6 remained very weak, aside from any other peculiarities pertaining to each of these positions: in Pos. 27 it was Black's shattered pawn formation on the kingside (for the end of this game see Pos. 290); in Pos. 28 it was Black's poor development, the non co-ordination of his two developed pieces, and the exposed king in the centre (problems that vanished completely after **15 ♗b5+!? axb5! 16 ♘xd6+ ♔f8! 17 ♘xc8 ♘c6 18 ♘d6 ♖d8 19 ♘xb5 ♕e7 20 ♕f4 g6**); and in Pos. 29 it was the critical relinquishing of d5, of which Reshevsky took immediate advantage by manoeuvring ♗f3-d5 (see Pos. 107). Interestingly, of these three encounters only Spassky was fortunate enough to save half a point! It seems that Fischer had developed a very refined sense as to the amount of pressure inelastic pawn structures could sustain without causing the position to collapse. One has to be constantly aware that such resolute decisions are very critical in nature. We consider now some more resolute pawn moves of a different kind.

30                                          W

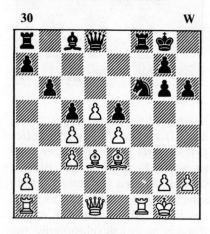

Gligorić described Fischer's **16 ... a5!** which came as the response to Spassky's **16 a4** in their 5th match game, World Championship, Reykjavik 1972 (Pos. 30) thus: "Played without hesitation, which illustrates Fischer's precise judgement".[7] In a sense, this is the kind of move that could be made either by a chess savant, or by a complete ignoramus, since if it is bad, it would normally turn out to be *extremely* bad, and if correct, there is a great likelihood it would be *highly* correct.

Or take, for instance, the next position: Pachman-Fischer, Havana Olympiad 1966 (Pos. 31).

31                                          B

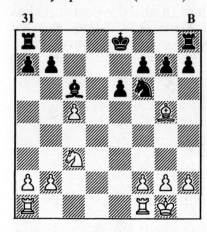

Fischer played **16 ... a5!** – neutralising White's pawn majority on the queenside – **17 ♖fd1 h5!**. With his powerful bishop on c6 Black wants to provoke pawn weaknesses on White's kingside by pushing ... h4-h3, as well as aiming to develop his rook via h5. (see also Pos. 53, 95, 288). Be it as it may, ... a5 followed by ... h5 (or vice versa) are remarkable for their rare occurrence in grandmaster games, and may remind one of a beginner's play. Don't some of the newcomers to the game tend to take unnecessary precautions with 1 ... a6 (*pace* Tony Miles![8]) and 2 ... h6 (not on grandmaster record, as yet)?

Or take his game (with the black pieces) against Saidy, Manhattan v. Marshall, Metropolitan League

1969 (Pos. 32):

32     W

33     W

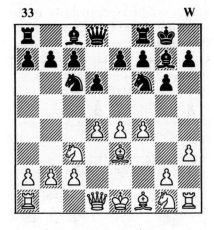

**12 h3 h5!** Here it is! **13 a3 a5!** And there it is, too! By forestalling g4 and b4 respectively, Black reduced White's options on both wings. (see also Pos. 116)

## THE G-PAWN

A move that was a Fischer peculiarity and kept appearing throughout his career was g4 (as White) or – though less often – ... g5 (as Black). If Fischer had any distinct bias towards a certain device, it was this one. As far as this move was concerned, he could lose his usual composure, restraint and good judgement, and give vent to a certain impulsiveness, which was seldom apparent otherwise.

He could carry it out as early as move 7 (White against Udovčić, Rovinj-Zagreb 1970, Pos. 33) – **7 g4**, which Trifunović marked with a '!?', writing: "This move can never be made by a quiet, positional player, for now White, willy-nilly, must attack. But when such a move is made by 'Great Bobby' it is twice as strong, for it provokes anxiety, confusion and fear."[9] Suetin, for one, was more sceptical about the move's value, and preferred to attach a '?!' to it.[10]

And he could also carry it out in the endgame, sometimes with dubious reasoning. Here (Pos. 34), against Smyslov at Monte Carlo 1967, Fischer plays **19 g4?**, which enables Smyslov, by playing **19 ... ☐g8**, to force White into playing **20 h3**, thus limiting White's manoeuvring abilities on the king-

**34**                                              **W**

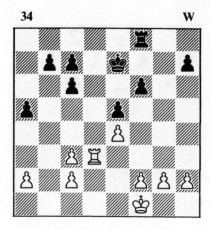

side considerably. (Fischer apparently had in mind the sequence ♖h3-h6, stopping ♔d6 or ♔e6 in view of g5!, and then reinforcing his position later by f3, h4, ♔e2, g5, etc.)

More common was the g4 pawn advance in the early middlegame. Anyone interested in the relation-

**35**                                              **W**

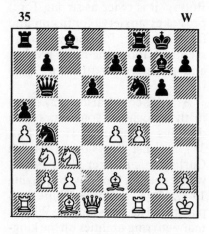

ship between chess moves and numerology would no doubt find it remarkable that the following five examples occur on the same move number – 13! . . .

Quite well known is his game (as White) against Korchnoi from the 1st cycle of the 1962 Curaçao Candidates (Pos. 35): **13 g4? ♗xg4! 14 ♗xg4 ♘xg4 15 ♕xg4 ♘xc2** and White's position was critical.

**36**                                              **W**

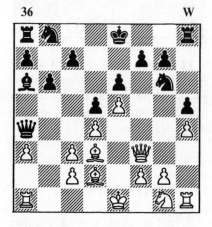

Next comes Fischer-Ivkov, Santiago 1959 (Pos. 36): **13 g4?!.** Mednis remarked: "Such thrusts at the French, before the completion of development, usually only lead to self-weakness. So also here."[11] The game continued: **13 ... hxg4 14 ♕xg4 ♗xd3 15 cxd3 ♘c6 16 ♕g5 ♘ce7 17 h5 ♘f5! 18 ♘e2 ♘ge7! 19 ♘g3 0-0-0**, and Black had a winning position.

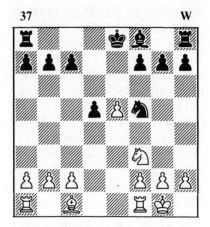

37        W

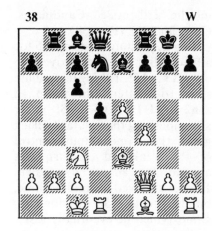

38        W

In quite a similar vein, Arthur Bisguier wrote in *Chess Review*, March 1963, of his game (as Black) against Fischer at the US Championship 1962-63 (Pos. 37): **13 g4**. "White hopes to mobilise his pawn majority, but he is weakening his pawn structure. All his subsequent pawn moves turn out to be weapons which cut both ways."[12] **13 ... ♘e7 14 ♗f4 c6 15 ♖fe1 ♘g6 16 ♗g3 ♗c5 17 c3 ♘f8 18 b4**. "Another weakening pawn move which might well have proved costly." **18 ... ♗b6 19 ♔g2 ♘e6 20 ♘h4 h5 21 h3**. "As a result of White's pawn weaknesses, Black's position is already distinctly superior . . . Simply 21 ... g6 should have been played [here]."

Fischer managed to win this game, as well as the next one (Fischer-German, Stockholm 1962, Pos. 38), though here too, **13 g4**

allowed his opponent to get some counterplay after **13 ... ♗b4 14 ♘e2 ♘b6 15 ♘d4 ♕e8 16 c3 ♗e7 17 f5 c5 18 ♘b5 d4! 19 ♗f4**, and now 19 ... ♗b7 20 ♖g1 a6! would have caused White some headaches. Instead of g4, the restraining 13 ♘a4 was indicated.[13]

13 g4 had graver consequences in Fischer's game against Keres,

39        W

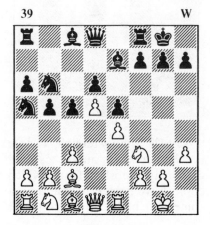

in the 3rd cycle, Candidates, Curaçao 1962 (Pos. 39).

**13 g4?.** Wishing to stop ... f5 for all time. But the price proves too dear: **13 ... h5!**. Taking immediate steps to "soften" the pawn **14 ♘h2 hxg4 15 hxg4 ♗g5!**. After accomplishing the first task, Black gets to the second: gaining control of the weakened dark squares around the advanced g-pawn. Fischer survived the middlegame, but had to face an inferior endgame, which he eventually lost.

The same move led to an immediate débâcle (not on move 13 this time, though!) in Fischer's game against Ivkov, Havana 1965 (Pos. 40).

♗c5! f5 34 f3 ♖d7 35 ♔e1 fxe4 36 fxe4 ♘a5 37 ♖b1! ♘c4 38 b3 axb3 39 axb3 ♖c7! 40 bxc4 (40 ♗g1 ♘d6!) 40 ... ♖xc5 41 ♖b4. This mistake led to another after **34 ... f5 35 gxf5 gxf5 36 exf5?**. It wasn't too late for a feasible defence: 36 f3 fxe4 37 fxe4 ♘a5 38 ♗c5 ♖d7 39 ♔e1, and White ought not to lose. **36 ... e4 37 ♔e1 ♘e5**, and White's position was beyond repair now. Fischer resigned on move 54.

Any critical study of one player's games is bound to bring out stylistic idiosyncracies. In Fischer's case, this advance of the g-pawn, was one of the most conspicuous.

**40**                                **W**

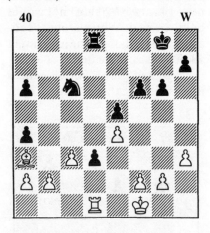

**34 g4??.** Simply terrible. It does not hinder ... f5, and it loses an extremely important tempo which could have helped to maintain a somewhat better ending after 33

## THE PAWN CHAIN I

The kingside pawn chain f2-g3-h4 (White) or f7-g6-h5 (Black) appears quite frequently in master play. It stems regularly from the structure f2-g3-h2 (or Black's corresponding one) where the h-pawn has advanced two squares. The rationale behind this advance is basically twofold: restrictive and offensive. Alexander Nikitin put it very concisely when explaining Kasparov's 16 ... h5! in his game against Agdestein, Interpolis 1989 (*NIC* 89/8): "A very useful move, restricting White's possibilities and threatening ... h5-h4". A structure needs no better approbation than this.

This formation appeared in quite a number of Fischer's games. Very enterprising and interesting was his decision to play for it in his game against Eliskases at Mar del Plata 1960 (Pos. 41).

**41** W

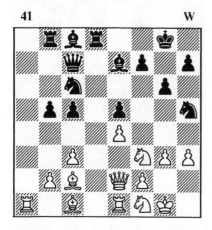

Bronstein-Reshevsky, Zürich Candidates 1953, had continued here 19 ♔h2. In his notes to the game, Bronstein discusses only the alternative 19 ♘e3.[14] Yet Fischer (White), seven years later, comes up with a completely new idea – 19 h4!. (At Mar del Plata, where Bronstein, too, was playing, Fischer told him this move was a 'tremendous improvement' over 19 ♔h2.)[15]

What was there in this advance that hadn't been attractive enough to draw Bronstein's attention to

it? 19 ♔h2 was certainly more solid in that it kept the white squares h3 and g4 under complete control, thus restricting the scope of Black's light-squared bishop, without taking yet any definite steps on the kingside. Fischer's committal advance was made with a view to another element in the position: he was interested in bolstering his control of g5 with a view to an eventual ♘f3-g5. He was obviously less concerned about any theoretical weaknesses this pawn formation would bring about, since he perceived that gaining control of g5 should outweigh any disadvantages it might procure. Another virtue of this advance is that it enables White, under various piece configurations, to push for h5 straight away, creating prospects for attack on the kingside, as mentioned before. In the game it was the first of these options which gave White a slight but enduring advantage after **19 ... ♗e6 20 ♘e3 c4 21 ♘g5! ♗xg5 22 hxg5 ♘a5 23 ♘g4 ♗xg4 24 ♕xg4**, etc.

Interesting, though for different reasons, was Fischer's employment of the chain in his game against Benko at the 4th cycle of the Candidates in 1959 (Pos. 42).

Here, White's h5 advance is of course excluded, and it is even questionable if White could make any active use of g5. Actually

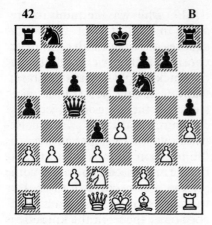

42 B

White's h4 is directed against Black's possibility of making use of g5, that is by playing ... g7-g5, an advance that might offer him some spatial advantages on that wing. These considerations are by no means established conventions, and might well be preferred by one player and rejected by another. Thus, as Fischer tells in *MSMG*, he was accused by Tal of "bad judgment" for preferring White's position here.[16] Such a verdict, in this type of position, must be given primarily with regard to both sides' pawn formations. Incidentally, Benko wasn't deterred by the presence of White's pawn at h4, and carried out the advance ... g7-g5 all the same. White had, though, slightly the better of it after **14 ... ♘bd7 15 ♗g2 ♘g4 16 0-0 g5 17 b4 ♕e7 18 ♘f3 gxh4 19 ♘xh4 ♘de5 20 ♕d2 ♖g8 21 ♕f4.**

That the dynamic advantages of the chain could turn into disadvantages was displayed most dramatically in Fischer's game against Keller, Zürich 1959 (Pos. 43).

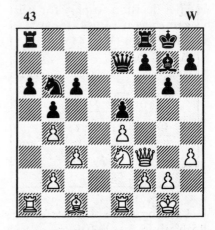

43 W

Fischer started shaping the chain by **20 g3**, to which Mednis pointedly remarked: "The move is bad enough by itself, as it provokes an attacking object for Black's f-pawn after ... f5 and ... f4. What is even worse is that it prepares the suicidal advance of the h-pawn."[17] There followed: **20 ... ♕e6 21 h4 f5 22 h5.** The h-pawn advances, but to whose advantage? **22 ... f4 23 ♘f1 gxh5 24 ♕xh5 ♖f6 25 ♘h2 ♖g6 26 ♘f3 fxg3 27 fxg3 ♖xg3+.** The white king was stripped of his shield and naturally couldn't survive thus unclad for long.

There are cases in which the chain, though being a prominent element in the position, might vouchsafe no visible or vital advantages. As in Fischer-Olafsson, 4th cycle, Candidates 1959:

44                                    B

Looking at Pos. 44, after White's 15th move, we observe the restrictive power of the chain. Black's dark-squared bishop and king's knight are limited in motion, and this cramps the whole of Black's

45                                    B

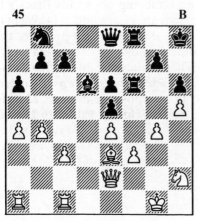

position on the kingside. In Pos. 45 we have the picture of the game 14 moves later, that is after White's 29th move. We realise the chain has advanced a step farther. How effective is such a chain here? Being more advanced, isn't it more restrictive as well? Remarkably enough, it isn't! It does still restrict Black's manoeuvring space on the kingside to some extent, but not drastically so. As a matter of fact, White's manoeuvring space on the kingside is at least as restricted. There is no action he could undertake on that wing (30 g5 would be positionally unjustifiable, since there isn't yet enough to sustain the solitary bishop on g5 after 30 ... hxg5 31 ♗xg5), and the knight at h2 has been relegated to the modest task of the f3 base pawn's protector. Black's weakness on g6 is, as yet, inaccessible to White's forces; and the question which pawn structure is the more vulnerable (Black's in view of the e6 and e5 pawns and the g6 square, or White's in view of the f3 pawn) can't be answered definitely at this stage.

For a structure similar to Pos. 44, see Pos. 236.

It is interesting to note that another player in whose games this formation occurred fairly often was Tigran Petrosian.[18] There is no need to stress the huge differences in Fischer's and Petrosian's chess outlooks, yet this structure's restrictive and space-gaining qualities perfectly conformed with the latter's style.

There is, therefore, some irony in the fact that when annotating their 2nd game from the Match of the Century, Belgrade 1970, Fischer commented about the position after Black's (his) 51st move (Pos. 46) that "the endgame is lost for White since his pawn structure on the kingside is weak"![19]

**46**                                **W**

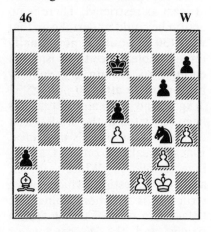

This, anyway, was demonstrated by **52 ♔f3 ♘f6 53 ♔e3 ♔d6**. The white king has to rush now to the queenside, yet he can't play 54 ♔d3 because of 54 ... ♔c5 55 f3 ♘h5[20] 56 g4 ♘f4+ 57 ♔c3 ♘e2+ 58 ♔b3 ♘d4+ 59 ♔xa3 ♘xf3 60 h5 ♘g5 61 ♗d5 ♔d4, and wins. **54 f4 ♘d7 55 ♗b1**. Again he couldn't play ♔d3-c3, since after

55 ... ♘c5+ the e4 pawn might fall. **55 ... ♘c5 56 f5. 56 ♔d2?** ♘xe4+ wins. This situation gave Black a free hand to manoeuvre ... ♘a6-b4, which won him the white bishop and, naturally, the game. (see also Pos. 184-6)

## THE PAWN CHAIN II

A different type of pawn-chain is the one that is exclusively restrictive. It is a chain (say, c3-d4-e5) that opposes an opponent's chain (c4-d5-e6, in this example). If left unaltered, this structure would obviously be completely static.

The pros and cons of such formations have to be considered with regard to a long-term strategy, since restricting the opponent's options is very likely to restrict

**47**                                **W**

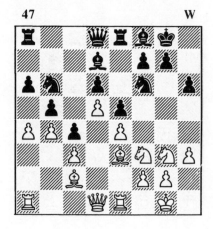

one's own options too. Thus, Trifunović, for instance, remarked about **20 a5** in Pos. 47 (Fischer-Gligorić, Rovinj-Zagreb 1970): "There is no more queenside play".[21] Since there are no great chances of creating central play either, White has to count on possibilities of creating some play on the kingside. As to Fischer's success in doing so, see Pos. 237.

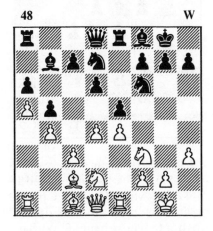

**48**　　　　　　　　**W**

A significant modification of the above, was Fischer's 10th match game against Spassky, World Championship, Reykjavik 1972 (Pos. 48). Here, after move 15, Black's (Spassky's) c-pawn is still at c7. This suggests that the tension on the queenside is far from being resolved yet. Indeed, the options of ... c5 (for Black) and c4 (for White) are very much to be kept in view, since both can change the features of the struggle

on the queenside, and across the whole board. The game proceeded: **16 ♗b2 ♕b8 17 ♖b1 c5 18 bxc5 dxc5 19 dxe5 ♘xe5 20 ♘xe5 ♕xe5 21 c4**, with a very tense position. (see also Pos. 318)

A certain spatial advantage was granted by such chains on the kingside in Fischer's games (with the black pieces) against Olafsson, 3rd cycle, Candidates 1959 (Pos. 49, after White's 28th move), and Lombardy, Monte Carlo 1967 (Pos. 50, after White's 40th move).

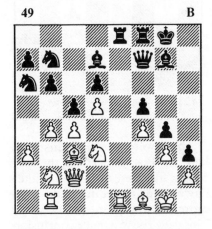

**49**　　　　　　　　**B**

It couldn't yield much in Pos. 49 since there was too little tension present in the position. With only the e-file open, Black could hope for no hegemony in the centre, and had to take the little that was left to be taken on the queenside: **28 ... ♗f6 29 ♖xe8 ♖xe8 30 ♖e1 ♖xe1 31 ♗xe1 cxb4 32 axb4 ♗d4+ 33 ♗f2 ♗xf2+ 34**

♕xf2 ♕f6. The queen dominates the long diagonal now. The pressure it puts next on White's queenside's pawns proves insufficient for winning purposes. 35 ♘d1 ♕a1 36 ♘e3 ♕c3 37 ♘d1 ♕xc4 38 ♘e5 ♕c1 39 ♘xd7 ♕xd1 40 ♕b2 ♕e1, draw.

46 ♕e3 ♗xb3 47 ♘xb3 ♘c4 48 ♕e2 ♘xe5 49 ♘c5 ♕e7 50 ♘xb7 ♘fd7 51 ♕d2 ♘c4 52 ♕c3 ♕e2 53 ♗xc6 ♘d2 54 ♕c1 ♘7e5, and White resigned. Mate is unavoidable.

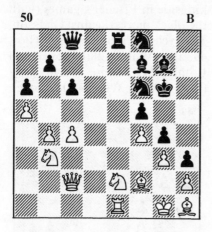

50      B

51      W

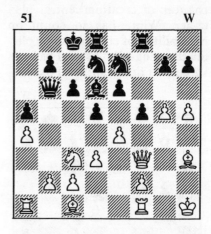

There were greater gains to be had in Pos 50. Here the two central files were open, and White's pawns on the queenside were more than just modestly weak. This gave rise to a quick conclusion: **40 ... ♘e4 41 ♗d4 ♗xd4+ 42 ♘exd4 ♘d6! 43 ♖e5.** This leads to an elegant solution, based on White's immobility on the king-side, and the weakness of the first rank. But even by correct play, i.e. 43 ♖xe8 ♕xe8, he couldn't have saved the game – the pawn on c4 is to fall next move. **43 ... ♖xe5 44 fxe5 ♕e8! 45 ♕e2 ♗xc4**

In Fischer-Kagan, Netanya 1968 (Pos. 51), Black has just played 15 ... f7-f5. After 16 gxf6 e.p. the position would have been opened up, but to whose benefit? With his two bishops, and threats at g7 and e6 after 16 ... ♖xf6 17 ♕g2, one would expect the answer to be "to White's", but after 17 ... h6! 18 f4 (18 ♕xg7?? ♖g8 19 ♕h7 ♘f8 picks up the queen) 18 ... ♖df8!, White can't play 19 e5 and Black gets reasonable counterplay. Fischer decides instead to support his two far-advanced pawns on the kingside by f4. **16 ♕g2! g6 17 h6 ♔b8 18 f4**, and we have the chain! There is no tension on the kingside any longer, and with his next move Fischer stabilises the centre, too. But there is a lot of play left on the queenside, and with cramped positioning of his pieces Black was unable to stand up against White's offensive there. 18 ... ♖fe8 19 e5 ♗c5 20 ♕f3 ♘c8 21 ♗g2 ♔c7 22 ♘e2 ♘b8 23 c3 ♘d7 24 ♗d2 ♘a6 25 ♖fb1 ♗f8 26 b4!, and White crashed through along the b-file.

## THE PAWN TRIANGLE

The importance of the role that 'holes' in the pawn structure played in Fischer's positional considerations was indicated by his remarks on his 13th move against Miagmarsuren, Sousse 1967 (Pos. 52), a game he analysed in depth in his column in *Boys' Life* (see p.52) in June 1968:

52　　　　　　　　　　　W

**13 a3**
Fischer: "Believe it or not, I actually spent more time on this innocuous push (15 minutes) than on any other move in the game! I didn't want to allow Black to get in ... a3, which would practically force me to reply with b3, thereby creating "holes" (weak squares) on c3 and d4. On the other hand, by stopping to meet his positional threat I am forced to postpone my own schemes for at least one move." And if for some readers 13 a3 might seem anything but remarkable, hearken then to how it was reviewed at the time by Robert Wade in the tournament book: "A big surprise. Following the Bronstein game [Bronstein-Botvinnik, 14th match game 1951], in which White played c3 on move 10, it has been accepted policy for White to leave the queenside pawns unmoved as long as possible to keep that wing blocked while he gathers together material for a strike on the king's wing."[22] So this decision went against 16 years of chess praxis! (see also Pos. 168, 172)

It was Fischer's policy to avoid, as far as possible, the creation of such pawn triangles, and induce their creation by his opponents. Pos. 53 (Pachman-Fischer, Havana Olympiad 1966), featured such a pawn triangle. How critical should White's position be assessed as in

**53**

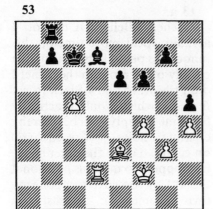

view of this? Well, Pachman for one, thought it was a hopeless one, and decided to resign at this point (after adjournment) without resuming the game. He explained his decision thus: "It could be argued that I resigned too early," he wrote in the German magazine *Schach-Echo*.[23] "Yet my analysis had convinced me that the position was completely lost. The black king marches via d8, e7, f7, g6 and f5 to g4, the bishop takes up his position at c6, and the rook infiltrates via the a-file or the d-file; and against all this White has no defence or counterplay whatever." (see also Pos. 31, 95, 288)

In many such endgames it would be the king's penetration to the centre of this triangle that would signal the coming end. The reason is quite easy to figure: The closeness of the pawns to each other make them an easy prey for the king. Against Tal at the Candidates in Curaçao 1962 (2nd cycle), Fischer (White) was ready to offer a pawn to create the triangle on Tal's kingside (Pos. 54).

**54**                              **W**

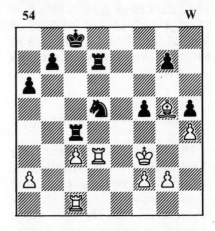

**28 ♖cd1!**. Forcing liquidation to ease the king's penetration of the kingside. **28 ... ♖xc3 29 ♖xc3+ ♘xc3 30 ♖c1 ♖c7 31 ♗f4 ♖c6 32 ♗e5 ♘d5 33 ♖d1 ♘f6 34 ♔f4 g6**, and the triangle has been established. Four moves later the king reached the heart of the triangle – g5: **35 f3 ♘d7 36 ♗d6 ♖c2 37 g3 ♖e2**. If 37 ... ♖xa2, then 38 ♖c1+! ♔d8 39 ♔g5 b5 (39 ... ♖e2 40 ♗c7+ ♔e7 41 ♔xg6 ♖e3 42 ♖d1! ♘f8+ 43 ♔xh5 ♖xf3 44 ♗d6+ ♔f7 45 ♖b1 b5 46 ♖a1 ought to win for White) 40 ♔xg6 a5 41 ♔f7! ♖e2 42 ♗c7+ ♔c8 43 ♗f4+ ♔d8 44 ♗g5+ and mates.

This winning line has been completely overlooked by the many annotators of the game.[24] **38 ♔g5.** The game remained quite interesting until White's win of the triangle's base pawn – g6: **38 ... ♖e6 39 ♗f4! ♘f8 40 ♖d6 a5 41 ♔h6! ♖e2 42 ♖d2 ♖e7 43 ♗d6 ♖h7+ 44 ♔g5 ♖f7 45 ♖b2 f4!? 46 ♗xf4 ♖f5+ 47 ♔h6 b5 48 ♗d6 b4 49 g4 ♖xf3 50 g5! ♘e6 51 ♔xg6,** and the rest was, as they say, a matter of technique.

**56**            **B**

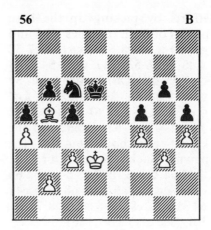

**55**            **W**

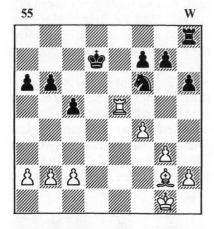

On reaching Pos. 55 against Taimanov in their 4th match game, Candidates 1971, Fischer played **25 ♗f1**, forcing the creation of the triangle by **25 ... a5.** After trading off rooks, some twenty moves later, the following position (Pos. 56), appeared on the board.

Had White's c-pawn stood on c4, instead of c3, we would get not only almost symmetrical pawn formations with four triangles, but – more importantly – a dead drawn position, since b5 would be inaccessible to White's king. Here White's advantage consists in this possibility, plus the fact that Black's other triangle – that on the kingside – is composed of pawns corresponding to the colour of the white bishop. This might well be the optimal advantage that two pawn triangles could offer the opponent – one being accessible to the king, the other to a piece. Here, with the material reduced to minimum, this factor proves decisive. White's triangle, on the other hand, is invulnerable, since Black's knight can't get at it. Play continued: **45 ... ♘e7 46 ♗e8 ♔d5 47 ♗f7+ ♔d6 48 ♔c4 ♔c6 49 ♗e8+ ♔b7 50 ♔b5** – and the king has arrived! A dozen moves later White was able to crown his efforts by picking up the base pawns of both triangles – b6 and g6: **50 ... ♘c8 51 ♗c6+ ♔c7 52 ♗d5 ♘e7 53 ♗f7 ♔b7 54 ♗b3 ♔a7 55 ♗d1 ♔b7 56 ♗f3+ ♔c7 57 ♔a6 ♘g8 58 ♗d5 ♘e7 59 ♗c4 ♘c6 60 ♗f7 ♘e7 61 ♗e8 ♔d8 62 ♗xg6! ♘xg6 63 ♔xb6**, and the knight was no match for the pawns. Black resigned after **63 ... ♔d7 64 ♔xc5 ♘e7 65 b4 axb4 66 cxb4 ♘c8 67 a5 ♘d6 68 b5 ♘e4+ 69 ♔b6 ♔c8 70 ♔c6 ♔b8 71 b6**, 1-0. (see also Pos. 156)

57                                    W

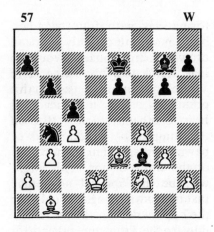

Position 57 shows the game Gheorghiu-Fischer, Siegen Olympiad 1970 after Black's 28th move. Wishing to simplify still further, Gheorghiu played **29 a3 ♘c6 30 ♗e4**, forcing the exchange of the light-squared bishops. (**30 ... ♗xe4 31 ♘xe4**). The Romanian Constantin Stefaniu, in his book *Fischer, Gheorghiu, Karpov*, tells that Fischer criticised White's 29th move after the game, indicating 29 g4.[25] As for the reason – well, it was the almost imperceptible weakening of White's pawn formation on the queenside. After **30 ... ♗b2!** we have Gheorghiu's own comment in his autobiography: "An excellent move, causing a slight weakening of White's pawn structure".[26] **32 a4** now saddled White with a pawn triangle on the queenside. Gheorghiu had to show great ingenuity to hold the issue in the balance in the next 26 moves, notwithstanding the drawish nature of the position (see further Pos. 161).

Yet it was not only in endgames that Fischer created or tried to exploit such weaknesses in the opponent's pawn structure. Against Durao at the Havana Olympiad 1966 he was ready to enter the following queenless middlegame

58                                    W

position (Pos. 58, after Black's 16th move, Fischer having the white pieces). He did so in view of Black's pawn triangle on the queenside, and the potentially weak squares on d6 and f6.

First he saw to fixing Black's triangle, since if Black is allowed to play ... a4 and ... b5, it could turn into quite a powerful phalanx. So: **17 a4!**. Next he traded the light-squared bishops and established a knight at c4: **17 ... ♖ad7 18 ♗f1 ♗xf1 19 ♔xf1 ♘de7 20 ♘c4**. This knight was later to bite at the triangle (pawns a5 and b6 – see Pos. 246). But there was some instructive manoeuvring to behold before that, for which the reader is referred to Pos. 118. (see also Pos. 149)

## THE KING'S INDIAN CENTRE

Throughout his career Fischer wavered between two alternative set-ups in the King's Indian Defence: one features a pawn centre, the other a centre occupied by pieces. This dilemma hit at the crux of his approach to the game. Both set-ups were dynamic, each in its own way. One was based on a mobile pawn centre, the other on active piece play.

In his game against Petrosian at the 1958 Portorož Interzonal

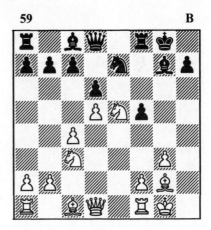

59           B

(Pos. 59) Fischer played **13 ... ♗xe5**, but later, when analysing the game in *MSMG*, he regretted that decision and thought that **13 ... dxe5**, keeping a fluid pawn centre, was preferable. He admitted he had been unnecessarily worried about a possible **14 c5**.[27] The way he played gave Petrosian an immediate hold on the important d4 square, while ousting Black's bishop from e5: **14 f4 ♗g7 15 ♗e3 ♗d7 16 ♗d4**. Moreover, Black now had little compensation for his inferior pawn formation on the kingside. (see also Pos. 194)

If d4 is one central square that Black might have to concede in this structure when opting for piece play (see also Pos. 63), e4 is another one. Fischer was not averse to doing so when meeting Najdorf at Mar del Plata 1959 (Pos. 60):

**60**　　　　　　　　**B**

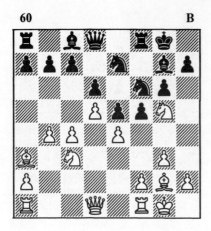

**13 ... fxe4 14 ♘cxe4 ♘f5 15 ♗b2 ♘xe4 16 ♘xe4 ♘d4 17 f4 ♗f5**, yet at the other end of his career, in his 4th match game against Larsen, Candidates 1971 (Pos. 61), he would take a different decision:

**61**　　　　　　　　**W**

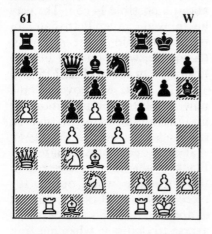

**18 exf5 gxf5**, on which Suetin remarked "18 ... ♘xf5 is also all

right, though after 19 ♘de4 ♗xc1 20 ♘xf6+ ♖xf6 21 ♖fxc1 ♘d4 White's control of e4 gives him a stable position".[28] Quite a similar sequence took place in the game, but with the important difference that White enjoyed no stability on e4: **19 ♗c2 a6 20 ♘de4 ♗xc1 21 ♘xf6+ ♖xf6 22 ♖fxc1 ♖af8 23 ♖b6 ♗c8 24 ♘e2 f4**. He does eventually give e4 away, but under much more propitious circumstances. **25 ♗e4 ♘f5 26 ♖c6 ♕g7 27 ♖b1 ♘h4 28 ♕d3 ♗f5**, and Black's pieces completely dominated the kingside.

Back again at Mar del Plata 1959, Fischer had to solve the problems of the following position (Pos. 62), ensuing this time from a Sicilian (Pilnik-Fischer, after White's 18th move).

**62**　　　　　　　　**B**

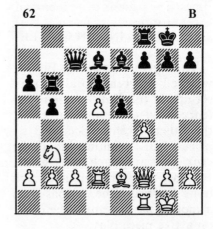

He played here **18 ... ♗f6**, arguing in *MSMG* that he didn't want to weaken e6 with 18 ... f5 19 c3 ♗f6 20 fxe5 dxe5 21 ♘c5, with equality.[29] Fischer also noted that in this line 20 ... ♗xe5 would have been answered by 21 ♘d4. This brings to mind Pos. 59, where the capture on e5 by the bishop disadvantageously lost hold of d4. And the structural similarities between these two positions, which are otherwise visibly different, coincide in respect to another point: in both it is the renunciation of c5 with which Black has to reckon. In this case it is the knight's move (21 ♘c5) and in the other it was the pawn's move (14 c5) by which White could take advantage of his new possession.

Within a space of seven weeks, Fischer faced the following two positions (Pos. 63 and 64) three times. The positions are identical, except for the elimination of both sides' dark-squared bishops in

63                                 B

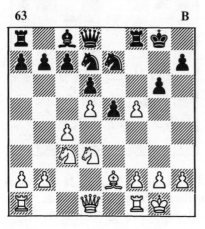

Pos. 63. That position (Reshevsky-Fischer, 1st match game 1961) illustrates the many problems this particular structure poses for Black.

Fischer captures on f5 with the pawn – **14 ... gxf5** – seemingly in order to maintain a fluid structure. After **15 f4** Black can play 15 ... e4, which, for the time being, does nothing to damage the structure, yet as in Pos. 59 and 62 it concedes d4 in the long run (the sole difference being the closed position here as compared with the semi-open positions there). Fischer plays **15 ... ♘g6**, but, inconsequently though it may appear, after **16 ♕d2 ♖e8 17 fxe5 ♘dxe5 18 ♘xe5**, he recaptures on e5 with a piece – **18 ... ♖xe5**, and not 18 ... dxe5. Here, as previously, this pawn capture would have given White the opportunity to make immediate use of c5 – 19 c5!. So, as in Pos. 59 he had to cope now with a compromised pawn structure on the kingside, the pawn on f5 being an obvious weakness. He found a way of solving his problem by sacrificing the pawn a few moves later, after having traded some minor pieces and having compromised White's pawn structure: **19 ♘b5 ♗d7 20 ♗d3 ♗xb5 21 cxb5 ♕d7 22 ♕f2 f4!? 23 ♗xg6 hxg6 24 ♕xf4 ♖ae8**, with a tenable position, notwithstanding his pawn deficit.

**64**                                    **B**

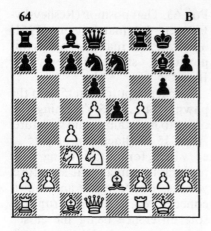

Fischer took a different decision (**11 ... ♘xf5**) in Pos. 64, which occurred twice: the first time in his 11th match game against Reshevsky, 1961 (see also Pos. 99), and then in his game against Gligorić at Bled that year, right after the untimely termination of Fischer's match with Reshevsky. Both games are included in *MSMG* (G. 28 and G. 30 respectively) and it is interesting to compare Fischer's comments to this position in both of them. The first is: "11 ... gxf5 keeping Black's pawn front mobile is very strong".[30] The second is: "In this line White gets a grip on e4, Black on d4. 11 ... gxf5 is more energetic."[31] Very strong, and more energetic than 11 ... ♘xf5 – we may wonder why he refrained from playing it! The answer is given by his remark to the next move in the game against

Gligorić, **12 f3 ♘f6**: "For 12 ... ♘d4 see game number 28. Both moves give Black a nice game."[32] In this light we understand "very strong and energetic" as posited against "a nice game". We may take this last to mean dynamic and lively piece play. Probably nothing can better illustrate Fischer's difficulty in determining which set-up ought to be regarded as preferable. It seems that he preferred the pawn capture (... gxf5) on principle, but felt more at home in the positions which arose from a knight capture (... ♘xf5).

Of considerable interest is also the following example, taken from D.Byrne-Fischer, US Championship 1966-67 (Pos. 65).

**65**                                    **B**

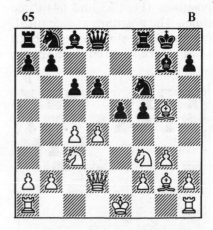

Fischer's **13 ... exd4** makes a rather strange impression. Why should Black spoil the elasticity

of his pawn formation in the centre? Has it to do with Fischer's approach to questions of pawn elasticity in general? Not very much. It all makes sense when we examine the alternative line 13 ... ♕e8 (13 ... ♘bd7 14 0-0 wouldn't make much difference) 14 dxe5 (14 0-0 ♘e4!) 14 ... dxe5 (14 ... ♘e4?! 15 ♘xe4 fxe4 16 ♘h4 ♕xe5 17 0-0! d5 – 17 ... ♕xb2 18 ♕xd6 is better for White – 18 cxd5 cxd5 19 ♗f4, with White having the advantage) 15 0-0, and the open d-file and half open e-file guarantee White favourable prospects. He would be able to put very useful pressure on the e-pawn, whether it is on e5 or e4. In the latter case, after the eventual exchange of pawns on f3, Black would have no compensation for his bad pawns on the kingside. After 13 ... exd4 – the move Fischer chose to play – he maintained a pawn majority on the queenside. There followed **14 ♘xd4 ♕e8+ 15 ♘de2 ♘bd7 16 0-0 ♘e5 17 ♕xd6 ♘xc4 18 ♕f4 ♘e5**, with a slight advantage to Black.

The problems dealt with here recur quite often in middlegames emanating from the King's Indian or related openings. How much prudence is still required in applying the standard and tested concepts associated with these structures was to be seen in,

among other games, Ivanchuk-Timman, Linares 1989.

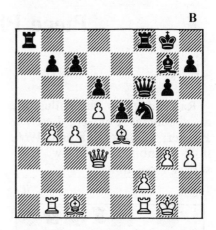

B

In the diagrammed position Timman played 22 ... ♘d4, a centralisation that in many cases is Black's recompense for conceding e4 to White. Timman, remarkably enough, attached a question mark to his move, and wrote: "A bad move. The knight is not positioned correctly on d4."![33] And indeed, after 23 ♔g2 ♖a4 24 h4 ♔h8 25 ♖b2, the knight had to retreat – 25 ... ♘f5, thus yielding White the initiative.

It is to be assumed that the positional questions surrounding this pawn structure and the piece activity linked to it will in all likelihood remain very much live issues and will continue to present a challenge as long as these openings are played.

# Piece Placement

Rarely does a position illustrate as vividly as Pos. 66, Letelier-Fischer, Leipzig Olympiad 1960, how combinations flow from superior positions.

**66**            **B**

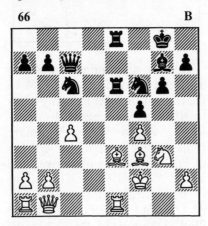

Let's compare both sides' piece deployment:

Queens: White's has limited scope on the b1-h7 diagonal, Black's is exerting pressure on the isolated f4 pawn, might incidentally attack the c4 pawn (after ... ♘b4 for instance), or reinforce the threats on the e-file by ... ♛e7.

Rooks: White's a1 rook is hemmed in, and the e1 rook plays as yet a protective role only. Black's rooks are doubled on the e-file, and constitute a threatening battery.

Minor pieces: The white bishops occupy important diagonals. One concrete threat is ♗d5. They are the only white pieces that have a say in the game. The knight, on the other hand, plays a very modest role at g3, and could have served better as a defensive piece at f1. Its present position would have been meaningful only if potential sacrifices at f5 were on. The only positive role it does play is in protecting e4, so that Black's ... ♘e4(+) could be answered by ♘xe4, when the recapture with the pawn (... fxe4) is compulsory, thus shutting down the e-file. In comparison with this, all the three black minor pieces occupy natural and good positions, which are boosted by an effective pawn structure, and especially the pawn on f5, which lends support to Black's activities in the centre.

As a matter of fact, Black has just completed his development, but he has deployed his pieces in such a way that they converge on the centre ready for decisive action. There is an invisible thread which binds them together to operate in concert. And that is, indeed, something which typified Fischer's approach to problems of piece placement, namely an aspiration to place them in an harmonious way, and create a co-ordination with regard to specific positional objectives. To return to the position at hand: Black's superiority in piece placement is so overwhelming that he can win the game as he pleases. One way is 21 ... ♘g4+ 22 ♗xg4 fxg4, with the deadly threats of 23 ... ♖xe3 and/or 23 .../24 ... ♗d4. A slight variation on this is 21 ... ♖xe3 22 ♖xe3 ♘g4+ 23 ♗xg4 ♗d4. Yet even 21 ... ♘d4 wins right away. Letting Black exchange on f3 fatally weakens the g4 square, and 22 ♗xd4 ♖xe1 (or 22 ... ♘g4+) is as bad. 22 ♗d5 again allows a pretty finish: 22 ... ♘xd5 23 cxd5 ♖xe3, etc. What Fischer played is by far the prettiest: **21 ... ♖xe3! 22 ♖xe3 ♖xe3 23 ♔xe3 ♕xf4+!!,** when another facet of the happy arrangement of the black pieces revealed itself – 24 ♔xf4 allows 24 ... ♗h6 mate! – Black controls all the squares around f4 except f3 and g3, which incidentally are occupied by white pieces. (see also Pos. 294)

Certainly more balanced is the following position (67), reached

after Black's 23rd move in Najdorf-Fischer, Havana Olympiad 1966.

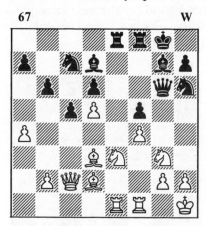

67                                    W

Najdorf once said: "Bobby just drops the pieces and they fall on the right squares".[1] In this relatively typical Benoni set-up Fischer has 'dropped' his pieces in optimally active positions: the bishops have good diagonals, the queen is well placed on g6, the rooks are in the centre, the knight on c7 puts pressure on the pawn on d5, while the other knight, without interfering in the activity of the other pieces, guards f5. This last is an important factor – Fischer tries to place his pieces so that they don't get in each other's way, as far as that is possible. What we get here, then, is a dynamic position, containing many objectives to play on: open lines and diagonals, weak pawns (on both sides, by the way, which promises sharp play) etc. (see also Pos. 223) The same considerations hold good for the next example – Suttles-Fischer, Palma de Mallorca 1970 (Pos. 68).

**68**              **W**

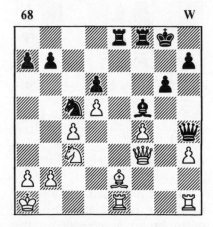

Not only do all the black pieces occupy active posts, but their harmonious convergence on the e- and f-files bears the unmistakable mark of a critical action. Black's dominance of the e-file in particular is very significant, making threats such as 27 ... ♘e4, 27 ... ♗e4, or 27 ... ♘d3 possible, or, even more elaborately, doubling rooks on the e-file and invading on e3. Furthermore the co-operation of the bishop on f5 and the knight on c5 can in some cases produce mating threats through manoeuvres such as ... ♕d8-a5. As in Letelier-Fischer (Pos. 66) we realise that well placed pieces may give rise to more than a single good plan.

(see also Pos. 155, 269)

Even in positions where there are no concrete plans, Fischer will seek to deploy his pieces effectively. Hort-Fischer, Palma de Mallorca 1970 (Pos. 69), looked like this after White's 26th move:

**69**              **B**

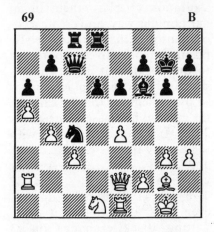

Three out of Black's six pieces are poised to attack c3, while the knight and the rook on d8 are plainly well deployed for anything that might take place in the centre. Black does not yet have a concrete plan as far as winning the pawn on c3 is concerned, but at this stage it isn't even necessary to form such a plan. By further strengthening his position and waiting for the right opportunity Black achieves his aim eleven moves later: **26 ... h5 27 h4 ♕d7 28 ♔h2 ♘e5 29 ♖c2 ♘g4+ 30 ♔h1 ♖c7 31 ♗h3 ♘e5 32 ♘e3 ♕a4 33 ♖b1 ♘c4 34 ♖a2 ♕c6.** Seemingly Black's set-up has remained unmodified. However, the slight difference in the position of the queen, and the fact that White has shifted his pieces to and fro less skilfully, is transformed into a concrete advantage now. **35 ♘xc4 ♛xc4 36 ♕xc4 ♖xc4**, and Black wins a pawn. (see also Pos. 110, 287)

So far we have been looking at examples of open or semi-open positions. Here is an example of a closed position (Pos. 70).

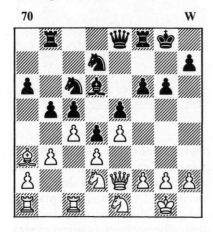

70                      W

How meaningful is better placement in positions like this one? (Petrosian-Fischer 6th match game, Candidates 1971). Black has the greater manoeuvring space, owing mainly to his advanced d-pawn, as against White's backward one. But besides this there are some visible differences in the deployment of the forces of both camps: Whereas White's pieces are not

organised for any concrete action on either side of the board, Black enjoys a great choice of such possibilities. He is the one to decide if and when to operate in the centre by advancing ... f5. He can play for various set-ups like, for example, ... ♕f7, ... ♖b7, and doubling rooks on the b-file, or ... ♕e7, ... ♖fc8, and ... ♘f8-e6, etc. There are other optional manoeuvres, which naturally wouldn't all be in accordance with every possible development of the position. In the actual game, as a result of the opening of the a-file by Petrosian's exchange on b5, Black's pieces became operative on the queenside through a different set-up: ♕f7 (ideally placed on the a2-g8 diagonal, ready to support the advance ... c5-c4; see Pos. 98)/ ♘a5/♘b6/♖a8/♖fb8. So even in a closed position like this, the advantage of having the better placed pieces, and the freer hand to manoeuvre and regroup, is quite significant. (see also Pos. 157)

Fischer tries to get superior piece placement right from the opening. Against Minić, at Vinkovci 1968, after the first five moves (Fischer playing White) – **1 e4 e5 2 f4 exf4 3 ♗c4 ♘e7 4 ♘c3 c6 5 ♘f3 d5** – a position similar to some main lines of the King's Gambit was reached, with the slight difference that Black's king's knight stood on e7 instead of the more common f6. Fischer therefore rejected the standard pawn exchange on d5, and played **6 ♗b3!**. Now the knight at e7 remained badly placed. In order to improve its position it was Black who had to exchange the central pawns – **6 ... dxe4 7 ♘xe4** – thus allowing White to centralise his knight in order for Black to centralise his own knight – **7 ... ♘d5**. By his timely attention to Black's misplaced knight, White gained a developmental advantage.

Against Robatsch's Centre Counter Defence (Varna Olympiad 1962) Fischer (White) developed the following elegant, quick, and efficient system: **1 e4 d5 2 exd5 ♕xd5 3 ♘c3 ♕d8 4 d4 g6 5 ♗f4! ♗g7 6 ♕d2!**. White has completed the development of his queenside and is ready to castle long. He has prevented the development of Black's knight to h6, which is one of his main instruments to pressurise the pawn d4 (... ♘f5). In the meantime he takes no decision as to which piece to play to b5 – a knight (to attack c7) or a bishop (to pin Black's knight after ... ♘c6), both of which remain important options with regard to Black's two possible captures of the gambitted pawn at d4.

The preceding examples have, hopefully, shown how well refined was Fischer's sense of piece place-

ment. Naturally, there are examples where that sense failed him. Few, however, where it did so as badly as in his game against Gligorić (White) at the Leipzig Olympiad 1960 (Pos. 71).

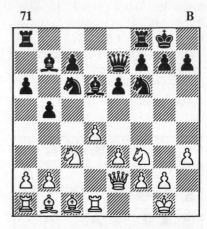

**71**　　　　　　　　　　　　**B**

**15 ... e5?**. This must be a mistaken concept as White hasn't played e4 yet, and that square can still be occupied by his minor pieces. But this misconception is less grave than the one it leads to next. Fischer has it in mind to play his knight back to d8, assuming he would be able to manoeuvre it swiftly to the centre via f7. **16 d5 ♘d8 17 ♘g5 h6 18 ♘ge4 ♘xe4 19 ♘xe4 f5 20 ♘xd6 cxd6 21 a4!**. The awkward positioning of the black pieces begins to tell. What Fischer thought would be a temporary retreat of the knight in order to regroup his pieces turns out to be a very useful opportunity for

White to develop his own pieces to ideal positions. 21 ... ♕e8 would be answered by 22 axb5 axb5 23 ♖xa8 ♗xa8 24 b4, or 24 ♗d3 b4 25 ♗b5 ♕f7 26 ♕c4 winning a pawn. **21 ... bxa4 22 ♖xa4 ♖f6 23 ♖c4! e4 24 b4 ♘f7 25 ♗b2 ♖g6?.** The last misplacement, and this time a fatal one. Fischer hopes to create some counterplay by this, followed by ... ♘g5, overlooking Gligorić's reply. Relatively better was 25 ... ♘e5 26 ♗xe5 ♕xe5 27 ♖c7 ♖f7 28 ♖xf7 ♔xf7 29 f3!, with advantage to White. **26 f4!**, and White won quickly after **26 ... exf3** in view of Black's weak pawn on f5.

**72** **B**

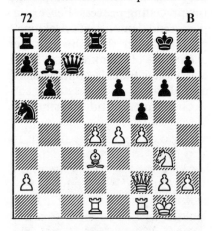

Against Spassky at Santa Monica 1966 (Pos. 72) he would play, quite uncharacteristically, **19 ... ♕f7?**, placing the queen at a square that offers no vistas for the future. Instead 19 ... ♕g7, as he himself later pointed out to his friend Bernard Zuckerman,[2] was called for.

**73** **B**

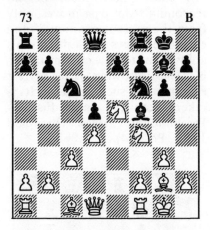

And at the same tournament, against Ivkov, he could play **12 ... ♗e4** (Pos. 73), on which Ivkov laconically remarked "Weak – the bishop is misplaced here".[3] And indeed after **13 ♗h3!** the bishop had nothing to do in the centre. (see also Pos. 284)

Piece placement is a dynamic process. One cannot place a piece on a certain square, and expect it to be optimally placed there for the rest of the game. Within a limited number of moves a piece's value may change drastically because of the altered features of the position. This demands of a player constant mental flexibility in replacing and regrouping the pieces according to the ever changing needs of the various positions that arise in succession over the board. Alekhine once remarked: "In chess there must be no reasoning from past moves, only from the present position,"[4] and everyone knows how difficult this adjustment to new circumstances is. The following is a perfect example of such a case. It is taken from the game Fischer-Ibrahimoglu, Siegen Olympiad 1970, (Pos. 74).

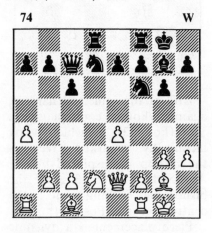

74                                    W

**15 ♘b3!.** In *L'Italia Scacchistica* Tatai writes: "Far stronger than the schematic 15 ♘c4. The knight on b3 watches over c5 and restricts Black's activity on the queenside."[5] True as this is, we shall soon realise that what Fischer had in mind reached beyond that. The knight at b3 is there for a short while only and for a limited purpose — that of not allowing Black to deploy his queen's knight

properly – neither 13 ♘b6 (14 a5) nor 13 ... ♘c5, nor 13 ... ♘e5 (which might have been Black's answer to 13 ♘c4, while now it is strongly met by 14 f4) is good. **13 ... b6 14 ♗e3 c5 15 a5 e5(?!) 16 ♘d2!.** The knight has nothing more to do at b3. All White wants now is to shift it one square to the right, namely c3, a process that requires three moves. **16 ... ♘e8 17 axb6 axb6 18 ♘b1 ♕b7 19 ♘c3.** After long manoeuvring the knight has finally reached its ideal square, eyeing both d5 and b5. **19 ... ♘c7 20 ♘b5!!.** One has to be mentally outstandingly flexible to play this move after completing the preceding process. Few examples could demonstrate Alekhine's precept better than this. Fischer exchanges off the knight in order to weaken Black's control of b5 and a6.

Great mental adjustment was

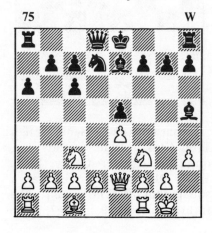

75                                    W

required of Fischer in the following case as well (Fischer-Alvarez, Mar del Plata 1960 Pos. 75).

Fischer plays here **10 ♘d1**, wishing to play ♘e3-f5 as quickly as possible. Yet he misses an important point: After **10 ... ♘c5 11 ♘e3** is wrong in view of 11 ... ♘xe4 12 ♘f5 ♗xf3 13 ♘xg7+ ♔f8 14 ♕xf3 ♘g5! – the knight attacks the queen while defending e6 against White's check. So White is forced to play **11 d3** first. But after **11 ... ♘e6!** 12 ♘e3 is again wrong because of 12 ... ♘f4, and neither is 12 g4 ♗g6 13 ♘xe5 ♘d4 14 ♕d2 f6 15 c3 fxe5 16 cxd4 ♕xd4 good for him. Now the ♘d1 is very badly placed indeed, and after **12 ♗e3** (threatening 13 g4) **12 ... ♗f6**, Fischer decides to play the knight back to c3 – **13 ♘c3**. However, Fischer's initial perception that the knight isn't well placed here hasn't changed. He decides to manoeuvre it now to c4, while keeping b3 as another option. It is worth mentioning that had he played 13 b3 and 14 ♘b2, then 14 ... b5 would have condemned the knight to a miserable fate. That's why the knight's voyage to c4 had to take the long route. There followed: **13 ... ♕e7 14 ♘b1 g5 15 ♘bd2 ♖g8**. If 15 ... b5 then 16 ♘b3 a5 17 a4!, with advantage. **16 g4! ♗g6 17 ♘c4**, and notwithstanding the long-winded regrouping, White had the initiative.

The following three examples are cases of structurally similar regroupings. The manoeuvring is very economical, and the main objective is the connection of the rooks, while the king is quite unconventionally placed in the centre in these semi-open positions.

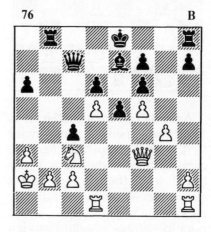

76             B

In Mednis-Fischer US Championship 1959-60 (Pos. 76), Black's bishop is evidently badly placed, and Fischer wants to transfer it to the more promising diagonal c1-h6. This needs some preliminary action: **20 ... h5!**. He protects the bishop from being attacked along the h-file, and breaks up White's pawns on the kingside. The price: a pawn and an open g-file for White. Yet if 20 ... ♗f8, then 21 h4 ♗h6 22 g5! fxg5 23 ♕h5, and Black is busted. **21 gxh5 ♗f8 22 ♖hg1 ♔e7! 23 ♕e2 ♗h6 24 ♖g4**

罝hc8. (see also Pos. 91)

77                                    B

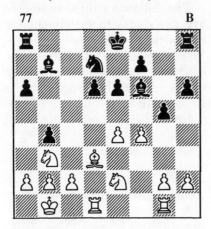

Against Troianescu at Netanya 1968 (Pos. 77) similar manoeuvring took place, except that here the dark-squared bishop was transferred from the kingside to the queenside. White is intending to play 19 ♘a5, to which 18 ... a5 is a poor preventive method in view of 19 ♗b5 ♗e7 20 f5!, and White has the advantage. His most immediate threat is 21 fxe6 fxe6 22 ♘c5!, winning the e-pawn. A standard solution would be 18 ... ♘c5. Fischer isn't satisfied with this. By the following regrouping he activates his pieces to the maximum: **18 ... ♗d8 19 g3 ♔e7!** defending d6, freeing the eighth rank for the rooks, and seeing to it that ... a5 could be played without fearing a pin with ♗b5. **20 c3 a5 21 cxb4 axb4 22 ♗c2 ♗b6 23 罝ge1 罝hg8!**. A short inter-

mezzo before taking up its regular position at c8. The threat is 24 ... gxf4 25 gxf4 罝g2, thus forcing White to loosen his grip on e5 by his next move. 23 ... gxf4 first would have been answered by 24 gxf4 罝hg8 25 ♘g3!, and White is okay. **24 f5 罝gc8**, with a tangible positional plus. After **25 ♘ec1 ♘e5**, all Black's pieces were splendidly placed. (see also Pos. 276)

78                                    W

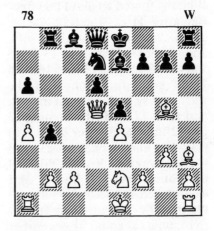

Against Matulović, some two and a half months later at Vinkovci, Yugoslavia, in a different variation of the Sicilian, Fischer's decision to apply a similar set-up was quite revolutionary (Pos. 78). On Matulović's **13 ♗xe7** Fischer captured back with **13 ... ♔xe7!**. Certainly quite a rare sight in this type of position. Gligorić, however, observed: "Black's reply ... speeds up his queenside piece development. The king is quite safe in the centre because of the fixed pawn centre."[6] In the next six moves, Fischer established the following set-up: ♘f6, a5, ♗a6, ♛b6, and ♖hc8; which bears great resemblance to the other two examples, and, one may add, is typical not only of Fischer's handling of various positions of the Sicilian, but of his approach to piece development in general: quick, effective and harmonious. (see also Pos. 197)

EXCEPTIONAL SET-UPS

Around 1966 (or probably even earlier), Fischer worked out a certain system which he employed on two occasions only. The first as Black against J.G.Soruco at the Havana Olympiad 1966 (Pos. 79), and the second as White against Andersson at Siegen 1970 (Pos. 80).

In both cases Fischer's set-up after eighteen moves is almost identical. It is quite a safe speculation that the initial impetus for this conception came about through his studies of the Sicilian Defence. The appearance of the English Opening (1 c4) and the Nimzowitsch Opening (1 b3) as White in his repertoire later in his

career might well have had something to do with this development and with his faith in the solid yet agressive qualities of this set-up. What makes it typically Fischerian is the rather bold and unconventional advance of the g-pawn (see Pos. 33-40).

For the time being it looks as though Fischer's activity on the g-file, and indeed on the kingside as a whole, is quite limited. But it all revolves around the timely advance of the g-pawn. In the first game this is the most immediate threat: 19 ... g4 20 hxg4 ♘exg4! wins; which frightened the Bolivian player into sacrificing incorrectly:

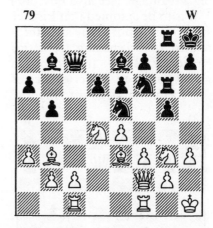

**79**          **W**

**19 ♘xe6?**, and after **19 ... fxe6 20 ♗xe6 ♘xe4 21 ♘xe4 ♖xe6**, White had to put down his weapons.

In the second game it took several preparatory moves before White advanced the pawn: **18 ...**

80              B

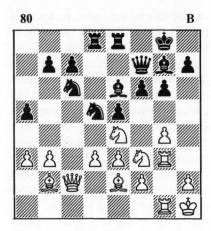

♘b6 19 ♘c5 ♗c8 20 ♘h4 ♘d7 21 ♘e4 ♘f8 22 ♘f5! ♗e6 23 ♘c5 ♘e7 24 ♘xg7 ♔xg7 25 g5!, with a big advantage. (see also Pos. 262)

It is to be assumed that Fischer studied in depth many structures related to or ensuing from this particular set-up. In two of his games, one can detect echoes of this formation. Against Gligorić,

81              B

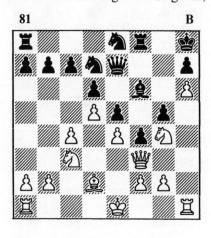

as Black at Monte Carlo 1967, he reached Pos. 81 after White's 16th move.

The following manoeuvre then took place: **16 ... ♖g8 17 0-0-0 ♖g6**. One would think Black's last move prepared ... ♘f8-g6. For some structural reason, however, Fischer prefers g6 to be occupied by the rook even in a position where the kingside is rather blocked, and the advance ... g4 is not in sight. This, in combination with his 23rd move, is strongly reminiscent of the two previous examples. **18 g3 c5 19 ♖dg1 ♘c7 20 ♘d1 b5 21 ♕e2 bxc4 22 ♕xc4 ♘b6 23 ♕e2 ♖ag8**.

82              W

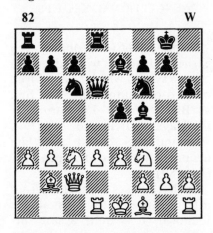

Against Tukmakov, at Buenos Aires 1970, Fischer's 1 b3 led to Pos. 82 after eleven moves. Black wished to go for simplifications in the centre by means of ... ♕e6 and ... e4. As Tukmakov mentions in

*Ajedrez*, the natural looking 12 ♗e2 would have enabled Black, after 12 ... ♕e6 13 ♘d2, to play 13 ... ♗g4! exchanging White's light-squared bishop, which defends the pawn on d3.[7] Fischer played **12 h3!** which, apart from preventing the above, made possible a rather unorthodox structure for this type of position – pushing g4 at this early stage. The game continued: **12 ... ♕e6 13 ♘d2 ♘d7 14 ♗e2**, and now, according to Tukmakov, correct was 14 ... ♕g6! (instead of his **14 ... ♔h8?**) 15 ♘de4 (15 g4 ♗e6) ♗e6 (15 ... ♕xg2? 16 ♘g3) 16 g4 ♗f8, and, remarkably enough, White's set-up is very much like the 'model' positions, with the exception that White hasn't castled yet. I see no plausible reason to doubt the correctness of Tukmakov's remarks, and it is more than likely that Fischer was consciously steering for this position.

# Material Considerations

From December 1966 to January 1970 Bobby Fischer was a regular contributor to the American scouts' magazine *Boys' Life*. In his articles he answered the children's questions, gave lots of practical advice, analysed games, and presented problems to solve, all in a very friendly and candid spirit. In the October 1968 issue, in answer to a reader's question, he advised him: "Concentrate on material gains. Whatever your opponent gives you take, unless you see a good reason not to."

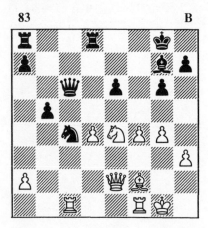

**83**           **B**

Analysing their exciting game at the Siegen 1970 Olympiad,
Spassky wrote about Fischer's **23 ... ♗xd4** in Pos. 83: "Fischer prefers to capture the pawn. Why? Simply because he would rather have an extra pawn. This little weakness in the American Grandmaster's style has been known to me for quite some time."[1] (see also Pos. 165, 258). On the strength of these two testimonies – Fischer's own, and one of his greatest rivals' – we seem able to contend without bias that Fischer's basic policy, as regards material considerations, was indeed "Take, unless you see a good reason not to".

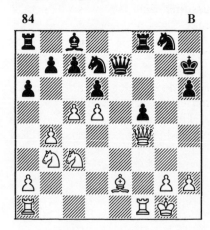

**84**           **B**

About Fischer's **20 ... dxc5** in his 3rd cycle game against Tal, Candidates 1959, Efim Geller remarked: (Pos. 84): "The different approach of the two grandmasters to one and the same position is most interesting. Tal stated that he did not consider this capture at all, since he considered that with the 'frozen' queenside, it was equivalent to suicide for Black to give up his last base."[2] And Tal in his autobiography, added that he thought Black was bound to play 20 ... ♘e5, on which there would probably have come 21 ♖ae1 followed by ♘d4, gradually preparing a kingside attack. Fischer, in his turn, captured on c5 without hesitation, evidently thinking that White had overlooked this, and that, with an extra pawn, he would have no difficulty in defending himself.[3] It is quite safe to assume that the reason "not to take" escaped Bobby this time. After Tal's **21 ♗d3!** there followed **21 ... cxb4 22 ♖ae1 ♕f6 23 ♖e6! ♕xc3 24 ♗xf5+**. White's attack flowed unchecked, and Black's material gains proved of no avail.

There are a number of cases in which Fischer can't resist material temptations, even, apparently, against his own better judgment. For a player of his sensitivity to principles of piece development, it is somewhat out of character to go pawn grabbing in the early stages of the game, allowing the opponent to disrupt the harmonious development of his pieces as in Fischer-Cardoso, Portoroz 1958 (Pos. 85):

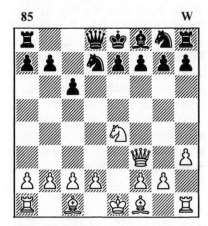

85                  W

**7 ♘g5** (in *MSMG* Fischer later indicated 7 d4)[4] **7 ... ♘gf6 8 ♕b3 e6 9 ♕xb7 ♘d5! 10 ♘e4 ♘b4 11 ♔d1**, and White's forces are deprived of any semblance of co-

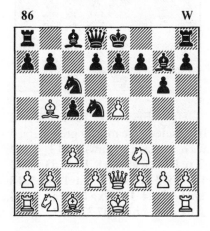

86                  W

ordination. The same held true for his celebrated encounter (as White) with Matulović at Palma de Mallorca 1970 (Pos. 86).

7 ♕c4 ♘c7 8 ♗xc6 dxc6 9 ♕xc5. Now he's a pawn up, but the price is very dear. 9 ... ♕d3 10 ♕e3 ♗f5 11 ♕xd3 ♗xd3, and Fischer had to muster all his ingenuity and will power in order to extricate himself from these dire straits – see Pos. 205.

At the same tournament he played the following game (Pos. 87 shows it after White's 12th move) against Uhlmann, a game that was "all meat".

87 B

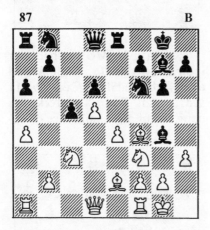

After Fischer's 12 ... ♘xe4! both sides were mostly preoccupied with counting pawns: 13 ♘xe4 ♖xe4 14 ♗g5 ♕e8 15 ♗d3 ♗xf3 16 ♕xf3 ♖b4 17 ♖ae1 ♗e5 18 ♕d1 ♕xa4 19 ♕xa4 ♖xa4 20 f4 ♗d4+ 21 ♔h1 ♘d7 22 ♖e7 ♘f6 23

♖xb7 ♘h5 24 ♔h2 ♗e3 25 ♗e2 ♗xf4+ 26 ♗xf4 ♖xf4 27 ♖b6 ♖xf1 28 ♗xf1 ♖d8 29 ♖xa6 ♔g7 30 ♗b5 ♔f6 31 ♗c6 ♔e4 32 ♖a7 ♖f8 33 ♖e7+ ♔d4 34 ♖d7 ♘f6, and White resigned. His pawn balance is negative. Seldom is a grandmaster required to do so little to win a game from a fellow grandmaster. But Fischer proved this might be a viable policy against an even mightier opponent – Tigran Petrosian. Their 9th and last game in the 1971 Candidates final had a comical flavour to it. Fischer took whatever he was given while Petrosian was engaged in deep manoeuvring, trying to weave a mating net around Fischer's king. By the time he almost succeeded, Fischer's material advantage had become so huge that he could beat off all of Petrosian's threats by benignly returning some of the material

88 W

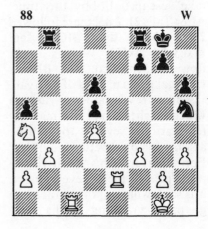

gained. We follow the game from its critical position after Black's (Petrosian's) 24th move (Pos. 88).

25 ♖c6 ♘f4 26 ♖d2 ♖fe8 27 ♖xd6 (one) ♖e1+ 28 ♔f2 ♖h1 29 ♔g3 ♘h5+ 30 ♔h4 g6 31 ♖xd5 (two) ♖e8 32 ♖xa5 (three) ♖ee1 33 ♘c3 ♘f4 34 ♔g4 ♘e6 35 ♖e5 f5+ 36 ♔g3 f4+ 37 ♔h4 ♔h7 38 ♘e4 g5+ 39 ♔g4 ♘g7. Now 40 ... ♔g6 41 ... h5 is mate, but meanwhile White has got 40 ♘xg5+! and after 40 ... hxg5 41 ♖xe1 ♖xe1 42 ♔xg5 ♘e6+ 43 ♔f5 ♖e2 44 ♖xe2 ♘xd4+ 45 ♔e5 ♘xe2 46 a4, Black had nothing else but to give up.

Yet Fischer's original statement shouldn't be taken at its face value, since no all-round player could ever afford to be that one-sided as regards any single aspect of the game. And though he could half-jokingly make remarks such as "13 h4? is too materialistic even for me"[5] with reference to Pos. 89 (Fischer-Bisguier, NY State Open Championship 1963; see also Pos. 2), he would, as a matter of fact, disdain taking or unnecessarily holding on to material in positions where this didn't fit in with other important features of the position, notably in positions where it hampered his own dynamic possibilities. As, for instance, in Fischer-Bukić, Skopje 1967, (Pos. 90).

90             W

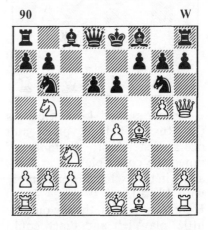

11 ♗xd6 would evidently have won a pawn, but after 11 ... ♗xd6 12 ♖d1 0-0 13 ♘xd6 ♕e7 (Boleslavsky)[6] or probably even better 12 ... ♘f4 13 ♕h4 ♘g6 14 ♕g4 e5 15 ♕g3 0-0 16 ♘xd6 ♕e7, White's position offers considerably scantier prospects than the game continuation: 11 ♗e3 a6 12 ♘d4 ♘e5 13 ♖d1 g6 14 ♕e2 ♗d7 15 h4, with a dynamic game where

89             W

White maintained a constant edge.

Remarkable in this respect was the decision Fischer took on his 17th move in his game (as Black) against Mednis, US Championship 1959-60 (Pos. 91).

**91**                                        **B**

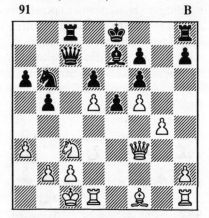

Fischer played **17 ... ♞c4**. As the Russian-Belgian priest and chess master Victor Sultanbeieff noted, he could play 17 ... ♞a4, and win the exchange quite simply with 18 ♜d3 e4 19 ♛xe4 ♞c5.[7] Here too, though, there would be little 'play' left and Black could face great problems in realising his material advantage. Instead Fischer preferred to let the game stay lively and dynamic. (see also Pos. 76)

Even more eloquent was Fischer's unwillingness to concede his clear dynamic edge for mere material gains in an earlier game, Fischer-Bhend, Zürich 1959 (Pos. 92).

**92**                                        **W**

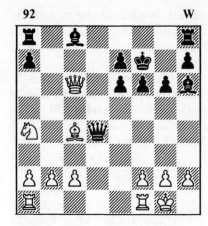

**16 ♜ae1!?**. No sworn materialist would have hesitated to take the rook: 16 ♛xa8 ♛xc4 17 ♞c3; but Fischer's move keeps the attack going, and is an apt precursor to later 'grand lines' (see pp.249-53). **16 ... ♜b8 17 ♝xe6+ ♚g7 18 ♝d5 ♝g5(!)**. 18 ... ♜b7 19 ♞c5! wins quickly. **19 ♜e4! ♛d2 20 ♜xe7+ ♚h6**, and only now did he become materialistic with **21 ♜xa7**, since 21 f4 (Euwe's preference)[8] 21 ... ♝h4! (Euwe's omission) leaves the issue a little unclear. For instance 22 g3? ♝h3! 23 gxh4 ♛d4+! and wins!

These last few examples, the many gambits Fischer played throughout his career, and other examples scattered in this book under different headings (see, for instance, Pos. 115, 156, 179, 253), point to the fact that Fischer's materialistic views were, in the final analysis, qualified if not strictly dualistic. It was more common with him to resort to materialistically oriented decisions when there was nothing better at hand than to do so indiscriminately. A characteristic example of this is the following (Pos. 93), played at Vinkovci 1968 between Fischer (White) and Hort.

93             W

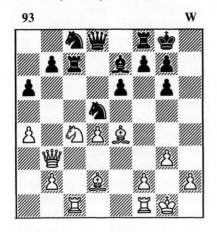

White's dynamic possibilities are very limited. As a matter of fact, it is Black who enjoys the more dynamic options. Either 22 ... ♗g5 (followed, after trading bishops, by ... ♘ce7), or 22 ... ♗f6 with the same idea, trying to exploit White's weakness at d4 and/or consolidate Black's d5 stronghold, are positional threats to be taken seriously. Going for material is White's only chance to hold his own, with chances of keeping options for more. **22 ♘a5** 22 ♗a5 is answered simply by 22 ... b6, when 23 ♗xd5? ♕xd5 loses material. **22 ... ♘cb6 23 ♗xd5 ♘xd5 24 ♘xb7 ♕b8 25 ♖xc7 ♕xc7 26 ♖c1 ♕b8 27 ♖c4.** Black threatened 27 ... ♗b4!, winning a piece. **27 ... ♖d8 28 ♗c3 ♖d7 29 ♘a5**, and White's pawn plus enabled him to enter a slightly favourable endgame.

# Timing

Timing in chess cannot be dealt with in isolation from other elements of the game. It is the correct timing in carrying out a certain plan which counts. A plan can become good by virtue of its correct timing, and vice versa – a plan that in principle might have been a good one in a certain position, can turn bad or ineffective if applied too early or too late. This is of special significance in sharp and positionally dynamic games. For Fischer, questions of timing were therefore of paramount importance, and it is no wonder he himself made the un-

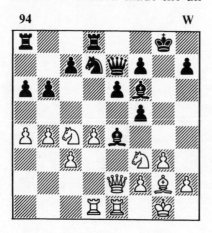

94                                    W

ambiguous statement that "chess is a matter of timing".[1]

Good timing is a mingling of alertness and a 'feel' for the game's rhythm. One would hardly think of a move like **19 g4!** in Pos. 94 (Fischer-Minev, Havana Olympiad 1966) if one's chess 'ear' were not sensitive enough to register all the positional 'sounds' present: the impending thrust ... c5; the fact that the black king is not as yet fully sheltered; the potentially weak black pawn on a6; the fact that the black queen is protected only once; and the somewhat shaky position of the bishop on e4, which if attacked now by ♘cd2 could not retreat in view of gxf5. It took Fischer only six moves to prove the perfect timing of this advance which, had it been carried out a move or two later in a slightly altered position, might have been of no significance whatever – **19 ... ♔h8 20 ♘cd2 fxg4 21 ♘xe4 gxf3 22 ♗xf3 ♖g8+ 23 ♔h1 c6 24 ♘xf6 ♘xf6 25 ♗xc6**, and Black is lost.

This game was played in the 10th round of the Havana Olympiad. In the next round, Fischer had the black pieces against Ludek Pachman. This is how the game looked after White's 14th move (Pos. 95).

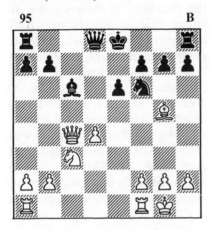

95           B

It is a roughly equal position, and indifferent moves such as 14 ... 0-0 or 14 ... ♖c8, might give White some chances for the initiative. For instance 14 ... ♖c8 15 ♕d3 ♕a5?! 16 ♗xf6 gxf6 17 ♖ae1 (inferior is 17 ♘e4 ♔e7!), and White stands better. It is the timely **14 ... ♕a5!** that Fischer played, which turned the scales slightly in his favour. He only had to calculate carefully that White gets nothing with 15 ♗xf6 gxf6 16 d5 ♗xd5 17 ♘xd5 (17 ♕d4 ♗c6! 18 ♕xf6 ♖g8 etc) 17 ... ♕xd5 18 ♕xd5 exd5 19 ♖ac1 ♔d7 20 ♖fd1 ♔d6 21 ♖c4 ♖ae8 22 ♖a4 a6 23 ♖a5 ♖e5 24 f4 ♖f5 25 g4? ♖g8. After Pachman's **15 ♕c5** the

middlegame was quickly transformed into an endgame: **15 ... ♕xc5 16 dxc5**. See further Pos. 31, 53, 288.

Fischer would normally take the position's bull by the horns at the first available opportunity. This has a good deal to do with his straightforward approach and his early bid for the initiative (see those chapters). The following example (Pos. 96), taken from Spassky-Fischer, Mar del Plata 1960, illustrates what this means as far as timing is concerned.

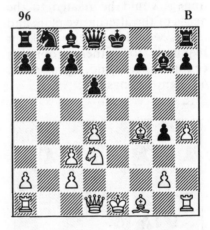

96           B

Concerning **10 ... c5**, Fischer remarked in *MSMG*: "Immediately nibbling at White's centre",[2] yet, interestingly, "Keres gives 10 ... 0-0 first". Here again, as elsewhere, the question of timing has to be related to other questions. It is the timing of the plan (or positional intention) to 'nibble at White's centre' (the centre pawn being the 'bull' in this case) that is at stake. After **11 ♗e2 cxd4 12 0-0 ♘c6 13 ♗xg4**, it transpired that that intention was carried out at the cost of Black's pawn on g4 – certainly a positional asset of some weight. Other players might have gone for a consolidation of that pawn with moves like ... ♗f5 and ... ♘d7-f6. In that set-up it would be the light squares e4, d5, and probably c4, that would become Black's positional targets. In this case, the question of timing would be related to the needs of the alternative plan, and ... c5 would be held back, if required, for other propitious circumstances and, *ipso facto*, different timings.

with precise timing of execution. "Very nice!" wrote Oscar Panno.[3] "It goes against the principle of not opening lines for the enemy's rooks". Fischer wants to decide the character of the endgame on either side of the board. It is important to do so before White plays ♖e2 and ♖fe1. If he plays it now, it might lead to a lost endgame on the queenside: 20 ♖e2 ♕d7 21 ♖fe1 ♔f7 22 ♖xe6? ♕xe6 23 ♖xe6 ♔xe6 24 dxc5 b5!, etc. The way Portisch played – **20 dxc5 bxc5 21 ♗f4 h6! 22 ♖e2 g5 23 ♗e5 ♕d8 24 ♖fe1** – allowed instead Black's pawn majority on the kingside to play a decisive role in the game's outcome.

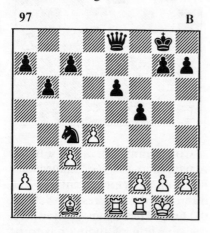

**19 ... c5** in Portisch-Fischer, Santa Monica 1966, Pos. 97, was doubtless the best plan, coupled

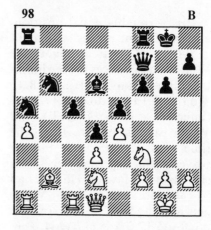

Fischer's decision in the next example (Petrosian-Fischer, Candidates 1971, 6th match game, Pos. 98) was received with mixed feelings and opinions. Fischer

played **25 ... c4**. Averbakh didn't know whether 25 ... ♖fc8 wasn't at least as good.[4] Korchnoi concurred,[5] whereas Shamkovich asked: "What has Black got after 26 ♗a3! ♗f8 27 ♖ab1?".[6] Here the timing of this advance is an affair of great consequence. Postponing it to a later stage would have changed the features of the whole game. From playing for the realisation of a concrete advantage – Black's passed d-pawn (and White's poor bishop at b2 – see Pos. 157) – it would have turned into a manoeuvring combat for the domination of the b-file and the mounting of pressure on White's isolated pawn on a4. In playing the advance of the c-pawn at this precise juncture, Fischer remains loyal to his positional vision of aiming for clear objectives without delay or undue preparation. And indeed, Black reached a highly advantageous position within the shortest time possible: **26 dxc4 ♘axc4 27 ♘xc4 ♘xc4 28 ♕e2** – see again Pos. 157. Another (earlier) moment of this game is Pos. 70.

The sharper a position gets, the more critical the factor of timing becomes. In tactical play correct timing is of course indispensible. In positional play it might have, as we have just seen, a lasting impact on the game's character. There are many cases however, in which the two – the positional and the tactical factors – sustain each other to make an indissoluble compound. Here are three examples.

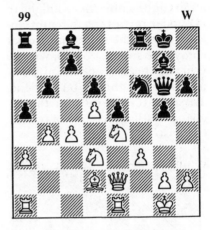

In the 11th match game between Reshevsky and Fischer, Los Angeles 1961, (Pos. 99), Reshevsky here plays **21 bxa5**, awaiting the seemingly forced and most obvious recapture **21 ... bxa5**. Positionally Fischer had in mind the plan of relocating his knight to f4 (after ... ♘h5). He spots that the particular configuration of the white pieces at this moment makes it possible for Black to interpolate the highly unpleasant **21 ... g4!**. The absence of the white rook from the f-file and the positioning of both his knights on the b1-h7 diagonal, allow the introduction of the following 'little combination' as pointed out by Fischer in *MSMG*:

22 axb6? gxf3 23 ♕xf3 ♘xe4 24 ♕xe4 ♗f5,[7] winning the rear knight. Whereas after the game continuation – **22 ♘df2 gxf3 23 ♕xf3 ♘h5** – Black succeeded in attaining his objective (knight to f4) under favourable circumstances: the knight on e4 no longer enjoys the support of a pawn, the g-file has been opened, and Black has some real threats on the f-file. These features won him the exchange within a couple of moves. (see also Pos. 64)

**100**                                    **W**

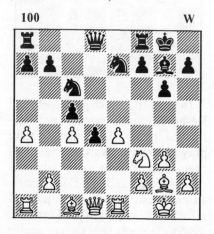

In Pos. 100 where Fischer had the white pieces against Hübner, at Palma de Mallorca 1970, White would certainly have liked to complete his development with 14 ♗f4, taking control of e5, to be followed by 15 h4, etc. But, as Hübner explains, White cannot afford to lose time: "White has to carry on energetically, for if he

does not, Black gets a superior position by playing 14 ... ♘b4 and 15 ... ♘ec6".[8] That's why Fischer plays **14 e5!** so as to be ready to counter Hübner's positional manoeuvre with a tactical one. As Hübner remarks about his **14 ... ♕d7**: "Had Black played his intended 14 ... ♘b4 now, he would have lost the exchange after 15 ♘g5 ♘ec6 (15 ... d3 16 ♖a3) 16 e6 f6 17 e7 ♘xe7 18 ♘e6". So the committal advance of the e-pawn took place earlier than usual in this type of position in order to create concrete threats as quickly as possible. (see also Pos. 234)

**101**                                    **W**

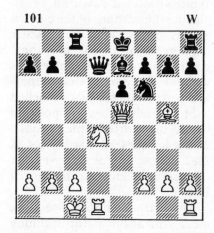

More complicated were the considerations that preceded Fischer's (White's) 14th move against Sarapu, Sousse 1967 (Pos. 101). Fischer played here **14 f4**, a move which Matanović thought was premature in view of 14 ... h6, when White has to exchange on f6, since 15 ♗h4 ♗d6 16 ♕e3 ♘d5 loses.[9] As indicated by me in *Chess Life*,[10] Fischer's intention must have been much more profound. He didn't wish to lose time with the preparatory 14 ♔b1 (the move Matanović suggested), and considered the timing of his offensive thrust correct, most probably on the grounds of: 14 ... h6 15 ♗h4! ♗d6 16 ♕e2!! ♗xf4+ 17 ♔b1 ♘d5 (Fischer had, of course, to consider other moves, like 17 ... ♕e7 and 17 ... g5. For instance 17 ... g5 18 ♘b5 ♕e7 19 ♘xa7 ♖c5 20 ♗e1! ♖e5 21 ♕c4

♕c5 22 ♕a4+ b5 23 ♘xb5!, etc) 18 ♘f5 ♕c6!? (18 ... 0-0? 19 ♖xd5! exd5 20 ♕g4 ♗g5 21 ♘xh6+!) 19 ♘xg7+ ♔f8 20 ♘h5, with advantage to White. This, in a way, was confirmed by Sarapu, who, in a later issue of *Chess Life*[11] informed the readers that Fischer had taken some 55 minutes on 14 f4 – for him quite probably a record for the time consumed on a single move. Again we have observed how the timing of a positional decision goes hand in hand with the tactical ramifications it entails. (see also Pos. 298)

This is discussed in greater detail in our final chapter, pp.249-58.

# Strategy

## STRATEGIC PLANS

We are more used to talking of tactical talent at chess than of strategical. Yet being a strategist takes as distinctive a talent as that of a tactician. One can as justly speak of a player's innate strategic gifts as another's tactical ones. Botvinnik, Petrosian and Andersson are good examples of the first case. Alekhine, Tal and Kasparov of the second. The difference, however, – and this is a rather significant one – is that the principles of chess strategy, being basically intellectual, are easier to acquire and cultivate than tactical principles (or, more correctly, tactical insight). Alekhine and Kasparov could develop into excellent strategists, whereas there is no example of the contrary.

Fischer can't be thought of as a strategist in the same sense as, say, Petrosian was. For him, as with other players of a universal style, strategic concepts are as relevant as other factors and have to be taken into consideration in relation to other elements of the position. Pos. 102 (Ader-Fischer, Santiago 1959) is a simple example to illustrate this.

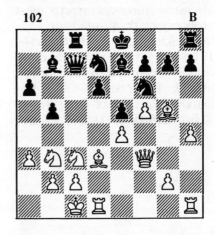

102            B

Fischer played **14 ... h5!**, fixing g4 as a permanent weakness. Yet he followed it up (after **15 ♔b1**) with **15 ... ♘b6**. A Petrosian would quite certainly have refrained from playing this way. For such a player the knight had to be left on d7 'on principle'. Why 'on principle'? Since the two knights on d7 and f6 constitute a single strategic unit to exploit g4, an exploitation that doesn't necessarily have to take place in the

64

very near future. The principle, however, is clear: The knight at f6 has to be defended by another knight so that any eventual exchanges on f6 would not lessen Black's grip on g4, leaving the possibility of ... ♘g4, ... ♘df6, to remain a constant element in the position.

Fischer, on the other hand, thinks in other terms. For him the dynamic possibilities of the position are of greater interest, and after **16 ♘d2?** (16 ♗xf6 was necessary) **16 ... ♘g4 17 ♗xe7 ♕xe7 18 ♘f1 ♖xc3! 19 bxc3 d5**, he managed to get an advantage of a different kind.

Extensive and systematic strategic schemes are not frequent in Fischer's games. A very fine example of one of those non-habitual cases was his game against Szabo, Havana 1965 (Pos. 103).

**103**             **W**

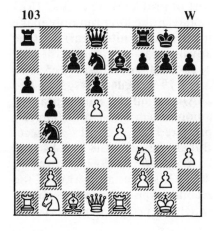

Fischer sees to a purposeful development of his queen's knight by playing **14 ♘a3 ♗f6 15 ♘c2** – in itself a proper manoeuvre since after 15 ... ♘xc2 16 ♕xc2, White's command of the c-file is likely to cause Black enduring positional concern. But what are White's options after **15 ... c5** – the move Szabo actually played? Fischer took about half an hour to decide on **16 ♘xb4!**. He must have worked out the strategic plan that unfolds from now to move 30 in detail. The alternative to this plan was to proceed with solid positional moves: 16 dxc6 e.p. 16 ... ♘xc6 17 ♘e3 (17 ♕xd6 ♘de5!) 17 ... ♘de5 18 ♘d5. No side can claim a real advantage, though White's prospects are probably slightly better. Fischer would not normally reject such a continuation, unless there is something better at hand.

There are three phases in his plan.

Phase 1: **16 ... cxb4 17 ♘d4 ♗xd4 18 ♕xd4**. White's pawn weakness on the queenside has been minimised. Now he has to create a passed pawn in the centre by means of f4 and e5. Phase 2 has to do with manoeuvring White's pieces to optimal positions before carrying out this advance: **18 ... a5 19 ♗f4 ♘c5 20 ♖e3 f6 21 ♖ae1 ♕c7 22 ♗g3**. There remains the question of timing: When to break through with f4 and e5.

Fischer decides to complete the regrouping of his pieces by moving his king to a safer place, and his queen to e2. There followed: **22 ... ♘d7 23 ♔h2 ♖fd8 24 ♖3e2 ♘c5 25 ♖e3 ♘d7 26 ♕d3 ♖ab8 27 ♕e2 ♖b7 28 ♔h1 ♘c5.** Everything has been prepared for f4 and e5. Phase 3 follows: **29 f4 ♖f8 30 e5.** White has achieved his strategic objective. If now 30 ... fxe5 31 fxe5 dxe5 32 ♖xe5 ♕f7 33 d6 ♘xb3 34 ♕g4, with a won position, or, as in the game, **30 ... f5 31 ♗h4! dxe5 32 fxe5 f4 33 ♖f3,** and his two connected passed pawns won.

Another game with a clear strategic build-up was Fischer-Unzicker, played at the Siegen Olympiad 1970 (Pos. 104).

**104**                      **W**

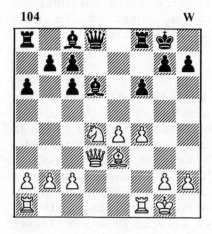

**14 f5!.**
This move is associated with a

very well defined plan. The pawn formation e4-f5-g4 which White is about to create, would enable him, after due preparation, to play for two types of possible pawn majorities: A – a three to two on the kingside, by pushing e5 and exchanging it for f6, as in the game; B – advancing g5 while having sufficient tactical threats to force Black to play ... fxg5, thus creating a protected passed pawn in the centre. There can be little doubt that Fischer thought at this stage in terms of endgame advantage, and in this respect the whole game can be regarded as a long liquidating combination.

**14 ... ♕e7 15 ♗f4! ♗xf4.**

White would go for an identical set-up with the one we are about to witness even if Black didn't exchange bishops. For instance: 15 ... ♖e8 16 ♖ae1, 17 g4, 18 ♕g3, 19 ♘f3, and Black faces the same sort of problems. 15 ... ♗c5 16 c3 would in the long run only make it easier for White to carry out the advance e5.

**16 ♖xf4 ♗d7 17 ♖e1 ♕c5 18 c3 ♖ae8 19 g4 ♕d6 20 ♕g3 ♖e7.**

Almost all the commentators, among them Euwe and Barcza,[1] preferred 20 ... c5 21 ♘f3 ♗c6. But after 22 g5! ♔h8 23 ♘h4 fxg5 24 ♕xg5 ♕f6 25 ♕g3 followed by 26 ♘f3, we get a position of the second type mentioned above, which seems even more critical for Black.

**21 ♘f3 c5 22 e5!.**

Typically, Fischer wastes no time in moving from the first strategic phase to the second.

**22 ... fxe5 23 ♖fe4 ♗c6 24 ♖xe5 ♖fe8 25 ♖xe7 ♖xe7 26 ♘e5 h6 27 h4 ♗d7.**

Euwe on the one hand, and Levy and Keene on the other,[2] maintain that 27 ... ♕d2 or 27 ... ♕d5 would have been correct here. But as Euwe mentions, White does retain the better endgame prospects after 27 ... ♕d2 28 ♕f2 ♕d5 (28 ... ♕xf2+ 29 ♔xf2 and ♔g3-f4, is also highly favourable for White – EA) 29 ♘xc6 ♖xe1+ 30 ♕xe1 ♕xc6.

**28 ♕f4 ♕f6 29 ♖e2! ♗c8** 29 ... ♕xh4 ♘g6 30 ♕c4+ ♔h7 31 ♘g6 ♖xe2 32 ♕xe2 ♗d7 33 ♕e7!, and the last stage has been reached. Fischer cashes in his advantage in elegant fashion:

**33 ... ♕xe7 34 ♘xe7 g5 35 hxg5 hxg5 36 ♘d5 ♗c6 37 ♘xc7 ♗f3 38 ♘e8 ♔h6 39 ♘f6 ♔g7 40 ♔f2 ♗d1 41 ♘d7 c4 42 ♔g3**, Black resigned.

Fischer might think up an elaborate strategic plan when other alternatives are less attractive. Against Arthur Bisguier at the Stockholm Interzonal 1962 (Pos. 105, Fischer Black) he had to get off the path that led to a draw by repetition:

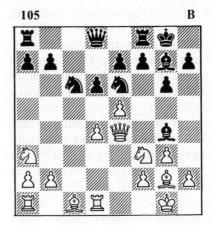

105      B

**13 ... ♗f5 14 ♕e1 ♗g4 15 ♕e4 ♗xf3!.**

Instead of a draw – a profound strategic decision! **16 ♗xf3 d5!!.** When a player makes such a move, he has to assess the consequences it might have on the structure of the position for many moves to come. The black bishop is likely to remain hemmed-in now for much of the game. **17 ♕e3** 17 ♕xd5? ♘exd4, and the e5 pawn is doomed to fall. **17 ... ♖c8!.** Indirectly mounting additional pressure on the pawn on d4. The white knight can't help in its defence (♘c2) owing to a possible ... ♘xe5!. **18 ♗g4 ♕b6 19 ♗xe6 fxe6 20 b3 g5! 21 ♗b2** 21 ♕xg5 ♘xe5 **21 ... ♖f5 22 ♖d2 ♖cf8**. It isn't necessarily this very position Fischer had in mind when playing 15 ... ♗xf3, but he must have envisaged this type of position at least in broad outlines, and have reasoned that the assets of Black's position outweigh its drawbacks. Such an assessment in a position where the central pawns of both sides are permanently fixed needs to be quite accurate, or else one would be quickly disillusioned. The most conspicuous disadvantage of Black's position is the schematic split between his forces on the kingside and those on the queenside, which can't be bridged, and only sacrificial motifs at e5 and f2 can bind the two wings together. For a discussion of what occurred in the next few moves (23 ♘c2 h6 24 ♕e2 ♖xf2 25 ♕xf2 ♖xf2 26 ♖xf2 g4) see Pos. 196.

Where a strategic assessment might have been less accurate was to be perceived in Fischer's game against the Icelander Ingi Johansson, played at Reykjavik 1960 (Pos. 106).

**106**                                   **W**

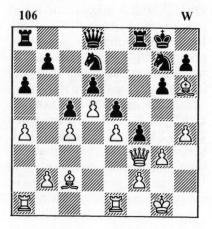

Black threatens 21 ... fxg3 22 ♕xg3 ♘f6-h5-f4. Fischer starts a strategic manoeuvre, taking this threat as a springboard. **21 g4!? ♕xh4 22 g5**. Now the bishop on h6 is worth 'only' the knight on g7, but the other bishop gets a promising future on the h3-c8 diagonal. **22 ... ♕h5 23 ♗d1 ♕xf3**. The attempt to activate the knight on g7 by 23 ... ♖f7 24 ♔g2 ♕xf3+ 25 ♗xf3 ♘h5 26 ♗g4 f3+ doesn't come off too well after 27 ♔h2! ♘f8 28 ♖a3. **24 ♗xf3 ♖fb8 25 ♗g4 ♘f8**. Here ends the first phase of Fischer's plan, and now begins the second – taking the initiative on the queenside: **26 b4!?** 26 ♖fb1 a5!, or 26 a5 b6 27 axb6 ♖xb6, and Black stands well. **26 ... cxb4 27 a5**. Johansson played now the weak 27 ... ♖c8, which resulted in a lost endgame after **28 ♗xc8 ♖xc8 29 ♖eb1 ♘d7 30 ♖xb4 ♘c5 31 ♗xg7 ♔xg7 32 ♖b6**. As he himself indicated in the Icelandic magazine *Skak* (November 1960) correct was 27 ... b6. This move might have put in doubt Fischer's strategic conception, since after 28 ♖eb1 bxa5 29 ♖xa5 it's not clear how White can carry out the c5 advance advantageously, without which his whole plan should be regarded as inadequate. Johansson gives 29 ... ♖a7 30 ♖b3 (30 c5 dxc5 31 ♖xc5 ♘e8 32 ♖c6 a5 33 d6 ♖d8 34 ♖d1 f3! 35 d7!? ♘xd7 36 ♗e6+ ♔h8 37

♗f8 ♖c7! 38 ♖a6 ♘g7! – EA) 30 ... ♖b6 followed by ... ♖c7. In this case we observe, then, a strategic plan of which the last stage was not developed to the full.

This has to do with similar aspects pertaining to the 'Grand Lines'. (see pp.249-53)

Fischer's strategic decisions, especially in the later stages of his career (1970-72), are in many cases directed towards the acquisition of the slightest advantage possible in order to try to capitalise on it in an endgame.

107                                    B

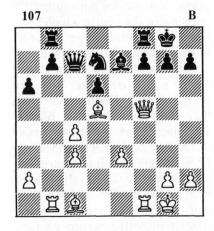

In Pos. 107 (Reshevsky-Fischer, Palma de Mallorca 1970) many players would have played 17 ... ♘e5 without thinking twice: The centralised knight can't be attacked by pawns, and it defends f7 while attacking White's weak pawn at c4.

As far as pawn structure is concerned, it is clear that Black has the better of it and this should play an important role in any strategic decision. Remarkably, Fischer, instead of moving his knight to this ideal position, develops a plan in which the knight is exchanged for White's light-squared bishop (admittedly a well placed piece as well), and the strongpoint on e5 is used to triple his heavy forces on the e-file: **17 ... ♘f6 18 ♗a3 ♖fe8 19 ♕d3 ♘xd5 20 cxd5**. White has now got rid of his problematic doubled c-pawn. Fischer tries next to fix the c3 pawn and stress the weakness of c4. Yet when Reshevsky manages to force some exchanges, including that of his c-pawn, it seems as though White enjoys total equality. **20 ... b5 21 e4 ♗f8 22 ♖b4 ♖e5 23 c4 ♖be8 24 cxb5 axb5 25 ♔h1 25 ♕xb5? ♕a7+ 25 ... ♕e7 26 ♕xb5 ♖xe4 27 ♖xe4 ♕xe4**. Black's strategy has proved justified in so far as White's pawns on a2 and d5 are weaker than Black's pawn on d6. But does he really have any tangible advantage to count on in this endgame? His main threats are 28 ... ♕e2 and 28 ... ♖e5. An attempt by White to force a draw by 28 ♕d7 ♕f4! 29 ♕b5 ♕e3 30 ♕d7, doesn't work because of 30 ... ♕f2!, which is similar to the actual game's end (**28 ♕d7 ♕f4! 29 ♔g1?? ♕d4+ 30 ♔h1 ♕f2**, 0-1).

Better is 30 ♗c1 ♕e2 31 ♕xe2
♖xe2 32 a3 ♗e7. Yet Black does
indeed maintain some endgame
advantage. For instance: 33 ♗f4
♖a2 34 ♖c1 g5!, or 33 h3 g5! 34
♔h2 ♔g7 35 ♖f3 ♗f6 36 ♗e3 h5!,
or if 36 ♖e3 ♗e5+ 37 ♔h1 ♖a2,
and in both cases White's position
isn't easy.

Fischer could rely on his highly
refined technique to drive home
such advantages. (see also Pos.
29, and for a discussion of this
topic 'Switching Advantages', pp.
105-11, and 'Playing for Space',
pp.111-14.)

## SEIZING THE INITIATIVE

As a rule Fischer does his best
to seize the initiative as early as
possible – that is, at the first
opportunity that comes his way.
This might be as early as the
opening phase.

In Pos. 108 (Addison-Fischer,
US Championship 1963-64) the
game is indeed still in that phase,
and both sides have to complete
the development of their pieces.
As for Black, quite in accordance
with the spirit of the position
would be the following set-up: ...
d6 ... ♘c6 ... ♗e7 ... 0-0 and ...
♗f6. The game would then revolve,
among other elements, around
the domination of e5. Fischer

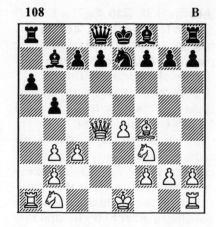

108                             B

plays, instead, for an immediate
decision in the centre which gives
Black an early initiative: **10 ... d5!**.
Putting the question to White –
"Shall we have a semi-closed
centre game, or rather an open
centre one?". Fischer perceives
that both would be to Black's
advantage. **11 e5**. Giving preference
to the first option. 11 exd5 ♘xd5
12 ♕e5+ ♕e7, leads to a queenless
game where Black has slightly the
better of it in view of his bishop
pair. **11 ... c5!**. With this move
Black's initiative becomes a fact.
12 ♕xc5?? ♘f5, and it's only
White who stays queenless this
time. From now on Black's pawn
majority on the queenside is a
prominent and dynamic factor.
(see also Pos. 3)

The next position (109) taken
from the game Porat-Fischer,
Netanya 1968, finds the game at

109 B

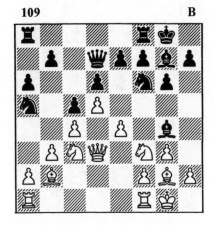

only a slightly more advanced
stage. Both sides have completed
their initial development. We are
about to cross the borderline
between the opening and the early
middlegame. Fischer sees to it
that he will be the one to set the
stage for the next phase of the
game. Without any further prepar-
ations (more conservative masters
would have played ... ♖fc8 and ...
♖ab8 first) he starts operating on
the queenside. **12 ... b5! 13 cxb5**.
The point after 13 e5 was 13 ...
bxc4 14 bxc4 ♗f5! 15 ♕e2 ♘g4,
with advantage to Black. If instead
13 ♘d2 ♖ab8 Black has obtained
an ideal position for this type of
opening. **13 ... c4!**. Another temporary sacrifice of a pawn, before
White plays ♖ac1 or ♘d2. White's
pawn at c4 will remain unpro-
tectable, and the strategically
important c4 square is about to

fall into Black's hands. **14 bxc4
♗xf3**. Of course not 14 ... ♖fc8 15
♘d2. **15 ♗xf3 ♖fc8 16 c5!**. An
ingenious attempt to check Black's
budding initiative by diverting
the Black forces to the b-file, and
thus gain some counterplay on
the c-file. **16 ... ♖xc5 17 ♘a4
♖xb5**. Material is equal, and
Black has the positional edge. It
yielded him a pawn after: **18 ♗d4
♖ab8 19 ♘c3 ♖b4 20 ♖ab1 ♕c8
21 ♖fc1 ♘xe4! 22 ♗xg7**. In
the Berlin newspaper *Tagesspiegel*
Porat gives the following alternative – 22 ♘xe4 ♖xb1 23 ♖xb1
♖xb1+ 24 ♕xb1 ♗xd4 25 ♕b4!
♕c1+ 26 ♔g2 ♘c4 27 ♗e2 "and
after winning back the pawn
White's position would be only
microscopically inferior", concludes Porat.[1] **22 ... ♘c5 23 ♕e3
♔xg7**, and 24 ... ♘d3 prevents 24
♕xe7.

Precise timing in seizing the
initiative was to be seen in the
next example as well. Incidentally,
it had to do with the same critical
square – c4. Hort, with the white
pieces (Palma de Mallorca 1970,
Pos. 110), wants to play his knight
to c4, which would help him
neutralise any possible Black initiative on the queenside. Moreover,
in the absence of his light-squared
bishop, Black's attempts to build
up pressure in the centre by
means of ... f5 and ... e5 are very
likely to fail. Fischer frustrates

Hort's plans, and in doing so he is the first to seize the initiative.

**110**                                    **W**

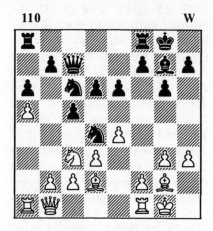

**111**                                    **W**

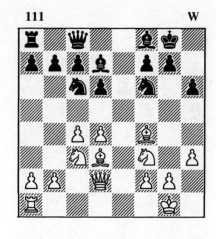

**16 ♘d1 c4! 17 dxc4 ♘e5.** As simple as it is effective. White can't defend c4 since Black's other threat is 18 ... ♘f3+. **18 ♗e3 ♘xc4 19 ♖a4 ♖ac8 20 ♗xd4 ♗xd4 21 ♕a2 ♗f6!**, and Black has the initiative owing to his control of the c-file and the concrete threats of 22 ... ♗d8 and 22 ... ♘d2. (see also Pos. 69, 287)

The last two cases have dealt with a "battle for c4". Fischer's game against Gheorghiu from Buenos Aires 1970 (Pos. 111) features a "battle for f5".

Should White succeed in bolstering his hold of the diagonal b1-h7, he might get some solid initiative. But how to go about it? The standard continuation 15 ♖e1 ♗f5 16 ♗f1 ♕d7 17 d5 ♘e7 18 ♘d4 ♗g6, doesn't do it, and offers White only a slight spatial advantage. Fischer plays to prevent ... ♗f5 in the first place. **15 d5 ♘b4.** Gheorghiu manoeuvres his knight to c5. He could keep the "battle for f5" on by playing 15 ... ♘e7. However, after 16 ♘d4 ♘f5 17 ♘ce2 ♘xd4 18 ♘xd4 c5 19 ♘f3 ♗f5 20 ♕c2 ♗xd3 21 ♕xd3, White can play against the weak black pawn on d6. **16 ♘e4.** By this move and the transfer of the other knight to d4 two moves later (**16 ... ♘xe4 17 ♗xe4 ♘a6 18 ♘d4!**), Fischer prevents ... ♗f5, and avoids the concession of the diagonal to Black. After that, White's initiative could no more be challenged (see p.119 and Pos. 120, 177). Could Black counter White's sixteenth move differently? 16 ... ♘xd3 17 ♘xf6+ is of course, out of the question. A plausible but insufficient alternative is 16 ... ♘h5, when there could follow 17 ♗b1 ♘xf4 18 ♕xf4 a5 (18 ... ♗e7 19 a3 ♘a6 20 b4 cramps Black drastically) 19 a3 ♘a6 20 ♘eg5! ♗e8 (20 ... hxg5 21 ♘xg5 f6 22 ♗h7+ ♔h8 23 ♗g6! mates in a couple of moves) 21 ♗h7+ ♔h8 22 ♗g6! f6 23 ♗xe8 ♕xe8 (23 ... hxg5? 24 ♘xg5! fxg5 25 ♕xf8+ ♔h7 26 ♖e1 and 27 ♖e7) 24 ♘e6 ♕f7 25 ♘fd4 ♘c5 26 ♖e1, with a strong bind.

112                                           B

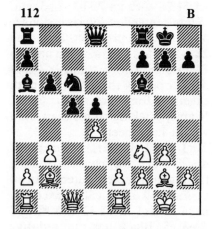

This (Pos. 112) is Fischer-Filip, Palma de Mallorca 1970, after White's 13th move. There is no reason to speak here of any distinct advantage or initiative for either side. Filip played 13 ... ♘xd4. This almost routine capture gave Fischer the opportunity to seize the initiative by exploiting a subtle positional nuance. 14 ♗xd4!. White has to play for a half-open d-file in order to be able to put

pressure on d5 after recapturing the pawn on d4. 14 ♘xd4 would make it possible for Black to return the pawn at d3 (e.g. 14 ... cxd4 15 ♕d2 d3!), thereby closing the d-file. For example, 16 ♗xf6 ♕xf6 17 exd3 ♕d4! 18 ♖ad1 ♖ae8 19 ♖e3 ♖e6!, and Black is fine. The somewhat indifferent game continuation – **14 ... cxd4 15 ♕a3 ♗b7? 16 ♖ad1** – enabled Fischer to carry out this plan. But even after the better move – 15 ... ♕c8 (suggested by Wade in the tournament book, though without supporting analysis)[2] – White would succeed in seizing the initiative: 16 ♖ac1 ♕b7 17 ♖cd1 d3 18 exd3 (18 e4?! ♗c3!) 18 ... ♖ae8 (or 18 ... ♖fe8 19 ♕a4!, while 18 ... ♖ac8 is answered by 19 ♘e5, with positional domination. A concrete threat is 20 ♗h3 ♖c7 21 ♘d7!) 19 b4!, with 20 ♕b3 to follow. In the game, after **16 ... ♗e7 17 ♕a4 ♕e8 18 ♕xd4 ♖c8 19 ♕f4 ♗f6 20 ♘d4 ♗e5 21 ♕e3 g6 22 ♘b5**, White's initiative had turned into a stable positional advantage.

So far we have seen examples taken from the earlier phases of the game. These are, as indicated before, the more common in Fischer's games. His bid for the initiative normally takes place between move 12 to 18. This stands in direct relation to the open nature of his play. In closed games, where piece development is slower, significant operations are generally possible only at a later stage of the game, so that the first opportunity to seize the initiative could come late in the twenties, which is what happened in Fischer's game (as Black) against Sherwin in the US Championship 1958-59 (Pos. 113).

**113**                            **B**

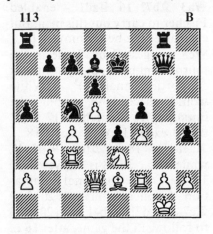

To be expected here are: on White's part the regrouping ♘c2, ♕e3, ♘d4; on Black's part ♕f6, ♖g7, ♖ag8, with a position that could be labelled 'dynamically balanced'. Fischer has no interest in establishing mere equilibrium and postponing critical decisions for a later stage of the game. He takes immediate steps to secure his hegemony in the centre and queenside. Quite imperative, for that purpose, is to forestall White's above mentioned regrouping. For

which reason he plays first **26 ... ♘a6!** heading for a collision with White's knight at b4. There is a certain tactical element which shouldn't escape our attention: rook c3, pawn a2, as well as White's knight, if it reaches d4, would all be protected by one and the same piece – White's queen at d2. Fischer takes advantage of the queen's overloading of defensive tasks. **27 ♘c2.** If 27 a3, then 27 ... ♘c5! 28 ♘c2 a4 29 b4 ♘b3, and White's intended ♘d4 is no longer an immediate prospect. **27 ... ♘b4 28 a3** 28 ♘d4 ♘xa2! (see note to Black's 26th move), and 28 ♘xb4 axb4, opening the a-file, are both excellent for Black. **28 ... ♘xc2.** Rightly sticking to his plan. Bad would have been 28 ... ♘a2? 29 ♖h3 ♕b2 30 ♖f1!, and Black doesn't get the chance to start fishing in troubled waters with 30 ... ♘c1. **29 ♖xc2 c5! 30 dxc6** *e.p.* **bxc6 31 ♖c1 ♖ab8 32 ♖d1 ♕f6 33 ♕e3 c5.** Black has the initiative on the queenside, and controls d4. White has very little to show against this.

'Material for the initiative' is a chess bargain of a long-standing tradition. In the nineteenth century players were ready to forsake a good deal of their army merely for the joy of beholding the remainder of the army nearing the enemy's king. As for the results of this flamboyancy – well, that was left for Dame Fortune to decide. This romantic approach has no adherents among top players nowadays, yet the gambit (chiefly pawn gambit) as a means for seizing the initiative will certainly stay as long as the game is played.

Fischer's attitude towards gambits was twofold: He liked to offer them, and he liked no less to accept them when offered! This reflects his basic attitude towards material questions in general (see 'Material Considerations', pp.52-7). When offering one – it would be in line with his approach to make a remark like "It's worth a pawn to open up the game", as in his game against Geller, Bled 1961 (*MSMG*, game 29). Gambitting the e-pawn in the Sicilian was something of a habit with him.

Our final two examples are taken from the two opposite poles of Fischer's career. The first, from the Candidates 1959, is a rather conventional gambit which yields the initiative as a matter of course. The other, from the Interzonal at Palma de Mallorca 1970, bears the unmistakable mark of a mature and self-confident master.

Keres-Fischer from the 3rd cycle of that Candidates, saw the following opening moves: **1 d4 ♘f6 2 ♘f3 g6 3 ♗f4 ♗g7 4 ♘bd2 c5 5 c3 cxd4 6 cxd4 d5!**. The bargain: the pawn on a7 and the

undeveloped knight, for White's actively placed bishop. It moreover brings about a swift development of Black's pieces. **7 ♗xb8 ♖xb8 8 ♕a4+ ♗d7 9 ♕xa7 ♘e4 10 e3 ♘xd2 11 ♘xd2 e5!** (Pos. 114).

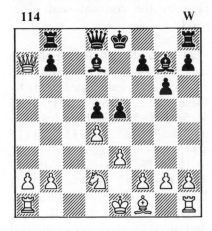

114       W

Black's initiative clearly makes up for his material deficit.

Against Smyslov, playing with the black pieces in the above-

115       B

mentioned Palma tournament, Fischer managed to gain some advantage right from the opening moves, owing to Smyslov's inaccurate play (Pos. 115).

Black can maintain his advantage by the conventional 12 ... cxd4.

Let us see:

a) 13 ♘xd4 (13 ♖c1? ♘cb4) 13 ... ♘xd4 14 ♕xd4 (14 exd4 ♗a6 15 ♘c4 – 15 ♘d3? ♘c3! wins by force – 15 ... ♖c8 16 ♖c1 b5! 17 ♘e5/e3 ♕a5+, with big advantage to Black) 14 ... ♗a6 15 ♘c4 (15 ♗f1? ♗b7 16 ♗g2 ♘xe3! wins, or 15 e4 ♕e7!! 16 exd5 exd5+ 17 ♕e3 ♕b4+ 18 ♕d2 – 18 ♔d1 ♖ae8! 19 a3 ♕b5! – 18 ... ♖fe8+ 19 ♔d1 ♕xd2+ 20 ♔xd2 ♖e2+ 21 ♔c1 ♖c8+ 22 ♔b1 ♖cc2 followed by ... ♗d3 wins) 15 ... ♖c8 16 0-0 ♖c5 17 ♖fd1 ♕c7, and Black's position is clearly the more dynamic.

b) 13 exd4 ♗a6 14 ♘c4 ♕f6 15 0-0 ♖ad8, with promising pressure on d4, and very well placed pieces.

Fischer opts instead for an unltra-sharp line, involving the gambit of a pawn, as a result of which Black's initiative attains more radical dimensions: **12 ... ♗a6! 13 dxc5 ♕f6 14 ♘c4 ♘c3! 15 ♘xc3 ♕xc3+ 16 ♔f1**. Black's initiative is strong enough for Fischer to be able to disdain 16 ... ♗xc4+, recovering the pawn.

White is behind in development, deprived of the right to castle, and will be subjected to constant pressure along the open files. (see also Pos. 123, 175)

## TYPICAL MANOEUVRES

Certain manoeuvres and positional patterns would recur in a player's games throughout his career, no matter how much chess knowledge and experience he had accumulated in those years. His technique might have been perfected through the years, his understanding sharpened, yet his basic inclinations might have remained to a considerable extent unaltered.

In the celebrated encounter between the Marshall and Manhattan clubs, US Metropolitan

**116**                                B

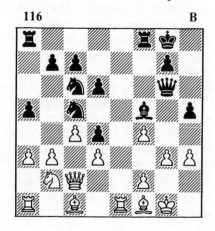

League 1969, Fischer met Anthony Saidy on the 1st board. After White's 18th move the game had reached Pos. 116.

Fischer (Black) carried out the following manoeuvre – **18 ... ♖a6! 19 ♗d2 ♖b6 20 ♗xa5 ♖xb3 21 ♗d2 ♖a8! 22 a4 ♖a6!**. (see also Pos. 32)

Thirteen years earlier, thirteen year old Bobby, playing at the 57th US Open Championship 1956, had used the same remarkable manoeuvring to bear down on his opponent's position (Fischer-S.Popel, Pos. 117):

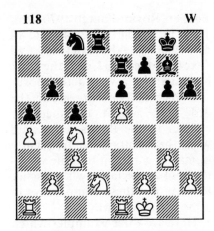

118 W

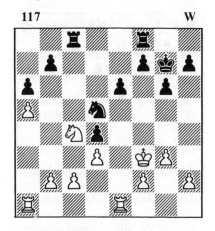

117 W

**22 ♖a3! ♖fd8 23 ♖b3 ♖c7 24 ♔e2 ♘e7 25 ♔d2 ♘c6 26 ♖b6 ♖d5 27 ♖a1! ♔f8 28 ♖a3 ♔e7 29 ♖ab3!**.

A modified version of this flank operation occurred on other occasions. For instance Fischer-Durao, Havana Olympiad 1966

(Pos. 118), saw: **24 ♖a3 ♖c7 25 ♖b3 ♖c6**, and soon the other rook performed a similar manoeuvre on the opposite flank: **26 ♘e4 ♗f8 27 ♔e2 ♗e7 28 f4 ♔f8 29 g4 ♔e8 30 ♖f1 ♖d5 31 ♖f3 ♖d8 32 ♖h3**. (see also Pos. 58, 149, 246)

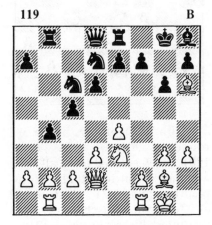

119 B

Another case was Smyslov-

Fischer, Rovinj-Zagreb 1970 (Pos. 119). **16 ... ♖b6! 17 ♘c4 ♖a6! 18 a3 ♘b6 19 axb4 cxb4 20 ♗e3 ♘xc4 21 dxc4 ♖a2**, and the rook has taken up a very active post.

Rook manoeuvring along the 3rd rank wasn't confined, of course, to the flanks only. And while this occurs rather frequently in master games, it became something of a speciality with Fischer to carry out these manoeuvres in a most efficient way.

Here are three examples which like the previous one, were all played in 1970.

**120**                                   **W**

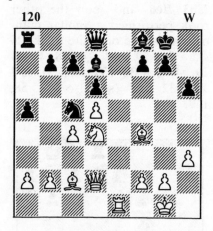

Against Gheorghiu, in the 3rd round at Buenos Aires (Pos. 120), Black seemed quite all right and was about to establish complete equality by 21 ... ♕f6 and 22 ... ♖e8, when Fischer's **21 ♖e3** disrupted his plans. Now 21 ... ♕f6 would be answered by 22

♖f3, and the queen is badly placed. After the game continuation: **21 ... b6 22 ♖g3 ♔h8 23 ♘f3!** (Pos. 177) the rook was temporarily offside, but was promptly returned to the centre (move 27), only to return decisively to the kingside (move 32) – see p.119, and see also Pos.111.

One round later Fischer was to play one of his most elegant sacrifices against Samuel Schweber. This was preceded by some deep rook manoeuvring, again on the kingside (Pos. 121).

**121**                                   **W**

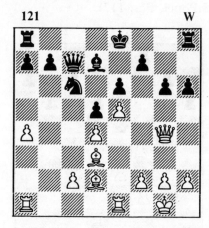

**17 ♖e3!**. More regular would have been 17 ♕f4. **17 ... 0-0-0 18 ♖g3!!**. An extremely subtle move. It seems so pointless that Euwe was later driven to dub it 'a rather indifferent move' meant to lull Black into playing 18 ... ♔b8.[1] But there was more to this rook manoeuvre than that. In the first place, it now prevents 18 ... f5, since 19 ♕xg6 ♖dg8 (19 ... ♘xd4 20 ♗xh6 ♕xe5? 21 ♗g7) 20 ♕xg8! is winning. Secondly, it enables White to meet a possible 18 ... ♘e7 by 19 ♕f3 ♘f5 20 ♗xf5 gxf5 21 ♖g7, when White's cryptic 18th move turns out to have been the first step in manoeuvring the rook to a dominant position on the 7th rank. All Fischer had to foresee was that after 18 ... h5 19 ♕f4 h4 20 ♖h3 (trotting along the 3rd rank, but not as aimlessly as it might seem at first glance) 20 ... g5 21 ♕xg5 (21 ♕xf7? g4) 21 ... ♘xd4 he should play 22 ♕f6! keeping his advantage, and not fall for 22 ♖xh4? ♘f3+!. **18 ... ♔b8 19 ♖f3!**. Unique manoeuvring artistry! As it turns out, this was a prelude to the following combination. But had Black defended passively (19 ... ♖df8) then 20 ♖f6! would come in with a strangling effect. **19 ... f5 20 exf6 *e.p.* e5 21 ♕g3 ♘xd4 22 ♖e3** – forced to return to his initial square (move 17). But watch what he had in store: **22 ... e4 23 ♖xe4!! ♕xg3 24 ♖xd4!! ♕g4 25 ♖xg4 ♗xg4 26 ♗xg6**, and White won the ending. (This whole process, in which the opponent might have got the impression he was dictating the events, only to realise too late that he had perfectly fallen in with Fischer's plans, is reminiscent of Fischer's active defensive artistry

– see Pos. 208-220).

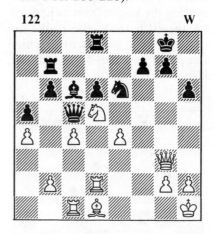

122          W

Against Taimanov, at Palma de Mallorca, Fischer played (Pos. 122) **31 ♖c3!**. On the third rank the rook stands optimally placed in anticipation of an eventual exchange on d5, as well as for the plan of playing ♗c2 without having to fear either ... ♕xc4 or ... ♘d4. White is now poised to answer that last move with ♕h4 and ♖g3, initiating a strong attack against Black's king. Taimanov's **31 ... ♘g5** led to **32 ♗c2 ♗xd5 33 ♖xd5 ♕c7 34 e5!**, giving White a superior position.

In three of Fischer's games one comes across a noteworthy manoeuvre: transferring a rook to the fourth rank along a file that is half-closed by his own knight, at the other end of which an opponent's rook is stationed. Fischer's rook enjoys the support of a pawn that isn't yet a passed one. By next moving the knight from its position on the fifth rank, the rooks are exposed to be traded, after which the pawn becomes a passed one. How did it look in practice?

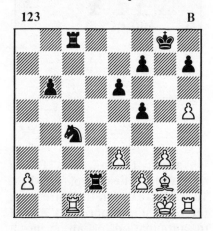

123       B

Smyslov-Fischer, Palma de Mallorca 1970 (Pos. 123): **26 ... ♖c5!**. Superior to 26 ... ♖xa2 27 ♖h4 b5 28 ♗f1 ♖a4 29 ♖d4, and Black is

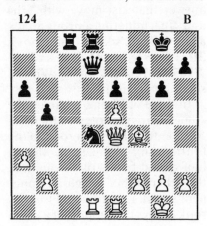

124       B

tied up. **27 ♖h4 ♘e5! 28 ♖xc5 bxc5 29 ♖a4 c4**, and the c-pawn became a decisive factor. (see also Pos. 115, 175)

Najdorf-Fischer, Buenos Aires 1970 (Pos. 124): **22 ... ♕d5**. Going for the same idea. White had better not reject the queen exchange since 23 ♕b1 is answered by 23 ... ♕b3! with either 24 ... ♘e2+, or 24 ... ♖c2 to follow, while 23 ♕e3 is strongly met by 23 ... ♖c2. **23 ♕xd5 ♖xd5 24 ♔f1 ♖c2 25 ♖d3 ♘c6! 26 ♖xd5 exd5 27 ♗h6 d4**, with some winning chances. (see also Pos. 183)

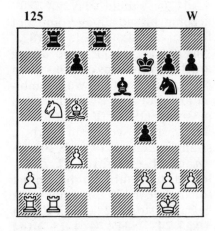

125       W

Fischer-Portisch, Havana Olympiad 1966, (Pos. 125) went: **22 ♖b4!**. The run-of-the-mill move was 22 a4. **22 ... ♗xa2 23 ♘xc7 ♖bc8**. This time the simplification offer is rejected. After 23 ... ♖xb4 24 cxb4, the b-pawn would have decided the game. **24 h4!** accentuating the strength of 22 ♖b4, and moving relentlessly towards a quick decision (see p.119). 24 ... ♘xh4 loses to 25 ♖xf4+ ♔g6 26 ♖xh4 ♖xc7 27 ♗b6. (see also Pos. 244)

There can hardly be a more suitable example to conclude this subject than the following one (Pos. 126). Fischer manoeuvres both his rooks with an agility that is more customary for fleet-footed minor pieces. The game is Fischer-Panov, Skopje 1967.

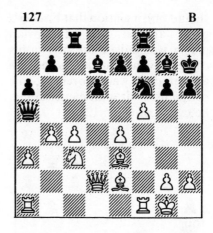

127　　　　　　　　　　B

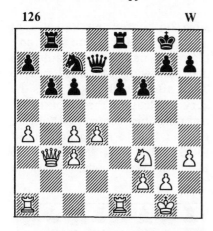

126　　　　　　　　　　W

18 ♖e4! a6 19 ♕c2 b5 20 axb5 axb5 21 cxb5 cxb5 22 ♘d2 ♖a8 23 ♖ae1 ♕d5 24 ♖h4! ♕f5 25 ♘e4 e5 26 ♖e3! h6 27 ♖f3 ♕h7 28 ♘xf6+! gxf6 29 ♖g3+ ♔h8 30 ♖g6!, Black resigned. (see also Pos. 15)

*The Centralised Queen*

About Fischer's **17 ... ♕e5** in their 2nd match game, Denver 1971 (Pos. 127) Larsen made the following observation: "Risky, but the only good move in this position . . . Probably [Fischer] has a special relationship with this maneuver ... ♕a5-e5. He got into serious trouble with it against Naranja in the Interzonal. Maybe it all has something to do with the game he lost in 1960, at the Leipzig Olympiad, where Muñoz from Ecuador surprised him with such a manoeuvre."[2] The queen seems indeed very uncomfortably placed at the centre, but after: **18 ♖ae1** (18 ♗f4/♗d4 ♘xe4!) **18 ... ♗c6 19 ♗f4 ♘xe4 20 ♘xe4 ♕xe4 21 ♗d3 ♕d4+**, the queen was out of danger. (see also Pos. 219). Without wishing to go into deep psychological explanations of the kind Larsen propounds here, one should only mention that Fischer's game against the Ecuadorian player was indeed the first in his career in which such a manoeuvre appeared. It was, moreover, one of the most dramatic encounters he ever lost (Pos. 128).

128                                    W

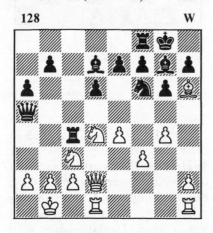

16 ♘b3 ♛e5!. The game's continuation proved how effective this manoeuvre was: **17 h4 ♖fc8 18 ♗f4 ♛e6 19 h5 b5 20 hxg6 fxg6 21 ♗h6 ♗h8 22 e5 b4!**, and Black's attack was irresistible.

Whether it was this game which impressed Fischer of the power of a centralised queen in a full-board middlegame or not, the manoeuvre does show up in a number of his games. Larsen mentions the game Naranja-Fischer, Palma de Mallorca 1970. Let's look at that example (Pos. 129).

Fischer played here **13 ... ♛f5**, luring White into playing **14 e4**

129                                    B

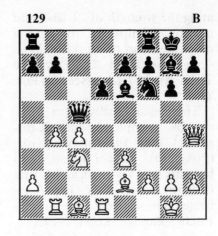

since he himself overlooked that after **14 ... ♛e5** White shouldn't play the natural but faulty 14 ♗b2 allowing 14 ... g5! but **15 ♖b3!** after which Black faces the very unpleasant threat of 15 f4, trapping his centralised queen. Fischer had to reconcile himself to **15 ... ♗d7 16 f4 ♛e6 17 f5! gxf5 18 exf5 ♛xf5**, when Naranja

130                                    B

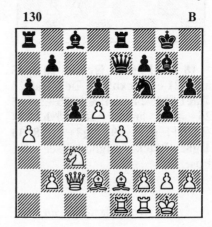

missed 19 ♘d5!, offering him much the better chances.

In the penultimate round of the same tournament, Fischer played against Gligorić (Pos. 130) **17 ... ♕e5 18 ♔h1 ♕d4**, taking greater risks than the position probably justified. After **18 f3 ♘h5** Gligorić blundered with **20 ♘b5? axb5 21 ♗xb5 ♕e5!**. Simply **20 ♘d1** would have forced Black to swallow his pride and retreat the queen to e5, leaving White with the superior position.

Greater precision and daring were involved in the following case (Kurajica-Fischer, Rovinj-Zagreb 1970, Pos. 131).

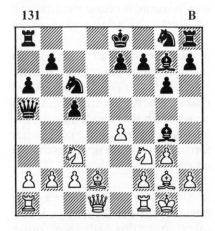

131                    B

White wants to play, obviously enough, 11 ♘d5, then 12 ♗f4. Fischer's unconventional way of countering this intention entails the transfer of his queen to the centre of the board. **10 ... ♖d8!?**

Suetin marked it – ?!. He was of the opinion that Black ought to play safe with 10 ... ♕d8, 11 ... ♘f6, etc.[3] **11 ♘d5 ♕a4 12 ♕c1 ♕xe4**. He might have been happy with the material gain – see pp. 52-7. But the manoeuvre holds, to be sure, more water. **13 ♘g5 ♕e5**. Again the queen finds itself very unpleasantly stationed at the centre, exposed to many threats along the e-file and the h2-b8 diagonal. But this time it was a calculated risk well worth taking. **14 ♗f4**. The critical juncture. Some commentators advised 14 ♖e1,[4] but after 14 ... ♕xb2 15 ♕xb2 ♗xb2 16 ♖ab1 ♗e5! (and not 16 ... ♗g7?) 17 ♖xb7 h6!, Black has nothing to fear. Another try was 14 ♗c3 ♘d4 15 ♖e1 ♕d6! (and not 15 ... ♕b8 16 ♘xf7!? ♔xf7 17 ♕g5, with wild complications that probably favour White). White has nothing convincing to show for the pawn. 16 ♘e4 ♕xd5! is doubtless better for Black.

**14 ... ♕xb2 15 ♕xb2 ♗xb2 16 ♖ab1 ♗e5 17 ♖xb7**. Here 17 ♗xe5 was thought to yield White some tangible advantage.[5] Far from this being the case, it only goes to show how precisely Fischer had to calculate the whole process: 17 ... ♘xe5 18 ♖fe1, is answered by 18 ... h6! 19 ♖xe5 hxg5 20 ♖xb7 ♔f8! 21 ♘e3 (21 ♘xe7? ♖d1+ wins, and 21 ♖xg5 ♗f5!

threatens 22 ... f6) 21 ... ♗e2 22
♖xc5 g4, with a tactical endgame
ahead. A sample line is 23 ♗f1?!
♗f3 24 ♖a7 ♘f6 25 ♖xa6 ♘e4 26
♖d5 ♖b8! 27 ♖b5 ♔g7! and the
threat of 28 ... ♖xh2! forces
White to concede the b-file by 28
♖xb8 (if 28 ♖aa5 then 28 ... ♘c3
first, and if 28 ♘g2 then 28 ...
♖bd8 29 ♗d3 ♘xf2!!) 28 ...
♖xb8, when Black's position is
probably winning.

The element of risk in all these
examples is considerable, and
centralising the queen in this way
can probably never be a completely safe manoeuvre. Yet when
it proves to be effective (as
in Fischer-Muñoz, Larsen-Fischer
and Kurajica-Fischer), its impact
on the further development of the
game is enormous.

For another interesting case see
Pos. 200.


## THE ART AND CRAFT
## OF LIQUIDATION

At the Buenos Aires 1970
tournament Fischer produced the
following example of an extremely
sophisticated liquidation process,
leading from an apparently even
middlegame to an advantageous
endgame (Pos. 132). The game is
Damjanović-Fischer after White's
22nd move.

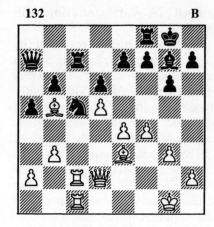

132                                   B

**22 ... ♕a8!**
Threatening 23 ... ♘xe4. He
invites White to exchange on c5,
which would increase the strength
of Black's bishop in view of its
prospective outpost at d4. White
would be virtually forced to
exchange if he plays now 24 ♗c6.
For after 24 ... ♕a6! 25 ♕g2 ♕d3!
Black is better, while on 25 ♖c4
he would have to reckon with the
imminent possibility of ... b5,
forcing him to give up the exchange
on c5.

**23 ♕e2 e5!**
After having driven away the
queen from the d-file, Black can
carry out this advance quite
safely, revealing another strong
point of his previous move. From
a8 the queen would send vicious
messages to the exposed pawn on
e4.

**24 dxe6** *e.p.*

Any opening of the e-file, either by White (fxe5), or Black (... exf4) would be in Black's favour.

**24 ... fxe6 25 ♖d1 ♖d8 26 ♗d4**

Notwithstanding the weakening of his central pawns, Black has gained a slight edge, owing to the potential of his d-pawn to become a passed one. Oddly enough, in *Ajedrez*[1] Damjanović claimed that 26 ♗c4 would have given White a winning advantage! Viz: 26 ... d5 (26 ... ♕xe4? 27 ♗xc5 ♕xe2 28 ♖xe2 bxc5 29 ♖xe6 ♗d4+ 30 ♖xd4! wins – EA) 27 exd5 exd5 28 ♗xc5 ♖xc5 29 ♕e6+ ♔h8 30 ♖cd2 (30 ♕xb6? ♖c6! – EA), etc. Yet it seems quite clear that after 30 ... d4! it is Black, if anyone, who has reason to claim the advantage. Let's see: 31 ♕xb6 ♖c6 32 ♕b5 ♖xd6 33 ♖d3 (or 33 ♗d3 ♖e8 34 ♖e2 ♖e3!) 33 ... ♖e8, and Black invades along the e-file. Best for White might be 33 ♗f1, so as to transfer the bishop to the long diagonal. 33 ... d3 doesn't work: 34 ♖xd3 ♗d4+ 35 ♖xd4! ♖xd4 36 ♕e5+. However, after 33 ... ♕a7 and doubling the rooks on the e-file Black would have the advantage.

After a preliminary phase, Fischer now initiates a systematic reduction of material on the board, fixing in the process the centre pawns.

**26 ... ♗xd4+ 27 ♖xd4 e5! 28 fxe5 dxe5 29 ♖xd8+**

Had he been aware of the subtleties of Fischer's plan, he would have kept rooks on the board by playing 29 ♖d5!.

**29 ... ♕xd8 30 ♗c4+ (!) ♔g7 31 ♗d5 ♘d7! 32 ♕f2**

It was too late to play 32 a4. Black would have some tangible advantage after 32 ... ♘f6 33 ♖d2 (33 ♖xc7 ♕xc7, then 34 ... ♕c5+, 35 ... ♕d4, etc) 33 ... ♖c1+ 34 ♔g2 ♕c7. White's move makes him the temporary boss of the c-file.

**32 ... ♖xc2 33 ♕xc2 b5!**

Played with a view to a possible queenless endgame, when Black would need b6 for his knight to prevent the white king's infiltration via c4. While serving this purpose, it also prepares ... b4, fulfilling two tasks: A – taking control of c3, B – forestalling any further pawn exchanges on White's part.

**34 ♔g2**

34 ♕c6 would change very little. Sure, the natural-looking 34 ... ♕b6+ is a grave mistake: 35 ♔g2! ♕xc6 36 ♗xc6 ♘c5 37 ♗xb5 ♘xe4 38 ♗c6, and this might well be a win for White. But simply 34 ... b4 keeps Black on top.

**34 ... b4 35 ♕c6 ♘f6 36 ♔f3 ♕d7!**

The last exchange, and the most important one. White cannot spurn it by means of 37 ♕c5, because of 37 ... ♕h3!! with two main lines: a) 38 ♕a5 ♕f1+ 39 ♔e3 ♘g4+ 40 ♔d2 ♕f2+ 41 ♔c1 (41 ♔d3 ♕d4+) ♘e3! 42 ♕c7+, ♔h6, and the co-operation of Black's queen and knight around the white king would be deadly; b) 38 ♕e7+ ♔h6 39 ♔e3 (39 ♕xf6?? ♕f1+) 39 ... ♘g4+ 40 ♔d3 ♕f1+! (40 ... ♕xh2 41 ♕h4+ poses greater problems) 41 ♔c2 ♕f2+ 42 ♔b1 ♕xh2!, and Black ought to win.

**37 ♕xd7+ ♘xd7 38 ♔e3 ♔f6 39 ♔d3 ♘b6 (see Pos. 133).**

133                              W

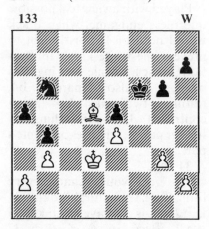

Notwithstanding Damjanović's claims that this is a drawn endgame,[2] it was won by Fischer, and analysis showed that White could not avert this. Due to the pawn formation Fischer has managed to set up, only Black has routes to the opposite camp (knight to c3), while both c4 and g4 – the squares from which White's king could

penetrate – can be defended by Black's knight placed on dark squares – b6 (d6) and f6 respectively. This factor alone must have been sufficient for Fischer to liquidate to this endgame. It does accord very well with his policy of playing for tiny spatial advantages in the endgame (see 'Playing for Space', pp.111-4 ).

Generally speaking, appropriate liquidation emphasises structural weaknesses (mainly those pertaining to pawn structure and the relative value of both sides' pieces), and inappropriate liquidation is that which would diminish the position's tension with no apparent benefits. In Fischer's games one finds many examples of both of these! Leonid Shamkovich once remarked that "Fischer is always glad to simplify for the sake of some advantage".[3] The example we've just seen illustrates this very well. The complete truth, however, is that Fischer was happy to simplify even without gaining any clear advantage. This is a hallmark of his style, and it can't always be sustained by objective reasoning. Only very rarely do we find an example of the contrary, namely a case where he ought to simplify and fails to do so. One such is his game with the black pieces against Unzicker, Santa Monica 1966 (Pos. 134).

134 B

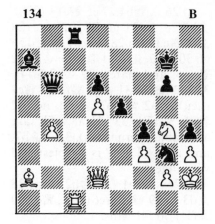

135 B

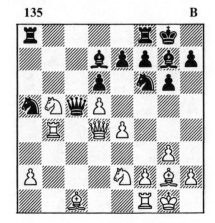

Fischer's **69 ... ♘e2** was dubbed by Unzicker "clever but artificial".[4] It must be regarded as a mistaken move since it led to a draw (**70 ♖e1 ♘c3 71 ♗b1 ♘xb1 72 ♖xb1 ♖c4 73 ♕e1**, etc), whereas, according to Unzicker "the simple line **69 ... ♖xc1 70 ♕xc1 ♘e2 71 ♕e1 ♘c3!** would have secured Black the win. In the long run White's position cannot be defended, considering the weaknesses of the pawns at b4 and d5 and the permanent mating threats on the diagonal g1-a7." To this could be added that after 72 ♘xe5, Black wins by 72 ... ♕e3! (not 72 ... ♘xa2 73 ♘c4!, draw).

More often we see Fischer liquidating too early rather than too late. In Pos. 135 (Szabo-Fischer, Buenos Aires, 1970), Fischer played **17 ... ♘xd5!?** at once, and after **18 ♕xc5 dxc5 19**

**♖b1 ♘b4 20 ♘c7 ♖a7 21 a3 ♖xc7 22 axb4 cxb4 23 ♖xb4 ♖c2**, enjoyed a very slight endgame advantage. By waiting another move and interpolating 17 ... ♖ab8!, he would have gained more: 18 a4, and only now, after the weakening of the a-pawn 18 ... ♘xd5!. This would have led to 19 ♕xc5 (19 ♕xd5 ♕xb4) 19 ... dxc5 20 ♖b1 ♘b6 21 ♗f4 (21 ♘ec3 ♘xa4!) 21 ... e5 22 ♗e3 ♘xa4, staying a pawn ahead.

Against Portisch at the 1962 Varna Olympiad (Pos. 136) Fischer played **26 ♕xb7?!**, expecting to retain some winning chances after **26 ... ♗xb7 27 ♖d7 ♗a6 28 ♗xa6 ♖xa6 29 ♖xf7** in view of Black's weak pawns. This, however, proved too slender an advantage to clinch a whole point, and the endgame was drawn twelve moves later. Refraining from simplifica-

**136** W

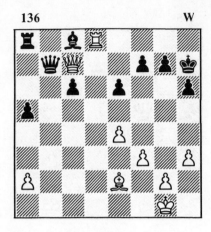

tion by 26 ♕d6! offered greater realistic chances for a win. White threatens 27 e5, 28 ♗d3+, and it is difficult for Black to organise a defence, considering the cramped positioning of his pieces. Here are a few sample lines:

a) 26 ... e5 27 ♕f8!, with the threat 28 ♗c4.

b) 26 ... ♕b6+ 27 ♔h2:

b1) 27 ... ♗b7 28 ♖d7 ♔g8 29 ♕e7, and wins.

b2) 27 ... ♕f2 28 ♗d3 e5 29 ♗c4! (29 ♕xe5? ♗xh3!! turns the tables) 29 ... ♕h4 (or 29 ... ♕d4 30 ♕f8! ♕xc4 31 ♕g8+ ♔g6 32 ♖d6+, and Black can't defend by 32 ... f6) 30 ♖f8! ♗xh3!? (or 30 ... ♕f4+ 31 g3! ♕xf3 32 ♖xf7) 31 g3! ♕h5 32 ♗xf7, winning.

c) 26 ... ♕b2 27 ♗f1 ♕c1 28 ♕c7 ♕e3+ 29 ♔h2 ♕f2 30 ♗d3, renewing the ancient threat of 31 e5+.

d) 26 ... ♕b4 27 e5 ♕e1+ (27 ... ♗b7 28 ♗d3+ g6 29 ♖d7, etc) 28 ♗f1 ♕e3+ (or 28 ... ♗b7 29 ♕d3+ g6 30 ♖d7 ♗a6 31 ♖xf7+ ♔h8 32 ♕xg6, and mates) 29 ♔h2 ♕f4+ 30 g3! ♕xf3 31 ♗g2 ♕f2 32 ♕c7 (neither 32 ♕xc6?? ♗b7!, nor 32 ♕f8 ♗b7!! 33 ♖xa8 c5!, are advisable alternatives). 32 ... ♗b7, and now 33 ♖d7 is simplest and winningest.

e) 26 ... ♕b1+ 27 ♔h2 ♕xa2 28 ♗d3 e5 29 ♕f8 ♕e6 (29 ... ♕d2 30 ♗f1!) 30 f4! wins.

Yet even without calculating these, or other, variations, it should be quite obvious that by playing 26 ♕d6 White would maintain a very strong grip on the position.

**137** B

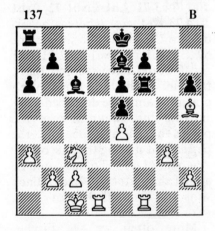

About the liquidation in the final stage in Fischer's game (as Black) against Tal, at Zürich 1959, Botvinnik commented (Pos. 137): **25 ... ♖d8** "Black's [ . . . ]

move involves an unnoticeable but quite essential oversight which results in White's obtaining a competent game (after an exchange of all four rooks which activates his king with a considerable advantage). Black ought to keep at least one pair of rooks on the board is he intends to play for a win." Botvinnik recommended 25 ... ♔f8! followed by ... ♔g7, ... ♖xf1, and ... ♖f8, when "[t]he strong black bishops and the weak white pawn on e4 make White's position difficult".[5] The way Fischer played it resulted in a quick draw. (see also Pos. 190, 231)

Fischer's predilection for simplifying, either properly or excessively, manifested itself right from the beginning of his career. Very characteristic is the following example, played at the US Junior Championship, Cleveland 1957

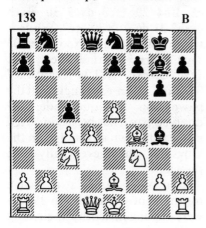

138       B

(Pos. 138).

The game is Schoene-Fischer, still in the opening phase. Clearly White's central pawns ought to become the rolls on which Black should feed. But are they there for breakfast, dinner, or supper? Bobby isn't selective. He starts buttering them in the opening, eats them up in the middlegame, and digests them in an early endgame.

Chessically, it would take thirteen moves of massive liquidation before Black could mark some advantage. But the liquidation process is highly advantageous this time, as it leads straight to an endgame where any material advantage is likely to be decisive: **10 ... cxd4 11 ♕xd4 ♘c6 12 ♕xd8 ♖xd8 13 ♖d1 ♖xd1+ 14 ♘xd1 ♗xf3 15 ♗xf3 ♘xe5 16 ♗xe5 ♗xe5 17 ♗xb7 ♘d6 18 ♗a6 18 ♗d5 e6 18 ... ♖b8 19 c5 19 b3 ♖b6 19 ... ♘e4 20 c6 ♖b6 21 ♗b7 ♘d6 22 b3 22 ♗a8 ♖b8 22 ... ♘xb7 23 cxb7 ♖xb7**, and this is evidently a winning endgame for Black.

The following two examples, both played in 1962, have one structural factor in common: White's pawn formation c4-d5 concedes Black the use of the strategically important outpost c5. By prompt liquidation Fischer makes optimal use of this.

Pos. 139 is taken from Blau-Fischer at the Varna Olympiad.

139                          B

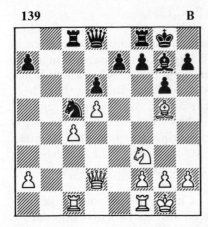

140                          B

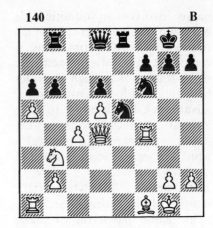

The game proceeded: **17 ... ♘e4 18 ♕e3 ♘xg5 19 ♕xg5 ♖c5 20 ♕e3 ♕c7 21 ♘d4 ♗xd4 22 ♕xd4 ♖c8**. The light pieces have gone, and Black has quickly tripled his heavy pieces on the c-file. **23 ♖c2 ♖xc4 24 ♖xc4 ♕xc4 25 ♕xa7**. As a consequence of the above, the pawn on c4 has fallen, and the pawn on d5 now awaits the same fate. All Black has to do is neutralise White's a-pawn. **25 ...♕e4! 26 h3** providing 'air'. 26 a4 ♖c5 27 ♕a8+ ♔g7 28 ♖d1 ♕d4! wins the d-pawn. **26 ... ♖c4!**. The advance of the a-pawn is now checked. Fischer went on to win the endgame.

Pos. 140 (Yanofsky-Fischer, Stockholm) saw the following development: **21 ... ♘g6 22 ♖f2 ♘e4 23 ♖e2 ♘c5 24 ♖xe8+ ♕xe8 25 ♖a3** 25 ♘xc5 bxc5 is better for Black, owing to his domination of

the b-file, and the limited scope of White's bishop. A black knight would outmatch it in almost any type of endgame. **25 ... ♘xb3 26 ♖xb3 bxa5**. The simplifications have led to Black winning a pawn on the queenside. For the time being the advantage is negligible, since the doubled pawn plays a very minor role. **27 ♖a3 ♕d8 28 c5 ♖b4 29 ♕c3 dxc5 30 ♕xc5 ♖xb2 31 d6 ♘f8 32 ♕c7**. White is worse off after 32 ♖xa5? ♘e6 33 ♕c3 ♕b6+ 34 ♔h1 ♖b1, etc. **32 ... ♕xc7 33 dxc7 ♖c2 34 ♖xa5 ♖xc7 35 ♖xa6**. After exchanging all the pawns on the queenside, the doubled pawn has been converted into a full pawn advantage on the kingside, which eventually won the game.

Two other games at the same tournament – Stockholm 1962 – were distinguished by their long series of liquidations, though with less success these times.

141           W

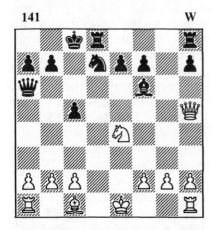

In Fischer-Pomar (Pos. 141), there occurred: **14 ♕e2 ♕e6 15 ♘xf6 ♕xe2+ 16 ♔xe2 ♘xf6 17 ♗e3 b6 18 ♖ad1 ♖xd1 19 ♖xd1 ♖d8 20 ♖xd8+ ♔xd8.** Within seven moves all but two pieces have been eliminated. Fischer pinned his hopes on the theoretical superiority of the bishop versus the knight in this endgame, all the more so, probably, when taking into account the fact that the three black pawns on the queenside are stationed on dark squares. Confident as Fischer must have been that such an advantage would suffice for a win, he was to fight for another 57 moves without success, before acquiescing to a draw.

Playing Black against Gligorić the next round, he even went as far as liquidating to a disadvantageous endgame, from a position that suggested no immediate unpleasantries for him (Pos. 142):

142           B

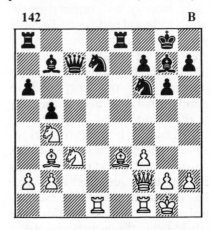

**18 ... ♗f8 19 ♘bd5 ♘xd5 20 ♘xd5 ♗xd5 21 ♖xd5 ♖xe3 22 ♕xe3 ♗c5 23 ♖xc5 ♕xc5 24 ♕xc5 ♘xc5 25 ♗c2 ♘a4 26 ♗xa4 bxa4.** Fischer was ready to play a long and inferior rook endgame after **27 ♖c1 ♖d8 28 a3 ♖d2 29 ♖c6 ♖xb2 30 ♖xa6 ♖a2 31 ♖xa4,** and was successful in holding it to a draw at move 81.

There is certainly nothing wrong with a player heading for these kind of simplifications in a number of games. It becomes, however, a double-edged weapon, to say the least, when adopted as a general policy. It is the personal view of this writer that Fischer's faith in his technical skills had by 1962 become more of a liability than an asset. Apart from a few creative outbursts at Varna and Curaçao that year, he showed very little by way of creativity, and relied ever more heavily on simplifying towards technical endgames. I believe that fundamentally he had the idea that he was superior to the top Soviet grandmasters in this respect, and probably had in mind outplaying them in this way at the Candidates.

Normally, liquidation brings about reduction in the position's tension. In the next two examples Fischer takes identical decisions. In both cases queens are exchanged, but at the same time the tension in the centre is, to a certain extent, intensified. Both, by the way, were played in 1962.

more play left with queens on the board after, for instance, 14 ♕e3 and 15 ♕h3. Fischer gives preference to the restoration of his pawn structure at the cost of eliminating the heaviest pieces. A couple of moves later it was he who saw to the relief of the tension in the centre: **14 ... ♕xd2 15 ♗xd2 ♗c6 16 a5 ♖ad8 17 ♗e3!? d4 18 ♗d2**, and White's slight advantage did not suffice for a win. (see also Pos. 232)

**144**                                  **W**

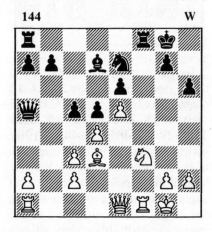

And against Petrosian (again as White) at Curaçao (Pos. 144): **17 c4**. A solution in the same spirit. The commentators were at odds as to the correct evaluation of the decision this time. Boleslavsky and Suetin criticised it. Boleslavsky[6] regarded it an outright mistake which aggravated White's position, preferring 17 ♔h1 instead. Suetin[7] added that in his willing-

**143**                                  **W**

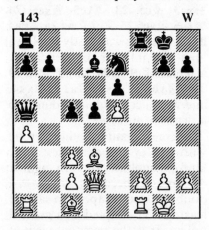

Against Uhlmann (Pos. 143), at Stockholm, Fischer (White) played **14 c4**. There would have been

ness to change the game's features, Fischer had headed for an endgame, where his pawns' weaknesses would make for a hard defence. Kan[8] thought it was anyway preferable to 17 ♕h4 ♖ae8, while, moreover, White had to take into account possibilities such as ... ♗a4, followed up by ... c4. P.H. Clarke[9] was of the opinion the move deserved an exclamation mark for its realistic approach. For him, Black's build-up on the queenside, nearing its completion with ... ♖ac8 and ... cxd4, had to be checked, and the sooner the better. The Romanian magazine *Revista de Sah*[10] held the same view, and maintained the same exclamation mark.

Whereas in the previous position (143) White had the somewhat better chances in an endgame because of his bishop pair and the pawn majority on the kingside, here he wouldn't enjoy the same advantages. Is this simplification wrong, then?

**17 ... ♕xe1 18 ♖fxe1 dxc4 19 ♗e4!?.** Clearly this move was on Fischer's mind when playing 17 c4. He apparently estimated his prospects as better, since had he wished to play for equality, he could do so by simply capturing on c4. After 19 ♗xc4, neither Suetin's 19 ... ♖ac8! (which White answers by 20 dxc5! ♖xc5 21 ♖ad1 ♗c8 22 ♗b3, and Black's

vulnerable pawn at e6 doesn't permit him to boast an advantage), nor Boleslavsky's 19 ... b5 20 ♗f1 c4 (with 21 ♘d2 ♘d5 22 ♘e4 followed by 23 g3, White has equality) seem convincing proofs to the contrary. **19 ... cxd4 20 ♗xb7 ♖ab8 21 ♗a6.** That was Fischer's point. After **21 ... ♖b4 22 ♖ad1** White recovers the pawn, and if Black plays inaccurately (22 ... ♖a4 23 ♖xd4!, or 22 ... ♘c6 23 ♘xd4 ♘b8 24 a3 ♖a4 25 ♗b5 ♗xb5 26 ♘xb5 a6 27 ♘c7), White indeed gains the advantage. It was Petrosian's turn to bring about further liquidation with **22 ... d3! 23 cxd3 cxd3 24 ♖xd3 ♗c6**, and the endgame has turned out to be slightly in Black's favour. His pieces occupy better positions. **25 ♖d4 ♖xd4 26 ♘xd4 ♗d5.** Even if Fischer hadn't blundered here (**27 a4? ♖f4**), and had played instead Petrosian's suggested 27 ♗f1 ♖f4 28 ♘b5,[11] he would have had some way to go before reaching complete equality.

Doubtful liquidation, again at the Candidates, Curaçao 1962, occurred in one of Fischer's most dramatic games – that against Keres in the 14th round (Pos. 145). **12 ... ♗g4.** Fischer (Black) concentrates on one structural element – creating a weak white pawn at e5. For this purpose he first has to see to it that White can't consolidate his centre by

**145** B

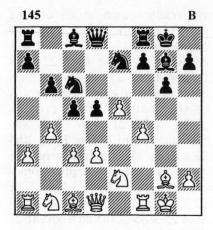

playing d4. In retrospect Fischer regarded another set-up – ... ♘f5 and ... ♘ce7, as better.[12] **13 h3 ♗xe2.** Bent on exchanging the bishop for the knight, so as to carry out his initial plan, Fischer rejects 13 ... ♗e6 followed by 14 ... ♕d7 and then ... f6, which, again, he was later to regret. **14 ♕xe2 f6 15 b5.** Practically forced, since White has no minor piece to defend e5, and both 15 exf6 ♗xf6 or 15 e6 f5, leave White's pawn formation in very poor shape. **15 ... ♘a5 16 ♘d2.** He wants to play d4, which he couldn't do at once because of 16 ... cxd4 17 cxd4 ♘b3. **16 ... fxe5 17 fxe5 ♖xf1+.** One exchange leads to another. Black couldn't put additional pressure on e5 by 17 ... ♕c7, since 18 ♘f3 ♘b3 19 ♖b1 ♘xc1 20 ♖bxc1 ♘f5 21 ♘g5! (and not 21 ♖fe1 ♗h6!), is better for White.

**18 ♘xf1 ♘b3.** Heading for the last exchange – that of the offside knight for White's dark-squared bishop. Keres played **19 ♖b1**, allowing Fischer to carry out his plan to the full. In an article in *Chess Life*[13] I gave 19 ♗g5!! as a better way to expose the inherent flaw of Fischer's uni-directional policy. Here is the analysis of the possibilities after this move: 19 ... ♘xa1. It is interesting to note that White, though being temporarily a rook down, may consider alternatives to the natural 20 ♗xe7. They all have two factors in common: trying to exploit the pin along the h4-d8 diagonal, as well as take advantage of Black's weakness on the a2-g8 diagonal.

a) 20 ♘e3 ♕d7! 21 ♕a2?! ♗xe5! (Simplest and best. 21 ... ♖e8 enables White to seize the initiative with 22 d4!), and White might at best equalise.

b) 20 ♕g4, trying to provoke Black into playing 20 ... ♔f8 21 ♘e3! h6 22 ♗xd5!, with advantageous complications. But 20 ... ♕c8! is difficult for White to meet satisfactorily, e.g. 20 ♕d1 (in case of 20 ♕f3 ♕f5! and Black has the better of it, or 21 ♗xe7 ♕xg4 22 hxg4 ♖e8, and Black ought to win) 21 ... ♘f5! 22 ♗xd5+ ♔h8 23 ♗xa8 ♕xa8 24 ♕xa1 ♕f3! 25 e6?! ♘g3!, and Black wins.

c) 20 ♕a2 ♗xe5 (if 20 ... ♖c8? 21 ♘e3! c4 22 ♘xd5 ♗f8 23 ♕xa1 cxd3 24 ♕a2 ♔h8 25 ♗f6+, and White wins, while 20 ... ♔h8 is strongly met by 21 d4!, when despite being an exchange down, White's prospects are preferable) 21 ♘e3!? ♗xc3 22 ♘xd5 ♗d4+ 23 ♔h1 ♔g7 24 ♘xe7 ♕f8, and the advantage is on Black's side. If White refrains from 25 ♗xa8, and plays instead 25 ♕d5, then 25 ... ♕f2!, or 25 ♕d2 ♔h8.

So, after the prosaic 20 ♗xe7 ♕xe7 21 ♗xd5+ ♔h8 22 ♗xa8 ♕xe5 23 ♕xe5 ♗xe5 24 c4, my article ended with the conclusion that "the endgame is drawn. Neither side can make any meaningful headway." When I showed it to Kasparov, a couple of months later, the World Champion's immediate reaction was "Drawn? Are you sure?", and off-handedly he suggested the very strong 24 ... ♗f4!. The idea is to restrain White's knight, while trying to profit from having the better remaining minor piece, plus the 2-to-1 pawn advantage on the kingside. However, it seems that White holds his own by a quick activation of his king: 25 ♔f2 ♘c2 26 ♔f3 g5 27 ♔e4! ♔g7 (if 27 ... h5 28 h4! ♘d4 29 hxg5 ♗xg5 30 ♘g3 h4 31 ♘f5, draw. Worse is 27 ... ♘xa3? 28 ♔d5!, and White picks up the pawn on a7) 28 ♔d5 ♘d4 (28 ... ♘e1 29 d4) 29 ♗b7 h5 30 ♗c8 ♔f6 31 ♔e4 etc.

This is, then, a case of faulty liquidation. The achievement of Black's objective, isolating White's pawn on e5, was done at the expense of weakening his own hold of the important d5 square.

Black should have taken advantage of his positional superiority at move 12 in other ways, as pointed out by Fischer in *MSMG*.

An excellent example of appropriate liquidation – that is, one which stresses structural weaknesses in the opponent's camp without incurring one's own weaknesses – was played by Fischer two years earlier, at Mar del Plata 1960. It was in his game with the white pieces against Olafsson (Pos. 146).

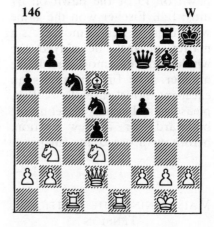

146                                    W

26 ♘a5!. A very timely liquidation offer, clearing the c-file, and preparing himself for a fight for control of e5. **26 ... ♘xa5 27 ♖xe8!**. Another subtle exchange.

It seems that he isn't really interested in e5. Why? Fischer is ready to renounce any claims for e5 for two other objectives he regards as more important: control of the c-file, and a further exchange of knights on f4, rightly assessing that as a result Black's greater structural problem – his weak d-, f- and h-pawns – would be rendered more critical. **27 ... ♖xe8 28 ♕xa5 h6 29 g3! ♔h7 30 ♘f4 ♘xf4 31 ♗xf4 ♕e6 32 ♗d2!.** Ready to switch his rook from the c-file to the e-file, while maintaining, for the time being, the threat of 33 ♖c7. **32 ... ♖c8 33 ♖e1 ♕f7 34 ♖e7!.** Reaping the fruits of his very proper action. Either the pawn on f5 or the pawn on b7 must fall. Fischer won the game within another eight moves. As a matter of fact, he played the whole game in a most instructive manner. The first part was an excellent model case of . . . Well, please wait! Let me just set up the billboard for a new section, before we proceed any further.

## MAINTAINING THE POSITIONAL TENSION

Right. Here we are. What I wished to say was that the first part of this game (Fischer-Olafsson, Mar del Plata 1960, that is), might be an excellent introduction to our present chapter.

In open and half-open positions it is essential to create and maintain some positional tension, for else the game might all too soon turn dull and eventless, offering no objectives to play for. Positional tension is normally the result of tension in the pawn structure. In closed games the mere presence of (usually) more pieces on the board wouldn't always bring about sufficient tension if there are no negotiation points between the two camps' pawn formations. Yet this is even more so in open and half-open games.

147                                     W

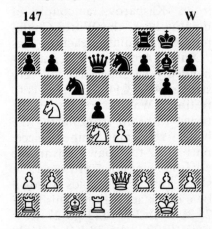

In Pos. 147, from the above game, it is evidently the mutual options of exchanging the central pawns which is the source of tension in the position. Once the pawns are exchanged, the tension would be completely resolved.

Fischer plays **14 ♘b3**.

For the sake of keeping the positional tension, he is ready to grant Black some domination in the centre in return for play on the weakened dark squares which are soon to be created on the queenside: a5, b6, c7, c5, and d6.

**14 ... a6 15 ♘c3 d4**

Black establishes a passed pawn on d4, and sets out to pressurise e4 by ... ♖ae8 and ... f5.

**16 ♘a4 ♖ae8 17 ♗f4!**

Very well timed. The bishop takes up this important position on the h2-b8 diagonal before Black plays ... f5. This required some precise calculations since the position gets tenser and richer in tactical possibilities.

**17 ... ♘d5 18 ♗g3 ♛e7**

Spassky, with whom Fischer shared first place in that tournament, was impressed enough by Fischer's play to analyse this game in the Russian Yearbook,[1] where he mentions the following alternatives after 18 ... f5 19 ♛c4 – A: 19 ... fxe4 20 ♘b6, and White wins a piece, B: 19 ... b5 20 ♛xd5+ ♛xd5 21 exd5 bxa4 22 ♘c5 (also good is 22 dxc6), with White's superiority.

**19 ♘ac5 ♚h8** 19 ... f5 20 ♛c4 – Spassky. **20 ♖e1 ♘b6 21 ♖ac1** threat: ♘xa6 **21 ... f5!**.

This expected thrust is coming now with the double threat of 22 ... f4 and 22 ... fxe4. A positional struggle from a half-open game can hardly get tenser than this.

**22 ♛d2 ♛f7!?**

Removing the queen from the e-file, and making ready to meet 23 ♘xa6 by 23 ... ♘c4!.

**23 exf5! gxf5 24 ♘d3**

After some manoeuvring, the tension in the centre has subsided. White's position is superior, primarily because of a better pawn structure. We have seen how Fischer turned it to good use in Pos. 146.

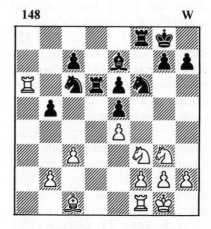

148                                    W

Keeping some tension in the late middlegame might well be an indispensible ingredient for maintaining winning possibilities in positions with level material. Reduction of material in a position where one does not have a clear advantage is bound to bring a drawn result ever nearer. For a player possessing an acute sense of economy and timing like Fischer to play a move like **19 ⌓h1** in Pos. 148 (Fischer-Smyslov, Havana 1965), wasting two tempi with regard to any probable endgame (the king would have to get back to the game via g1), is quite exceptional and needs a good reason behind it. More natural seems 19 ⌓e3, and if 19 ... ⌓d4, then 20 ⌓a7. But watch: 20 ... ⌓xf3+ 21 gxf3 ⌓d7 (not 21 ... ⌓d8? 22 ⌓c5, or 21 ... ⌓e8 22 ⌓b7) 22 ⌓b7 c6 23 ⌓xd7 (23 ⌓b6 ⌓c7, and White has to defend against ... ⌓a8 and ... ⌓d7). 23 ... ⌓xd7 24 ⌓a1 ⌓c5 25 ⌓d1 (25 ⌓a6 ⌓b8! 26 ⌓a8 ⌓d7, etc.) 25 ... ⌓xe3 26 fxe3 ⌓b8!, and all the advantages White once had have dissipated without leaving a single trace. The endgame is totally drawn. By forestalling ... ⌓d4, Fischer maintained enough positional tension, which prevented the game from fizzling out into drawish wastelands: **19 ... ⌓d7 20 ⌓e3 ⌓d8 21 h3 h6 22 ⌓fa1 ⌓db8 23 ⌓a8 ⌓d1+ 24 ⌓h2 ⌓xa1 25 ⌓xa1 ⌓d7 26 b4 ⌓f7 27 ⌓f1 ⌓d6 28 g3 ⌓f6 29 ⌓1d2 ⌓e7 30 ⌓a6 ⌓b8 31 ⌓a5 c6 32 ⌓g2**. So he gets back via g2, after all! **32 ... ⌓bd7 33 ⌓f1 ⌓c8 34 ⌓e1! ⌓e8 35 ⌓d3! ⌓c7 36 c4!**, and the pressure White has subtly built soon won him the game.

Although the right policy would usually be, as we have seen, to maintain the tension as long as there are no technical or tactical solustions in sight, Fischer's greater peculiarity was in detecting when this was superfluous. Even as early as the opening stage, sometimes.

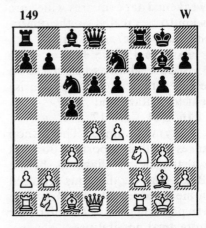

149                          W

For many players the positive tension in the centre in Pos. 149 (Fischer-Durao, Havana Olympiad 1966), and the spatial advantage White enjoys in this particular formation (which can be attributed, in the main, to the position of both sides' pawns on the d-file), would have been good enough reasons to wave aside any possible deliberations of altering this *status quo*, for as long as it is not made necessary by new circumstances.

Fischer thinks differently. By resolving the tension in the centre right away – **9 dxc5 dxc5** – he aims at creating a weak spot (d6) in Black's camp: **10 ⌓e2 b6 11 e5!**, and, at the same time, he renders e4 an ideal strategic post for a white knight. True, Black could react differently: 10 ... e5 (instead of ... b6) with a Kings Indian position with colours reversed. He would be then two tempi behind (one for colour, one for advancing the e-pawn twice) and it would then have been the weak d5 square that would serve as White's positional objective in that formation. (see also Pos. 58, 118, 246)

As a matter of fact, the other side of this tendency of Fischer's, is that in many of his games we come across middlegames in which there is too little positional tension left. This, quite naturally, was more apparent in games where he had the black pieces, when he couldn't aspire to more than equality after the opening.

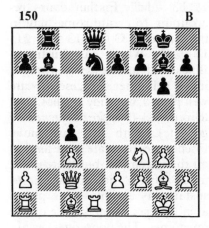

150        B

In R.Byrne-Fischer, US Championship 1962-63 (Pos. 150), for instance, both sides' pawn formations are almost identical, creating a near-symmetrical position. Black can only boast some greater space in view of the non-symmetry on the c-file, and White's pawn there might be slightly the weaker of the two, since it finds itself in the range of Black's dark-squared bishop. Yet these disadvantages may be compensated for by a certain advantage: the free square d4, and its supportive c-pawn, can be of good use for attractive centralisations of either the bishop ( ♗e3-d4) or the knight. Fischer takes the first tactical opportunity to force exchanges that put White on the defensive for some time. But the lean cow of this position can't be forced to produce more than she is able to, and eventually she is milked to an early draw. **13 ... ♕a5 14 ♖xd7 ♗xf3.** Now 15 ♗xf3 is strongly met by 15 ... ♕xc3. **15 ♗e3 ♗xg2 16 ♔xg2 ♗xc3 17 ♖c1 ♗b2 18 ♖b1 c3 19 ♖xa7 ♕d5+ 20 ♔g1 ♕f5 21 ♕xf5 gxf5 22 ♖c7,** and the game was agreed drawn a couple of moves later.

Greater ingenuity was required of Fischer in his game (as Black) against Reshevsky from the 1st round of the Santa Monica 1966 tournament (Pos. 151). The result, though, was the same.

151                                    B

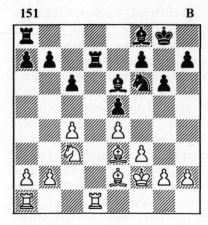

**17 ... b6**

An innocent looking move. It seems to have two purposes: a) protecting a7, thus enabling ... ♖ad8; b) strengthening Black's hold on c5 in readiness for the possible manoeuvre ... ♘d7-c5 or ... ♗c5.

**18 b3 ♖b7!**

It turns out that Fischer had nurtured another idea; instead of doubling rooks on the d-file, he removes the rook in order to create some tension on the queenside. He reckons that White's domination of the d-file could not tip the scales in his favour.

**19 ♘a4 ♘d7 20 ♘b2 b5!**

It would be, of course, quite impossible to break White down by this, since his position is too solid to crack so easily; but Fischer is exerting the maximum pressure his position can offer.

**21 cxb5 cxb5 22 ♖dc1 a5**

His light-squared bishop is directing its arrows at the pawns on a2 and b3, and he hopes that a timely advance of the a-pawn would bear some fruit. He played next 23 ... ♗a3!? and 24 ... b4, fixing White's pawns on the queenside, but the later advance of his a-pawn proved insufficient to force White's hand.

At times, Fischer failed altogether in creating any reasonable tension with which to breathe life into his game.

A case in point was his game with the black pieces against Victor Ciocaltea at Havana 1965. Let's follow it up to the early middlegame.

**1 e4 ♘f6 2 e5 ♘d5 3 d4 d6 4 c4 ♘b6 5 exd6 cxd6 6 ♘c3 g6 7 h4 h6** Ciocaltea recommended 7 ... h5.[2] **8 ♗e3 ♗g7 9 ♕d2 ♘c6 10 d5 ♘e5 11 b3 ♘bd7**. Fischer starts regrouping to create some play in the centre. **12 f3 ♘c5 13 ♘h3 ♗f5 14 ♘f2**. White has frustrated Black's intentions to sink a knight into d3. Fischer's pieces are quite well placed, but they can easily be driven back (b4, ♗e2 followed by g4, etc). With his next move Fischer tries to create some tension on the queenside, but there is not much there, position-wise, to sustain his actions – his pieces aren't poised to make use of the open lines. The consequences are quickly discernible: **14 ... b5 15 cxb5 ♕a5 16 ♖c1 0-0 17 ♘a4! ♕d8**. An admission of failure. Besides suffering material loss, Black's position offers very limited active chances. There are certainly no signs of positive tension on Black's side.

For the sake of historical truth, it should be mentioned that Fischer played the opening unprepared. This game, like all the others he played at the Havana 1965 tournament, was played by cable, Fischer sitting at the Marshall Chess Club in New York, his opponents in Havana. Through a mistake in transmission, Fischer's 1 ... ♘f6 was played as a response to his opponent's 1 d4. Only when White's next move appeared to be the improbable 2 e5, it became clear that Ciocaltea had played 1 e4. Remarkably, Fischer refused to retract his first move.[3] He fought on, from the above position, to an honourable draw.

Not known are the reasons for Fischer's disappointing performance in the first round at the tournament in Skopje, Yugoslavia, 1967. There, Black against Ilievski, he had a promising position in hand after White's 15th move (Pos. 152).

Black stands better, mainly with regard to White's pawns on c4 and d4, which can quite easily be put under pressure.

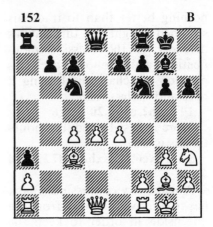

152 B

**15 ... ♘d7 16 e5 ♘b6 17 ♖b1!**
A clever reply. a1 is for the bishop. The pawn on b7 is perhaps for the rook.

**17 ... ♘a4?!**
Fischer immediately resolves the little tension he has created in the last two moves. He might have been a little apprehensive about 17 ... ♕d7 18 e6! fxe6 19 ♕g4 (19 ♘f4?! ♖xf4!) 19 ... g5 20 d5! ♗xc3 (20 ... exd5 21 ♗xd5+! with advantage) 21 dxc6 bxc6 22 ♖bd1, which is clearly better for White. But with the simple 17 ... e6, Black maintains an edge, and keeps the positional tension in the centre and the queenside sufficiently potent to play for a win.

**18 ♗a1 ♘b2**
The way Black has played left him with the pawn on d4 as the sole positional objective he could still hope to exploit. He has, then,

nothing better than to trade his stranded knight for this pawn's defender. Yet the excessive simplifications which follow scorch this position to charcoal, leaving a bare and lifeless field.

**19 ♗xb2 axb2 20 ♗xc6**

More or less forced, but nonetheless good.

**20 ... bxc6 21 ♖xb2 ♕d7 22 ♘f4 ♖ad8**

A necessary concession. Black has to remove this rook from the queenside in order to keep the other guarding f7. 22 ... c5 would have yielded nothing: 23 dxc5 ♕xd1 22 ♖xd1 ♗xe5 23 ♖b7, and if 23 ... ♖fb8, then 24 c6!, while 23 ... ♖xa2 is answered by 24 ♘d5!, and in both cases White stands better.

**23 e6! ♕xd4 24 exf7+ ♖xf7 25 ♕xd4 ♖xd4 26 ♖c2**, and the game soon ended in a draw.

Whatever problems Fischer had to face in order to cope with his own simplifying tendency he ultimately turned to great benefit by developing an extraordinarily subtle art, in which he, like very few other players, could register the slightest fluctuations in the ever-changing flow of a game's 'positional charge' even at its lowest pitches.

Already as early as 1959 we see him turning out the following extremely fine example, where he manages to get more than 'something' out of seemingly 'nothing' – a simple, tensionless position. The game is Fischer-Bisguier, US Championship 1959-60 (Pos. 153).

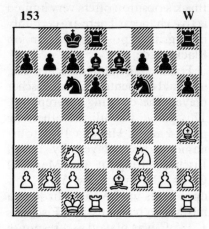

153      W

**13 ♗c4**

Not just to attack f7 but, more importantly, to start mounting pressure along the e-file.

**13 ... ♖df8!**

The right rook. Not just to defend f7, but, no less importantly, to vacate d8 for the bishop.

**14 ♖de1!**

The right rook! Black will soon get the opportunity to capture with his knight on d5 and c3. It is essential that the capture on c3 happen *without* threatening the rook at d1.

**14 ... ♗d8 15 d5!**

Activating the knight on f3 at the cost of blocking the a2-g8 diagonal. It prepares, moreover, a positional sacrifice of a pawn.

**15 ... ♘b8 16 ♘d4!**

The knight is heading for b5, but there are also threats like ♘e6 in the air. By the way, by playing thus he unprotects his bishop on h4 – a factor that plays an important role in the following sequence.

**16 ... ♖e8!**

Confronting White on the e-file, and sidestepping 16 ... ♘xd5? 17 ♗xd8 ♘xc3 18 ♗e7, etc.

**17 ♘db5 ♗xb5 18 ♗xb5!**

Tempting but wrong was 18 ♘xb5 a6 19 ♘a7+ ♚d7 20 ♗d3 g6 21 c4 (with the idea of ♗c2-a4+) 21 ... ♖xe1+ 22 ♖xe1 ♘xd5! 23 ♗xd8 ♘b4, and Black wins.

**18 ... ♖xe1+ 19 ♖xe1 ♘xd5! 20 ♘xd5 ♗xh4 21 g3 ♗g5+**

21 ... ♗d8 leads, after 22 ♘e7+ ♗xe7 23 ♖xe7 ♖f8 24 ♗c4 ♘c6 25 ♖xf7 ♖xf7 26 ♗xf7, to a better endgame for White.

**22 f4 c6 23 fxg5 hxg5!**

Bisguier has played excellently, probably so far in a way that couldn't be improved upon. Naturally, this makes young Bobby's performance all the more impressive. 23 ... cxb5 would have been met by 24 ♖e7 ♘c6 25 ♖c7+ ♚b8 26 ♖xf7 hxg5 27 ♖xg7, and White should win, while 23 ... cxd5 would have brought about a curious endgame: 24 ♖e8+! ♖xe8 25 ♗xe8 f6 26 gxh6 gxh6, when White, despite being a pawn down, has good winning chances.

**24 ♖e7!**

The process commencing with 14 ♖de1 has been carried out to its completion. If, on the other hand, 24 ♘e7+, then 24 ... ♚d8 25 ♗d3 ♖e8, equalising. It is interesting to watch how almost imperceptibly Fischer succeeded in turning a tensionless position into a very tense one, rich in possibilities, of which he knew to pick out the most advantageous.

**24 ... cxd5 25 ♖xf7**

White has the edge. By ingenious play, Bisguier managed to hold it to a minimum, though losing in the end.

This artistry effected one of its most delicate manifestations in the second match game between Fischer (White) and Taimanov, Candidates, Vancouver 1971 (Pos. 154).

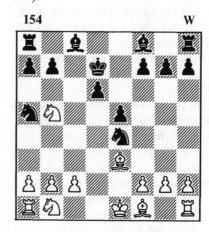

154           W

**12 ♘1c3!**

Suggested by Nikitin in his monograph on the Sicilian,[4] although never tried out in practice before this game. It takes a player of extremely refined chess knowledge to be able to justify this approach. White not only refrains from capturing on a7, but develops his queen's knight while offering it for exchange. Normally, one liquidates when enjoying material advantage. Here the process is reversed, and Fischer is in no hurry to get even as regards levelling material. He wants first to create as much tension as possible in the centre, reckoning that this would cramp Black even more. He will level material only when other gains have been accomplished.

**12 ... ♘xc3 13 ♕xc3 ♔d8 14 ♘b5**

There again! Yet it is not going to touch either the pawn on a7 or the pawn on d6! It is there only to increase White's pressure! A remarkable conception.

**14 ... ♗e6 15 0-0-0**

Should White commit the slightest inaccuracy Black might get the upper hand. For instance: 15 ♗xa7?! ♔d7!, and Black plays either 16 ... ♘c6 or 16 ... ♘c4 according to White's next move – 16 0-0-0 is answered by the first, 16 ♗b6 or ♗e3, by the second.

**15 ... b6 16 f4!**

Again refraining from any capture, instead building up yet more pressure in the centre. As a number of commentators have pointed out, White would get nothing from either 16 ♘xa7 ♔c7! 17 ♘b5+ ♔c6, or 16 ♘xd6 ♗xd6 17 ♖xd6+ ♔e7, etc.[5] The advance of Black's pawn to e4 would now give White an important tempo, gaining him the advantage: 16 ... e4 17 ♘xa7 ♔c7 18 ♘b5+ ♔c6 19 ♘c3! f5 (19 ... d5 20 ♗b5+ wins the pawn on d5. Two other alternatives are: 19 ... ♘c4 20 ♗xc4 ♗xc4 21 ♖d4!, or 19 ... ♗c4 20 b3! ♗xf1 21 ♖hxf1 f5 22 ♖d5 g6 23 ♖fd1, both leading to White's advantage) 20 ♘b5!, and Black is beset with tremendous problems. Protecting the pawn by 16 ... f6 is bad, too: 17 fxe5 fxe5, and White now does capture on d6, leaving Black with an isolated pawn on e5.

**16 ... exf4 17 ♗xf4 ♘b7 18 ♗e2!**

Still maintaining the tension. 18 ♘xd6 would have led to a dead drawn position: 18 ... ♘xd6 19 ♗xd6 ♗xd6 20 ♖xd6+ ♔c7 21 ♖d1 ♖ad8. As Robert Byrne showed, forcing White to capture on d6 after 18 ♗e2 would result in a lost endgame for Black: 18 ... a6 19 ♘xd6 ♘xd6 20 ♗xd6 ♗xd6 21 ♖xd6+ ♔c7 22 ♖hd1 b5 23 ♗f3 ♖a7 24 ♖c6+ ♔b8 25 ♖dd6 ♗c8 26 ♖b6+ ♔c7 27 ♖dc6+ ♔d8 28 ♖b8 ♖c7 29 ♖xa6.[6]

**18 ... ♗d7 19 ♖d2 ♗e7 20 ♖hd1**

♗xb5 21 ♗xb5

Black is relieved of the threat on d6, but now White, with his light-squared bishop in command of e8, starts piling on the e-file without having to face immediate simplifications there by ... ♖e8, and thus prevents possible 'depletion' of the position's tension.

**21 ... ♔c7 22 ♖e2 ♗f6 23 ♖de1 ♖ac8**

Directed against the threat of 24 ♖e7+! ♗xe7 25 ♖xe7+ ♔b8 26 ♗a6, winning. White has achieved his aim, but how to make further progress? By simple yet subtle play Fischer manages to elicit further concessions from Black.

**24 ♗c4 ♖hf8 25 b4! a5 26 ♗d5 ♔b8 27 a3**

It transpires that Black can't hold on to his material advantage any longer. Moves like 27 ... ♔a7 or 27 ... ♗c3 are answered by 28 ♖e7!, and 27 ... ♖c7 by 28 ♗xb7!. Doing nothing would help just as little. After for instance, 27 ... h6? 28 ♖e4 Black runs very quickly out of effective moves. Taimanov decides to return his material surplus by playing **27 ... ♖fd8 (!)**. The positional tension Fischer has created could no longer be maintained, and has to be converted into material gains since 28 ♖e4, for example, allows Black to consolidate on the seventh rank by 28 ... ♖d7! (not 28 ... ♗c3? 29 ♖e7!). However, **28 ♗xf7** more

than vindicated Fischer's tactics. Even the simplifications that now finally took place (**28 ... ♗c3 29 ♗d2 d5 30 ♖d1 d4 31 ♗xc3 ♖xc3 32 ♔b2 d3 33 ♔xc3 dxe2 34 ♖e1**), didn't offer Black equality.

A masterful performance by Fischer in maintaining the slightest positional tension, right from the opening to the late middlegame.

## SWITCHING ADVANTAGES

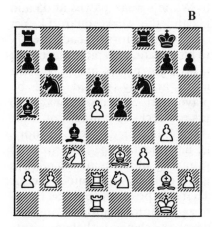

B

Of his 21 ... ♗a6 in the above position, taken from the 1st match game, World Championship 1951 against Botvinnik, David Bronstein wrote: "It is a pity to have to part with a good position; this is a trait which is probably characteristic of every artist . . . Instead of playing so "beautifully" (bishops at a6 and a5, knight at b6), Black could have exchanged off the white knights: 21 ... ♗xe2 22 ♖xe2 ♗xc3 23 ♗xb6 axb6 24 bxc3 g5 and then ... ♘d7 with a winning position."[1] Why did Bronstein miss this line? Apparently because he judged the position according to one set of criteria, and couldn't mentally switch to another set. After White's 21st move Black stands better. He has the half-open f-file (and will soon have the c-file), and the better pawn structure, with regard to White's weak pawns at d5 and f3, and the weak square f4. Yet one of the factors that add greatly to his advantage is piece placement – his light pieces are by far the more actively placed, and by playing 21 ... ♗a6 he wants to take direct advantage of this, threatening 21 ... ♘c4. In short, he must have judged the position primarily in terms of the relative value of both sides' minor pieces. That this position could be transformed into another one, in which the elements that constitute Black's advantage are of a different nature, didn't occur to Bronstein, or, put another way: it didn't present itself as a possibility in his thinking process. This isn't a question of calculating moves. It is a question of conceptual thinking. And in this case conceptual thinking has a lot to do

with the question to what extent one is flexible enough to shift from one way of thinking to another.

Fischer was very agile when it came to bartering one advantage for another, a process which usually entails simplification.

155                                    B

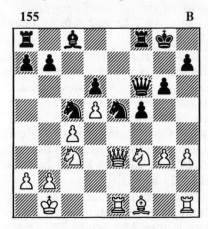

What strikes one in Pos. 155 (Suttles-Fischer, Palma de Mallorca 1970), are the weak white pawns on the kingside. In any endgame they might be White's greatest problem, and especially the pawn on g3. One would thus expect Black to maintain the pawn formation on the kingside intact until a later stage of the game. Since he has already gained some other advantages, Black could consolidate them, for example, by the following natural sequence: 22 ... ♘xf3 23 ♕xf3 ♗d7 24 ♗d3 (24 b4?! ♘a4 25

♘xa4 ♗xa4 26 ♖e6 ♕d4! is good for Black) 24 ... ♖ae8, and with 25 ... ♖e5 (or 25 ... ♕d4) following next, he could take control of the e-file, increasing his spatial advantage. To imagine that Black should, on his 22nd move, push his f-pawn, would occur to most experienced players only with respect to a possible tactical twist. In this position, such a twist would occur if the following attacking sequence could have led to decisive results: ... ♗f5+ ... a5 ... a4 ... ♘b3+ ... axb3+, etc. Very few, if any,would consider 22 ... f4 in association with a purely positional plan. Black had a comfortable edge, which he could increase by standard developing moves; why should he seek to change the features of the position and, in doing so, relieve White of his greatest problem? One answer was given by the game's continuation: **22 ... f4 23 gxf4 ♘xf3 24 ♕xf3 ♕h4** 24 ... ♗f5+ 25 ♔a1 a5 26 ♘b5 a4 27 a3, and Black has nothing decisive – he has merely compromised his pawn formation on the queenside. **25 ♗e2 ♗f5+ 26 ♔a1 ♖ae8.** All Black's pieces occupy ideal positions (see Pos. 68). The way Fischer now brings his rooks into play speaks volumes for the correctness of his approach: **27 ♖c1 ♗e4!.** Instead of e5, Black now uses e4 as his 'lever point' on the e-file. **28 ♘xe4 ♖xe4 29 ♖h2**

**♖fxf4 30 ♕c3 ♕e7 31 ♗f1 ♖e3**, and the black forces excercise complete domination (see further Pos. 269). So, an advantage in pawn structure that was to be exploited in an unspecified future, was 'exchanged' for a concrete and immediate positional domination. This, no doubt, is a good objective reason for embarking upon this process. The other answer to the above question is a more subjective one: in the later stages of his career, Fischer didn't care very much whether switching from one advantage to another had a complete positional rationale behind it. He was motivated mostly by his wish to steer for positions in which he would feel the most comfortable. This was more evident in the next three examples, all from very well-known games.

156                                    W

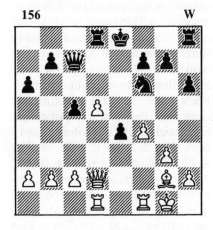

Fischer-Taimanov, 4th match game 1971, (Pos. 156), saw **19 ♖fe1 !?/?!**. Here the transformation of advantages is uniquely Fischerian. Probably no other top player would have played so, unless he had made an accidental blunder. All the principles of chess strategy that have been learnt and applied in the past two centuries, dictate the protection of White's advanced passed pawn by 19 c4. Moreover, since Black can't do the same as far as his passed pawn is concerned (namely, protect it by a pawn), this asymmetry would very soon tell: 19 ... 0-0 20 ♖fe1 ♖fe8 21 ♖e2 followed by 22 ♖de1.

No matter how actively (or ingeniously) Black plays now, the e-pawn must fall very shortly without any visible compensation. This must be considered objectively better than what Fischer had played, as the realisation of White's decisive advantage in this line ought to be easier and quicker than in the actual game (Fischer won 51 moves later – see Pos. 56). How is one to explain Fischer's preference for the technically long and delicate endgame that ensued after **19 ... ♖xd5 20 ♖xe4+ ♔d8 21 ♕e2 ♖xd1+ 22 ♕xd1+ ♕d7 23 ♕xd7+ ♔xd7 24 ♖e5 –?** And how does one reconcile this with Fischer's approach to material questions at large? Probably the best answer, and one that is also

sustained by the next example, is that Fischer considered 19 c4 all too briefly to take stock of its virtues, looked into the line he eventually played, found it apparently much to his liking, and was ready to transform a 'passed pawn' advantage into a 'slightly better endgame' one, relying on his ability to cash in such advantage. This, however, is a stage when a player of the highest class is so sure of his powers that he no longer cares for the objective value of his moves, as long as they land him in, for him, easy to handle positions.

This might be interpreted as carelessness, or even superficiality, and this is how some grandmasters indeed saw it. Larsen, for instance, wrote in *Chess Canada*, August 1971: "It seems to me that Fischer's play is rather superficial, as if he doesn't even try to find the "truth" in many positions. Petrosian says that Fischer played better chess many years ago and I understand what he means."

Petrosian was proved wrong in the Candidates match he played with Fischer a month later, but that there had been a change in Fischer's attitude in comparison with "many years ago" was borne out by two critical moments in their games. The first was after Petrosian's (White's) 28th move in the 6th match game (Pos. 157).

157 B

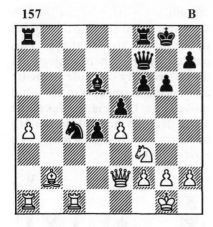

A number of commentators maintained that 28 ... ♖fc8 would have increased Black's advantage here (which consists of greater space, more active pieces, and a protected passed pawn). But 29 ♖c2 seems strong enough to hold White's position, in view of possible pins on the c-file. For instance: 29 ... ♔g7 (the king leaves the a1-g8 diagonal and the 8th rank for the tactical reasons that become clear in the next couple of moves) 30 ♖ac1! (30 a5? ♗b4 31 a6 ♕d7! and Black wins) 30 ... ♖xa4 31 ♘d2! d3! 32 ♕xd3 ♘xb2 33 ♕xd6 ♖d4 34 ♕a6, and White has succeeded in achieving equality. Yet much stronger for Black is Korchnoi's suggestion: 28 ... ♘a5![2] White's cramped position doesn't allow him to coordinate his pieces for meeting the threat at b3 and Black's threatened domination of

the c- or the b-file. White would most certainly collapse in the middlegame if he does nothing to alleviate Black's pressure by steering for an endgame: 29 ♗a3 (if 29 ♖ab1 ♖fb8, and Black's domination becomes increasingly annoying, while 29 ♘d2 ♗b4! wins an exchange by force) 29 ... ♗xa3 30 ♖xa3 ♖fc8; however, the endgame that now ensues is decidedly unfavourable for White. As Averbakh showed after both 31 ♕d1 ♕b7 32 ♘d2 ♖xc1+ 33 ♕xc1 ♖c8 34 ♕a1 ♖c2, and 31 ♖aa1 ♘b3 32 ♖xc8+ ♖xc8 33 ♖b1 ♕c4 34 ♕xc4 ♖xc4[3] Black maintains a clear endgame advantage which could be translated quite easily into a win. Instead of that Fischer decided on trading his beautiful knight (28 ... ♘xb2) for White's almost worthless bishop. Shamkovich thought that he was indeed "unexpectedly exchanging off a poor bishop . . . but Fischer is very fond of rook and bishop versus rook and knight . . ."[4] Factually this isn't correct. This type of endgame doesn't occur in greater frequency in Fischer's games in comparison with other endings. It was apparently thought to be so in retrospect, after the three examples given here, and two games against Taimanov: at Palma de Mallorca 1970, and the 1st match game 1971. I think we have to agree with the Cuban

Jesus Suarez, who wrote in *Jaque Mate*: "Fischer has been called by Najdorf 'a photocopy of Capablanca'. Here he proves that he is capable of copying the Cuban genius's defects as well."[5] Why throw away so much of one's advantage, and what for?

Ironically, the only commentator who fully supported Fischer's move was Bent Larsen: "The clearest solution. As the white knight cannot get to the blockade square d3, the Black d-pawn is very strong now", he wrote. Even if one agrees that by transforming his solid strategic advantage into a slight endgame advantage Black still retained some winning chances, it shouldn't escape our attention that here again Fischer had to play an extremely delicate endgame after **29 ♕xb2 ♖fb8 30 ♕a2 ♗b4 31 ♕xf7+ ♔xf7 32 ♖c7+ ♔e6 33 g4**, where the issue remained for a long time very close to equality. That he felt himself very much at home in that phase of the game was clear enough, and eventually he won this endgame on move 66. Yet, as in the previous example, Fischer must have glanced at 28 ... ♘a5 only very cursorily. It couldn't have escaped him, had he truthfully searched for the objectively best plan, that Black's superiority after that move was more significant than in the line he chose to play. (see also Pos.

70, 98).

And we move to the next game of the match, the 7th that is. This is a happy case where subjectivity and objectivity coincide to create a chess masterpiece. On the 22nd move (Pos. 158) Fischer takes the same decision he took in the 6th game (or – viewed differently – 60 moves earlier):

**158**                                     **W**

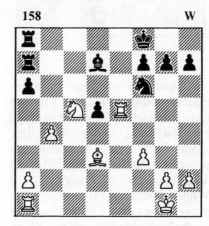

**22 ♘xd7+**. "Surprising that this exchange of the good knight for the bad bishop is so devastating", wrote Reuben Fine.[7] "[Fischer] often has recourse to the opportunity to transform one type of advantage into another. Thus in the given situation he lightly parts with the strong knight, exchanging it for Black's rather bad bishop, and gets a position of a qualitatively different nature, where it will already be White's bishop that dominates the black knight", explained Lev Polugayevsky.[8] Robert Byrne, who was in Buenos Aires, reported that this exchange "was completely overlooked by the press-room group of grandmaster analysts. Najdorf, in fact, criticised it (!) suggesting instead the incomparibly weaker 22 a4."[9] It was the same Najdorf, who, a few months later, in the tournament book, extolled this decision in one word: "Magistral!"; and Suetin, Petrosian's second in that match, openly confessed that he was considerably surprised during the game "when Fischer, almost without thinking . . . exchanged the pride of his position, his knight at c5, for the 'bad' bishop".[11] So besides the surprising decision, the move was made almost instantly! And yet within twelve moves the game was over! 22 ... ♖xd7 23 ♖c1 ♖d6 24 ♖c7 ♘d7 25 ♖e2 g6 26 ♔f2 h5 27 f4 h4 28 ♔f3 f5 29 ♔e3 d4+ 30 ♔d2 ♘b6 31 ♖2e7 ♘d5 32 ♖f7+ ♔e8 33 ♖b7 ♘xb4 34 ♗c4 1-0. Hardly could any finale be more elegant and incisive. Without in any way wishing to dim the brilliance of his performance, it seems quite safe to assume that the motives underlying Fischer's decision in playing 22 ♘xd7+!! were very similar to those of playing 28 ... ♘xb2?! in the previous game. Luckily their application in this game brought

about a quick decision as compared to the two other protracted endgames. (see also Pos. 6, 285)

## PLAYING FOR SPACE

While the pursuit of space in the middlegame is, as we shall see on pp.120-7, a quality dyed in the wool of Fischer's style, it becomes a conscious element in his endgame play: there he often deliberately steers for positions in which he has a tiny spatial advantage on which he tries to capitalise with the aid of his peerless technique. Let's observe here three typical examples.

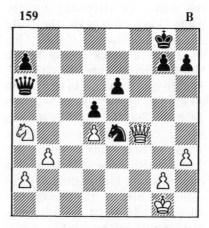

159   B

In Uitumen-Fischer, Palma de Mallorca 1970 (Pos. 159), the position is well-nigh equal. There is not much Black can look

forward to in the line 27 ...  ♛d3
28 ♛b8+ ♚f7 29 ♛f4+ (simplest),
and Black has no way out of
perpetual check. Fischer trades
queens. There is very little material
left on the board then, but one
factor might yet boost Black's
winning ambitions – White's weak
pawn at d4. **27 ...  ♛d6 28 ♛xd6
♘xd6 29 ♘c3 ♘f5 30 ♘e2**. After
30 ♘b5 a6 31 ♘c7 ♘xd4 32
♘xa6, a complicated endgame
ensues, in which the better player
is likely to win. Evidently Uitumen
prefers not to challenge his adversary to this test. **30 ... ♘e3! 31 ♚f2
♘c2**. With minimal material present, Black has created a position
of maximum squeeze. He attacks
d4 in such a way that neither can
the pawn be defended by the
white king, nor can the king
attack the black knight. This
should give Black's king a free
hand to manoeuvre. **32 ♚f3 ♚f7
33 ♚f4 ♚f6 34 h4 h6 35 h5 ♘e1 36
g3 ♘c2 37 ♚g4 e5 38 dxe5+ ♚xe5
39 ♚f3 ♘b4** 39 ... d4 40 ♘f4 and
Black can make no progress.
Thus far Black has increased his
spatial advantage and created a
passed pawn. Unfortunately, this
could not bring in the bacon after
**40 ♘c1 ♚d4 41 g4**, because of a
certain tactical possibility White
had in response to 41 ... ♚c3,
namely 42 ♘e2+ ♚b2 43 ♘d4
♚xa2 44 ♘e6 ♚xb3 45 ♘xg7 d4
46 g5! ♘d5 (46 ... d3? 47 ♘f5 d2

48 ♚e2, and White wins!) 47 ♚e4
♚c4 48 ♘f5 d3 49 ♘e3+ (or 49
♘d6+ ♚b3! 50 ♚xd3 hxg5 51 h6
♘f6 etc) 49 ... ♘xe3 50 ♚xe3 ♚c3
51 gxh6, draw. The game was
agreed drawn however after **41 ...
a5 42 ♘e2+ ♚e5 43 ♘c1**, ½-½.

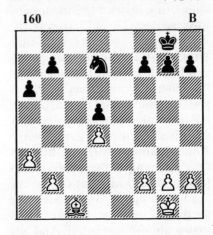

160                                    B

Fischer was more successful
in his game against Anthony
Saidy, played in the eleventh and
last round of the US Championship
1963-64. Fischer, with 10-0, had
to win this endgame (Pos. 160), in
order to 'get even' with some all-
time records. But on what can
Black (Fischer) base his winning
hopes in this position? As in the
above game, Fischer seeks, first,
to combine two elements: attack
White's weak central pawn, and
at the same time limit the white
king's space. Here this is done by
the simple manoeuvre ... ♘f8-e6,
followed up by ... h5. Such a set-

up admits White's king no entry squares into Black's camp (besides a5! – yet even this square can be defended, if ever it becomes necessary, by ... b6, and Black's position is hermetically sealed). What characterises these two endgames, then is Fischer's utilisation of the single piece he's left with for attacking, and at the same time the reduction of his opponent's space. In this way the relative value of his own piece increases compared with the opposite one. However, these types of endgames are still very difficult to win, since such an advantage might prove in practical terms too small.

There are, basically, two kinds of pawn formations that White could choose between on the kingside: h3-g4-f3, or h3-g2-f3. Saidy chose the second, enabling Fischer to place his pawns on h5, g5 and f4, and break through at the right moment with ... g4: **24 ♔f1 ♘f8 25 ♔e2 ♘e6 26 ♔d3 h5 27 ♗e3 ♔h7 28 f3 ♔g6 29 a4 ♔f5 30 ♔e2 g5 31 ♔f2 ♘d8 32 ♗d2 ♔g6 33 ♔e3 ♘e6 34 ♔d3 ♔f5 35 ♗e3 f6 36 ♔e2 ♔g6 37 ♔d3 f5 38 ♔e2 f4 39 ♗f2 ♘g7 40 h3 ♘f5 41 ♔d3 g4! 42 hxg4 hxg4 43 fxg4 ♘h6**. Here the game was adjourned, and Saidy sealed **44 ♗e1**, a move that gave Fischer the opportunity to crown his efforts with a well-crafted finish: **44 ... ♘xg4 45 ♗d2**

**♔f5 46 ♗e1 ♘f6 47 ♗h4 ♘e4 48 ♗e1 ♔g4 49 ♔e2 ♘g3+! 50 ♔d3 ♘f5 51 ♗f2 ♘h4 52 a5 ♘xg2 53 ♔c3 ♔f3 54 ♗g1 ♔e2 55 ♗h2 f3 56 ♗g3 ♘e3!**, and White resigned. Subsequent analysis showed that by **44 ♔e2** White could hold the endgame: he places the king at f3, plays the bishop back to g1 after the knight's capture on g4, and later liquidates the two pawns left on the kingside by g3.[1]

It seems though that by playing for the first of these formations, White's task might have been facilitated. After **24 ♔f1 ♘f8 25 g4!?** the black king can't penetrate on the kingside and the weakening of White's pawn formation is quite meaningless in view of this. Black would find it very difficult to make headway there: ... f5 and ... h5 are met by f3 and h3 respectively, and the black knight's possible infiltrations via f4 and g5 are, naturally, checked by the bishop.

In Gheorghiu-Fischer, Siegen Olympiad 1970 (Pos. 161), Black enjoys a tiny spatial advantage that consists of the more advanced pawn on the g-file, and the closeness of his king to the centre. However, the pawn on a7 is attacked at the moment, and 45 ... ♘c6 gives White the time to play his king to the centre – **46 ♔d3** – after which Black's advantage seems, for all practical purposes,

161           B

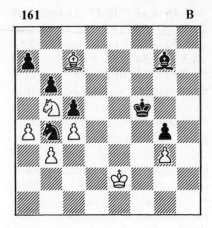

non-existent.

Yet even less attractive seems 45 ... a6 46 ♘d6+ ♚e6 47 ♘e4 (inferior is 47 ♘e8 ♗e5! which favours Black) 47 ... ♚f5 48 ♘d2 ♗e5 49 ♗xb6 ♗d6 50 ♘f1! etc. In fact Fischer did play **45 ... ♘c6!**, on which Gheorghiu remarked that for all its apparent innocence the move conceals great subtlety. After 46 ♚d3 Gheorghiu gives: "46 ... ♗e5!! 47 ♗xe5 ♚xe5 48 ♚e3 a5, with a winning endgame for Black".[2] Let's take this line a bit further and see what exactly he meant: 49 ♘c3 ♘d4 50 ♘d5 ♘f5+! 51 ♚f2 ♚d4! 52 ♘xb6 ♚c3 53 ♘d7 ♚xb3, and now: a) 54 ♘b6 ♚b4! zugzwang! b) 54 ♘xc5+ ♚xc4 55 ♘e4 ♚b4 56 ♘f6 ♘h6 57 ♚e3 ♚xa4 58 ♚f4 ♚b4 59 ♘d5+ ♚c4 60 ♘b6+ ♚d3 61 ♚g5 (or 61 ♘a4, when Black wins by manoeuvring his king to h3) 61 ...

♚e3 62 ♚xh6 ♚f3, and Black wins. Gheorghiu saw this in time and reacted creatively: **46 ♘xa7!**, which resulted in a draw: **46 ... ♘xa7 47 ♗xb6 ♘c6 48 a5 ♘b4 49 ♗xc5 ♘a6 50 ♗d6 ♚e6 51 ♗f4 ♗f8 52 ♗d2 ♗d6 53 ♚d3 ♗xg3 54 b4 ♗d6 55 ♚e4 ♗f8 56 c5 ♘xc5 57 bxc5 ♗xc5 ½-½.** (see also Pos. 57)

Fischer's policy in such endgames couldn't lead exclusively to wins, of course. Yet it taxed his opponents' creativity and technical skills to the maximum.

## THE ROLE OF AESTHETICS

That aesthetics plays a role in chess has been attested by many players. It is quite common to see players base their decision on the 'look' of a given move no less than on its content.

Tal, for example, remarks about his 24th move in his 4th match game against Timman, Hilversum 1988: "Of course I also saw 24 ... ♖xb4, but for aesthetic reasons I didn't want to make unnatural moves in this position".[1] And Karpov – a player whom no one could possibly accuse of being aesthetically biased – would also give preference, at times, to aesthetic (or quasi-aesthetic) ideas. Analysing a game against Ian

Rogers in his book *Chess at the Top*, he confessed about one of his decisions that "the paradoxical nature of this idea greatly appealed to me".[2] The degree to which a player has recourse to aesthetic considerations varies greatly from one player to another. Nimzowitsch, for one, had a sympathy for 'ugly' moves, provided they were logical. To the charge that his moves were ugly he once replied: "Beauty in chess after all is said and done exists only in the thought".[3] Larsen in the sixties made it a speciality to play eccentric moves, provided they were reasonably strong. And there are players like Timman, who, while having a sensitive eye for the aesthetic aspects of the game, would never, as a rule, play a move merely for its aesthetic value.

A distinctly aesthetic style can be the result of either a highly refined intuition, as was the case with Capablanca, or of a belief in the intrinsic value of aesthetics, as is the case with Fischer. Between these two one finds a player like Smyslov, whose style represents a combination to a certain extent of the two approaches.

A deep-rooted belief in the intrinsic value of aesthetics in chess corresponds with a common attitude in other fields. This is, basically, a belief that on a more profound level there ought to exist some meaningful correlation between Beauty and Truth. Uldis Roze, a modern biologist, gave a very apt description of this sense in his science: "Much of the work on control of bacterial protein synthesis was carried out in the Paris laboratories of Jaques Monod and François Jacob. Their experiments are among the most elegant in the literature of molecular biology and offer clear proof that *the aesthetic sense functions as strongly in science as it does in the arts*"[4] (my italics). And Roger Penrose, one of the foremost phsyicists of our time, has expressed the opinion that "aesthetic qualities are important in science, and necessary, I think, for great science".[5] If in science, why not in chess?

Generally speaking, a rough distinction can be made between two kinds of aesthetics in chess – static and dynamic. Static aesthetics pertains mainly to piece placement, when one can review the co-ordination and tension between the various pieces in much the same way as one can examine a composition in the plastic arts. Fischer certainly derives great aesthetic pleasure, as do many other players, from the following typical Sicilian set-up (Pos. 162).

**162**

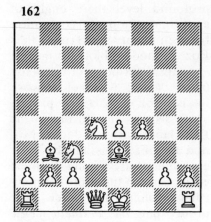

**163**                                    **W**

He played his dark-squared bishop only very rarely to g5, and never stationed his light-squared bishop at a2 (after advancing a3). It is to be assumed that the compact placement of the pieces in and near the centre and the fact that this conforms with the general aesthetic norms of lines (b3-c3-e3, and later a queen at f3) and triangles (c3-d4-e3) strongly appealed to him, and influenced his adherence to this set-up throughout his career.

A player would hardly start thinking of a move like **7 ♘d5!** in Pos. 163 (Fischer-Najdorf, Varna Olympiad 1962) if the view of the two centralised white knights hadn't given him great aesthetic satisfaction, and the prospect of another knight 'joining in' (7 ... ♘xe4) wouldn't have offered him a true aesthetic thrill. 7 ...

♘xd5 would, on the other hand, eliminate two of the knights, but leave the third safely and beautifully centralised. Of course, 7 ♘d5 had other virtues as well, as the course of the game demonstrated (it threatens 8 ♘xf6+, and prepares the advance c4), but the basic motive and incentive for playing it must have been aesthetic. (see also Pos. 179)

Is such a policy always justifiable? Certainly not always, and as a matter of fact quite a few of Fischer's inaccuracies could be traced to an aesthetic bias. Here are three instructive examples:

Against Gligorić, Siegen Olympiad 1970 (Pos. 164) Fischer continued **24 ... ♖e5?!**. The possibility of this elegant centralisation, in which the rook doesn't block the way of the dark-squared bishop (as would have been the case had

**164** B

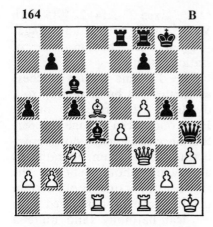

it stood on g7), and the fact that ... ♖fe8 can follow immediately, must have diverted Fischer's attention from the fact that 24 ... ♗xd5 wins a clear pawn, since 25 exd5?? loses on the spot: 25 ... ♖e3 26 ♕f2 ♖xh3+. (see also Pos. 199)

**165** B

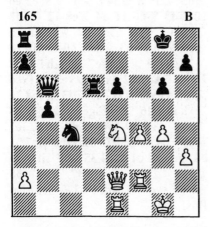

Two rounds earlier at the same

Olympiad, Fischer had (as Black) this position against Spassky (Pos. 165). In a couple of publications Spassky indicated 27 ... ♖c6 as the right move here.[6] Fischer played **27 ... ♖d4**. Yet even if this position were ever to be reached by Fischer again, I very much doubt he would take Spassky's recommendation. 27 ... ♖c6 is so un-Fischer-like in its clumsy appearance that it is hardly probable Fischer would ever shift the rook to that square. Everything in him would have revolted against it. The unaesthetic configuration of the black pieces on the queenside after 27 ... ♖c6, and the great imbalance between that wing and the opposite wing and the centre, must have constituted a repellent sight for Fischer. His centralising move 27 ... ♖d4 serves the same 'justice' to the rook – and the aesthetic value of the whole position – as did 24 ... ♖e5 in the previous example. And that wasn't yet the mistake which lost the game for Black. (see also Pos. 83, 258)

In the game Fischer-Bertok, Rovinj-Zagreb 1970 (Pos. 166) play went **20 g5?! ♘e4 21 ♘xe4 dxe4 22 ♕c3 ♗d4 23 ♕b3 ♗xb2 24 ♕xb2 ♖xd2**, when Black had a chance to equalise completely. After **25 gxh6** Bertok pointed out the defence 25 ... **♕g6!** 26 ♗xe4 ♕xh6.[7] An endgame would

**166** W

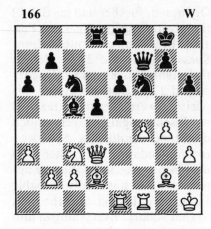

not offer White any advantages: 26 ♕xg7+ ♕xg7 27 hxg7 ♖xc2 28 ♖g1 ♖c3! etc. Every player is familiar with the inherent aesthetic (and in many cases positional) merits of the rook pair occupying two adjacent files (f and e, e and d, d and c, etc). Here Fischer is simply too eager to keep them placed at f1 and e1 that he overlooks the much stronger 20 ♖d1!. Not only does the rook protect the bishop on d2, thus preparing more carefully the g5 thrust which would now gain greatly in force (concretely, the threat is: 21 g5 ♘d7 22 f5!, and if 22 ... ♘de5 23 fxe6 ♕xe6 24 ♕xd5!); it also makes possible a bishop transfer to h4 via e1, and puts additional pressure on d5. Black remains very limited in his counterchances at this stage. For instance 20 ... e5? 21 fxe5 ♘xe5

(21 ... ♖xe5 22 ♗f4) 22 ♕f5, with White having a clear advantage.

These were, then, examples of static aesthetics.

The dynamic nature of chess aesthetics can be compared to a dynamic art form like music. Here one doesn't judge the performance as a note-by-note/move-by-move continuum, but rather as a flowing whole. Whereas the static aesthetic quality of a certain position can be compared to a musical harmony (and quite a complex one at that sometimes!), the dynamic side is the game's melody.

Let's take these three games:

Fischer-Petrosian
*1st Game, Belgrade 1970*
1 e4 c6 2 d4 d5 3 exd5 cxd5 4 ♗d3 ♘c6 5 c3 ♘f6 6 ♗f4 ♗g4 7 ♕b3 ♘a5 8 ♕a4+ ♗d7 9 ♕c2 e6 10 ♘f3 ♕b6 11 a4 ♖c8 12 ♘bd2 ♘c6 13 ♕b1 ♘h5 14 ♗e3 h6 15 ♘e5 ♘f6 16 h3 ♗d6 17 0-0 ♔f8 18 f4 ♗e8 19 ♗f2 ♕c7 20 ♗h4 ♘g8 21 f5 ♘xe5 22 dxe5 ♗xe5 23 fxe6 ♗f6 24 exf7 ♗xf7 25 ♘f3 ♗xh4 26 ♘xh4 ♘f6 27 ♘g6+ ♗xg6 28 ♗xg6 ♔e7 29 ♕f5 ♔d8 30 ♖ae1 ♕c5+ 31 ♔h1 ♖f8 32 ♕e5 ♖c7 33 b4 ♕c6 34 c4 dxc4 35 ♗f5 ♖ff7 36 ♖d1+ ♖fd7 37 ♗xd7 ♖xd7 38 ♕b8+ ♔e7 39 ♖de1+ 1-0 (see also Pos. 253)

Fischer-Gheorghiu
*Buenos Aires 1970*

1 e4 e5 2 ♘f3 ♘f6 3 ♘xe5 d6 4
♘f3 ♘xe4 5 d4 ♗e7 6 ♗d3 ♘f6 7
h3 0-0 8 0-0 ♖e8 9 c4 ♘c6 10 ♘c3
h6 11 ♖e1 ♗f8 12 ♖xe8 ♕xe8 13
♗f4 ♗d7 14 ♕d2 ♕c8 15 d5 ♘b4
16 ♘e4 ♘xe4 17 ♗xe4 ♘a6 18
♘d4 ♘c5 19 ♗c2 a5 20 ♖e1 ♕d8
21 ♖e3 b6 22 ♖g3 ♔h8 23 ♘f3
♕e7 24 ♕d4 ♕f6 25 ♕xf6 gxf6 26
♘d4 ♖e8 27 ♖e3 ♖b8 28 b3 b5 29
cxb5 ♗xb5 30 ♘f5 ♗d7 31 ♘xh6
♖b4 32 ♖g3 ♗xh6 33 ♗xh6 ♘e4
34 ♗g7+ ♔h7 35 f3 1-0 (see also
Pos. 111, 120, 177)

Fischer-Portisch
*Havana Olympiad 1966*
1 e4 e5 2 ♘f3 ♘c6 3 ♗b5 a6 4
♗xc6 dxc6 5 0-0 f6 6 d4 exd4 7
♘xd4 c5 8 ♘b3 ♕xd1 9 ♖xd1
♗d6 10 ♘a5 b5 11 c4 ♘e7 12 ♗e3
f5 13 ♘c3 f4 14 e5 ♗xe5 15 ♗xc5
♗xc3 16 bxc3 ♘g6 17 ♘c6 ♗e6 18
cxb5 axb5 19 ♘a7 ♖b8 20 ♖db1
♔f7 21 ♘xb5 ♖hd8 22 ♖b4 ♗xa2
23 ♘xc7 ♖bc8 24 h4 ♖d2 25 ♗b6
f3 26 ♗e3 ♖e2 27 ♘b5 ♖a8 28 h5
♘e5 29 ♖f4+ ♔e7 30 ♖d1 ♖c8 31
♖e4 ♔f6 32 ♖d6+ ♔f5 33 ♖f4+
♔g5 34 ♖xf3+ 1-0 (see also Pos.
125, 244)

The 'melodious' quality of these
three games is easily discernible.
Everything runs smoothly and
coherently from the first move to
the last, creating an extremely
satisfying whole. In the first of the
three it was the forming of the
queen-bishop battery on the b1-
h7 diagonal, the early conquest
and consolidation of e5 by 15
♘e5 and 18 f4, the dark-squared
bishop's transfer to h4, the timely
opening of the f-file (21 f5), the
quick manoeuvring of the knight
to g6, the occupation of the e-file
by the heavy pieces (queen and
rook), and finally the opening up
of the centre (34 c4), which all
flowed successively, as in a well
written musical piece in which
each motif continued and completed the previous, forming an
impressive well balanced and
integrated composition. In the
second, it was the conquest of the
centre by 15 d5, 16 ♘e4 and 18
♘d4, the quick manoeuvring of
the gook to g3, the centralisation
of the queen (24 ♕d4), and, after
that, the re-centralisation of the
knight followed by its prompt
transfer to the kingside, and the
final assault starting with 32 ♖g3,
which created the same effect.
The third game was of a more
poignant aesthetic, and in a way
more eccentric (or chessically –
'excentric'). The king's knight's
tour to the edge of the board (10
♘a5), the completion of the
initial piece development as early
as move 13 with Black's queenside
pawns as targets, the neat tactical
blow in the centre (14 e5!), the
peculiar position-picture at move
17 with the squares c3-c8 all
occupied by pawns and pieces,

the second 'eccentricity' of the knight (19 ♘a7!) followed by the de-centralisation of the rook from d1 (20 ♖db1), only to be manoeuvred to b4 two moves later, thus securing a pawn win, the very fine 24th move, combining as it did attack and defence, the final co-ordinated action of both rooks to create a mating net, these all left the impression of being one complete and concordant whole.

Having said all this, I believe one essential thing has been left unsaid. Since these three very well played games quite obviously weren't meant to be art products, what place should aesthetics occupy in their evaluation? After all, these games, like any other game, could be judged and evaluated by the effectiveness of their plans and moves, and the introduction of other criteria seems redundant and unnecessary. To this can be given the following answer: in these games, as in many other games of Fischer's, one of the keys to understanding and evaluating them lies in the *organisation* of the games' 'plans and moves'. All three were played in such a way that any positional and tactical idea was carried out by minimal means and was condensed into the shortest sequence of moves possible. Not a single move was superfluous, not any of these games' phases could be

shortened by a single move. They were supreme examples of economy in chess. What we have perceived as dynamic aesthetics, was primarily the effect of Fischer's surpassing economical conduct of the games. This is certainly not an exclusive criterion by which to judge dynamic aesthetics in chess. It is in many cases one of the most pertinent, however.

Aesthetics may not be indispensible for playing good chess; but, to paraphrase Penrose, it might well be necessary for producing great chess.

Our next section deals with some other analogies of this relationship.

## THE POETRY OF EMPTY SQUARES

Botvinnik has called Kasparov a chess poet. He didn't specify what kind of poet he had in mind. But I guess he meant an epic one, passionate, colourful, of a broad vision, a chess Rustaveli.

Fischer is a poet of a different kind: airy and restrained. His art reminds one of his compatriot's, the poet Robert Frost: never opaque, always simple and economic, coherent yet possessing a discreet beauty. It was he, Fischer, who said of another World Champion, Alexander Alekhine: "There is nothing light or breezy about [his style]",[1] and by that he expressed what for him was most important – his positions had to breathe. It is this 'pneumatic' quality of his games which distinguishes his style of play probably more than any other quality. In order to explain this quality, let me start by quoting two comments that I believe to be very apropos in our present discussion.

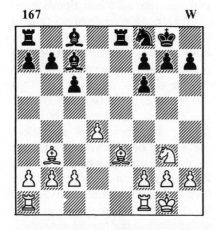

The renowned critic Hans Kmoch, whom I'll quote again in this chapter, wrote about Fischer's **16 d5!** in Pos. 167 (Fischer-Barcza, Stockholm 1962): "The exchange of this pawn, rather than establishing it as passed with the aid of c4, is one of the major points of White's strategy. *Clearing more roads for his pieces* while maintaining his compact pawn structure,

White increases the significance of his basic advantage."[2] (my italics) (see also Pos. 4)

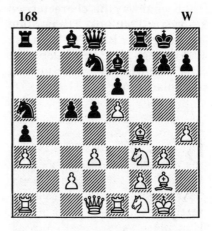

Even more revealing is Robert Wade's comment in the tournament book of the Sousse 1967 Interzonal, concerning Fischer's 15th move in his game against Miagmarsuren (Pos. 168) **15 ♘e3.** "It is noteworthy that Fischer does not press on with h5-h6 as this tends to lead to a semi-blocked king's wing, with only a limited field of approach for White. Holding the pawn back *leaves more space for the white pieces to manoeuvre.*" (my italics) This is it! This comment touches on one of the principle secrets of Fischer's art. I shall return to this example later. I confine myself here to one remark only: it is this "space to manoeuvre" that Fischer constantly pursues which gives his games their fresh and breezy character.

The following example exemplifies in what way this characterised his personal outlook. The position is the one after Black's 11th move in Fischer's (White) celebrated game against Tal at the Leipzig Olympiad 1960 (Pos. 169).

**169**                                     **W**

In *MSMG* Fischer observed his 12th move thus: "**12 ♗b5!** – harmoniously pursuing development without losing time. Also playable is 12 ♗f4 ..."[3] etc. Years before the publication of *MSMG*, grandmaster Efim Geller annotated the game for the German magazine *Schach*,[4] and this is what he saw in Fischer's move: "12 ♗b5? – It is well known that 12 ♗f4 leads to White's advantage. 12 ♗b5 is, besides, disadvantageous since Fischer will have to exchange his bishop in order to

protect his e5 pawn, which is bad for his position."

We are faced with a riddle: how come two classical approaches to one and the same problem could be so diametrically opposed to each other? For Geller, as for the majority of players, e5 is much too important a stronghold to risk, and pretty much in accordance with the Nimzowitsch principles, has to be protected now, and over-protected ( ♖e1) later. Fischer, who earlier had refrained from playing f2-f4 so as not to shut in his dark-squared bishop, is interested, first of all, in granting this bishop maximum space to manoeuvre (it was played to g5 two moves later). He is ready to risk his grip in the centre, but not render the bishop a scopeless piece at f4 or g3, modestly facing its own centre pawn. The centre itself might remain, for Fischer, less stable and potentially more fluid, where e5 may change into an 'empty square' for enhancing the manoeuvring options of White's pieces.

These diverging views clashed again in both sides' notes after **12 ... ♗d7 13 0-0 0-0-0**. Geller attached a question mark to Black's last move, and wrote: "It is remarkable that Tal doesn't make use of the opportunity offered him to grab the central pawn. After 13 ... ♘xe5 14 ♘xe5

♛xe5 15 ♗xd7+ ♚xd7 White would have found it quite difficult to hold his position." Fischer, in his annotations, went one move further – 16 ♛d3! – and found that this "keeps White on top"!

It was Tal who, acting as silent judge, explained his 13th move in a wider context: "The most critical moment of the game. At this point I spent about 40 minutes assessing the position arising after 13 ... ♘xe5 14 ♘xe5 ♛xe5 15 ♗xd7+ ♚xd7 16 ♛d3 ..." And he takes this line further "16 ... ♖ac8 17 ♖b1 ♚c7 18 ♖b5! ♚b8 19 ♗e3, and White has activated his forces. It is very difficult for Black to set his central pawn mass in motion".[5] This, in a sense, not only vindicates Fischer's assessment of this particular variation, but of his whole approach to the positional questions of piece activity and the centre in this set-up. An approach he was able to prove worthy of acclaim in his 1st match game against Larsen, Candidates 1971 (Pos. 170).

Fischer had had positions similar to this one on other occasions,[6] but here his approach is developed most thematically. **13 ♗a3! fxe5 14 dxe5 ♘cxe5 15 ♘xe5 ♘xe5 16 ♛d4! ♘g6 17 ♗h5!**. All of White's pieces have sprung to life at the cost of his central pawn. One has to be quite insensitive to weather changes to fail to take note of the

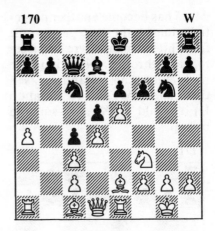

**170**　　　　　　　　**W**

light and gentle breeze moving across the opened centre (or is it actually Pan playing his flute in its hollow squares?).

Be it one or the other – this is exactly the kind of position Fischer aspired to, and would willingly have played whenever given the opportunity. White's queen already occupies a central post, and for the other square that has just been 'emptied' – e5 – let us turn to Jan Timman's comment after **17 ... ♚f7 18 f4**:

"I assume that a player like Karpov or Romanishin," he writes in *The Art of Chess Analysis*,[7] "would continue less energetically with 18 ♖e3 or even 18 ♖e5 to continue the attack in a half-open position purely on the dark squares after a possible exchange on g6".

We see, then, the immediate results of White's policy: besides

d4, e5 has become another potentially important strategic outpost
for White to manoeuvre his pieces
to, and through. Now it is the
rook that can establish itself
there; later (see Pos. 317, variation
II) it would be the dark-squared
bishop.

**171**                              **W**

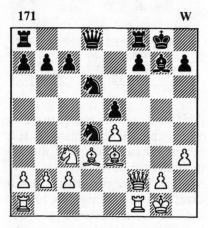

This (Pos. 171) is the position
after Black's 14th move of one of
Fischer's best known games – the
one against Pal Benko at the
1963-64 US Championship. The
position seems roughly equal,
and Black (Benko) is about to
play 15 ... f5.

One would expect White to
take some drastic measures to
stop that move. Yet Fischer plays
**15 ♕g3**. Hans Kmoch reported
about this decision in *Chess
Review*: "15 ♕g3! – The most
difficult move of the game. Fischer
played it after prolonged delibera-

tion, checking on the consequences
of both 15 g4 and 15 ♕g3 f5 (and
probably some other possibilities)".[8] Now, we just have to bear
in mind Fischer's partiality to the
advance of the king knight's
pawn (see pos. 33-40), to understand how great was the likelihood
he would indeed play, or at least
consider, 15 g4 in this position.
Remarkably enough, he doesn't
mention this possibility at all(!)
neither in his initial annotations
to thte game in *Chess Life*,[9] nor in
*MSMG*.[10] Besides the move played,
he refers only to 15 ♘d5 and 15
♘e2 as possible alternatives. Why
doesn't he mention 15 g4-? – the
answer is given by the game's
continuation. For Fischer it must
have been quite self evident that
g4 had to remain an 'empty
square' for the coming manoeuvre
of the queen:

**15 ... ♔h8** 15 ... f5 16 ♗h6 leads,
according to Fischer, to a slightly
better endgame for White. **16
♕g4!**. Among its other virtues,
this prevents 16 ... f5. **16 ... c6 17
♕h5!**. h5 is without doubt the
most active outpost the queen
could occupy in this set-up, and
she couldn't have reached it by
any other manoeuvre (with the
exclusion of the quite ridiculous
♕f2-e1-d1-h5). In the brief and
brilliant epilogue that followed,
her majesty played an extremely
important role there: **17 ... ♕e8 18**

♗xd4 exd4 19 ♖f6!! ♔g8 20 e5 h6 21 ♘e2, and Black resigned. Apart from the effectiveness of that manoeuvre, there is a cryptic beauty to it – three 'creeping moves' (if we use Kotov's terminology)[11] played one after the other with the fastest piece. One should probably better speak of an exceptional 'creeping manoeuvre' in this connection.

For a more 'expanded' queen manoeuvre we shall have to return to Pos. 168. (Fischer-Miagmarsuren, Sousse 1967). After 15 ♘e3 ♗a6 16 ♗h3 d4 we get the following position (Pos. 172).

172               W

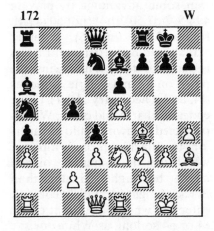

Where should one play the knight on e3 to? The impulse of the majority of players of this sharp line of the Closed French would be to get the knight closer to the black king by 17 ♘g4. Fischer, with restraint that is typical of a true classical artist, plays 17 ♘f1!. To his young readers at *Boys' Life* magazine (see p.52), he explains: "The horse beats a strategic retreat – temporarily. It is headed for the "hole" on e4 now that Black's d-pawn can no longer guard that square."[12]

This is one side of the story. There is another as well: at g4 the knight would have stood in the way of the queen's path to her destined outpost – h5. Instead of blocking this diagonal, Fischer now clears it of other obstacles: 17 ... ♘b6 18 ♘g5! ♘d5 19 ♗d2 ♗xg5 20 ♗xg5 ♕d7 21 ♕h5. Jokingly, Fischer remarked: "Make way for the heavy artillery". But this, indeed, was the final objective he had set for this phase of the game. This is by no means to say that it was the 'only', and not necessarily even the 'best' line. It was, of the many alternative lines possible, the most Fischerian in its reliance on 'empty squares'. And it had a most elegant sequel, too: 21 ... ♖fc8 22 ♘d2. Enter the horse! 22 ... ♘c3 23 ♗f6! ♕e8 24 ♘e4 g6 25 ♕g5 ♘xe4 26 ♖xe4 c4 27 h5 cxd3 28 ♖h4! ♖a7 29 ♗g2! dxc2 30 ♕h6 ♕f8 31 ♕xh7+!! 1-0 (see also Pos. 52)

In Petrosian-Fischer, 8th match game, Candidates 1971 (Pos. 173), 19 ... c4 perhaps wasn't bad. It was, at its worst, old-fashioned:

173                    B

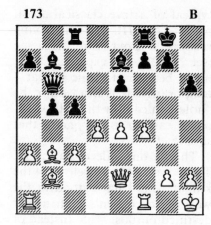

174                                    W

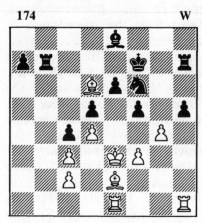

20 ♗c2 a5 21 f5 exf5 22 ♖xf5 ♗g5
23 ♖af1 (23 a4 b4 24 cxb4 axb4 25
♖b5 ♕a6 26 ♖xb4 c3! 27 ♕xa6
cxb2!! might win for Black, and
23 ♗c1 ♗xc1 24 ♖xc1 b4 is quite
promising for him) 23 ... ♖ce8 24
e5 ♗d5. Black's right lung (queenside) remains as yet full of smoke,
but there is no indication of
sickness. Fischer, anyway, dispels
any signs of such disturbances by
**19 ... cxd4! 20 cxd4 b4 21 axb4
♗xb4**, and after Petrosian's **22
d5?** (Korchnoi mentioned 23 ♖f3
as correct here)[13] he made use of
the newly-emptied c3 by playing
**22 ... ♗c3!**. This won him a pawn
after **23 ♗xc3 ♖xc3 24 ♗c2 exd5**.
(see also Pos. 271)

However, even an excellent
poet may turn out some bad
poetry sometimes. And that happened to Fischer in his game (as
White) against Mednis at the US

In Pos. 174 White could maintain some advantage by playing
49 g5 ♘d7 50 ♖h4! (not 50 f4 h4!,
followed by ♘f8-g6). Whether
this should be sufficient for a win
is hard to tell. White wins the
pawn on h5 in a couple of moves
(f4, and if necessary ♖eh1). In the
endgame that would ensue, White's
protected g-pawn, would be superior to Black's passed a-pawn,
while the dark-squared bishop
might be slightly better than
Black's knight (the knight couldn't
enter the white position at either
e4 or g4 so long as White doesn't
push g6). Yet Fischer's aversion
to blocking g5 and f4 by pawns
beguiled him into playing the
inferior **49 gxf5**. Since he had one
good continuation at his disposal,
we are inclined to think that he
considered this one even better,

that is, one that might have offered good winning chances! This is a very instructive case to illustrate how a player's style (and a player of that high level, at that!) can give rise to such a biased judgment, so as to distort it even when the issue at hand is quite clear-cut. For Fischer g5 and f4, together with e5, had to remain 'empty squares' for his pieces (the dark-squared bishop, the king, and possibly a rook) to manoeuvre. Objectively, he could hardly have reckoned on winning the game after **49 ... exf5**, notwithstanding Black's weak pawns on the fifth rank. White's superior piece activity offers at the very best barely adequate compensation for what is in effect a two pawn deficit. Kmoch thought that now "the issue is in the balance",[14] while Mednis opined that "there can be no doubt that Black must now win"![15] Certainly a remarkable

difference of opinion. Yet with Fischer favouring, in all probability, White (at least during the game), we have one of the most curious cases on record of differences in expert opinion of one and the same position!

The end of the story is well known: Fischer had to resign on move 73. Kmoch might be right that he failed to utilise his chances properly in this ending (**50 ♖h4?** instead of manoeuvring his bishops to f4 and h3 respectively), but his greater error was to steer for this endgame in the first place.

In this case his poetry of the empty squares was in discord with the nature of the position.

There was greater harmony in, among others, Pos. 149 (with regard to e4 and the d-file), Pos. 155 (pay heed to h4, e4, f5, and the e-file) and Pos. 178 (with emphasis on e4, f5 and of course the c-and the d-files).

# Clarity

It is customary to speak of Fischer's clear and lucid style. As a matter of fact, Fischer's style has become almost synonymous with clarity and lucidity in chess. The examples I've chosen should indicate clearly and lucidly enough the ways in which this distinguished him from other players.

**175**                                        **B**

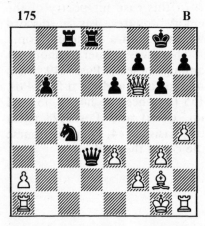

In Smyslov-Fischer, Palma de Mallorca 1970 (Pos. 175), there occurred **23 ... ♛f5!**. Gligorić, in *Chess Life & Review* (March 1971) remarked: "Black made this move without hesitation, illustrating the efficiency of Fischer's technique. White's only active piece will be traded off. Black is subject to no illusion as to continuing the king hunt and goes rather for an increased advantage in the endgame after the queens go. Also, there was some threat of 24 h5."

A question that might arise, however, is: "if this is typical of Fischer, what would other players have played here?". Black's superior position might very well offer other possibilities of which other players would have made use, thus maintaining Black's advantage by other methods. In what way, then, can we recognise Fischer's 'hand' here? A player of a distinct tactical disposition would have considered trying, á la Tal, to force White's hand by tactical means, that is – a knight sacrifice at e3. But 23 ... ♘xe3 24 fxe3 ♖c2 25 ♛f3 ♛c3 26 ♖f1, and Black's attack comes to a halt. Would a postponement of one move in sacrificing the knight make any difference? Let's see: 23 ... ♛d2 24 h5 ♘xe3 25 hxg6 (25 h6? ♘f5) 25 ... ♖c1+ 26 ♗f1!!. The disillusioner! More in line with Black's expectations was: 26 ♖xc1 ♛xc1+ 27 ♔h2 ♛xh1+!! 28 ♔xh1 (28

♗xh1 ♘g4+) 28 ... ♖d1+ 29 ♗f1 ♖xf1+ 30 ♔h2 ♘g4+ 31 ♔g2 ♘xf6, and Black wins. After 26 ♗f1, however, too many black pieces remain under attack, and he loses material by force. So, a king hunt is indeed a short-lived adventure in this case, and any top class player would have realised this almost instantaneously when checking the above line.

A player of another temperament, someone whose approach is similar to that of, say, Anatoly Karpov's, would most probably have directed his attention not to e3 but to a3, attracted by the strong positional move 23 ... ♘a3!. Without lessening the tension of the position, Black restricts White's options, and increases the spatial domination of his own pieces. After 24 h5 ♕c3! 25 ♕xc3 ♖xc3 Black's control of the open c-and d-files plus the fact that b1 isn't accesible to a white rook, give him a considerable endgame advantage. For a player of this approach, the further restriction of White's mobility by the containment of the a-pawn, would be a most significant factor. If analytically disposed, he might very well substantiate his observations by calculating this line a little deeper, making sure that 26 h6 ♔f8 27 ♖h4 ♔e7 28 ♖d4 (or 28 ♖b4 ♘c2 29 ♖c1 ♘xb4 30 ♖xc3 ♘xa2 31 ♖b3 ♖d6, etc) 28 ...

♖xd4 29 exd4 ♔d6! 30 ♔f1 ♘b5 31 ♖d1 ♖c4 32 d5 e5 indeed offers Black excellent winning chances.

Another solution is more in Capablanca's style. Well, I guess Capa himself, like Fischer, would not have hesitated, and would have played 23 ... h5! on general grounds.[1] Black keeps all his positional advantages, and is ready to trade his knight for the bishop so as to increase the activity of his rooks. It could have led to 24 ♗f1 (24 g4?! ♖c5 25 ♗f1 ♕d6! threatening 26 ... ♘xe3! is very strong, while 25 gxh5? leads to 25 ... ♖f5 26 ♕e7 ♖xf2! 27 ♕xd8+ – 27 hxg6 ♖xg2+! – ♕xd8 28 ♔xf2 ♕d2+, winning) 24 ... ♕d5 (24 ... ♕d2 is premature: 25 ♗xc4 ♖xc4 26 ♖b1! ♖d6 27 ♖b2! equalises) 25 ♗xc4 (25 ♗g2 ♕d2!) 25 ... ♖xc4 26 ♔h2 ♕d2! (taking advantage of the fact that 27 ♖hd1 ♕xd1! ought to win for him, Black now centralises his second rook) 27 ♖hf1 ♖d5!, and in this position Black enjoys classical advantages of piece co-operation, aided by simple tactical threats (28 ... ♖f5), without conceding any positional gains to his opponent.

Fischer's choice is as clear, yet not as 'clean'. Black's pawn formation gets (after **24 ♕xf5 gxf5**) a sharper twist (see also 'Pawn Structure', Pos. 14-29). In a sense, it is the most direct and simple solution – Black trades off queens without waiting another move. While not being as airtight as the line proceeding from 23 ... ♘a3!, it achieves something very important straight away, namely establishing a rook on the second rank: **25 h5 ♖d2**, after which Black's superiority is no longer in doubt (see also Pos. 115, 123).

Clarity in this line, as well as in the following examples, is the result of decisions taken on general positional grounds, without calculating the consequences of these decisions in terms of concrete variations too deeply. Of course, these positional considerations, besides being sound, have to be sustained by a powerful positional insight.

**176**       **W**

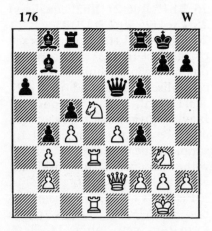

Take a look, for instance, at Pos. 176 (Fischer-Johannessen, Havana Olympiad 1966). The positional insight of the majority

of players wouldn't have carried them further than realising White's domination of the d-file, his good knight at d5, and his somewhat better pawn structure, mainly with regard to his e-pawn as against Black's pawn at f4. Very few, if any, would have taken note of Black's weakness at e6 (which, for all practical purposes, seems negligible at this stage), and the possibility of the c5 pawn becoming a concrete positional target in the very near future. It takes a player of an exceptionally sharp positional insight to see how White can turn these factors into a palpable advantage within a very short sequence of moves, and, moreover, do so while swapping the pawn on e4 for Black's 'weakling' on f4. Fischer's solution started with the seemingly harmless **27 ♘h5**. What might have appealed to many other players, on the other hand, is the possibility to create immediate tactical threats by **27 ♘f5!?**. The threat at e7, and the cover this knight provides for the queen for a ♕g4, look very promising elements. And indeed they are! As the following variations show, the complications that arise after this move are in White's favour:

I) 27 ... ♖fe8 (27 ... ♗xd5 28 cxd5 ♕e5 29 d6, is highly dangerous for Black) 28 ♘fe7+! ♖xe7 29 ♘xe7+ ♕xe7 30 ♖d7 ♕xe4 31

Ξd8+!, and White wins material.

II) 27 ... Ξce8 28 ♕g4 g6 29 ♘c7!! ♗xc7 30 Ξd7, and now:

a) 30 ... ♕xe4 31 Ξg7+ ♔h8 32 Ξxh7+!! ♔xh7 33 Ξd7+ Ξe7 (33 ... ♔h8 34 ♕h4+) 34 Ξxe7+ ♕xe7 35 ♘xe7 ♗e4 36 ♕h3+! ♔g7 37 ♕d7 Ξd8 38 ♘f5++ and mates.

b) 30 ... ♗xe4 31 ♕h4 h5 32 ♘g7! ♕e5 33 ♘xe8 Ξxe8 34 Ξe1!, winning material by f3.

c) 30 ... ♔h8 31 Ξxc7 ♗xe4 32 ♕h4 (32 Ξdd7? Ξxd7!) 32 ... ♕g8 33 Ξdd7 h5 34 ♘h6 g5 (or 34 ... ♗f5 35 f3!) 35 ♕xh5 ♕g6 36 ♘f7++ and wins.

It is, however, in this last line that Black can put up some resistance: 31 ... Ξd8! (instead of 31 ... ♗xe4), and the issue remains quite unclear: 32 Ξe7 (Not 32 Ξxd8 Ξxd8 33 Ξxb7 ♕xe4, and Black wins! Or 32 Ξxb7 ♕xe4! 33 Ξe7 ♕xf5 and Black is alright) 32 ... ♗xe4! (32 ... ♕c8 33 Ξxd8 Ξxd8 34 h3! ♗xe4 35 ♕h4 h5 35 ♕h4 h5 36 ♕xf6 mates) 33 Ξxe6 ♗xf5 34 Ξxd8 Ξxd8 35 ♕e2 ♗xe6. This might well be a won endgame for White, but it would take greater efforts to turn it into a win, than the way it happened in the game. After 27 ♘h5!, Johanessen played **27 ... Ξce8**. 27 ... Ξfe8 could lead to 28 ♘hxf4 ♗xf4 29 ♘dxf4 ♕xe4 30 Ξe3 ♕c6 31 ♕g4! Ξcd8 32 Ξxd8 Ξxd8 33 Ξe7 g6 34 ♘d5! ♗c8 35 ♕f4, and wins. There followed: **28 ♘hxf4**

♗xf4 29 ♘xf4 ♕xe4 30 Ξe3 ♕c6 31 Ξe6!. Clearer and simpler it can't be. It is remarkable how decisive this (again deceptively quite harmless looking) move is. Now 31 ... Ξxe6 loses to 32 ♕xe6+ ♕xe6 (or 32 ... ♔h8, which drops the vital c-pawn: 33 ♕xc6 ♗xc6 34 ♘e6) 33 ♘xe6 Ξc8 34 Ξd7. **31 ... ♕c8 32 h4 g6 33 Ξe7**, and White, threatening now among other things 34 Ξd6 and 35 Ξxf6, won by: **33 ... Ξxe7 33 ... ♕c6 34 ♘d5! 34 ♕xe7 Ξf7 35 Ξd8+ ♔g7 36 ♘e6+**, Black resigned.

Clear, lucid, and instructive, is also the next example, from Fischer-Gheorghiu, Buenos Aires 1970, Pos. 177.

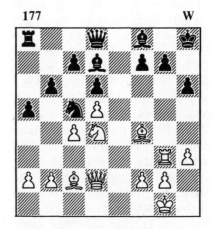

177                                    W

**23 ♘f3!**. Played with a view to using d4 for the centralisation of the queen. All Fischer wants is to force a queen exchange on f6, after which Black's ruined kingside would signal a quick decision. Interestingly, he gives preference to this clear positional plan over the one starting with the subtle tactical retreat 23 ♗e3!, in which d4 could be used for the bishop's centralisation, with grave consequences for Black: a) 23 ... ♕e7 (or 23 ... ♕e8 24 ♘b5! ♗xb5 25 ♗d4! which is similar to the main line) 24 ♘c6! ♗xc6 (24 ... ♘e4 25 ♕d4! ♗xc6 26 ♗xe4 wins) 25 ♗d4! f6 (25 ... ♕h4 26 ♕c3!) 26 dxc6, and Black's position is critical; 26 ... ♖e8 is answered by 27 ♕f4!, and 26 ... ♘e4 leads to 27 ♕d3 f5 (27 ... ♖e8 28 f3) 28 ♖e3 ♕h4 (or 28 ... ♕f7 29 ♖xe4! fxe4 30 ♕xe4 ♕g8 31 ♕g6 with mate to follow) 29 g3! ♕xh3 30 ♖xe4! fxe4 31 ♕xe4 ♔g8 32 ♕h7+ ♔f7 33 ♕g6+ ♔g8 34 ♗f5, winning Black's queen; b) 23 ... ♕h4 24 ♘f3 ♕xc4 25 ♗d4 f6 26 ♘h4 ♕xd5 27 ♕xh6+!! gxh6 28 ♗xf6+ ♗g7 29 ♖xg7!, and wins. Fischer's plan unfolded as follows: **23 ... ♕e7.** Black must try to take control of e4. After 23 ... ♕f6 White certainly plays 24 ♗e3! and then 25 ♗d4, 26 ♕xh6+! **24 ♕d4!.** This not only threatens 25 ♗xh6, but precludes 24 ... ♘e4 as well. 24 ♗e3, on the other hand, would relieve Black of all his troubles: 24 ... ♘e4 25 ♕d3 ♗f5! 26 ♖g4!? ♖e8! (26 ... ♗xg4 is by no means a mistake either). **24 ...**

♕f6 25 ♕xf6 gxf6. For what followed next, turn to p.119, and see also Pos. 111, 120.

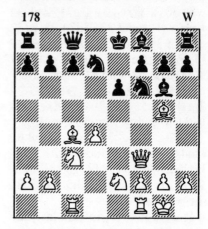

178                                      W

11 ♘f4 in Pos. 178 (Fischer-Addison, Palma de Mallorca 1970) would be, for many, about the only move to consider seriously. White's threats against e6 are certainly not to be taken lightly. There are five ways to prove that this is indeed a weighty affair:

a) 11 ... ♗e7 12 ♗xe6 fxe6 13 ♘xe6 ♔f7 14 ♗xf6! gxf6 (14 ... ♘xf6 or 14 ... ♗xf6 are answered by 15 ♘g5+ ♔f8 16 ♘b5) 15 ♘d5!, with a tremendous attacking position.

b) 11 ... ♗d6 12 ♘b5 ♘e4 13 ♘xd6+ ♘xd6 14 ♗xe6 0-0 15 ♘xg6 hxg6 16 ♗d5, and the threat of 17 ♗e7 isn't easy to counter. For instance 16 ... ♖e8 17 ♗f4! and White wins.

c) 11 ... ♘b6 12 ♗b3!, and the

combination of the threats ♗xf6, d5, and ♖fe1 is very menacing. If 12 ... ♗e7 12 ♖fe1, and 12 ... 0-0 isn't playable in view of 12 ♘xe6!.

d) 11 ... c6 12 ♖fe1, and again looming clouds gather around the black king.

e) 11 ... ♗f5 12 ♖fe1 ♗e7 13 d5 ♘xd5 (13 ... e5 14 ♘e6!) 14 ♘fxd5 ♗xg5 15 ♕xf5 ♗xc1 16 ♖xe6+! fxe6 17 ♕xe6+ ♔f8 18 ♘xc7 ♘e5 19 ♕d6 mate.

However, instead of heading for positions featuring thematic sacrificial motifs at e6, Fischer decides the centre's character with other aims in mind. **11 ♗xf6 gxf6.** If 11 ... ♘xf6 12 d5 e5 13 ♗b5+ ♘d7 14 ♘g3 or 14 ♖fe1. **12 d5! e5 13 ♗b5 ♗e7 14 ♘g3.** The way Fischer has played makes it pretty clear what White is going to do next: squeeze Black on the weakened light squares and exploit the uncastled position of the king. From the technical point of view the game might well be considered won for White. Everything is now extremely clear and well defined. There followed: **14 ... a6 15 ♗d3! ♕d8 16 h4 h5 17 ♗f5! ♘b6 18 ♘ce4! ♘xd5 19 ♖fd1,** and Fischer won in a few moves.

How clear-sighted Fischer is capable of being even in the wildest positions, is illustrated by a certain side-line in his game against Najdorf, Varna Olympiad 1962 (Pos. 179). White (Fischer)

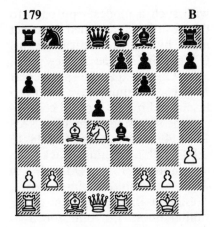

179        B

has just gambitted away his e4 pawn, and Black can collect another one by a bishop desperado at g2. Let's see first how Fischer approaches this position, and then go on to compare this with other commentaries. In *MSMG* Fischer gives this line: "12 ... ♗xg2 13 ♔xg2 dxc4 14 ♕f3 ♘d7 [Fischer doesn't mention 14 ... ♖a7, but after 15 ♗e3 ♖d7 16 ♖ad1 White's positional advantage is overwhelming] 15 ♘f5 ♖g8+ (if 15 ... e6 16 ♖xe6+! fxe6 17 ♕h5 mate) 16 ♔h1 e5 (if 16 ... e6 17 ♕c6 threatening ♖xe6+) 17 ♗e3 with a winning bind despite the two-pawn deficit".[2] A very clear, simple-looking, yet decisive line, isn't it?

A few other grandmasters who annotated the game before and after the publication of Fischer's book, were not apparently satisfied with such a modest approach to this position, and wished to extract more by radical tactical means. O'Kelly in *Europe Echecs* gives, after 12 ... ♗xg2, the spectacular 13 ♘e6. He must have been too fascinated by the tactical complications resulting from 13 ... ♕c8 14 ♗f4! fxe6 15 ♕h5+ ♔d8 16 ♗b3 "with a winning attack",[3] to take note of 13 ... ♕d7 14 ♗f4 ♖g8!, and White is simply lost.

Gideon Barcza thought along similar lines.[4] For him, too, Fischer's 13 ♔xg2 must have seemed too naive for such a rich position. He offered his version of a spectacular White win by 13 ♕a4+ ♘d7 14 ♘f5 ♗e4 (14 ... e6 15 ♕c6 threatens 16 ♖xe6+) 15 ♘d6+ exd6 16 ♗xd5 f5 17 ♖xe4+! fxe4 18 ♕xe4+ and 19 ♗xa8, with evidently the better endgame for White. Again Black can improve on this line with 14 ... ♕b6! when 15 ♗f4 is answered by 15 ... ♖g8! (16 ♘d6+ ♔d8 17 ♘xf7+ ♔c8 and Black ought to win!), and 15 ♗e3 is met by 15 ... ♕e6!. Best is probably 15 ♔xg2 (the same move after all!) though White has hardly any compensation for his two-pawn deficit after 15 ... dxc4 16 ♖d1 (or 16 ♕xc4 ♖g8+) 16 ... ♕b7+ 17 ♔h2 e6, etc.

Leonid Shamkovich accepted Fischer's 13th move, but rejected his 15th. In his book *The Modern Chess Sacrifice* he indicated (from

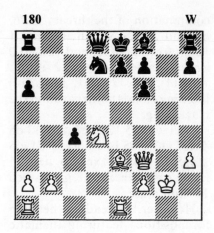

**180**                          **W**

Pos. 180) 15 ♘c6[5] instead of Fischer's more positional 15 ♘f5. He wished to elicit decisive threats from the position after 15 ... ♕c8 16 ♗h6!. As in the two other suggestions, this too actually boomerangs on White. 16 ... ♖g8+ leads to either: a) 17 ♔h1 (or 17 ♔h2 ♕c7+ first) 17 ... ♕b7 18 ♗xf8 ♔xf8 19 ♖xe7 ♘e5!!, and Black comes out on top; or b) 17 ♔f1 ♘b8!! 18 ♘xe7 ♗xe7 19 ♖xe7+! (not 19 ♕xa8 ♕xh3+ 20 ♔e2 ♕d3 mate) 19 ... ♔xe7 20 ♖e1+ ♔d7! 21 ♕xa8 ♘c6! 22 ♖d1+ ♔e6, with a draw as the most likely result. 21 ♕d5+ ♔c7 22 ♗f4+ ♔b6 23 ♗e3+ ♔c7 24 ♕a5+ offers nothing more than a perpetual. (see also Pos. 163)

The comparison of these four approaches doesn't, of course, mean to imply that clarity in handling such positions is a necessary pre-condition for success. It does indicate, though, how more effective such an approach might prove to be at times, even in sharp positions. Fischer's policy involved the following:

a) Capturing the bishop at g2.

b) Placing the queen at f3 from where it dominates the h1-a8 diagonal, and attacks f6.

c) Knight to f5.

After these three simple steps, Black's position was already critical. None of the other approaches achieved anything similar. Ironically, they all came closer to losing the game for White! . . .

Let me conclude this chapter with the words of one of the tactical wizards of the post-war era, David Bronstein: ". . . [It] does not mean that you must forcibly attempt to decide the battle by a combination, even where there is no place for it. Clear, logical positions, while they contain less emotion, have their own unique charm, and with the passing of the years I have come to appreciate this better."[6] In our last case it wasn't so much a clear position as a clear way of thinking in a position that had the potential of becoming extremely unclear, had it been handled more fancifully.

# Straightforwardness

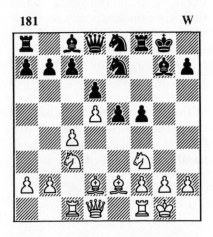

Of Taimanov's **12 ♘g5** in his 1st match game against Fischer, Candidates 1971 (Pos. 181) opinions diverged. Tal commented: "By intruding with the knight at e6 White compels his opponent to give up his white-squared bishop. Of course, you have to figure that the isolated pawn will sooner or later fall prey to the enemy, but during this time it will be easy to deploy the pieces advantageously."[1] Robert Byrne, on the other hand, attached a question mark to the move, and wrote: "There was still a chance to transpose into the

preferable line of the third game with ♕b3 or to try Korchnoi's idea b4 [Byrne is referring to the 3rd match game, Korchnoi-Geller, Candidates 1971], but Taimanov is intent on a positional gambit of a type with which he has had considerable success in the past. Unfortunately for him, Fischer refutes it at once."[2] Whether one adopts one view or the other, or considers the following a refutation or not, the one important thing is that it happens 'at once', without any circumventory manoeuvring: **12 ... h6 13 ♘e6 ♗xe6 14 dxe6 ♕c8 15 ♕b3 c6 16 ♗h5 ♕xe6 17 ♕xb7 ♘f6 18 ♗e2 ♖fb8 19 ♕a6 ♖xb2** (see also Pos. 25). It is this swift and straightforward action that typifies so many of Fischer's games. True, it might at times prove somewhat crude when a more intricate approach is called for, as for instance in his game against Korchnoi, Rovinj-Zagreb 1970 (Pos. 182). Fischer's **16 ♕e3** was criticised by Korchnoi,[3] who indicated instead 16 ♖ac1. Korchnoi's **16 ... ♗f6!** (not 16 ... ♕a5? 17 ♗xe6!) brought about another

182 W          183 W

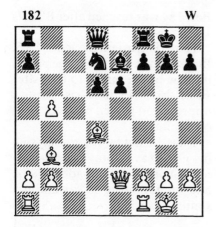          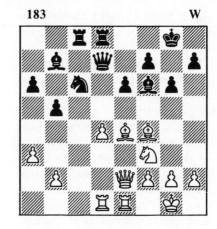

straightforward response: **17 ♗xa7 ♕a5 18 b6?**. Fischer might have expected now 18 ... ♗xb2, which Korchnoi assessed as equal after 19 ♖ab1 ♗a3 20 ♗c2 ♗c5 21 ♕d3 g6 22 ♕b5. But again Korchnoi's subtle **18 ... ♗d8!** set greater problems for White. After **19 ♖ad1** had Korchnoi played 19 ... d5 (instead of **19 ... ♘xb6?**) 20 ♕d2 ♕a6!, as pointed out by him, the advantage would be Black's.

Yet this very approach was one of Fischer's strongest weapons. Against Najdorf at Buenos Aires, 1970 (Pos. 183), Fischer (Black) has just played **18 ... ♗e7-f6**. White could play 19 d5, equalising immediately. But we have to assume that Najdorf estimated his position as better, since he gave preference to **19 ♘e5**. An experienced player like him must have expected Fischer to play in accordance with the 'spirit of the position' 19 ... ♕e8 (not, of course, 19 ... ♕e7? 20 ♘xc6 ♗xc6 21 ♗xc6 ♖xc6 22 d5! etc). He might have reckoned with a slight White advantage after 20 ♕e3, or even 20 ♘g4 ♗g7 21 ♗g5!?. Fischer's move – **19 ... ♗xe5!** – certainly came as a surprise to him. This straightforward capture shows little respect for chess culture and conventions. By giving up his vital bishop, Black remains awfully weak on the dark squares on the kingside. As it turned out, however, Fischer concretely saw that after **20 dxe5 ♘d4! 21 ♕e3** (21 ♖xd4 ♕xd4 22 ♗xb7 ♕xf4 23 ♗xc8 ♖xc8, with a slight advantage for Black) **21 ... ♗xe4 22 ♕xe4 ♕d5!**, Black's initiative on the c- and d-files would more than outweigh his position's other weaknesses, and it would be White who'd have to fight to hold the issue in the balance. (see futher Pos. 124).

We have to appreciate Fischer's straightforwardness against its appropriate background. Fischer happened to be active at a time when the general tendency in the chess world, and especially that of the dominant Soviet School, was still very heavily inclined towards over-sophistication in chess. Nowadays, with the more vigorous and direct chess outlook of Kasparov, this is no longer prevalent. But in the years that preceded him and Karpov, that approach used to be the order of the day among the reigning chess elite.

Here is a classical example of an encounter between Fischer and one of its most prominent representatives – Tigran Petrosian. In their second game at the Match of the Century, Belgrade 1970,

**184**                    **W**

Pos. 184 was reached after Black's 13th move.

Here Petrosian played **14 c5**. Black is forced to exchange pawns in view of the threat 15 b5. After **14 ... bxc5 15 bxc5**, is White's unprotected passed pawn an asset or liability?

Isaac Kashdan, when analysing his game (as White) against Herman Steiner from Pasadena 1932, had the following to say about a similar decision:

**W**

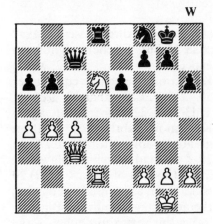

33 c5! – "This had to be carefully analysed. Such an advance, *if it does not bear an immediate fruit may result in the pawn becoming a weakness.*"[4] (my italics)

There is very little reason to believe Petrosian thought his c-pawn would become a weakness, let alone that it would fall within eight moves, without offering the slightest compensation in return.

How come that a subtle strategist like him made such a faulty assessment of as crucial a point as this one? After **15 ... ♘a5 16 ♘a4 ♗c6 17 ♕c2 ♘b7**, Petrosian explains: "When I analysed the position after the thirteenth move I could not see any refutation of the plan 14 c5, although I didn't like it much. Black's sixteenth and seventeenth moves are very strong. It seems that it isn't easy to defend the pawn on c5." Was it really so? Are we to believe that Petrosian couldn't foresee moves like 16 ... ♗c6 (attacking the only piece that defends the c5 pawn), and 17 ... ♘b7 (retracting the attacked knight, and attacking c5 again)? This seems hardly credible. These two moves are simply too obvious for an ex-World Champion to overlook. It must have been 15 ... ♘a5! (Fischer's exclamation mark, by the way. Petrosian passes over this move without any comment)[6] which he either overlooked or underestimated.

White's 14 c5 could be retrospectively justified only if he should have succeeded in exploiting Black's weakness at d6. A quick transfer of a white knight to d6 is therefore mandatory. Petrosian must have based his plans on either 16 ♘b5 or 16 ♘e4. The move he was reluctant to play in the game – 16 ♘a4 – was a grave concession, and an admission of

his plan's failure. The question that remains to be answered, then, is why should 15 ... ♘a5 (see Pos. 185) have taken him by

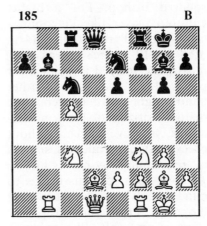

185                                    B

surprise? On the surface of it, 15 ... ♘a5 is quite a natural move. The knight defends the attacked bishop while opening the c-file for the rook to attack c5, and the h1-a8 diagonal for the bishop to prevent ♘e4, from where the knight would protect c5 and aim to plant itself at d6. Yet such a straightforward approach to the position's problems was, apparently, not in line with Petrosian's expectations. The set of positional considerations mentioned above is quite concrete in nature. There are some abstract considerations as well, which must have played a greater role in Petrosian's thinking. Viewed abstractly, 15 ... ♘a5 might well be considered a rather weak move. The bishop at b7 remains exposed to White's attack while the knight at a5 is placed within the range of White's dark-squared bishop. For a highly cultured player like Petrosian a 'sophisticated' retreat like 14 ... ♗a8 (as 19 ... ♕e8 in Pos. 183) must have seemed a much wiser policy. 15 ... ♘a5, on the other hand, might well have remained on the horizon of his consider-ations, a move which, without checking its consequences, smacks of 'refutability' by moves like 16 ♖b5, or 16 ♘b5. This brings to mind Karpov's words that "during the period of Petrosian and Spassky chess became 'soft'. Players began to have too much respect for each other . . ."[7] The straightforward 15 ... ♘a5 might have been too 'hard' for Petrosian to take into serious consideration. Only after Fischer had played it might he have realised that 15 ♖b5 leads nowhere after 16 ... ♗c6, while after 16 ♘b5 ♖xc5 17 ♘xa7 ♕a8! Black clearly has the better of it. After the 'softer' 15 ... ♗a8, on the other hand, White gets things his way: 16 ♘e4. If now 16 ... ♘e5 (16 ... ♘d4 17 ♘xd4 ♕xd4 –17 ... ♗xe4 18 ♘xe6! – 18 ♗e3 remains better for White), then 17 ♘xe5 ♗xe5 18 ♗h6 ♕xd1 19 ♖fxd1 ♖fd8 (19 ... ♖fe8 20 ♘d6!) 20 ♗g5 ♖xd1+ (or 20 ... ♗xe4 21 ♗xe4 f6 22 ♗e3 etc) 21 ♖xd1 ♘c6

22 ♖d7, with a delightful endgame for Petrosian to play. Better for Black might be 16 ... ♘d5 or 16 ... ♘f5, though White maintains his edge after 17 ♖b3!.

Fischer's straightforward ap-proach caused Petrosian a second upset in the game, fifteen moves later. Eduard Gufeld once wittily remarked that "[i]n every move (good or bad) there is an idea (good or bad)".[8] This could be extended even further: one can make a good move with the wrong idea in mind and *vice versa*.

**186**                                    **W**

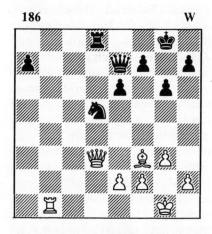

Petrosian's **30 ♕d4** (Pos. 186) was an excellent example of the latter case. The idea behind the move is subtle, yet the move itself proves quite weak in view of Fischer's reaction. What might have been Petrosian's idea? He had, as a matter of fact two, I guess – one quite obvious, the other a more concealed one. White's most immediate threat now is 31 ♗xd5, when Black can't recapture with the rook in view of 32 ♖b8+, winning at once. The second idea behind this move was most probably the following: White would have loved to place his queen at a6, checking the advance of the a-pawn and creating threats on the b-file. The immediate 30 ♕a6 would give Black the opportunity to improve his position by 30 ... ♕c5! when 31 ♖b7 is strongly met by 31 ... ♕c1+ 32 ♔g2 ♘f6!, and 31 ♔g2 by 31 ... ♘b4 32 ♕a3 a5. Petrosian wants to induce Black to play ... ♘b6. Admittedly, Black would thus close off the b-file against a white invasion there, yet at the same time the knight would be decentralised, and, more importantly, ... ♕c5 would be excluded since the knight at b6 would now interfere in its defence of the a7 pawn. Thus, after 30 ♕d4 ♘b6, we would have witnessed a Petrosian finesse – 31 ♕a1! – followed up by 32 ♕a6!, when Black would find it extremely difficult to realise his advantage.

This fine idea was straight-forwardly refuted by Fischer's **30 ... e5!**. Again we have to assume that this move had occupied only a marginal place in Petrosian's pre-considerations, and once again

we are obliged to ask "How come?" If in the former case Petrosian presumably might have overlooked 15 ... ♘a5, here such an oversight was simply out of the question. 30 ... e5 is too elementary to overlook. Petrosian could only have underestimated its strength. On what grounds? – on the theory that it would loosen Black's grip on d5 to his disadvantage. This is only of theoretical importance in this position, since White merely loses space and is unable to take advantage of it by 31 ♕xd5 in view of 31 ... ♖xd5 32 ♗xd5 e4!? (not 32 ... a5? 33 ♖b7 ♕e8 34 ♖a7! etc), and White's game is hopeless: 33 ♖b7 ♕c5 34 ♗xe4 a5 35 ♖b8+ ♔g7 36 ♖a8 ♕c4! 37 ♗f3 (37 ♗d3? ♕c1+ 38 ♔g2 ♕c6+) 37 ... a4, winning. On the other hand, after the game continuation **31 ♕c4 ♘b6** the intended 32 ♕a6 would mean very little, given the further advance of Black's e-pawn. Fischer had a clear advantage after **32 ♕c2** 32 ♕b4 ♕e6! **32 ... ♖c8 33 ♕d3 ♖c4 34 ♗g2 ♕c7**. (see also Pos. 46)

Like excessive sophistication, so might an out-and-out straight-forward policy be at times detrimental to one's position. We have seen this in Fischer's game against Korchnoi from Rovinj-Zagreb 1970 (Pos. 182). Here are three other examples sharing a common theme: an all too fast occupation of the central square e5. The first is taken from Fischer's game (as White) against Gligorić at the Varna Olympiad 1962 (Pos. 187).

187            W

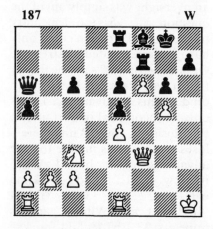

Before embarking on any operations in the centre or the kingside, White, as Gligorić pointed out,[9] would do best to consolidate his options by manoeuvring his knight to g4 (♘d1-e3-g4). By tackling the position 'head on' Fischer, instead of bolstering his chances, decreases them: **25 ♕g3? ♕b6 26 ♕xe5? ♕xb2.** Now the knight is pinned, and the centralised queen has to stay motionless, since an unmotivated move would enable Black to improve his position by ... e5. His immediate threat is 27 ... ♗b4.

**27 ♖ad1 h6!.** Black's game comes to life. He dismantles the protection of White's f-pawn and opens the h-file. Note that a

knight at g4 would have forestalled such activities. Fischer, apparently discouraged by these developments, went quickly downhill. **28 ♖e3 ♗b4 29 gxh6 ♕xc2 30 ♖g1 ♔h7 31 ♕g3 ♖g8 32 e5 ♗xc3 33 ♖xc3 ♕e4+ 34 ♖g2 ♖d8 35 ♖e3 ♕b1+ 36 ♔h2 ♖d1,** and Black won.

188            W

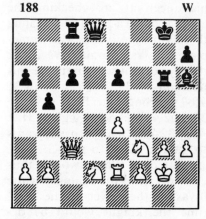

In Fischer-Portisch, Santa Monica 1966 (Pos. 188), it was by **28 e5?!** that Fischer wished to take immediate advantage of the weakened f6 and d6 squares. This was coupled, of course, with the idea of playing the knight to e4 next. However, by doing so he a) relinquished d5 to Black, b) gave up e5 as a potential outpost for a knight, c) let go of the opportunity to play 28 ♘b3 "in order to get the knight to c5. Black could not play 28 ... c5 29 ♘xc5 b4 because of 30 ♕d3." (Portisch)[10]. The game continued: **28 ... ♕d5 29**

♘e4 ♗g7 30 b3 ♖f8 31 ♕c2 ♖f4, and the knight had to retrace its steps: 32 ♘ed2. (see also Pos. 257)

189　　　　　　　　　　W

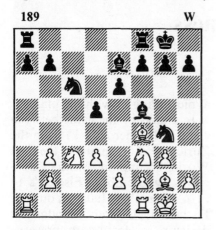

Fischer-Polugayevsky, Palma de Mallorca 1970 (Pos. 189) saw **13 e4**, again with a view to a quick and straightforward decision in the centre, intending to push e5 directly after this advance. Polugayevsky wrote: "if Fischer had foreseen the consequences, he would not have been in a hurry to make this move. The quiet 13 ♖fc1 looks more unpleasant for Black."[11] The continuation was as follows: **13 ... dxe4 14 dxe4 ♗g6 15 e5**, and Black got strong counterplay by **15 ... ♗d3 16 ♖fd1 ♗c2 17 ♖fc1 ♗xb3 18 h3 g5!**.

# Alertness

It was said about Fischer that "he plays best without an opponent". This, in a sense, is one of the greatest compliments he ever received. Its falsity speaks for his ability to carry out his plans smoothly enough to evoke the impression that he cares little for prospective counterplans of his opponent.

Being alert is a prerequisite to any sensible planning, as no plan can succeed if met by a superior counterplan. Moreover, trying to guess what's in the opponent's mind would certainly help one to avoid falling in with his plans.

In analysing the game between Tal and Fischer (Black) from the Zürich 1959 tournament, the then World Champion, Mikhail Botvinnik, wrote about Fischer's **18 ... ♘e5** in Pos. 190:[1] "Youthful Fischer adopts a truly Grandmaster decision, preferring to preserve his positional gains and avoiding the doubtful complications which could arise after 18 ... ♘e3 19 e5 (or even 19 ♖xf7) – complications towards which White has been much too obviously striving." Curiously, Botvinnik himself seemingly didn't pay great attention to the difference between his two suggested alternatives, something which youthful Bobby must have done at the board. After 19 e5?! Black gets the upper hand with 19 ... ♘xf1 20 ♗xg6 (20 exd6 ♕xd6 21 ♘db5 ♕f4+!, or 20 ♖xf1 ♖g7!, etc) 20 ... ♗g5+ 21 ♔b1 ♘d2+. Instead, 19 ♖xf7!! would have led to another Tal masterpiece: 19 ... ♔xf7 (if 19 ... ♖g5 20 ♖xe7+ ♔xe7 21 ♕xh6, or 19 ... ♘xd1 20 ♖f3!) 20 e5 ♘f5 (two

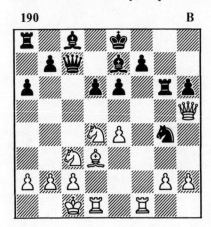

190　　　　　　　　　　B

144

other alternatives are a) 20 ... &g5
21 ©e4!! ©xd1+ 22 ©xg5+ hxg5
23 ♕h7+! ♖g7 24 &g6+ ♔f8 25
♕h8+, mating; b) 20 ... ©xd1 21
♕xg6+ ♔f8 22 ♕xh6+ ♔e8 23
&g6+ ♔d7 24 &f5!, winning in
all variations) 21 ©d5!! (21 g4?!
&g5+ 22 ♔b1 ©h4, is hard to
crack) 21 ... &g5+ (21 ... exd5
fails to 22 e6+!, and 21 ... ♕d8 to
22 ©f4 ♕g8 23 ©xf5 exf5 24
&c4+, while 21 ... ♕c5 leads to 22
©xe7 ©xe7 23 &xg6+ ©xg6 24
♖f1+ ♔g7 25 ♖f6, with a mate to
follow) 22 ♕xg5! ♖xg5 (no better
are 22 ... ♕xc2+ or 22 ... hxg5) 23
©xc7 ♖b8 (23 ... ©xd4 24 ©xa8
dxe5 – 24 ... ♖xe5 25 &g6+ ♔xg6
26 ♖xd4 ♖d5 27 ♖g4+! ♔f7 28
♖c4! – 25 ©b6 ♖g8 26 &e4,
winning the endgame) 24 ©xf5
exf5 25 &c4+ ♔g7 (or 25 ... ♔f8
26 ♖xd6! ♖xg2 27 ♖d8+ ♔e7 28
♖h8!, etc) 26 exd6 &d7 27 &e6
&c6 28 d7 ♖d8 29 &xf5!, with a
won endgame for White. (see also
Pos. 137, 231)

It is this situation that we
will rarely behold in Fischer's
games, that he becomes the reluctant co-author of a chess
masterpiece. And if anything might
stand as evidence for a player's
keen alertness, this fact does so. It
matters very little whether the
opponent he is facing is the
magician from Riga or a lesser
rival from a small town in Yugoslavia called Bitolj.[2]

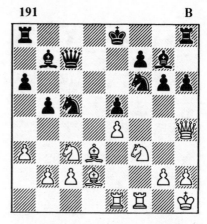

In Ničevski-Fischer, Skopje 1967
(Pos. 191), most natural and good
seemed 16 ... ♖d8. It would
indeed have been so, had it not
been for White's rather unexpected,
hidden shot 17 ©xe5!!. Black
goes downhill in a most elegant
fashion: 17 ... ♕xe5 18 ©d5! g5
(18 ... ©h5 is answered by 19 ♕f2,
or if 18 ... ©xd3 then 19 &c3 with
advantageous complications for
White) 19 ♕f2 ©xd3 20 cxd3 0-0
(if 20 ... ♕xb2, then 21 ♕c5! &f8
22 ♕c7 forces resignation) 21
©xf6+ (not 21 &c3 ©g4!) 21 ...
♕xf6 22 ♕xf6 &xf6 23 ♖xf6
♖xd3 24 &c3 ♔h7 loses to 26
&b4 ♔g7 27 ♖ef1. Fischer's **16
... g5 17 ♕g3 ©h5** stopped all
this.

Someone who would undoubtedly have liked to find in Fischer a
less alert opponent was his lifetime
rival, Samuel Reshevsky. Here are
two moments from their games.

**192**                    **B**

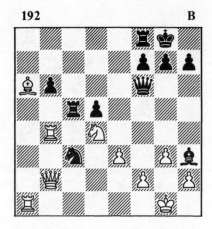

At the US Championship 1963-64 (Pos. 192) it was Fischer's move as Black. No move suggested itself more than 28 ... ♖b8, protecting the attacked b6 pawn. But wait! Reshevsky had set a very sly trap: 29 ♗f1! ♗xf1 30 ♖xb6!!, flattening Black on the spot. And what if Black refuses to play into White's hands? With 29 ... ♗c8 (29 ... ♗d7 30 ♖a6, while 29 ... ♗g4 30 f3 ♗xf3? 31 ♖xb6!! is a variation on the same theme) he might introduce another beautiful white combination: 30 ♖c1 ♘e4 31 f3 ♖xc1 32 ♕xc1 ♘c5 33 ♕xc5!!, and again White wins very convincingly. Black can play, of course, 32 ... ♘d6 (instead of 32 ... ♘c5), but his position remains highly unattractive after 33 ♘c6 ♖b7 34 ♖f4 ♕g5 35 ♕a3. Fischer's **28 ... b5** avoided this. Also see Pos. 261.

An alert player with a keen eye for both tactical and positional elements would naturally be doubly watchful.

A couple of years before the above game, in their notorious 1961 match, the following position (Pos. 193) was reached after White's (Reshevsky's) 19th move in the 3rd game.

**193**                    **B**

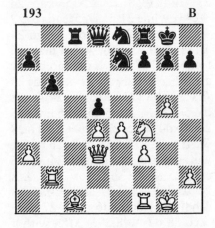

White strives for a very active set-up on the kingside, with (♗e3) ♖g2 and h4 'on the agenda' for the next couple of moves. His knight stands, for the time being, quite well-placed at f4. Yet, should it be provoked (by, say, ... ♘c7-e6), it would willingly take up an even more active post at h5.

Fischer takes the very timely opportunity to play **19 ... ♘g6!** when neither 20 ♘xd5, nor 20 ♘h5, work, in view of the neat tactical possibility: 21 ... ♖xc1! 22

♖xc1 ♕xg5+.

No player is able to see 'everything'. One is limited by one's own criterions and tendencies. There hasn't been a player, and there never will be one, whose way of thinking would enable him to encompass all the relevant ideas possible in any position. That, as a matter of fact, is the thing which makes the game such a fascinating mental engagement, being, as it is, an encounter between two very different types of consciousness, each with its own distinctive particularities. As far as alertness is concerned, this means that there will always be certain ideas that will slip past one's attention, and be left for the creativity of the opponent to take advantage of.

A case in point is Pos. 194, taken from Fischer's game against Petrosian (White), Portoroz 1958.

**194**                          **W**

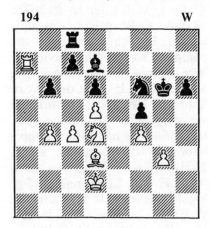

Fischer has managed to put up a stiff and reliable defence. His main concern was, as can be seen from this position, to hold together his weak pawns on the kingside, and primarily the pawn on f5. He had to pay attention to manoeuvres like ♘f3-h4+ and, under some circumstances, the advance g3-g4 (if, for instance, Black were to play now 45 ... ♘h5?, then 46 g4 ♘xf4 47 ♘xf5! ♔f6 48 ♘xd6! etc). As for the centre and queenside, the situation seems more or less stable and there is no reason to suspect a breakthrough on that side of the board. An advance of the c-pawn might well cost White not only that pawn, but the pawn on d5 as well. And yet – **45 c5!** – Petrosian had descried a method to create another weakness in Black's camp – e5! It seemed so unlikely a moment before that Fischer honestly had to admit that "[t]his pawn sac caught me completely by surprise".[2] Fortunately, his position was still tenable, notwithstanding the disclosure of new weaknesses: **45 ... bxc5 46 bxc5 dxc5 47 ♘f3! ♔f7! 48 ♘e5 ♔e7 49 ♘xd7 ♘xd7 50 ♗xf5 ♖f8! 51 g4**, and by 51 ... ♘f6![3] Black could achieve a technical draw. (see also Pos. 59)

(An interesting oversight, since the move 49 c5, "emptying" the e5 square for the white knight, would have been very much in

Fischer's style, and he would surely have considered it as White. Was Fischer so attuned to Petrosian's "cat and mouse" play that he did not expect Petrosian to play like . . . Fischer? – Editor).

**195**                                    **B**

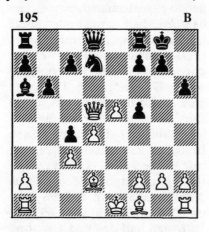

Intriguing and far from obvious is Fischer's decision in Pos. 195 (Saidy-Fischer US Championship 1965-66). Black is temporarily a pawn up, which White wants to win back by 15 ♗xc4. The most natural way to protect the pawn is by playing 14 ... ♕e7. This prevents 15 ♗xc4 by virtue of 15 ... c6! 16 ♕xc6 ♖ac8, winning a piece. Natural though it might look, Fischer must have been alert to another White possibility: 15 ♕c6! – one of those 'creeping moves' that are so easily overlooked when one has to play them, let alone prevent them! The endgame after 15 ... ♕e6 16 ♕xe6

fxe6 17 ♗e2, doesn't offer Black decidedly better chances, and 15 ... ♘xe5 doesn't deliver conclusive results either. But let's see first what Fischer did do. He played **14 ... ♖e8!!**, inviting White to take advantage of the weakened f7 square so that he can capture now on c4 without having to take ... c6 into consideration. Saidy complied, and Fischer unleashed a pretty and effective liquidating combination (see next chapter). However, the interesting question is: "What if Saidy hadn't taken up that invitation?". After all, White does better to leave Black's bishop blocked by its own pawn (c4), and go for another pawn – at f5. Fischer was certainly alert to that possibility, and as a reply to 15 ♕f3 had 15 ... ♕c8! up his sleeve. Now 16 ♕xf5 is answered by 16 ... ♘xe5! (17 ♕xc8 ♘d3+ + 18 ♔d1 ♘xf2+), while after 16 ♗e2 ♘f8 17 0-0 c5, Black clearly stands better. But this isn't yet the complete story. What about 15 ♕c6-? Now 15 ... ♖e6 can well be answered by 16 ♕f3, or even 16 ♕a4 b5 17 ♕c2, with reasonable counterplay. Black, however, has the following handsome combination at his disposal: 15 ... ♘xe5! 16 dxe5 ♖xe5+ 17 ♗e2 (17 ♗e3 f4, or 17 ♔d1 ♖d5 winning) 17 ... ♕e8! 18 ♕xe8+ (18 ♕f3 ♗b7! 19 ♕xb7 ♖xe2+ 20 ♔d1? ♖d8, etc) 18 ... ♖axe8 19 ♗e3 f4, and Black wins. What seemed a most straight-forward combination demanded Fischer's alertness to two positional moves: ♕c6 and ♕f3.

Alertness to potential resources on the part of his opponent was called for in Fischer's game (as Black) against Bisguier, Stockholm 1962. (Pos. 196).

**196**          **B**

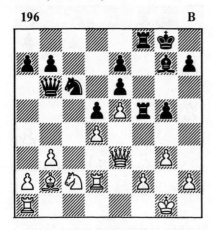

**23 ... h6!.** Black wants to dislodge the queen from e3 by ... ♖f3, and then play ... g4 ... h5 ... ♗h6. But why not play 23 ... g4 straight away? Since after 24 ♖f1 h5 (24 ... ♖f3 25 ♕g5!), White has 25 f4!. If Black refrains from 24 ...

gxf3 *e.p.* he might lose by gradual suffocation – his bishop is a worthless piece, and apart from some token activity he could show on the c-file, his pieces lack prospects for any co-ordinated activity elsewhere. But if he does play 24 ... gxf3 *e.p.* then 25 ♖df2 followed by 26 ♖xf3 (or 26 ♔h1 first) easily equalises for White. After Fischer's move, Bisguier played **24 ♕e2.** Interestingly, 24 ♕e1 could have led to 24 ... g4! 25 ♘e3 ♖f3 26 ♘xg4 h5 27 ♘e3 ♗h6, threatening 28 ... ♘xe5!. Bisguier's move prevented ... g4, but enabled Fischer to liquidate to a better endgame by **24 ... ♖xf2!** viz: **25 ♕xf2 ♖xf2 26 ♖xf2 g4 27 ♗c1 ♕b5 28 ♗f4 ♕d3 29 ♖d2 ♕g6 30 ♘e1 h5 31 ♘g2 ♔h7 32 ♖ae1 ♘d8 33 ♘h4 ♕e8 34 h3 gxh3 35 ♔h2 ♘f7 36 ♔xh3 ♗h6 37 ♖c2 ♕g8 38 ♖f1 ♕g4+ 39 ♔h2 ♘g5,** etc. (see also Pos. 105)

These last two examples are typical of a player of universal style, whose attention is simul-taneously directed towards various facets of the position which arises over the board.

# Reducing the Opponent's Options

"If you want to play for a win give your opponent counterplay!" was some advice once given by Karpov.[1] Fischer, as we shall see, fully conforms to it whenever the risks taken by allowing the opponent counterplay keep the game alive enough to stir up fighting chances where he indeed could hope to win (see pp. 176-84).

However, this doesn't mean that the precondition of any winning attempt should be to satisfy one's opponent's offensive intentions! On the contrary, whenever winning aspirations could be carried through to fulfilment straightforwardly, one should of course attempt to do so while reducing the opponent's counterplay.

In his game against Matulović at Vinkovci 1968, Fischer reached, as Black, the following position (197) after White's 20th move.

Black's better developed pieces allow him to mount immediate pressure along the c-file, as well as on the e4 pawn. He could combine the two by playing 20 ... ⌶c4, and 21 ... ♛c6, followed by ... ⌶c8.

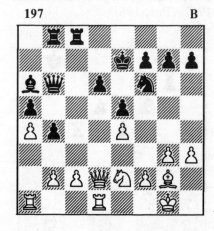

197      B

Fischer notes, however, White's options for some counterplay on the kingside, which might confuse the issue unnecessarily, e.g. 20 ... ⌶c4 21 g4 ♛c6 (Capturing on e4 with either the knight or the rook enables a quick transfer of White's knight to f5, and a position is reached where White has quite a lot to say. It is this 'speech' of his opponent that Fischer wants to hush to a minimal 'background noise'.) 22 ♘g3 g6 23 ⌶ac1 ⌶c8, and the threat of 24 ... ⌶d4 can be met by 25 c3 only. Black's advantage remains unquestionable, yet

White isn't without chances, notably tactical ones, consisting of moves like ♗f1 or even ♘f1-e3 that try to cash in on Black's weak pawn at d6. Fischer thwarts all this by playing **20 ... h5!**. (For this advance, see also Pos. 30-32). It is interesting to note that there is an implicit 'give and take' deal here, which is characteristic of Fischer's policy of switching one advantage for another (as we have seen in that chapter, pp.105-11). The 'Give' now is: "Give up any hope of counterplay on the kingside". The 'Take' is: "Take your chance to play 21 b3, by which ... ♖c4 is stopped". The only unfairness one can point out in this deal, and the likes, is a certain imbalance between the Give and Take ...! **21 b3 ♗xe2!**. An instructive way of claiming another 'Give' to his balance. White surrenders c3, and with it the half-open c-file, after which his options on both wings are reduced still further. He pinned his hopes on **22 c4!**, either holding the position half-closed, or getting some chances in the centre (after 22 ... bxc3 *e.p.* 22 ♘xc3 etc). Fischer is willing to part with his excellent bishop in order to obstruct these last chance-giving options of White. There followed: **22 ♕xe2 ♖c3 23 ♖d3 ♖bc8 24 ♖xc3 ♖xc3 25 ♔h2 ♕c5 26 ♖a2**, and by now White was reduced to a mere onlooker. (see also Pos. 78)

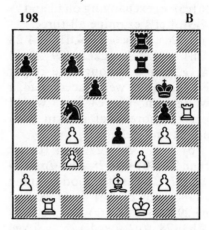

**198**          **B**

In Uhlmann-Fischer, Havana Olympiad 1966 (Pos. 198) the cardinal question after White's 26th move was: "Which minor piece is the better – White's bishop or Black's knight?" Examining the position superficially, one would probably tend to affirm the superiority of the second player's piece. At c5 the knight is ideally placed, while the bishop is tied down to the defence of the f3 pawn. However, White need only play ♗d1-c2, and the impression might change drastically. Suddenly the knight becomes a passive piece, tied down to the defence of his pinned pawn on e4. Can Black make any use of the time it would take White to play his bishop to c2, in order to activate his knight? There are three possible manoeuvres to hand: a) 26 ... ♘e6-f4; b) ... ♘d7-f6(e5); c) exchanging on f3 and ... ♘e4. Let's examine all three.

a) 26 ... ♘e6 27 ♗d1 ♘f4 28 ♖h1 exf3 29 gxf3 (29 ♗xf3 ♘xg2!), and although the knight is again quite well placed on f4, a white bishop at e4 or f5 would play a more vital role in both attack and defence.

b) 26 ... ♘d7 27 ♗d1 (better than 27 ♖b7 ♘f6 28 ♖h3 ♘xg4 29 ♖xa7? ♖b8! with good winning chances; or 27 ♔e1 ♘e5! 28 ♖b5 c5 29 fxe4 ♖f4! etc) 27 ... ♘f6 28 ♖h3 (28 ♗c2 ♘xg4!) 28 ... ♘xg4 29 ♔e2 exf3+ 30 gxf3 ♖e7+ 31 ♔d2 ♘e3 32 ♗e2, with chances for both sides, and the same holds true for 30 ... ♘e5 31 ♗c2+ ♔g7 32 ♗e4!.

c) 26 ... exf3 27 gxf3 ♘e4 28 ♔g2! ♘xc3 (28 ... ♘d2 29 ♖bh1!) 29 ♗d3+ ♔f6 30 ♖e1! and White should win – look how the relative value of the knight versus the bishop has changed! In all these variations the bishop is the piece that keeps White's game alive. Fischer decides that in order to cut down any options White might have, best would be to eliminate the bishop at the cost of an exchange. This reduces Black's options too, but from now on it's only he who has any winning chances at all. There happened: **26 ... exf3 27 gxf3 ♖xf3+!? 28 ♗xf3 ♖xf3+ 29 ♔e2**

♖g3 30 ♖h8 ♖xg4, and by accurate defence Uhlmann succeeded in drawing this endgame.

That wasn't the case in Fischer's game (again as Black) against Gligorić in the next Olympiad – Siegen 1970 (Pos. 199). Generally speaking, we have here a similar case with both sides having a pair of rooks and a minor piece. The difference is in White's inferior position. Yet, here too, it is the minor piece with which he can hope to get some counterplay.

**199**                **B**

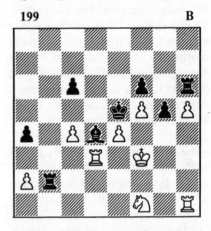

Black's most obvious move – 43 ... ♖xa2 – will be answered by 44 ♘h2!, when the threats at g4 and possibly f3 begin to play some part. For instance: 44 ... ♖f2+ 45 ♔g3 ♖xh2 46 ♖xh2 ♔xe4 47 ♖hd2 (47 ♖a3? ♗e5+) 47 ... ♗e3 48 ♔g4!, and the issue is far from being settled yet. Fischer cuts down White's options with **43 ...**

Xxh5! 44 Xxh5 Xf2+, reaching a technically won endgame: **45 ☗g3 Xxf1 46 Xh8 ☗xe4 47 Xa3 Xg1+ 48 ☗h2 Xc1 49 Xxa4 Xc2+ 50 ☗h1 c5 51 Xa3 ☗xf5**, and Black won fifteen moves later. (see also Pos. 164)

It is a remarkable fact that in these two games reduction of the opponent's counterchances was achieved by means of an exchange sacrifice. As we shall soon see, this became well-nigh a custom with Fischer, whether on the offensive or on the defensive. Gligorić seems to have been much under this impression when he explained Fischer's 21st move in his 17th match game (playing with the black pieces) against Spassky, World Championship, Reykjavik 1972 (Pos. 200):

**200**                 **B**

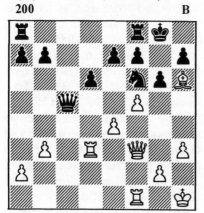

**21 ... ♛e5.** "Black remains faithful to his concept of giving up an exchange for a very solid position and some positional compensation. But, after White's 21 ☗h1, Black could well play 21 ... Xfc8 22 fxg6 fxg6 23 g4 (23 Xd5 ♛c3) 23 ... ♛e5, attacking White's e4."[2] This mild criticism was in sharp contrast with other views. Reuben Fine, for one, found that "21 ... ♛e5??" was "[a] totally unexpected sacrifice of the exchange with no apparent chess rationale behind it"[3], while Robert Byrne, in *Chess Life & Review*,[4] opined thus: "21 ... ♛e5?! – there is some risk of Black losing now because he gets only one pawn for the exchange in the coming endgame". I suspect that besides Gligorić very few were aware of the fact that Fischer willingly entered such endgames.

Tal had expressed his shock when the envelope of the adjourned position of his first cycle game against Bobby in the 1962 Curaçao Candidates (Pos. 201) was opened.

**201**                 **B**

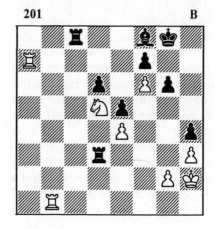

"I adjourned the game with an advantage, but Black's sealed move came like a thunderbolt: 41 ... ♖xd5!! 42 exd5 ♗h6, and Black, by placing his bishop on f4, supporting it with his g-pawn, and giving up his e-pawn by ... e4!, obtained an impregnable position".[5] The same radical methods of reducing his opponent's options were employed by Fischer at the same tournament against Efim Geller. Geller-Fischer, 3rd cycle, Curaçao 1962 (Pos. 202)

202                              B

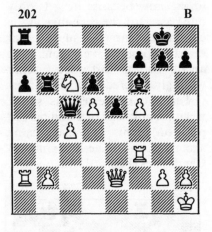

saw: **27 ... e4!!**. White threatened both 28 ♖a5 and 28 b4. Fischer played his move with the intention of giving up his rook on b6 for the knight. 27 ... ♖b7 would have been answered by 28 b4 ♕b6 29 ♖fa3, etc. **28 ♖f4 e3! 29 b4** 29 ♖a5 ♖xb2! **29 ... ♖xb4 30 ♘xb4 ♕xb4 31 ♕d3 a5 32 ♖f1 ♕c3 33 ♕xc3 ♗xc3**, and nothing has been left

of White's proud position. A draw is inevitable. This approach had almost yielded a whole point in Fischer's game against Vassily Smyslov in Round 14 of the Bled 1959 Candidates (Pos. 203). White's

203                              B

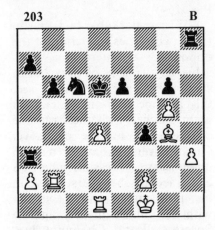

(Smyslov's) position looks quite healthy and promising, with threats such as 32 ♖e2 ♖e8 33 d5!. However: **31 ... ♖axh3!**, and Smyslov had to muster all his ingenuity to hold the endgame. **32 ♗xh3** 32 ♖e2?? ♖h1+ **32 ... ♖xh3 33 ♔e2 ♔d5 34 ♖b3 ♖xb3 35 axb3 ♘xd4+ 36 ♔d3 e5 37 b4 a5 38 bxa5 bxa5 39 ♖b1 e4+ 40 ♔c3 e3 41 fxe3 fxe3 42 ♖b6** 42 ♖d1? e2 43 ♖xd4+ ♔e5, and Black wins. **42 ... a4 43 ♖xg6! a3 44 ♖a6 ♘b3 45 ♖xa3 e2 46 ♖a1!!** draw.

Fischer was more successful in his game against Anthony Saidy from the US Championship 1965-66 (Pos. 204). With an elegant

204                          B

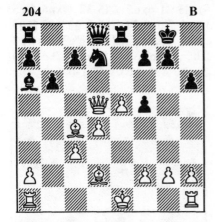

combination Fischer liquidates to a won endgame where his rook and bishop are superior to White's two rooks. This was prepared well in advance (see Pos. 195), and left White with no counterplay whatsoever. **15 ... ♘xe5! 16 ♕xd8.** No choice. 16 dxe5 ♕xd5 17 ♗xd5 ♖xe5+ is even worse for him. **16 ... ♘xc4+ 17 ♕xe8+ ♖xe8+ 18 ♔d1 ♘xd2 19 ♔xd2 ♖e2+ 20 ♔c1 ♖xf2.** Black's domination of the second rank was turned in a few moves into a gross material force – White's pawns on the kingside were all eliminated.

Reflecting over Pos. 200, one may say now with greater conviction that Fischer must have considered Spassky's bishop at h6 as the one piece whose presence on the board might have still offered White some potential winning chances. This, besides,

might have been based on calculation as well. After 23 ... ♕e5 in Gligorić's line, there could follow 24 g5! ♖c2 25 ♕f4 ♕xe4+ 26 ♖df3!, or 24 ... ♘d7 25 ♕f7+ ♔h8 26 ♖df3!, and Black is in trouble.

Fischer's knowledge and insight assured him that all reasonable White options in the actual game could quite easily be checked. And that indeed proved correct: in the endgame after **22 ♗xf8 ♖xf8 23 ♖e3 ♖c8 24 fxg6 hxg6 25 ♕f4 ♕xf4 26 ♖xf4 ♘d7**, Black had little to fear.

This pattern, like others discussed in the book, may of course occur in games of other players as well. In Ulf Andersson's games, for instance, one often comes across a typical exchange sacrifice of a rook against an actively posted knight, for similar purposes to Fischer's. Three examples:

W

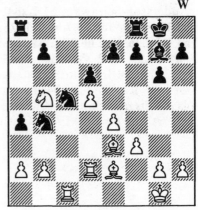

Andersson-Larsen, Linares 1983

Andersson-Larsen: **18 ♖xc5!** dxc5 **19 ♗xc5 ♘xa2 20 ♗xe7 ♖fc8 21 f4 ♗f8 22 d6 ♘b4 23 ♗h4 ♖c1+ 24 ♔f2 ♘c6 25 ♘c7 a3 26 bxa3 ♖xa3 27 e5 h6 28 ♗f6 ♔g7 29 ♗e7 ♗f8 30 ♘d5 ♖a8 31 h4 ♖c5 32 ♘f6+ ♔g7 33 ♗xf8+ ♖xf8 34 ♘d7 1-0**

♘xd5 **31 cxd5 ♗f5 32 ♕xb6 ♖c5 33 a5 ♖dc8 34 ♖b3 fxg3+ 35 fxg3 e4 36 ♘xe4 ♖c2 37 ♕e3 ♕a4 38 ♖b7 ♖8c7 39 ♖xc7 ♖xc7 40 ♘xd6 ♖c2 41 ♘xf5 1-0**

W

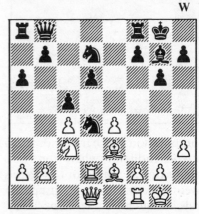

Andersson-Vaganian, Skelleftea 1989

W

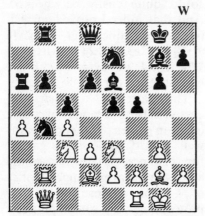

Andersson-Seirawan, Linares 1983

Andersson-Seirawan: **22 ♖xb4!** cxb4 **23 ♕xb4 ♕d7 24 ♖b1 ♖d8 25 ♕b3 ♔h8 26 ♘c2 h6 27 ♘b4 ♖a5 28 h4 f4 29 ♔h2 ♔h7 30 ♘bd5**

Andersson-Vaganian: **17 ♗xd4!** cxd4 **18 ♖xd4 ♗xd4 19 ♕xd4 ♕a7 20 ♕xd6 ♖ad8 21 ♘d5 ♔g7 22 ♖d1 ♕c5 23 ♕g3 a5 24 ♕c3+ f6 25 ♘f4 ♕e7 26 ♕xa5 ♕xe4 27 ♖d4 ♕e7 28 ♕c7 ♔h8 29 ♗f1 ♕e5 30 ♖xd7 ♖xd7 31 ♕xd7 ♕xf4 32 ♕xb7**, and White won.

# Playing to Win

The will to win at chess is as essential a quality as any particular talent in order to achieve sporting success. Fischer's will to win, as is quite well known, was exceptionally forceful, and it accounted for many of his competitive achievements, giving him a significant psychological edge over the majority of other players, whose will to win, and endure the hard labour this entailed, was considerably less than his.

Besides games where the issue was more a question of nerve attrition (as in his endgame against Geller, Palma de Mallorca 1970, and against Taimanov in their second match game, Candidates 1971), the will to win played in his games a most important role as far as creativity was concerned.

As we shall see in the next chapter, Fischer was at his most creative when having slightly inferior positions. We could get a better insight into the psychological aspects of this phenomenon and its relation to the will to win by examining the following example (Pos. 205). It is a quite familiar

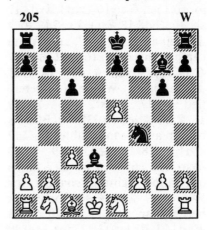

205        W

one, taken from the celebrated encounter between Fischer (White) and Milan Matulović, Palma de Mallorca 1970. After some poor opening play (see Pos. 86), Fischer landed in this unattractive position. His pawn plus doesn't really seem to make up for the visible drawbacks of his position. One gets the impression that White is virtually paralysed here. In *Informant* Matulović shows how beautifully White's king could be helped to end his brief sojourn on this board: 14 g3?

♗e2+ 15 ♔c2 ♘h3 16 d4 (or 16 f4 ♘f2 17 ♖g1 ♗d1 mate) 16 ... ♘xf2 17 ♖g1 ♗d1+ 18 ♔d2 ♗h6 mate![1] Black's distinct lead in development doesn't allow White to consider preparatory moves such as 14 h3. After 14 ... 0-0-0! (better than 14 ... ♗xe5 15 g3 ♗e2+ 16 ♔c2 ♘e6 17 d4, which is roughly equal) 15 g3 ♗e2+ (superior to 15 ... ♘e6 16 ♘xd3 ♖xd3 17 ♔e2! ♖hd8 18 ♘a3 ♗xe5 19 ♘c4 ♗f6 20 a4 c5 21 h4!?, and White can hold his own) 16 ♔c2 ♘d3 17 ♘a3 (17 ♘xd3 ♗xd3+ 18 ♔d1 ♗xe5 leaves White completely tied up) 17 ... ♘xf2 (17 ... ♘xc1? 18 ♖xc1 ♗xe5 19 d3!, and Black's bishop at e2 is in trouble) 18 ♖h2 ♗d1+ (18 ... ♗d3+ 19 ♘xd3 ♘xd3 20 e6! fxe6 21 ♖e2 holds out some fighting chances for White) 19 ♔b1 ♘e4 (somewhat better than 19 ... ♘d3 20 ♘xd3 ♖xd3 21 ♖h1 ♗f3 22 ♖e1, etc) 20 d4 (20 e6 f5!) 20 ... ♘xg3, there is nothing to compensate White for the pawn deficit, and the exposed position of his king on the b1-h7 diagonal.

This is one of those positions many players would have written off as hopeless, mentally giving them up, playing on with the clear presentiment that it is actually all to no avail – White is bound to lose some ten to fifteen moves from now. They would be ready to kick themselves later for their sloppy opening preparation, or look for other pretexts for their ill luck in the opening. With that approach, realistic though it might seem, one would doubtlessly lose the game. The creative process is impeded, and it is in a difficult position such as this where creativity is most needed. It is only through a tremendous will to win (or, in the first instance, not to lose), that one would hit upon a brilliant idea like the one Fischer finds here.

It would sound very simplistic, of course, and quite untrue, to assert that someone doesn't lose a game unless he's psychologically given it up. On the other hand, we have to bear in mind that the immense richness of the game allows for subtle, unexpected, and fantastic ideas, as well as for unimaginative, bad, and mistaken ones, to lie dormant side by side in one and the same position. And it remains up to the individual player to transfer them from latency into actuality. It stands to reason then, that a creative player with a strong will to win, would be quicker than a player of a different disposition to realise hidden resources in critical positions.

The idea that Fischer comes up with succeeds in doing the almost impossible: transforming an apparently lost position into quite a promising one; **14 ♘xd3 ♘xd3 15 f4!!**. This introduces a number of new elements into the position. As a result the position has to be assessed anew. First, it is the way in which White's two weak pawns have been connected to form a strong unit in the centre, that requires our attention. Either of these pawns – White's e- and f-pawns – were doomed to fall shortly. Yet now neither of them can be captured. See: 15 ... ♘xf4 16 d4 ♘xg2 17 h4! and 18 ♖h2 nets the knight. This audacious strengthening of White's centre entails a second, no less important, element: a temporary rook sacrifice – 15 ... ♘f2+ 16 ♔e2 ♘xh1 17 d4, and after 18 ♗e3 and 19 ♘d2, a good deal of material will have been claimed back, and White's chances might well be preferable.

Of his previous advantages, Black now has only his knight at d3 to pride himself on. There followed: **15 ... ♗h6 16 ♔c2 ♘xc1**, and again White is in some trouble. True, not as grave as three moves earlier, but the consequences of indifferent play could be as grave now as then. After 17 ♔xc1 Black wins back his pawn with a spicy dividend: 17 ... ♗xf4 cashes in either the e5 pawn or the h2 pawn, in view of the pinned d-pawn. Again an ingenious treatment is called for, which now as before Fischer doesn't fail to incorporate. Here it is in the shape of **17 ♖e1!**. By defending the e5 pawn, White is ready to meet 17 ... ♗xf4 by 18 g3. At the same time he keeps the black knight detained – e2 is taken away from it. This solution is certainly more dynamic than 17 g3 ♘e2 18 ♖f1 0-0-0 19 ♔d1 (19 ♘a3 g5! 20 f5 g4, or 19 ♖f2 ♘g1, etc) 19 ... ♘xf4 20 gxf4 ♖d3, and White's position is unenviable. Fischer is ready to risk another pawn for greater dynamic options. Now after the desperado 17 ... ♘xa2 18 g3! ♘xc3 19 bxc3, the position was evaluated by Matulović as unclear but about even.[2] For the pawn, Black has to cope with a hemmed-in bishop as against White's knight that would soon take up a lovely post at e4. The game continued: **17 ... 0-0-0 18 ♔xc1 ♗xf4 19 g3 ♗h6 20 ♔c2**. White is out of any immediate danger. Later, Fischer again tried to win from a slightly inferior position, risking the game's peaceful outcome. Yet this is a risk a player with a powerful will to win constantly confronts. His decisions are bound to be irrational at times. For instance, against Korchnoi at Sousse 1967 (Pos. 206).

Material would remain even after 21 ... ♖xb8 22 ♔xd1, with Black (Fischer) having somewhat the better prospects; for example 22 ... ♘d6 23 ♔c2 ♖e8 24 ♖e1 c4!

**206** B

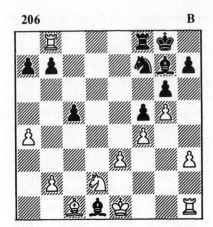

**207** B

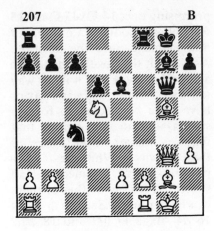

25 ♘b1! (25 ♘f3?! ♘e4) with ♗d2-c3 coming up next, is a plausible sequence. Fischer might have feared that an endgame of this type would sooner or later peter out to a draw. He gave preference to a continuation that he thought offered Black a sharper edge: **21 ... ♗xa4(?!) 22 ♖xf8+.** He must have believed the 3-to-1 pawn majority on the queenside and the presence of the two bishops gave Black real winning chances, or at least much more so than the conventional continuation above. Put to the test, this almost cost him the game. Only his stiff resistance, and Korchnoi's slightly inaccurate play in the last seven moves before time control, prevented a loss.

As much as willing the win was a rule with Fischer, exceptional cases where he didn't do his most to win, or look for an effective line to forestall an imminent loss, occurred, albeit rarely. One such exception was his game with the black pieces against Benko, Buenos Aires 1960 (Pos. 207). In the last round of a most disappointing tournament Fischer, clearly dispirited, couldn't muster enough will power to stand up to a rather mild offensive. He went under in a very straightforward fashion: **21 ... ♕f7? 22 ♗h6 c6 23 ♗xg7 ♕xg7 24 ♕xg7+ ♔xg7 25 ♘c7 ♔f6 26 ♘xa8 ♖xa8 27 b3**, and Black resigned.

Considerably more stubborn was the not so hard to find line starting with 21 ... ♔h8. Let's see: 22 ♘xc7 (22 ♘f4 ♕f7 23 ♘xe6 ♕xe6 24 ♗xb7 ♖ab8, is a dynamic equality) 22 ... ♗e5! 23 f4 (or 23 ♕h4 ♖f5! 24 f4 ♘e3!, with great complications. For instance 25

♘xa8 ♗xf4 26 ♖xf4 ♖xg5, or 25 ♗e4 ♗d4!, or 25 ♘xe6 ♘xg2 26 ♔xg2 ♕xe6 27 fxe5 ♖xg5+! 28 ♕xg5 ♖g8, etc) 23 ... ♗d4+ 24 ♔h2 ♖ac8 25 ♘xe6 ♕xe6 26 e4 ♘e3, which isn't at all bad for Black.

Instances like this one were, to be sure, few and far between in Fischer's career, whereas the extremities of cases like the previous one (Pos. 206), are to be justified, in a way, by Fischer's sportive record. For more risk-taking decisions see the chapter dealing with that subject, pp.176-84, and of relevance also are Pos. 307-11.

## ACTIVE DEFENCE AND COUNTERPLAY

In Fischer's case, to make a distinction between 'active defence' and 'active counterplay' would be quite an arbitrary affair. An analogy will probably make it clear why.

Imagine a football (Am. soccer) team in which the three defending players are not only capable of dismantling the opponent's attacks, but in no time they dribble past the attackers and pass the ball on to their own attacking players on the opponent's ground.

The same holds good for Fischer's artistry in this respect. The agility with which he usually dismantles his opponent's attacks, and at the same time initiates his own counterplay, is exemplary.

As far as ingenuity is concerned it can reasonably be argued that with regard to active defence and counterplay, Fischer excels not only in comparison with other great masters, but also when comparing it with other qualities of his own style. He is without doubt at his most ingenious when active defence and counterplay are called for. As we shall see in the next couple of examples, the question that constantly presents itself in these cases is: is Fischer defending, or is he actually attacking? And the very possibility of posing such a question speaks eloquently for his outstanding mastery in this field.

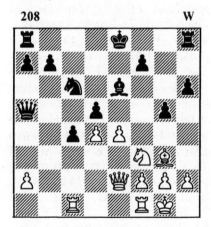

208         W

Against the Chilean Osvaldo Bazan at the Mar del Plata 1960, he reached Pos. 208 as Black, after having played the first part of the game very enterprisingly. In exchange for the pawn he has won, Black has compromised his kingside pawn structure, and his king is quite unsafely situated, as yet, in the centre. Bazan played 17 ♗c7!, rightly expecting to have some initiative after 17 ... b6 18 ♖fe1. Note, by the way, that 17 ♖fe1 at once would have given Black the opportunity to castle long. Interestingly, Fischer took up the challenge, and let White open the e-file without any further ado after:

**17 ... ♕xc7 18 exd5**

Hasn't he actually played right into his opponent's hands? 18 ... ♕d7 19 dxe6 ♕xe6 20 ♖fe1! ♕xe2 (20 ... ♔d7? 21 d5! wins at once, and 20 ... 0-0-0 21 ♕xe6 fxe6 22 ♖xe6 ♘xd4 23 ♖xc4+ ♘c6 24 h4! leaves White with the better prospects) 21 ♖xe2+ ♔d7 22 d5 ♘a5 23 ♘e5+ ♔c7 24 d6+!, or 21 ... ♔f8 22 ♖xc4, both offer White the better chances in the endgame. While 18 ... 0-0-0 19 dxe6 (19 dxc6 b5!, and Black can hold his own) 19 ... ♘xd4 20 ♘xd4 ♖xd4 21 ♕e3! gives a very promising position, e.g. 21 ... ♖f4 22 ♖fd1!, or 21 ... ♕f4 22 exf7, or 21 ... ♖d3 22 ♕xa7, or 21 ... ♖h4 22 g3, etc. So Black is left with very little choice if he wants to fight for survival, which explains why he

plays **18 ... g4(!) 19 ♘d2 ♘xd4 20 ♕e4**. And now everything seems just as White wanted it to be. Yet Fischer's next move makes it pretty clear that it was his opponent who was playing into his hands all along!

**20 ... ♕f4!!**

And we have to ask: is Fischer defending, or is he actually attacking?

**21 ♖xc4**

No matter how White plays, the position soon liquidates to an advantageous endgame for Black. For instance 21 ♕xf4 ♘e2+ 22 ♔h1 ♘xf4 23 dxe6 ♘xe6 24 ♖xc4 h5, while 21 dxe6 loses to 21 ... ♕xe4 22 ♘xe4 ♘e2+; whereas 21 ♕e1 allows Black to consolidate his advantage with 21 ... b5.

**21 ... ♕xe4 22 ♘xe4 ♘e2+ 23 ♔h1 ♗d7 24 ♖e1 ♔f8!**, and Fischer converted his material advantage into a full point.

**209**         **W**

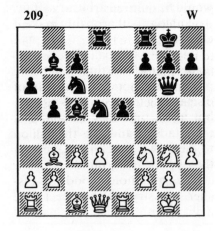

Even more complicated is the next example, which had been played two years earlier, at Portorož 1958, against the Hungarian veteran Laszlo Szabo, who had the black pieces (Pos. 209).

A brief glance at the position is enough to give us the correct impression that Black has the better of it. He has completed his development, and his pieces occupy excellent positions: two effective bishops, a rook at d8 that sends vicious messages along the d-file (most resoundingly to the weak pawn on d3), an ideally posted queen that reinforces the threats of both the rook and the dark-squared bishop (an immediate threat is 15 ... ♕xg3), and a centralised knight at d5 that is ready to jump at the appropriate moment to f4.

It seems that White, after having played the opening rather poorly, should entertain no aggressive ideas in this position, and would rather do best to find a plan to neutralise Black's initiative, as far as that is possible.

And indeed his position, for all its drawbacks, does offer such a possibility in the shape of the solid and good 15 ♗g5!. (After 15 ♘e4 ♗e7 the knight would soon be repulsed by ... f5). Let's see to what extent he succeeds in defending himself after this move:

a) 15 ... ♖d7 (15 ... ♖d6 16 ♘e4) 16 ♖xe5!! ♘xe5 17 ♘xe5 ♕xg5 18 ♘xd7 ♘xc3! 19 ♕g4!, or 18 ... ♘e3 19 ♕h5!, and Black has some reason for concern here.

b) 15 ... h6? 16 ♗xd8 ♕xg3 17 ♗h4.

c) 15 ... f6 16 ♘e4! ♗xf2+ (16 ... ♗b6 17 ♘h4) 17 ♘xf2 fxg5 18 ♘xe5, and White is all right.

d) 15 ... ♘f4! is the only attempt to keep some initiative. 16 ♗xf4 ♖xd3(!) 17 ♘h4 (not 17 ♕e2 exf4 18 ♗c2 fxg3!) 17 ... ♖xd1 18 ♘xg6 ♖xa1 19 ♖xa1 hxg6 20 ♗g5. There are very good chances White could hold this position to a draw, notwithstanding his slight material disadvantage.

It is remarkable that fifteen-year-old Bobby rejects this quite safe defensive line in favour of an ultra-sharp continuation that holds much greater risks, yet much greater promises too.

**15 d4!!**

Certainly the most daring solution to the position's problems, if a solution it indeed is. For how can you describe as a "solution" a move that not only does nothing to resolve White's problems, but renders the existing ones more critical? There can be no doubt that the d-pawn would not enjoy a long life after this advance, in view of its immediate exposure to the combined threats of the black pieces. Yet when we follow this line as it unfolds, it becomes abundantly clear that Fischer took note of all the possible resources Black could summon for his attack. It was, at the same time, the only possibility for White to aspire to a win if Black overreached, or if he missed some tactical finesse along the way.

**15 ... exd4 16 cxd4 ♘bd4**

Besides attacking d4, he clears the diagonal of the bishop on b7.

**17 ♗e3 ♘xd4! 18 ♘xd4 ♗xd4 19 ♗xd4 c5 20 ♗xc5!!**

So this was Fischer's point. By giving up the queen for rook and bishop, he quickly completes his development, and creates dangerous threats of his own.

**20 ... ♖xd1**

He can't try for more. 20 ... ♛c6? loses to 21 ♛f3!.

**21 ♖axd1 ♘d3**

And now 21 ... ♛c6? is bad in view of 22 ♘e4, when again it is White who comes out on top.

**22 ♗xf8 ♘xe1 23 ♖d8! h5 24 ♗b4+ ♚h7 25 ♖d6!**

Now he isn't satisfied with the draw that results from 25 ♗xe1 h4 26 ♖d4 hxg3 27 ♖h4+ ♚g8 28 ♖f4!. Quite a remarkable turn of events!

**25 ... ♛b1!**

He sidesteps Bobby's sly attempt to lure him into 25 ... f6? 26 ♗xe1 h4 27 ♖d4, with an easy win.

**26 ♖d1**, and the game was drawn in a few moves.

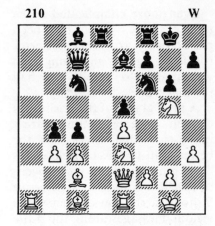

In his game against Charles Kalme at the US Championship 1958-59, Fischer (White) was faced with a most ingenious innovation. (Pos. 210). Kalme's last move – 20 ... b4!? – would certainly have enjoyed a better reputation had it not been for the decisive way in which Fischer refuted it. Had it not been for this immediate death blow, it might have taken many tries to find the right way to meet Black's imaginative bid to seize the initiative.

Before joining Fischer in his long search for the dynamic roots of this position, let's check first various other possibilities:

a) 21 cxb4 cxb3 22 ♗xb3 ♘d4 23 ♛a2 (or 23 ♛c4 ♛xc4 24 ♗xc4 h6 25 ♘f3 ♘xf3+ 26 gxf3 ♗xb4 and 27 ... ♗xh3) 23 ... ♗xb4 24 ♖d1 h6 25 ♘f3 ♘xf3+ 26 gxf3

&xh3, and Black is a pawn to the good.

b) 21 ♘xc4 bxc3 22 ♕e3 ♘d4! 23 ♕xc3 &b4!, and Black wins the exchange. Or 22 &e3 ♘d4 23 &xd4 exd4 24 e5? ♘h5!, and 25 ... d3 will win.

c) 21 bxc4 bxc3 22 ♘d5 ♘xd5 23 cxd5 ♘d4 24 ♕d1 (if 24 ♕d3 &d7), and Black stands better.

d) 21 &d2 h6 22 ♘f3 bxc3 23 &xc3 cxb3 24 &xb3 ♘xe4 25 ♘d5 ♘xc3 (but not 25 ... ♖xd5 26 ♕xe4!), and Black is a clear pawn up.

e) 21 ♘d5 ♘xd5 22 cxd5 ♖xd5, and now: I – 23 ♕xc4 ♖c5 24 ♕h4 &xg5 25 &xg5 ♖xc3. White has no compensation for the pawn. II – 23 bxc4 ♖d8 24 ♘xh7 ♔xh7 25 ♕h5+ ♔g7, and White would have a draw at best.

There are very few players who would see all this, and still ask themselves: "How do I manage to *win* this position?" Most would be happy to find a good defensive possibility. Not so Fischer. Looking, as always, for active counterplay, he finds a ten move deep line, which involves a piece sacrifice. And when the storm subsides, it transpires that White has a superior endgame position in hand.

**21 ♕xc4! h6 22 ♘d5 ♘xd5 23 exd5 hxg5 24 ♕xc6 ♕xc6 25 dxc6 bxc3 26 ♖xe5 &f6 27 ♖ea5 ♖fe8!** (Pos. 211).

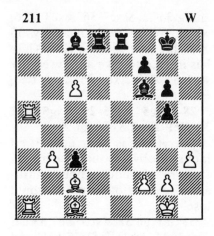

211       W

Very sharp. Both Fischer and Kalme must have foreseen this position well in advance. Kalme probably at home, Fischer when entering this variation with 21 ♕xc4. For his pawn, Black has some serious threats. If, for instance, 28 ♔f1, then 28 ... ♖d2!! (but not 28 ... &f5 29 c7!) 29 &xd2 cxd2 30 ♖d5 (or 30 ♖d1 ♖e1+!) 30 ... &xa1 31 ♖xd2 &c3, and Black ought to win. 28 &e3 leads to a complicated endgame with double-edged positions: 28 ... ♖d6 29 c7 (29 ♖c5 &f5! is another, quite unclear possibility) 29 ... ♖c6 30 ♖c5 ♖xc5 31 &xc5 ♔h7! 32 ♔f1 (the tempting 32 ♖a8? loses to 32 ... ♖e1+ 33 ♔h2 &e5+ 34 g3 &b7!) 32 ... &e5 33 &b6 (33 ♖e1? &a6+ 34 ♔g1 &h2+ wins, while 33 ♖a7 is answered by 33 ... &f5!) 33 ... ♖e6 34 &a5 ♖a6, and Black is threatening 35 ... ♗xc7 36 ♗xc3 ♖c6, which White can't meet by 35 ♗d3 because of 35 ... c2!. White has instead to take a draw earlier with 34 ♖a8 ♖xb6 35 ♖xc8 ♖c6, etc.

**28 ♗xg5 ♗xg5 29 ♖xg5 ♖d2 30 ♖c1 ♖ee2 31 ♗xg6!!**

Everything is clear now. It all looks so obvious that one hardly stops to take note of one remarkable fact: any other move would lose!

**31 ... fxg6 32 ♖xc3 ♔h7 33 b4! ♖e1+ 34 ♔h2 ♖xf2 35 b5!**, and the two connected passed pawns proved superior to Black's bishop.

No less exciting is the following, taken from Fischer's game against Filip, Candidates, Curaçao 1962 (Pos. 212).

**212**                               **W**

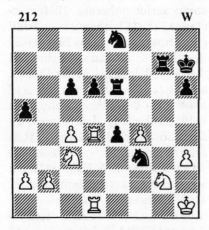

White's (Fischer's) position looks difficult, and it would look even more so after 32 ♖xe4 ♖eg6 33 ♖e2 (33 ♖xe8 ♖xg2 mates at g1 or h2) 33 ... ♖g3, *fini*.

**32 f5!**

Freeing f4 for the knight in case of 32 ... ♖g3, and also a couple of other future events . . .

**32 ... ♖e5**

Acting under the illusion that he is likely to win material or mate White's king. After 32 ... ♘xd4 33 fxe6 ♘xe6 34 ♘xe4 ♖d7, he has a draw for the asking.

**33 ♖xe4 ♖xf5**

Deliberately giving up the knight. As we have seen in other examples, Fischer is willing to fall in with the plan his opponent imposes on him. One gets the impression that he acts passively, under the full command of his adversary. This quality made his art an extremely dangerous weapon. Usually, when his opponent started realising what was happening, it was all too late. (see also remark to Pos. 121).

**34 ♖xe8 ♖g3**. If 34 ... ♖fg5 35 ♖f8 ♖g3 36 ♖xf3 **35 ♘f4!!**. Fischer's extremely subtle and problem-like resource. He is killing three birds with one stone: a) defending h3; b) vacating g2 for his king; c) enabling the other knight to gain an important tempo by forking Black's rooks on e2.

**35 ... ♖xf4** 35 ... ♖fg5 is met by 36 ♘ce2. **36 ♘e2 ♖xh3+ 37 ♔g2 ♖fh4 38 ♖xd6**.

It's too late to ask now whether he is defending or attacking. It is obviously the latter. Besides winning a pawn he threatens mate in two starting with 39 ♖e7+. It's not just ironical that it is White who all of a sudden has a mating attack. It's quite incredible! **38 ... ♘e1+ 39 ♔f1 ♖h1+ 40 ♔f2 ♖4h2+ 41 ♔e3 ♖h3+ 42 ♔e4 ♔g7**, and Black resigned. After 43 ♖e7+ ♔f8 44 ♖a7 he soon gets mated.

From a much earlier day comes our following example. It's Fischer's over-the-board meeting with Arpad Elo, the "father of the Elo system", at the New Western Open, Milwaukee 1957 (Pos. 213).

**213** B

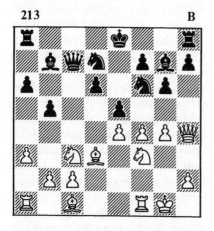

White (Elo) threatens to get a strong initiative with 14 g5 and 15 f5. How should Black tackle the situation? Very wild is 13 ... h5 14 g5 (14 fxe5?! hxg4 15 exf6 ♘xf6!,

etc) 14 ... ♘g4 15 h3 (safer than the immediate 15 f5 gxf5 16 exf5 d5) 15 ... ♕c5+ 16 ♔g2 (16 ♔h1? exf4!, and Black stands better) 16 ... ♘e3+ 17 ♗xe3 ♕xe3 18 f5 gxf5 19 ♖ae1 ♕b6 20 exf5, and White has the edge. Too timid is 13 ... h6. White's prospects are better after either 14 ♕g3 or 14 f5 g5 15 ♕g3.

Perfectly playable, however, is 13 ... d5!?, when Black enjoys a free game, where his chances are by no means inferior to White's. Characteristically, Fischer chooses, even at that early stage of his career, a line that offers the sharpest active counterplay.

**13 ... exf4!?**

Positionally a very committal decision. He opens the a1-h8 diagonal for his bishop, clears e5 for his knight, and takes the sting out of White's impending pawn storm. At the same time though, this seriously weakens the pawn on d6.

**14 ♗xf4 0-0!**

14 ... ♘e5 15 ♘xe5 dxe5 16 ♗g5, with advantage to White.

**15 ♕g3**

Quite logical, of course. In all probability he expected now the 'only' move 15 ... ♘e8.

**15 ... ♘e5! 16 ♘xe5 dxe5 17 ♗xe5 ♕c5+ 18 ♖f2**

18 ♔h1 is strongly met by 18 ... ♘xe4!.

**18 ... ♘h5!**

And the defence turns into attack! Fischer's plan now consists of a couple of very neat tactical blows that lead to a superior endgame. By the way, 18 ... ♘xg4? 19 ♗xg7 ♘xf2 20 ♗xf8 would have won material for White.

**19 ♗d6**

Virtually forced, since 19 gxh5 ♗xe5 followed by 20 ... ♗d4 wins the exchange.

**19 ... ♕xc3! 20 bxc3**

No better is 20 gxh5 since after 20 ... ♕xb2 21 ♖af1 ♗d4 22 ♗xf8 ♖xf8 23 ♕c7 ♗xf2+ 24 ♖xf2 ♕c1+ 25 ♔g2 ♕g5+ 26 ♔f1 ♗c8, the white king comes under cross-fire of both the queen and the bishop.

**20 ... ♘xg3 21 ♗xf8 ♖xf8 22 hxg3 ♗xc3 23 ♖b1 ♗d4**, and Black's superior pawn structure proved sufficient for a win.

**214**                                    **B**

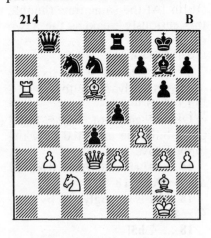

Another example of bold defensive play is to be seen in Donner-Fischer, Bled 1961 (Pos. 214).

White has two nasty threats: 27 ♖a8! and 27 ♖c6. Fischer could extricate himself from these by playing the simple 26 ... ♕b5. After 27 ♕xb5 ♘xb5, there could follow either:

a) 28 ♗c6 d3 29 ♗xb5 (29 ♘b4? d2) 29 ... dxc2 30 ♖c6 (30 ♗a3 ♗f8! 31 ♗c1 ♖d8) 30 ... exf4 31 ♗xf4 (31 ♖xc2 fxe3! 32 ♔f1 ♖e6) 31 ... g5! 32 ♗d6 (32 ♗xg5 ♖e5) 32 ... ♖e6, which is about equal; or –

b) 28 fxe5? d3 29 ♘d4 d2 30 ♗f3 ♘xd6 31 exd6 (31 ♖xd6 ♘xe5 32 ♗d1 elicits 32 ... ♗h6!, etc) 31 ... ♖xe3, and Black wins.

Fischer, however, plays **26 ... ♘c5!? 27 ♗xc5 e4!**, and once again we are faced with the question "is he defending, or is he actually attacking?" One thing is beyond doubt – if in the line after 26 ... ♕b5 White wouldn't have any great trouble finding the right way, here he could very easily go wrong. And his first opportunity to do so presents itself at this juncture: on 28 ♕c4 comes 28 ... ♘xa6 29 ♕xa6 d3 30 ♘d4 d2 31 ♕e2 ♖c8 32 b4 ♖xc5!, and Black wins. Donner played, instead, the correct **28 ♗xe4**, after which followed **28 ... ♘xa6 29 exd4!**. Donner rises to the occasion. He gives up the exchange in the most profitable way – creating two connected passed pawns on the queenside. His chances would have been considerably drearier after 29 ♕xa6 ♖xe4 30 ♗xd4 ♗xd4 31 exd4 ♕xb3, and White's end is near.

We see how Fischer constantly forces his opponents to respond creatively to the challenges his extremely active defences set. It shouldn't escape our attention, at the same time, that this approach can involve considerable risk on his part. For more about this see pp.176-84 in our next chapter. Here, for example, it was White who had theoretically the best chances after 29 ... ♘xc5 30 dxc5 ♕c8 31 c6 ♕xh3, which Fischer managed to neutralise later.

**215**                                B

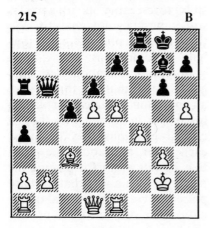

A very systematic example of active defence appeared in the 4th cycle Korchnoi-Fischer encounter from Curaçao 1962 (Pos. 215).

**25 ... dxe5!**

The beginning of a most ingenious defensive plan. First, Fischer clears the 6th rank in order to be able to recapture on g6 with a piece, if necessary, since doing so with a pawn carries great risks (and this time merely negative ones: hxg6, ♖h1, ♕g4-h4, etc). Yet once again, by playing the way he plays, he takes other risks: White's central pawns become a strong positional factor. Black will have to find a way to neutralise this.

**26 dxe5 a3!**

A very important move in connection with the overall scheme: the bishop on c3 has to be divested of its pawn protection.

**27 b3 ♕b7!**

The third step – attacking d5. As the pawn can't advance, neither now nor on the next move, its exchange for Black's e-pawn is inevitable.

**28 ♕f3 e6!**

The point of this simple-looking but far from obvious plan is that White cannot play 29 d6 because of 29 ... ♕xf3+ 30 ♔xf3 ♖xd6! 31 exd6 ♗xc3.

**29 ♖ad1 exd5 30 hxg6 ♖xg6 (!) 31 ♖xd5 ♕c8**

The chances are even. The game was drawn ten moves later.

We have again to go back a few

years for our next example, which is from Fischer-Tal, Portorož 1958 (Pos. 216).

**216** W

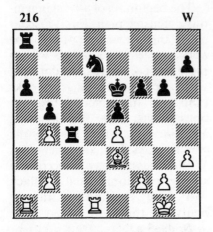

It seems that the only way White could defend both b4 and e4 is by playing a rook to c1, so as to strike back at c6 after the black rook captures one of those pawns. 29 ♖ac1 is better than 29 ♖dc1, which is answered simply by 29 ... ♖xe4!. So, after 29 ♖ac1 ♖ac8 (not 29 ... ♖xe4? 30 ♖c7! ♖d8 31 ♗c5! wins, or 30 ... ♘f8 31 ♗c5 ♔f5 32 ♖f7 ♘e6 33 ♗e7 ♖d4 34 ♖e1! e4 35 f4!! wins) 30 ♔f1 f5, White is still alive, but he can't kick too hard. He has an arduous defensive task before him that offers very little by way of active counterplay, let alone winning chances.

Fischer comes up with another idea – giving up the two pawns on the queenside for the full activation

of his rooks.

**29 ♖d2! ♖xb4 30 ♖ad1 ♘f8 31 ♖d6+ ♔f7 32 ♖b6!**

First he doubled the rooks on the d-file, now he doubles them on the sixth rank. They couldn't be activated more vigorously than that.

**32 ... ♖xb2 33 ♖1d6 a5 34 ♖b7+! ♔g8 35 ♖xf6?**

Fischer's policy has brought him to the verge of victory, but now, in severe time trouble,[1] he stumbles. 35 ♗h6! with the idea of 36 ♗g7, 37 ♗xf6, 38 ♖g7+, would have crowned his efforts with a full point.

The quality of placing the pieces in such a way that they would co-operate exceptionally well under certain, highly specific circumstances which weren't possibly foreseeable in advance, is sometimes beyond analysis. We then refer to a player's mysterious 'gift' for doing this.

Botvinnik said about Petrosian and Karpov that the former had an unexplainable talent for placing his pieces in such a way that in critical positions they defended each other, and about the latter that he has a gift for placing his pieces in such a way that they are poised to create positional domination. He suspected that neither of them was aware of how he accomplished it. The same could be said about Fischer's gift for creating positions in which active chances for defence and counterplay were regularly present.

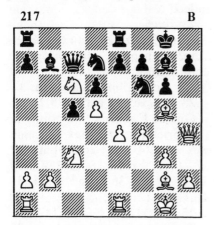

**217** **B**

In Johannessen-Fischer, Havana Olympiad 1966 (Pos. 217), White threatens to break through in the centre. There seems to be no reason to doubt his well-marked initiative, and it looks as though Black would indeed face great difficulties in many possible sequences emanating from this position. Yet with one little move – **18 ... ♔h8!!** – Fischer established a definite fact: Black would stand better in all likely continuations!

It isn't just the difficulty of finding a move like 18 ... ♔h8 that should evoke our wonderment. More than that it is the creation of a position in which such a move could prove so effective that demands our recognition. It must be assumed that when heading for

this position Fischer sensed that the exposed white king and the somewhat awkward placement of his bishop at g5 (although it is active, it is 'stuck' between the queen at h4 and the pawn at f4) would be two factors that would act in Black's favour. It is still puzzling how decisive these two factors are, and how marvellously Black's pieces start to co-operate once White carries out his intended plan.

What is the king actually doing at h8?

It helps to do three things: firstly, the bishop on g5 now runs some risk of being trapped by ... ♘g8, and ... f6. Secondly, some tactical possibilities of White's, based on a knight check on e7, are eliminated. Thirdly, the advance of White's e-pawn (e5-e6) wouldn't terminate with a capture on f7 (exf7) *with check.*

**19 e5**

There was little time left for strengthening the position with 19 ♖ad1. Black replies 19 ... ♘g8!, and if 20 ♘xe7 ♘xe7 21 ♗xe7 f6! 22 ♘b5 ♕b6, Black wins a piece.[2]

**19 ... dxe5 20 fxe5**

Isaac Boleslavsky was still under the impression that White's position was superior, when he gave this move a '??', and recommended instead 20 ♘xe5!. He further gave a) 20 ... ♔g8 21 ♘c6!; and b) 20 ...

♘xe5 21 fxe5 ♘d7 22 e6 fxe6 23 ♖xe6 ♗f6 24 ♖ae1; as proof of White's advantage.[3] This mistaken view only highlights the subtlety of Fischer's play.

After 20 ... ♔g8 (back again!), the 'solid retreat' 21 ♘c4, instead of Boleslavsky's 21 ♘c6, enables Black to gain the advantage by 21 ... ♘b6!. For if 22 d6!? ♕c8! 23 ♘xb6 axb6 24 ♗xb7 (24 dxe7 ♘g4!) 24 ... ♕xb7 25 dxe7 ♘g4!! 26 ♕xg4 ♗d4+ 27 ♔f1 ♕h1+ 28 ♔e2 ♕g2+ 29 ♔d3 ♕xb2 30 ♖ac1 ♖a3, and Black wins. If on the other hand White wishes to follow Boleslavsky's suggestion of 21 ♘c6, Black plays 21 ... c4!, and after 22 ♔h1 (22 ♘xe7+? ♖xe7 23 ♖xe7 ♕c5+) 22 ... ♕b6! 23 ♖ab1 (now 23 ♘xe7+ is met by 23 ... ♖xe7! 24 ♖xe7 ♕xb2 and wins) 23 ... e6!, Black has much the better of it. For example, 24 b3 exd5 25 ♘e7+ ♖xe7! 26 ♖xe7 d4 (not 26 ... ♕b4 27 ♘xd5!) 27 bxc4 ♗xg2+ 28 ♔xg2 ♕c6+ 29 ♘d5 ♘xd5 30 cxd5 ♕c2+ 31 ♔f3 ♕xb1 32 ♖xd7 ♕f1+, and mate next move.

**20 ... ♘xd5! 21 ♘xd5 ♕xc6**

With the king at h8 he doesn't have to fear ♘xe7+.

**22 e6**

This still looks quite ominous for Black . Yet we again realise that Fischer's sense and foresight were correct. Black's counterattack proves to have more punch than White's attack.

**22 ... ♘e5**

After 22 ... fxe6 23 ♘f4 Black is indeed lost.

**23 ♖xe5**

23 exf7 ♖f8! 24 ♘f4 (24 ♖xe5 ♗xe5 transposes into the game continuation) 24 ... ♘f3+ 25 ♗xf3 ♗d4+!, and Black wins.

**23 ... ♗xe5 24 exf7 ♖f8 25 h3**

One of Fischer's fine points in this brief but complex skirmish was: 25 ♘f4 ♗d4+ 26 ♔h1 ♖xf7!! 27 ♗xc6 ♗xc6+ 28 ♘g2 ♖f2 29 ♖g1 ♗xg2+ 30 ♖xg2 ♖f1+ 31 ♖g1 ♖xg1, mate.

**25 ... ♖xf7 26 ♘f4 ♖xf4!!**

The *coup de gràce*. After 27 ♗xc6 ♗d4+ 28 ♔h2 ♖f2+ 29 ♔g1 ♖xb2+ White's predicament would grow by the move. Johannessen decided to resign.

There is also something quite deceptive about the next example – Fischer-Czerniak, Netanya 1968 (Pos. 218). The exceptionally smooth transition from the early middlegame to the late makes it difficult to appreciate Fischer's artistry. Yet for its sophistication, originality, and complexity, the play that follows presents perhaps one of the most distinctive examples of active defence in the whole of chess literature.

Czerniak has played the opening phase with great verve, and he is about to start with an offensive in the centre with ... e5. There can be

218                 W

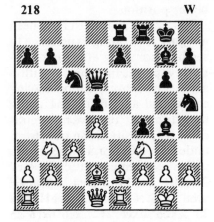

no mistaking that by Black's doing so, the d5 pawn would suffer the consequences, and after an exchange on e5, this pawn would remain a very weak point in Black's pawn structure. There can be no mistaking either the fact that the initiative would be in Black's hands. Or would it? Well, before watching Fischer's magical manoeuvring, let's see first the alternatives White had here. In order to prevent 15 ... e5 White can play 15 ♘e5. But after 15 ... ♗xe2 16 ♕xe2 f3! 17 ♘xf3 e5! Black has a very good game for the pawn.

Another possibility is the modest looking 15 ♗c1!?, when 15 ... e5 is answered by the standard 16 dxe5 ♘xe5 17 ♘bd4, with quite a sound position, but nothing more.

**15 ♘c1!!**

It isn't very easy to define

genius at chess. This though is a very good example of it. The plan Fischer contrives here is a combination of positional elements which viewed one by one are each a *deja vu* idea. Put together, they are an exceptional 'never seen before' conception. To begin with – the knight is headed for d3 to support the other knight for an eventual ♘f3-e5. But isn't it a move too late? Black, of course, is going to play ... e5 *before* White plays ♘d3.

**15 ... ♗xf3 16 ♗xf3 e5**

Black's position looks like an attacking player's dream. After 17 dxe5 ♘xe5 18 ♗xh5 gxh5 19 ♕xh5 ♖e6! (19 ... f3? 20 ♘d3! fxg2 21 ♗f4!), White is not long for this world: ... f3, ... ♖h6, and ... ♖fe8, are all hovering like black crows over his head. Refraining from 18 ♗xh5 is better, but White's game remains rather prospectless. And allowing Black to play ... e4 is simply out of the question.

**17 ♕b3!!**

Now we realise that 15 ♘c1!! had another side to it – that of vacating b3 for the queen, which hits at d5 straight away. This sally looks quite natural, but does White actually prevent 17 ... e4 in this way? – not at all! White intends to meet Black's threat with an intriguing queen sacrifice: 17 ... e4 18 ♖xe4 (superior to 18

♗xe4 ♖xe4 19 ♖xe4 ♘a5 20 ♕a4 dxe4 21 ♕xa5 f3, when Black has good attacking chances for the pawn) 18 ... ♘a5 19 ♖xe8! ♘xb3 20 ♖xf8+ ♗xf8 21 axb3, with a strong dynamic edge for White:[4] eg. 21 ... a6 22 ♘d3 ♗h6 23 ♘c5 ♕c6 24 ♖e1, with either 25 ♖e6, or 25 ♖e5 followed by 26 c4, coming next.

**17 ... exd4 18 ♘d3!**

We have seen this thousands of times since High Priest Aaron (Nimzowitsch) issued, in the late twenties, his commandment: "Thou shalt blockade thine enemy's pawns by a knight!" Here the move serves not so much to blockade the pawn – Black is free to play 18 ... dxc3 anyway – as to connect the rooks and threaten 19 ♖xe8 ♖xe8 20 ♗xh5 gxh5 21 ♗xf4.

**18 ... ♖d8(!)**

He must have thought he had outplayed his opponent, after all. Everything is protected (19 ♕xb7 ♘a5 20 ♕xa7 ♘c4 21 ♗c1 dxc3), and he has won a pawn, hasn't he? What now, then?

**19 c4!**

The culmination of White's plan. The piquant point is that now the knight *is* blockading the passed pawn, as though Fischer was saying: "I'm not evading classical principles – I'm just implementing them my way!" More important, however, is that he recovers the pawn with the

better position.

For Czerniak it must have been a highly frustrating experience to see his promising attacking position evaporate into thin air within a mere five moves, without having committed any mistake. He was unfortunate to observe how miraculously a position can transform under the hand of a chess giant.

White threatens 20 cxd5 ♘e7 21 ♗b4. So: **19 ... dxc4 20 ♕xc4+ ♔h8 21 ♖e6 ♕b8 22 ♖ae1! ♖c8 23 ♗xc6 ♖xc6 24 ♖xc6 bxc6 25 ♕xc6 ♕c8 26 ♕xc8 ♖xc8 27 ♔f1 ♗h6 28 ♖c1 ♖xc1+ 29 ♗xc1**, and with White having a fast and effective pawn majority on the queenside, Black had no chance of holding the endgame.

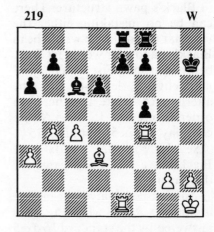

219     **W**

The final example has a curious story to it. Pos. 219 was the one reached after Black's (Fischer's) 27th move in the second match game between Fischer and Larsen, Candidates 1971. Larsen played here 28 ♖xf5. A couple of months after the match, he published an analysis of the game in *Chess Canada*,[5] quoting a line that had been indicated by a Dutch player,[6] which showed that White could have gained a winning advantage after 28 ♖e3 ♖g8 (he has to do something about 29 ♖g3, 30 ♖h4 mate, or 29 ♖g4, 30 ♖h3 mate – EA) 29 ♗xf5+ ♔h6 (29 ... ♔g7 30 ♗e6!) 30 ♗h3, and now on 30 ... ♖g7 (30 ... ♔g7? 31 ♖g3+ ♔f8 32 ♗e6!) 31 b5!! axb5 32 cxb5, Black is left with two sad alternatives:

a) 32 ... ♗xb5 33 ♖h4+ ♔g5 34 ♖b4!, and White wins a piece owing to the threat ♖g3+.

b) 32 ... ♗d5 33 ♖h4+ ♔g5 34 ♖d4 ♗e6 35 ♗xe6 fxe6 36 ♖xe6, and White should win the endgame.

**220**            **B**

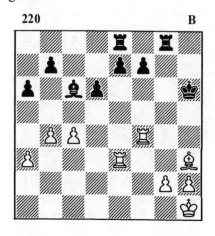

It is remarkable to see how Larsen – a player known for the richness of his creative ideas – could miss a move as simple as 30 ... d5! in Pos. 220, a move on which Fischer had presumably based his defence.

Black forsakes the f7 pawn in order to create a passed pawn. For instance, 31 ♖xf7 dxc4 and if 32 ♖fxe7? the c-pawn triumphs: 32 ... ♖xe7 33 ♖xe7 c3 34 ♖e1 (34 ♖e3/♖e2 ♖e8!) 34 ... c2 35 ♖c1 ♖d8 36 ♗g4 ♖d2, and Black wins. Instead of 32 ♖fxe7, 32 ♔g1 is preferable. Black holds his own with 32 ... e6! and 33 ... ♗d5. It remains an interesting endgame with chances for both sides.

Two other tries are 32 ♖f4 ♗d5 followed by 33 ... e6, as in the last line, and (the faulty) 31 c5? e5 32 ♖xf7 d4, and Black's pawns roll to promotion. (see also Pos. 127).

And so there is an instructive lesson to learn from the closing example of the present chapter. The common assumption is that creative ideas might appear with greater ease in cases of attack than in cases of defence; we are inclined to think more in terms of linear solutions ('only' moves) when a defence is called for. Such a linear solution was in this case 30 ... ♖g7. There are, of course, exceptions to this rule. Lasker and Korchnoi have been particularly adept at spotting the creative possibilities of a defensive situation. The difference between them and Fischer is that Fischer has no sympathy whatever for defending cramped positions. His great artistry lies in transforming those positions into 'playable' ones as quickly as possible.

## TAKING RISKS

One usually takes risks when this offers better prospects than the safe alternatives. There are, basically, two kinds of risk-taking: a) the one that can be calculated with high exactitude, and the risk consists in the theoretical unpredictability of the position, being complicated in nature; b) the one in which the consequences of a decision are difficult to calculate, and the risk is taken mostly for the sake of sharpening the battle. In this case we can observe a certain psychological factor at play, namely, that the player taking the risks is optimistically disposed towards believing in his better abilities to make use of the new opportunities arising on the board. To the first category belong the following three examples.

In Perez-Fischer, Leipzig Olympiad 1960 (Pos. 221), capturing the bishop on g5 is certainly quite a risky affair for Black, yet Fischer

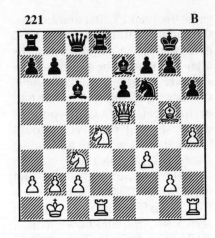

221                           B

carefully and cold-bloodedly calculated that after **15 ... hxg5 16 hxg5 ♗d6 16 ... ♘h7? 17 ♕h2** wins **17 ♕e1 ♘e8 18 ♕h4 ♔f8 19 ♘f5!? exf5 20 ♖de1 ♕e6! 21 ♖xe6 fxe6 22 ♖e1 ♔e7!**, Black would be out of any serious danger, with a better material balance, and so he decided it was a risk worth taking.

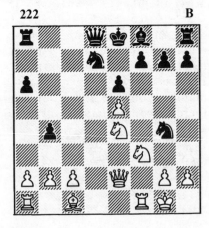

222                           B

There was apparently some misunderstanding about Fischer's decision in the next game (Lehmann–Fischer, Havana 1965, Pos. 222). **14 ... ♘gxe5!** "Here is the crucial move of the opening and of the entire game," wrote Kmoch in *Chess Review*.[1] However, this move was seemingly based on sound calculations which for some reason escaped the attention of the annotators at the time,[2] who were under the unanimous impression that the risks Fischer had taken were far too great. Kmoch and Najdorf[3] thought that now "15 ♗g5! makes Black's [defensive] task extremely difficult", yet after 15 ... ♕b6+ (better than the suggested 15 ... ♘xf3+ 16 ♕xf3 ♘e5, methinks) 16 ♔h1 ♕b5 (much as in the actual game, which went: **15 ♘xe5 ♘xe5 16 ♗g5 ♕b6+ 17 ♔h1 ♕b5! 18 ♕e1 ♗e7**) 17 ♕f2 (17 ♕xb5 axb5 18 ♘xe5 ♘xe5 19 ♘f6+ gxf6 20 ♗xf6 ♘g6) 17 ... f5!, the position remains complicated, but the risks taken seem quite justified. Black is a pawn up (with a 4-to-2 majority on the kingside) and there is no immediate threat to his king.

A line that extended longer, and had an element of risk that was considerably greater, involved the game Najdorf-Fischer, Havana Olympiad 1966 (Pos. 223). White's pawn on d5 is isolated and weak.

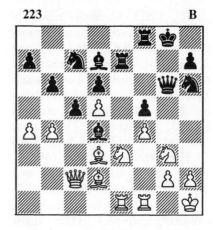

223 B

If Black could manage to win it and escape unscathed, with the booty, his position might well be a won one. This requires, though, a very bold decision – giving up the bishop on d4 for White's knight on e3, after which an unchallenged White dark-squared bishop at c3, accompanied by its 'comrade' at c4, could create a dangerous presence, one that might prove even lethal. The margin of unpredictability remains quite large in such decisions, no matter how far ahead one calculates, and for that reason the majority of players would probably have rejected it out of hand as a matter of principle. Fischer, in contrast, plays: **26 ... ♗xe3! 27 ♗xe3 ♖fe8 28 bxc5 bxc5** a bad risk is 28 ... ♖xe3 29 ♖xe3 ♖xe3 30 cxb6 axb6 31 ♕xc7 ♗xa4 (31 ... ♖xd3 32 ♕xd7 ♖xg3 33 ♖e1!) 32

♗xf5! ♘xf5 33 ♕c8+ ♖e8 34 ♕xf5, and White has winning chances. **29 ♗d2 ♖xe1 30 ♖xe1 ♖xe1+ 31 ♗xe1 ♘xd5!**, and contrary to initial appearance, Fischer proves that it shouldn't be Black who comes a cropper after **32 ♗c4 ♕e6 33 ♗c3 ♗c6 34 ♕b3 ♔f7 35 ♕b8 ♘g8 36 h3 ♘ge7 37 ♕h8 ♕h6**. As a matter of fact, Black's material advantage won him the game. (see also Pos. 67)

To the second class belong the following examples. In these cases, one relies to a greater degree on positional considerations, and the risks one takes are motivated less by provable lines than by the player's will to win.

**224**                                    **B**

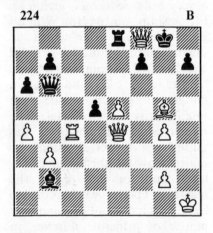

Against Taimanov at Buenos Aires 1960 (Pos. 224) for instance, Bobby rejected the safe and sound 35 ... ♖xf8, solely because that would have reduced any winning aspirations to nil: 36 ♕xd5 ♕g6 37 ♗f6 ♕h6+ 38 ♔g1 ♕e3+ 39 ♔h1 (39 ♔f1? ♗c3) 39 ... ♕h6+. And if 37 ♗d2 ♖e8 38 ♖e4 b5!. Black should have no problems in drawing (39 axb5 axb5 40 ♕xb5 ♖d8! 41 ♕e2 – 41 ♖e2? ♖xd2! wins – 41 ... ♖xd2 42 ♕xd2 ♕xe4 43 ♕xb2 ♕e1+ 44 ♔h2 ♕h4+), but hopes of a win no longer dwell in the position. Instead he plays **35 ... ♔xf8!?/?!**, pinning his hopes on the greater complexity of the position as compared with the one following 35 ... ♖xf8, and he expects to be the one to extract more out of that situation. Yet the risk he runs now is immense, and for the next phase of the game it remains doubtful whether it was really a risk worth taking: **36 ♕xh7 ♗xe5**. Certainly not 36 ... dxc4 37 ♕h8 mate. **37 ♖f4! ♕e6 38 ♖f1 b5?**. Ironically, Bobby is the first to go wrong in the route he chooses. He counted, in the first place, on his passed d-pawn as a source of winning possibilities, but the tactical possibilities inherent in the position are not to be taken lightly. Taimanov indicates 38 ... ♗g7 39 ♗c1 (39 ♗d2? ♕xg4) 39 ... ♕e7 40 g5 ♕b4!, with equality.[4] **39 axb5?**. And Taimanov returns the compliment. By opening the a-file, he gives Black what he was playing for – more manoeuvring space there. He could prove Fischer's assessment to have been too optimistic by playing 39 ♖e1!, with a dangerous bind. White threatens both 40 ♗h6+ ♔e7 41 ♗g7 and 40 ♗f4 (Taimanov). The actual game was drawn after Fischer's stubborn defence, on move 87.

225                 B

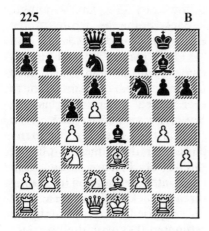

As in the previous example, so here (Pos. 225) and in the next one, the prospect of a quick and eventless draw coming up drives Fischer to risk-taking decisions. It is worth mentioning that he does so here, at the age of fifteen (the game was played at Portoroz 1958, Fischer having the black pieces) when facing an experienced grandmaster like Yuri Averbakh. Compare this with his game against Szabo from the same event, Pos. 209. The continuation 14 ... g5 15 ♘xe4 ♘xe4 16 ♘xe4 ♖xe4 17 ♕c2 (Averbakh)[5] would make a draw most likely. Fischer

plays instead **14 ... a6!?** so as, by not blocking the h4-d8 diagonal by 14 ... g5, to leave room for a possible queen sortie, and at the same time prepare ... b5. The risk he takes by playing thus has to do with a White offensive on the kingside: **15 h4 b5 16 g5** now winning a piece by force **16 ... b4 17 gxf6 bxc3 18 ♘xe4 ♖xe4 19 fxg7 ♕xh4.** For the sacrificed piece, Black has generated serious threats against the white king. Again, this did not ultimately avert a drawn result, which this time however comes quickly. **20 ♔f1** White has to stay vigilant. As Zagoriansky showed, Black gets the upper hand after 20 ♖g3 ♖ae8 (eg. 21 ♔f1 ♕h1+ 22 ♖g1 ♕h3+ 23 ♖g2 f5 24 ♗f3 c2! 25 ♕e2 ♖d4 etc – EA), or 20 ♕c1 cxb2 21 ♕xb2 ♖xe3, or 20 ♖g4 ♖xg4 21 ♗xg4 ♘e5.[6] **20 ... cxb2 21 ♖b1,** draw.

226                 W

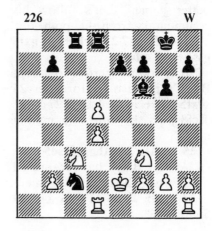

That the psychological effect of such a policy may be long and lasting (even well beyond the game session), is illustrated in the game Fischer-Yanofsky, Netanya 1968 (Pos. 226). White's pawn at d5 is doomed to fall, no matter how he plays. Fischer decides to take the opportunity to centralise his king so as to pose as many technical problems for Black as possible, while at the same time running a certain risk that the king would feel quite uncomfortable in the centre before the position reduces to a simplified endgame. **20 ♔d3!?**. There are, of course, many equalising lines here. One of them is 20 g3 ♘b4 21 ♖a1 ♘xd5 22 ♖hc1, etc. **20 ... ♘b4+ 21 ♔e4 ♖d6**. Analysing the game for the Israeli magazine *Shahmat*,[7] Yanofsky remarks here: "Threatening to double rooks and win back the pawn with the better game." Let's follow his commentary from this point on. **22 ♘e5 ♗g7 23 g4 f5+! 24 gxf5 gxf5+ 25 ♔f4**

"It is too dangerous to accept Black's pawn offer for after 25 ♔xf5 ♖f6+ 26 ♔e4 ♖xf2 27 ♖hg1 ♖cf8 puts the king in a mating net."

**25 ... ♖f8 26 ♖hg1 ♘xd5+**

"At last Black has recaptured the pawn with the better game."

**27 ♘xd5 ♖xd5 28 ♘f3 ♔h8 29 ♖ge1 ♗f6?**

"After having outplayed his opponent, Black now misses the win. Best was 29 ... ♗h6+ 30 ♔g3 ♖g8+ 31 ♔h3 ♗f4! when White cannot overcome Black's winning, either by 32 ... ♖d6 followed by 33 ... ♖h6 mating or 32 ... ♖b5 followed by 33 ... ♖b3 winning."

Back home he wrote to the editor of *Canadian Chess Chat*: "If I had [played 29 ... ♗h6+] this game would probably have been the most brilliant game I have ever played".[8] Perplexing as it is, Yanofsky seems to have been subject to a delusion for many days after the game. By playing ♔d3-e4-f4 Fischer must have taken into consideration the mating threats Black might create against the exposed king, but rightly estimated they would all be tractable. As the editor of the magazine further reports, "Moe Moss asks how the win goes after 29 ... ♗h6+ 30 ♘g5. We cannot see any clear line because the knight can be supported by h4, and if 30 ... ♗xg5+ 31 ♔xg5 ♖g8+ 32 ♔f4 ♖g4+ 33 ♔f3 ♖gxd4 34 ♖xd4 ♖xd4 35 ♖xe7 ♖b4 36 ♖e2 or 36 ♖e5 seems to hold." This is certainly a most dramatic example of how a player can overestimate his chances in view of a deliberately equivocal line played by his opponent – a phenomenon Emanuel Lasker, for one, knew how to make the utmost use of time and again throughout his long career. Interestingly, after **30 ♘e5 e6 31 h4 ♖c8 32 ♘f7+ ♔g7 33 ♘g5 ♗xg5+ 34 ♔xg5 ♖c6 35 ♖e5 ♖cd6 36 ♖xd5 ♖xd5 37 f4 ♖b5** Yanofsky writes in *Shahmat*: "Black must counter White's superior king position as otherwise he is in danger of losing the game. White threatened ♖e1 and if ♖d6 then d5! is strong." Nothing could vindicate Fischer's way of playing more eloquently than this. He succeeded in posing great problems for his opponent in a seemingly innocuous endgame, owing to the risks he had been ready to take. The game was eventually drawn on move 47.

Sometimes Fischer would take a certain risk so as to avoid facing a risk of a different kind.

227              B

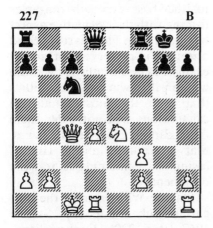

In Mednis-Fischer US Championship 1963-64 (Pos. 227) Black

would gladly play as 'positionally' as possible, since his advantage in terms of pawn structure is very graphic indeed. A plausible manoeuvre would be ... ♘e7-d5, and if (after 14 ... ♘e7) White answers 15 d5, Black blockades the pawn on d6 – 15 ... ♘f5 (16 ♕b4 b6 17 d6? c5!). However, White has the open g-file at his disposal, and he can sharpen matters considerably after 15 ♖hg1! ♔h8 (15 ... ♘d5? 16 ♕xd5 ♕xd5 17 ♘f6+) 16 ♘g5 ♘d5 17 ♖de1 c6 18 ♖e4 etc. In order to forestall such possibilities, Fischer is willing to concede White a certain freedom of action. He hopes that by taking the risks he is taking now, the sharp position which soon appears on the board would offer Black the better chances: **14 ... ♕h4 15 ♔b1 ♕f4!? 16 d5 ♘e5 17 ♕xc7.** Black will win back the sacrificed pawn, but now White's d-pawn becomes a force to be reckoned with: **17 ... ♖ac8 18 ♕d6 ♖cd8 19 ♕c7 ♖c8 20 ♕d6 ♖fd8 21 ♕e7 ♘xf3 22 d6,** with a very tense struggle ahead. (see also Pos. 8)

Most enterprising is Fischer's approach in the next example (Burger-Fischer, US Championship 1965-66, Pos. 228).

**26 ... ♔g7 27 ♘d2 ♖h8 28 ♖h1 ♖h7!!.** Taking considerable risks on the . . . queenside!

He could have played it much safer with 28 ... ♕h5, maintaining

**228**                          **B**

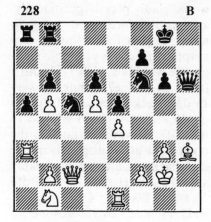

some advantage after 29 ♔f1 g5
(or interpolating 29 ... ♖ac8 30
♖c3 first. Not, by the way, 30
♗g2 ♘cxe4!!) 30 ♗g2 ♕g4,
though he has to stay watchful for
♘c4 – a move that is likely to
cause Black problems. Incidentally,
if White plays for it too early after
Black's 28 ... ♕h5, he finds
himself in narrow straits: 29 f3
♕g5 30 ♘c4 ♘h5 31 ♗g4 ♘xg3!
32 ♕c1! ♕xc1 33 ♖xc1 ♘e2 34
♖ca1 ♖h7!! 35 b4 ♖ah8, etc. **29
b4 ♘b7 30 ♘f1**. Wasn't it possible
for White to force matters on the
queenside? – apparently not, since
30 ♕c6 ♕xd2 31 ♕xb7 ♘xe4
favours Black: 32 ♕xb6 ♕xb4, or
32 ♖f3 ♖f8 33 bxa5 (33 ♕xb6
♕xb4!) 33 ... ♕xa5 (Kmoch).[9]
The slight delay involved in the
move actually played is sufficient
for Black to build up threatening
pressure on the kingside, though

it remains far from clear who
would finally get the upper hand.
**30 ... ♖ah8 31 ♖f3 axb4 32 ♕c7**
Fischer must have calculated long
in advance all the risks involved
in this infiltration of the white
queen. **32 ... ♘c5 33 ♖xf6**. The
following tempting alternatives
both fail: a) 33 ♕xd6 ♘cxe4 34
♕xe5 ♕g5! 35 ♕d4 ♕xd5, winning. b) 33 ♖h2 b3! 34 ♗e6
♕xh2+! 35 ♘xh2 ♖xh2+ 36 ♔f1
b2! 37 ♕xf7+ ♔h6, winning. **33 ...
♔xf6 34 ♕xd6+ ♔g7 35 ♕xe5+
♔g8 36 ♘e3 ♕g7 37 ♕b8+ ♕f8
38 ♕xb6 ♘xe4**. The danger is
over, and with it White's game.
Fischer estimated and calculated
both the risks and the chances
superbly. White resigned on move
46.

This example is akin in nature
to the first type of examples
dealing with the calculative aspect
of risk-taking. There is still a third
one that is preserved for a very
exclusive class of players – those
whose will to win is so tremendous
that even the most exhaustive
calculations will not deter them
from sailing close to the wind,
that is, running a real risk of
losing the game only to test the
opponent.

Playing White against the Bul-
garian Luben Popov at Skopje
1967 (Pos. 229), Fischer disap-
pointedly reached a position where
it was best to settle for a draw by

229 W

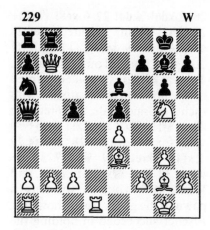

repetition: **18 ♕c6 ♖c8 19 ♕d6 ♖d8 20 ♕c6 ♖dc8 21 ♗d2.** Objectively, this can only be criticised since now White, and not his opponent, comes close to losing the game. Fischer trusts his ability to find an effective defence if necessary. There is one subtle point he isn't certain his opponent will detect, and he is tempted to take this great risk just in order to check it out. **21 ... ♘b4 22 ♕xa8 ♖xa8 23 ♘xe6 ♕b6!.** That's the point. After 23 ... fxe6 24 a3 there would remain an open battle where the better player might still win. **24 c3 ♘c2 25 ♖ac1 ♕xb2.** It looks as though White's losing. Fischer manages to save the game in time. **26 ♘c7 ♖b8 27 a4 ♕a2 28 a5!** forcing further liquidation, and ensuring the draw: **28 ... ♕xa5 29 ♖xc2 ♕xc7 30 ♖a1 ♗f8 31 ♖ca2 ♖b7 32 ♗e3 ♔g7 33**

♖a6, and a draw was agreed shortly afterwards.

Fischer's next opponent was forced into showing greater ingenuity. It was Wolfgang Uhlmann (White), facing Fischer at the Siegen Olympiad 1970, (Pos. 230).

230 W

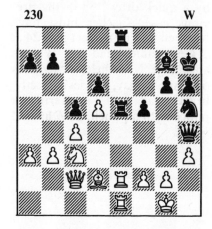

On Uhlmann's **24 ♖xe5** Fischer captured back with the bishop. In *Chess Canada* of November 1970 they published the commentaries of a number of local players alongside those of Mikhail Tal's, whose original commentary appeared in the Russian *64*.[10] The opinions reproduced here are very revealing.

Tal: stronger was capturing with the rook. It seems to me that Fischer overestimated the power of the threat 25 ... ♗d4.

Coudari: by taking with the bishop Fischer is obviously keeping the position as complex as possible, and shows a determined will to win.

Kuprejanov: interesting was 24 ... ♖xe5, although this leads to simplification.

No doubt after 24 ... ♖xe5 the game would have been concluded by a quick draw. As in the previous case, Fischer must have foreseen that by correct play 24 ... ♗xe5 would lead to White's advantage. Nonetheless, it requires of White to play, besides correctly, bravely as well, answering a punch with a punch. **25 ♘b5! a6!**

**26 ♘xd6! ♗d4! 27 ♘xe8! ♕xf2+ 28 ♔h2!**. White is mated after 28 ♔h1 ♘g3+ 29 ♔h2 ♘f1+ 30 ♖xf1 ♗e5+, as pointed out by Coudari. Tal was obviously too enchanted by the position to be satisfied with such a prosaic finale, and preferred 28 ... **♕f1+??/!! 29 ♖xf1 ♘g3+ 30 ♔h2 ♘xf1+ draw!! 28 ... ♘f4 29 ♗xf4! ♕xe1! 29 ♕xc2? 30 d6 wins. 30 ♕c1 ♕xe8 31 ♗xh6**, and White came out of the fray a pawn to the good. Again, however, Fischer succeeded in holding the draw.

# Practical Chances

Exploiting Practical Chances

**231**            **B**

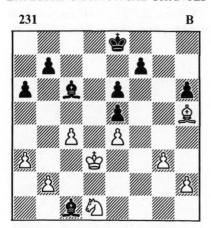

At the international tournament at Zürich 1959, sixteen-year-old Fischer reached in the last-round game this position (Pos. 231) against the eventual winner – Mikhail Tal, who had the white pieces. It was Fischer's turn to play, and he played **33 ... ⌔f8**. This decision aroused the criticism of the then World Champion, Mikhail Botvinnik.

In *Chess Review* of September 1959, Botvinnik wrote: "This move is difficult to understand. Black's bishop on c1 with now be cut off from its camp, and it will

be Black's turn to play to force the draw." (see also Pos. 137, 190). Keres, in the tournament book,[1] concurred. What Botvinnik thought preferable was the straight-forward drawing line: 33 ... ♗a4 34 ♘c3 ♗c6, and White has nothing better than repeat moves, since 35 ♔c2 ♗e3 is undoubtedly better for Black. After Fischer's move, on the other hand, it was Black who had to force the draw if White played correctly, i.e. **34 h4**, threatening 35 ♔c2, which Tal indeed played. It is remarkable, how both the grand veterans totally missed young Fischer's point: when playing 33 ... ♔f8, he must have cared very little who would be the one to force the draw, so long as it offered him a last practical chance to play for a win – had Tal missed 34 h4, there would have followed 34 ... f5!, and Black would enjoy a comfort-able edge. This principle, namely, exploiting any practical chance a position offers, was embraced by Fischer from the beginning of his career. As we have just seen, even players of the highest calibre sometimes fail to appreciate this stance correctly, and might even go as far as giving preference to a 'moral' policy which holds that the better-standing side oughtn't be the one submitted to the disgrace of begging the draw. For Fischer, this argument was of no relevance. If there still existed some chance of changing the game's outcome in his favour – it had to be taken.

White's favour. **22 ... g5(!) 23 fxg5 ♗xg2(!) 24 ♖xg2 ♘xg2 25 ♔xg2 ♖f2+ 26 ♔g3 ♖xd2 27 ♖xb7**. This is certainly not a serious attempt at winning the game, but it is worth the try. **27 ... ♖f7 28 ♖b8+ 28 ♖xf7 ♔xf7 29 ♗xh7 ♖e2**, etc. **28 ... ♔g7 29 ♖e8 ♖df2 30 ♖xe6 ♖7f3+**, and Black forces a perpetual check. (see also Pos. 143)

232                                    W

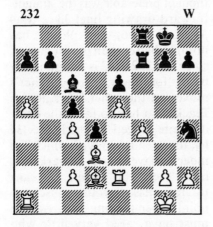

233                                    W

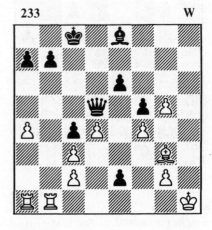

In Pos. 232 (Fischer-Uhlmann, Stockholm 1962) it is quite clear that Black's forces are poised for carrying out the move ... g5. In order to meet the move successfully, White should only play 22 ♖d1, ensuring an impasse for both sides. Fischer realises that the one practical chance that holds out some promise consists of giving Black what he wants. **22 ♖b1!**. No other move bears any potential of turning the scales in

Against the same opponent, Fischer (White) had faced difficult problems two years earlier, at Buenos Aires 1960 (Pos. 233). His position offered very little survival prospects. With 33 ... ♗c6 and 34 ... ♕e4, Black threatens to paralyse White completely. By then marching with his king to the kingside, and picking up some pawns on the queenside, he would ensure his win. Fischer doesn't wait that long. The position does offer yet another practical chance: **33 ♖b5!** ♗xb5 33 ... ♕e4 is answered now, of course, by 34 ♖e5. **34 axb5 ♕xb5 35 ♖e1**. After eliminating the e2 pawn, White gains some counterchances with his g-pawn. **35 ... a5!** Uhlmann employs the most common and sensible tactics in such situations – pushing one's own passed pawn. Ultimately both White's and Black's passed pawns will fall, after which the material imbalance is bound to take its toll: **36 ♖xe2 a4 37 ♖xe6 a3 38 g6 ♕d7 39 ♖e5 b6 40 ♗h4 a2 41 ♖e1 ♕g7 42 ♖a1 ♕xg6**, and White gave up in view of 43 ♖xa2 ♕h5 44 g3 ♕d1+ 45 ♔h2 ♔b7!, and he is short of moves. Black threatens 46 ... ♕b1, and if 46 ♖b2, then 46 ... ♕a1! 47 ♖b5 ♕xc3 48 ♖xf5? ♕xc2+, winning the rook. Be it as it may, 33 ♖b5 was his last practical chance to hold the game. (see also Pos. 306)

**234**                               **W**

Taking stock of the best practical chances involves, in many cases, quick adjustment of one's frame of mind to new circumstances. Having blundered away a piece for two pawns in his game (as White) against Hübner at Palma de Mallorca 1970 (Pos. 234), Fischer, seemingly unintimidated by these developments, strives nonetheless to grab the last winning chances, symbolic though they are. **32 ♕xa7?**. Larry Evans, who was in Palma de Mallorca as Fischer's second, testified that this was a simple oversight.[2] Incidentally, many commentators[3] regarded it a deliberate liquidation, since how else could one explain the fact that it was Fischer who rejected the perpetual after **32 ... ♘e4! 33 f3 ♘d6 34 ♕xc5 ♘xb7**, with 35 ♕e5+ –? Instead he began scraping the last morsels of practical chances the position contained: **35 ♕d4+ 36 ♔g8 36 ♔f2 ♕e7 37 ♕d5+ ♔f8 38 h5 gxh5 39 ♕xh5 ♘c5 40 ♕d5 ♔g7 41 ♕d4+ ♔f7 44 ♕d5+**, and the draw was finally agreed upon. (see also Pos. 100)

## TRAPS

Fischer's traps should be regarded in the main as quasi-traps, another form of making the most of his practical chances. By and large, he abstained from setting a trap if this didn't concur with the general features of his position. Here are a couple of examples.

**235**                              **W**

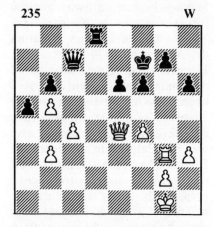

There is hardly a way by which White could possibly pose any problems for his opponent in Pos. 235 (Fischer-Pachman, Leipzig Olympiad 1960). Fischer spots a something-to-nothing chance to do just that without in any way tampering with his position's good foundations. He decides to put his opponent to the test. **36 ♕h7 ♖g8**. Not 36 ... ♔f8?? 37 ♕h8+ **37 ♕g6+ ♔e7??** Pachman falls into it. After 37 ... ♔f8 38 ♕e4 ♔f7/♔e7 Black is alright. **38 ♕xg7+!** and Black had nothing else but to resign. The pawn endgame after 38 ... ♖xg7 39 ♖xg7+ ♔d6 40 ♖xc7 ♔xc7, is hopeless for him.

Fischer-Ciocaltea from the next

**236**                              **W**

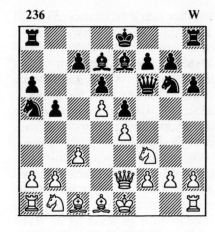

Olympiad (Varna 1962, Pos. 236) witnessed the same principle. **13 g3 0-0 14 h4!**. As we have already seen (pp.24-8), the pawn chain f2-g3-h4 is a set-up that recurs in quite a number of Fischer's games. He is willing to employ it here since besides its other virtues it makes possible the trapping of Black's queen if he plays a move like . . . **14 ... ♖fc8??** which Ciocaltea happened to play! 14 ... ♗d8 was necessary. **15 ♗g5!** and Black's queen is gone. ("Believe it or not, I lost to this 'player' in the finals!", wrote a nettled Bobby from Varna to his friend Bernard Zuckerman[1] – see Pos. 17, 283).

Fischer's **34 ♖h6!** against Gligorić (Rovinj-Zagreb 1970, Pos. 237) was practically best. There was, anyway, nothing to lose by it, so why not try it? Gligorić failed to take note of Fischer's sly

**237** W

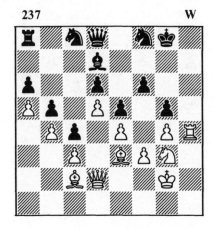

intention, and fell into the trap: **34 ... ♔g7? 35 ♖xf6!**, and he resigned. 35 ... ♔xf6 36 ♗xg5+, and 35 ... ♕f6 36 ♘h5+ were good enough reasons to do so. This position became something of a challenge for analysts who wished to demonstrate that Fischer had a winning plan anyway. Meaning well, they fell into a trap deeper than the one Gligorić had fallen into . . . Trifunović gave 34 ... ♘h7 35 ♘h5 ♕f8 36 ♗xg5!! (Vuković mentioned[2] 36 ♖g6+ ♔h8 37 ♖g7, but after 37 ... ♕xg7! it would be quite difficult to prove a forced win for White). 36 ... fxg5 37 ♘f6+! ♕xf6 (37 ... ♘xf6 38 ♕xg5+ ♕g7 39 ♖g6 ♘e8 40 ♖xg7+ ♘xg7 41 ♕d8+ ♗e8 42 ♕c7! wins more material – EA)[3] 38 ♖xf6 ♘xf6 39 ♕xg5+, etc.[3] Pretty as this variation is, it unfortunately contains a certain

hole: by 37 ... ♔f7!! Black saves the game, viz: 38 ♖xh7+ ♔xf6 39 ♖xd7 ♖a7 40 ♖xa7 ♘xa7 41 ♕f2 ♘c8 48 ♔f1 ♕h6 is as dead drawn as any book draw. (see also Pos. 47)

Gligorić had also been Fischer's victim in one of the deepest traps he ever set, and from the psychological point of view something quite extraordinary for a sixteen-year-old youngster, irrespective of chess talent. It was played in the 1st cycle of the Candidates, Bled 1959.

**238** W

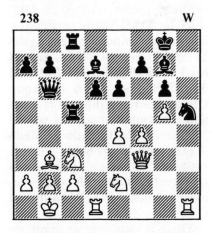

White's set-up in Pos. 238 is apparently aimed at breaking through with f5. By playing **23 ♕d3** Fischer signals that he has given up hope of carrying out his plans on the kingside now, and has switched his attention to the centre. Moreover, it would be quite natural for the second player to believe White blundered (and Gligoric was quick to react: **23 ... ♗xc3 24 ♘xc3 ♘xf4**) since a) Why anyway should White give up the very pawn on which he pins his hopes to crack Black's position? b) Why should one play his queen to d3 while she's so beautifully placed at f3 – normally you don't assume that this move (♕f3-d3) is a prelude to a symmetrical one (♕d3-f3) two moves later. The point was, however, that the disappearance of Black's dark-squared bishop proved a cardinal factor. After **25 ♕f3!** ♘h5 **26 ♖xh5!** White carried out his attack unhindered – **26 ... gxh5 27 ♕xh5 ♗e8 28 ♕h6 ♖xc3 29 bxc3 ♖xc3 30 g6 fxg6 31 ♖h1 ♕d4 32 ♕h7+**, 1-0. With hindsight Gligorić pointed out in the tournament book that correct was 23 ... ♗e8 24 ♕xd6 ♕xd6 25 ♖xd6 ♗xc3, with a probably tenable endgame.[4] In actuality, even the strongest grandmaster could succumb to such a diabolic positional trap.

There is only one example on record in which Fischer sets a trap that serves for no other purpose but that. It occurred in his 9th match game with Reshevsky 1961 (Pos. 239).

Fischer plays **27 ... ♖c8** which is quite unmotivated except for the simple trap 28 ♗xa7 ♖a8. Kmoch rightly labelled it a trap of

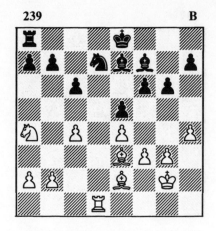

239                         B

a 'kindergarten grade'.[5] Ironically, it was Bobby who was to fall into a similar trap (of a primary school grade, perhaps) snatching with his bishop a corner pawn. Recall when and where?[6]

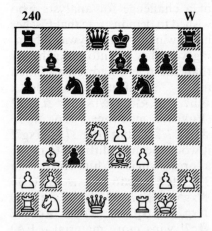

240                         W

More in his style is the trap in Pos. 240, taken from his game as White against Sherwin, US Championship 1957-58. Fischer was in mind of playing the following three-move sequence: ♘xc6, ♘xc3, ♖c1. The regular course would have been: 13 ♘xc3 0-0 14 ♘xc6 ♗xc6 15 ♖c1. He takes the opportunity to set a trap by playing first **13 ♘xc6**, so that if Black answers with 13 ... cxb2? White gets a winning advantage with 14 ♘xd8 bxa1=♕ 15 ♗d4 ♕xd4+ 16 ♕xd4 ♖xd8 17 ♗a4+ ♔f8 18 ♕b6 ♗c8 19 ♖c1. Fortunately Sherwin did not oblige, and Fischer went on to produce one of his finest victories in that championship.

A most piquant trap Fischer set was the one that remained behind the scenes in his game against Foguelman at Mar del Plata 1960 (Pos. 241).

**241**                                    **B**

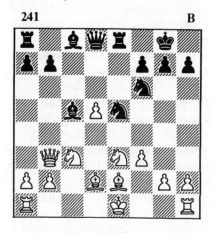

Black (Fischer) is a pawn down. He gambited it away on the 9th

move, and he can now recover it by 14 ... ♘xf3+. Fischer prefers though to win a different pawn. He plays **14 ... ♘g6! 15 ♘c2 ♘h4**, inviting White to defend his pawn at g2 by 16 ♔f1. What he must have had up his sleeve was 16 ... ♘g4! (Very tempting is 16 ... ♕d7, with the intention of forcing a quick and highly elegant mate after 17 ♗b5 ♕h3!! or 17 ... ♘xf3!!. However, 17 ♕c4! makes it much more difficult for Black to prove the correctness of this move: 17 ... ♘xg2 18 ♕xc5 ♕h3 19 ♔f2!, etc) 17 fxg4 ♗xg4!, and suddenly the white king is stripped of all defences. The threat 18 ... ♕f6+ forces 18 ♔e1 (18 ♕c4 is met by 18 ... ♕f6+ 19 ♕f4 ♕xc3!!, or 19 ♗f4 ♕g6!), but then 18 ... ♕f6 (still!) 19 ♔d1 ♖xe2!! 20 ♘xe2 ♕f2 21 ♕c4 (21 ♖e1 ♘xg2 22 ♕g3 ♕xg3 23 hxg3 ♖e8!, or if here 22 ♕c4 then 22 ... ♗f3!) 21 ... ♕g2 22 ♖e1 ♘f3! 23 ♔c1 ♖c8! would seal White's fate.

This is, besides, an excellent example of a trap that is in complete agreement with all of the position's elements. After Foguelman's **16 0-0-0!** Fischer captured the g2 pawn, a pawn that was far more important than the one of f3 he could have captured two moves earlier. Apart from that, capturing on f3 would have brought about undesirable liquidations.

# Tactics

## TACTICAL INSIGHT

That Fischer was a very gifted tactician is borne out by the many combinations he played throughout his career. Tactical insight is less subject to learning and development than strategic insight, yet in many players – and Fischer is a good example of it – it might undergo evolution along with the overall progress and maturity of one's style. Back in 1961 he could still be engaged in producing a piece of raw tactics such as this one (Pos. 242, Pachman-Fischer, Bled):

15 ... f5!? 16 ♘d5 fxg4 17 ♘xc7 gxh3 18 ♗d5+ ♔h8 19 ♘xa8 ♘e7 20 ♗e3 h2+ 21 ♔h1 ♗h3 22 ♘c7 ♘f5 23 ♘e6 ♖f6 24 ♘xg7 ♘xe3 25 fxe3 ♖xf1+ 26 ♕xf1 ♗xf1 27 ♖xf1 ♔xg7 28 ♖f7+, draw.

With the years, an ever-growing sophistication of tactical motifs found place in his games. When a player no longer falls back on tactics to solve sharp positional problems, and resorts to tactical measures only when they are objectively the most appropriate means to do that, his combinations are likely to gain in depth and beauty. They are no longer there to patch together remnants of otherwise unpromising positions, nor are they small shovels with which to dig traps for the opponents to fall into. They are simply the most logical, incisive and often elegant ways to conclude a game, or bring about an advantageous development. Here is a very fine example: Fischer-Panno, Buenos Aires 1970 (Pos. 243).

242 B

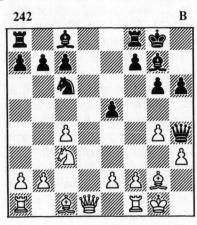

192

243                         W

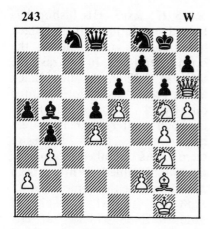

28 &e4!!. The commentators were impressed by the elegance of this move, yet failed to take stock of its depth.[1] For the less subtle tactician there was another plausible possibility: 28 ♘xh7!? ♘xh7 29 hxg6 fxg6 (29 ... ♘f8 30 g7 ♘g6 31 ♘h5 wins) 30 ♕xg6+ ♔h8 31 ♕xe6 ♘e7 (31 ... ♘g5 32 ♕h6+!) 32 ♘f5 and White might well win, though with some labour. Fischer's choice is more imaginative, profound and, indeed, elegant. It is pretty obvious that the bishop is taboo – 28 ... dxe4 29 ♘3xe4 mates Black before long. At e4 the bishop creates the threat of ♘h5 after the pawn exchange on g6, and also prevents ... &d3 – a move Black would gladly have played at the first appropriate moment, since the bishop would overprotect his most sensitive points on the b1-h7 diagonal (e4,

g6, h7), and give some hope for a future ... &b1. Panno's answer – 28 ... ♕e7 – gave Fischer the opportunity to carry his attack through to a neat finish: 29 ♘xh7! ♘xh7 30 hxg6 fxg6 31 &xg6 ♘g5 32 ♘h5 ♘f3+ 33 ♔g2 ♘h4+ 34 ♔g3 ♘xg6 35 ♘f6+! ♔f7 36 ♕h7+, and Panno resigned – it's mate next move. But the elegant-looking 28th move concealed much more than that; before playing that move Fischer must have calculated the consequences of 28 ... &e8!?. White is compelled to continue the attack, because retreats such as 29 &d3 or 29 &b1 permit Black to put up a real defence with 29 ... ♕c7!. So: 29 hxg6 hxg6 (29 ... fxg6 30 ♕xf8+!) 30 ♘h5! gxh5 31 ♘h7! (White has plenty of room to go wrong at this stage. On 31 &h7+ ♘xh7 32 ♘xh7 Black has 32 ... f6! 33 ♘xf6+ ♔f7 34 ♕xh5+ ♔e7 35 ♕g5 ♔f7. White also gets nowhere if he tries 33 exf6 ♕c7 34 ♕f8+ [he slides down the slippery slope of defeat with 34 f7+ ♔xf7 35 ♕f8+ ♔g6 36 ♕g8+ ♕g7 37 gxh5+ ♔h6+!] 34 ... ♔xh7 35 ♕xe8 ♘d6 36 ♕xh5+ ♔g8 37 ♕g6+ ♔f8) 31 ... ♘xh7 32 &xh7+ ♔h8 33 &d3+ ♔g8 34 ♕h7+ ♔f8 35 ♕h8+ ♔e7 36 ♕f6+ ♔d7 37 gxh5!!. Only in this way can White ensure his win, and Fischer must have foreseen it when playing his 28th move. The h-pawn can't be stopped.

With rare exceptions (like his spectacular queen sacrifice against Schweber from the same tournament as the above game – see Pos. 121, or his 1st match game against Larsen, Candidates 1971 – see 28 ♗c5!! in Pos. 317), Fischer's tactical approach, especially from the mid-sixties on, was not geared to creating spectacular shots by which to knock down his opponents, but rather, like a well-experienced boxer, he was interested more in the introduction of some timely left-rights or short upper-cuts whenever the occasion was right and ripe for it. Let's look first at Fischer-Portisch, Havana Olympiad 1966 (Pos. 244).

♗xe5 15 ♗xc5. His bishop has turned very influential, and Black has become vulnerable in the open central files. In contrast, the tame 14 ♗d2 would allow Black a 'free breath', as Gligorić pointed out, by 14 ... ♖b8. Could Black fare better after Fischer's 14 e5! by playing 14 ... fxe3 –? It doesn't seem so. As a number of commentators maintained,[2] White gets an advantage all the same after 15 exd6 exf2+ 16 ♔xf2 0-0+ 17 ♔g1 cxd6 18 ♖xd6 ♗f5 19 ♖e1, etc. (see also p.119 and Pos. 125)

The following example is also typical of Fischer's tactical skill (Fischer-Ivkov, Palma de Mallorca 1970, Pos. 245).

244                                    B

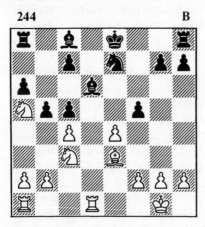

245                                    B

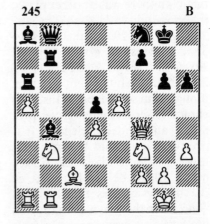

Portisch plays **13 ... f4**, and faces the unpleasant riposte: **14 e5!**. After this extremely well-timed and correct 'short' blow, Fischer gets things his way – **14 ...**

Ivkov plays **35 ... ♗c3**, hoping to tie White down on the b-file and answer 36 ♖a3 by (perhaps) 36 ... ♖xa5!?. Fischer's elegant **36 ♘c5!** dispels all illusions. Black doesn't get the chance to play 36 ... ♘e6 (37 ♘xa6 wins), and after the short four-rook skirmish, White is the one to say the last word: **36 ... ♖xa5** worse is 36 ... ♗xa1 37 ♘xb7, 37 ♘xb7 ♖xa1 38 ♖xa1 ♘e6 39 ♕f6!. Simplest. After 39 ♖xa8 ♕xa8 40 ♕e3 ♘xd4! 41 ♘xd4 ♕a1+ 42 ♔h2 ♗xd4 White would have found it more difficult to realise his advantage had his opponent insisted on playing on. In the game, Black resigned after: **39 ... ♗xa1 40 ♘d6 ♕c7 41 ♗xg6! ♕c1+ 42 ♘e1! ♕xe1+ 43 ♔h2 ♘g5 44 ♗xf7+!** 1-0.

Fischer's games are replete with such 'little combinations'. In many cases they are simply the most immediate and effective, though not necessarily difficult to find, solutions.

246 W

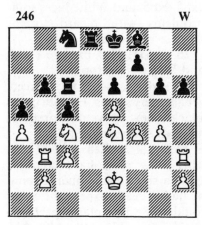

In Fischer-Durao, Havana Ol-

ympiad 1966 (Pos. 246), there followed: **33 ♘xa5! ♖c7** – it is mate in two after 33 ... bxa5 34 ♘f6+ ♔e7 35 ♖b7+. Now, after **34 ♘c4 ♖a7 35 ♘xb6 ♘xb6 36 ♖xb6 ♖da8 37 ♘f6+ ♔d8 38 ♖c6! ♖c7 39 ♖d3+ ♔c8 40 ♖xc7+ ♔xc7 41 ♖d7+ ♔c6 42 ♖xf7**, White's material advantage is decisive. But the end was also very cute: **42 ... c4 43 ♘d7 ♗c5 44 ♘xc5 ♔xc5 45 ♖c7+ ♔d5 46 b4!**, and Black is in an inescapable mating net. If 46 ... cxb3 *e.p.* then 47 ♔d3 with 48 c4+ to follow, and if 46 ... ♖xa4 47 ♔e3 and 48 ♖c5 mates. (see also Pos. 58, 118, 149)

At the last round of the Olympiad he had the following position against the Cuban Jimenez (Pos. 247, Fischer is White).

247 W

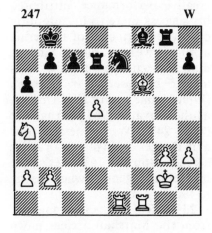

As Fischer mentioned in the Cuban magazine *Jaque Mate*,[3] 29 ♗xe7 ♗xe7 30 ♖f7 would allow

Black to counter with 30 ... ♗b4!.
With a neat little stroke he
eliminates this: **29 d6!**. Also winning was 29 ♘c5 ♖xd5 30 ♖xe7
♗xe7 – not 30 ... ♖xc5 31 ♖e8+
♔a7 32 ♗d4 – 31 ♗xe7 ♖d2+ 32
♖f2, etc. But this is certainly not
as incisive as Fischer's method. **29
... cxd6 30 ♗xe7 ♗xe7** 30 ...
♖xe7? 31 ♖xf8+! **31 ♖f7**. Now
there is no possibility of ... ♗b4,
and Black loses a piece by force:
31 ... ♖e8 32 ♘b6 ♖c7 33 ♘d5 –
so Black resigned.

These last examples illustrated
cases of one-sided blows, where
Fischer encountered no effective
opposition. Polugayevsky, who
regarded his drawn game with
Fischer at Palma de Mallorca
1970 (see Pos. 189) as a good
creative performance, attributed
his success there to his adoption
of Fischer's principle of answering
a blow with a blow. Such a
mutual exchange of blows was
also to be observed in Fischer's
(White) game against Hein Donner,
at the Havana 1965 tournament
(Pos. 248). We witnessed how
ably Fischer could put up an active
defence (pp.161-76). Let's see
his tactical ingenuity when having
to face it himself.

**23 b3 ♖c8!** Donner has emerged
from the Marshall a clear pawn
down, without much in the way of
counterplay. Yet from this moment
on he turns out a most imaginative

248                                    W

defence. 27 ... cxb3 28 axb3
followed by 25 c4 would have
been quite hopeless for Black.

**24 bxc4 ♗d6! 25 ♕b6!** Blow for
blow. Playable but certainly inferior was 25 ♖f3 ♗c5 (25 ...
♗g4? 26 ♕xg4 ♕xd2 27 ♖xf7!!)
26 ♕f4 ♕xf4 27 ♖xf4 ♗d3 28
cxb5 axb5, and White faces some
problems with regard to the
defence of his pawn on c3.

**25 ... ♗f4!** 25 ... bxc4 26 ♕xa6,
and White is on top.

**26 ♕xh6 ♗xh6 27 f4!**. Forced,
yet also very strong. He anticipates
Black's next move and prepares
his own surprising 29th.

**27 ... g5! 28 ♖e5 ♗d3 29 c5!!**.
This blow must have come as
quite a shock to Donner. Even if
he hadn't really expected Fischer
to fall in with his plans by 29 fxg5
♗g7!, something like 29 ♗h3
♖ce8! would have been much

more 'in line'. It takes great tactical vision to think up a move like 29 c5, all the more so as it had to be foreseen a good number of moves ahead. **29 ... ♖xc5 30 d6! ♖xc3 31 d7**, and the d-pawn decided the issue: **31 ... gxf4 32 ♖ae1 ♗g7 33 ♖e8 ♗d4+ 34 ♔h1 ♗f6 35 gxf4 1-0**

At the same tournament Fischer's tactical vision manifested itself in another game, in another way: Doda-Fischer (Pos. 249).

**249**                    **B**

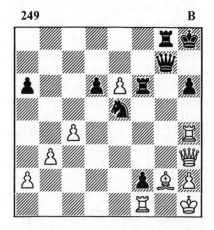

**33 ... ♘f3!**. "Normal" would have been 33 ... ♘d3!, intending 34 ... ♘f4, which was, to be sure, pretty decisive too (34 ♕g3 ♖g6 35 ♕e3 ♘e1! etc). Yet here we have to deal with a very interesting case of tactical imagination: though the a1-h8 diagonal is blocked by two pieces, Fischer envisages that the queen could be operative on that diagonal as well as on the g-file. **34 ♖h5 ♘d2! 35 ♖xf2 ♖g6!!**. Simple and beautiful. The threat 36 ... ♕a1+ can't be met. **36 ♖hf5 ♕a1+**. White resigned, for if 37 ♖f1 ♘xf1 38 ♖xf1 ♕xf1+! 39 ♗xf1 ♖g1 mate.

Many other examples of Fischer's tactical skills and insight are found in other chapters. See, for instance, Pos. 172, 208-218, 228, 230, 238, 319-321.

## DOUBLE-EDGED AND SPECULATIVE CHESS

Was Fischer a poor tactician, or was he a superb one? Did he play complicated positions with ease, or could he find his way there only with great difficulty?

These questions might seem misplaced after the last chapter, yet, strangely enough perhaps, these two extreme views were held simultaneously by different observers. The eminent critic, Hans Kmoch, for one, was a devout believer in Fischer's tactical gifts throughout his career. "Fischer seems to like complications. At any rate he has more than once demonstrated his fabulous ability to remain in the saddle even if the situation becomes very wild", he wrote on one occasion.[1] And on another one: "Fischer relies on his stupendous virtuosity to find his way in any complicated position".[2] Najdorf remarked about one of Fischer's moves in his match against Petrosian, Buenos Aires 1971: "This is characteristic of Fischer's style, his courting complications".[3] And when reviewing Fischer's career, Paul Keres wrote about the fifteen-year-old boy: "In complicated positions Bobby hardly had to be afraid of anybody".[4] Unless we assume that a player's talent might regress with the years for some reason, it seems a safe conjecture that for Keres, Fischer hardly had to be afraid of anybody in complicated positions up till his World Championship match with Spassky in 1972.

This view of Keres' was quite exceptional among the top Soviet grandmasters at the time. For Geller, Tal and Spassky, for

instance, Fischer's Achilles heel was precisely his lack of orientation in complicated positions!

Of Fischer's **19 ♕f1** in his game against Geller, Skopje 1967 (Pos. 250) ("A hard move to find – it took around 45 minutes", Fischer in *MSMG*)[5] Spassky, annotating it in the newspaper *Soviet Union Today*, had written: "White is losing his head, for else he would have certainly chosen 19 e5, which offers very reasonable attacking chances".[6]

Fischer, according to this view, was apt to lose his head in 'irrational' positions, and this was most evident in his two notorious losses with the white pieces to Efim Geller in 1967. We shall soon return to the one just quoted. Let's first take a look at the earlier encounter, at Monte Carlo that year (Pos. 251).

250                              W

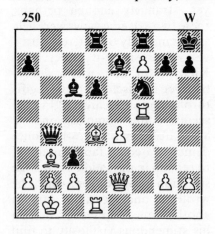

251                              W

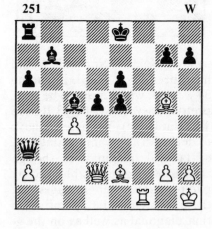

For a top grandmaster to reach this position as Black is, to say the least, quite irresponsible. One is of course entitled to play as one wishes, but what value does a game have when, after nineteen moves, a player finds himself completely at the mercy of his opponent, and can only hope to be saved by one or two side-lines, should his opponent stumble and overlook them? This, I believe, is speculative chess at its worst.

Fischer played **23 ♗g4?**, and lost after **20 ... dxc4 21 ♗xe6 ♛d3! 22 ♛e1 ♗e4!! 23 ♗g4 ♖b8 24 ♗d1 ♔d7 25 ♖f7+ ♔e6**, 0-1. Geller ought to be given credit for finding this highly inventive possibility, yet objectively Black's position after move 19 should have been beyond repair, and it must have been the abundance of winning lines which led Fischer astray. It is a well-known phenomenon that when a player has to choose between a number of winning options, the chance he will fail to notice a slight (yet sometimes significant) difference between one continuation and another grows in proportion to the number of those options.

In his book *The Application of Chess Theory*, Geller examines three alternatives: a1) 20 ♖f3, leading to an endgame which "Black can successfully defend"; b) 20 ♗d1 (Lilienthal's suggestion),

leading to a sharp endgame which "White should win"; c) 20 ♛c2, about which Geller remarks: "After the game I pointed out this attacking possibility to Fischer".[7] O'Kelly in *Europe Echecs*, gives a different version: "After the game Fischer pointed out that by playing 20 ♛c2 he would have 'an easy win'".[8] It seems unlikely Fischer failed to take note of this attacking possibility in his long think before playing his twentieth move. This move leads to a number of possible wins for White. One of them was played out over the board three months later, between Tal and Bogdanović, at Budva 1967: 20 ... e4 21 ♗g4 ♗e7 22 ♛f2 0-0-0 23 ♗f4 ♗d6 24 ♗xe6+ ♔b8 25 ♛b6 ♗xf4 26 ♛xd8+ ♔a7 27 ♖b1 ♛d6 28 ♗xd5 ♗xd5 29 ♛xd6 ♗xd6 30 cxd5, 1-0.

Besides the three possibilities above, in which Black could barely hold his own in a single line, other moves strongly come into consideration:

a) **20 ♖b1 ♗c6** (20 ... ♖b8? 21 ♖b3 ♛a4 22 ♛b2! ♗d4 23 ♛b1 ♛c6 24 ♛xh7, wins) **21 ♖b3 ♛a4 22 ♛c2!**, and the simultaneous threats at h7 and d5 aren't easy to meet.

b) **20 ♗h5+ g6 21 ♗g4 dxc4 22 ♖f6!?** (22 ♖f7 is best met by 22 ... ♗d5!). White has a promising attack, but probably no forced win.

c) **20 ♗f3!**. This (like the previous), wasn't mentioned by Geller or other analysts. It might well be White's simplest and quickest winning process:

c1) 20 ... e4 21 ♗xe4!! dxe4 22 ♕f4 ♔d7 23 ♕f7+ ♔c6 (23 ... ♔c8 24 ♖d1 ♔b8 25 ♖b1 wins, or 23 ... ♗e7 24 ♖d1+) 24 ♕xe6+ ♗d6 (Black can choose another end: 24 ... ♔c7 25 ♖f7+ ♔b8 26 ♗f4+ ♔a7 27 ♖xb7+! ♔xb7 28 ♕d7+ ♔b6 29 ♕c7 mate) 25 ♕d5+ (not 25 c5?! ♕d3!, complicating matters) 25 ... ♔b6 26 ♖b1+ ♗b4 27 ♕d6+ ♔g7 28 ♖xb4 and wins.

c2) 20 ... ♗e7 21 cxd5 exd5 22 ♗xd5 ♖d8 (22 ... ♗xg5 23 ♗f7+ ♔f8 24 ♕xg5 is hopeless) 23 ♗f7+ ♔f8 24 ♗b3+ ♔e8 25 ♕f2!, with a winning attack.

c3) 20 ... ♗d4 21 ♖b1 ♗c6 (21 ... ♖a7 22 cxd5 ♗xd5 23 ♗xd5 exd5 24 ♕c2 ♕c5 25 ♕f5! is very strong) 22 cxd5 ♗xd5 23 ♗xd5 exd5 24 ♕c2. White has the following threats: 25 ♕c6+, 25 ♕xh7, 25 ♕f5, 25 ♖b7. Black cannot attend to all of them successfully. For instance: 24 ... ♕c5 25 ♕xh7 ♖a7 26 ♕h5+! ♔d7 27 ♖c1! ♕b6 (27 ... ♗c3 28 ♕h3+, while 27 ... ♕f8 is met by 28 ♕h3+ ♔d6 29 ♕a3+!, and 27 ... ♕a3 by 28 ♕f7+ ♔d6 29 ♕f8+) 28 ♕f7+ ♔d6 29 ♕g6+ ♔d7 30 ♕xg7+ ♔e6 31 ♕f6+ ♔d7 32 ♕e7 mate. Another line is 24 ... ♔d7 25 ♖b7+ ♔e6 26 ♖e7+ ♕xe7 27

♗xe7 ♔xe7 28 ♕c7+ ♔f8 29 ♕d6+, winning Black's rook next.

c4) 20 ... ♕b4 21 ♕c2! e4 22 ♗h5+ g6 23 ♖b1 ♕a5 24 ♕b2! ♗c6 25 ♕h8+ ♔d7 (25 ... ♗f8 26 ♕f6! ♗d7 27 ♖f1) 26 ♕g7+ ♔c8 27 ♗g4 ♖a7 28 ♗xe6+ ♗d7 29 ♗f4! ♗b4 30 ♕f8+!.

To maintain that a player's carelessness when facing so many advantageous continuations is a sign of a want in his capabilities is quite far-fetched. And if one does criticise Fischer for not seeing 20 ♕c2, how then should he account for Geller's overlooking 20 ♖b1, 20 ♗h5+, 20 ♗f3 (and perhaps a number of other possibilities the position may still offer)? This, to sum it up, isn't merely a complicated position. It is, in the first place, a *won* position for White in which some lines are more complicated than others, and in which one, incidentally, is a losing line.

When so many roads lead you to Rome, choosing one that would finally sink your car in the Tiber is a matter of probablistic accident. In everyday life we have insurance companies to deal with such accidents. In chess we have points and tables in which they are reflected. Fischer's record doesn't allow for other than probablistic interpretations of such misfortunes.

And on to the next game.

This (Fischer-Geller, Skopje 1967) is an example of speculative chess at a much higher level. Here, quite exceptionally for him, Fischer, too, was engaged in a speculative piece sacrifice. This is how the game went:

**1 e4 c5 2 ♘f3 d6 3 d4 cxd4 4 ♘xd4 ♘f6 5 ♘c3 ♘c6 6 ♗c4 e6 7 ♗e3 ♗e7 8 ♗b3 0-0 9 ♕e2 ♕a5 10 0-0-0 ♘xd4 11 ♗xd4 ♗d7 12 ♔b1 ♗c6 13 f4 ♖ad8 14 ♖hf1 b5 15 f5 b4 16 fxe6 bxc3 17 exf7+ ♔h8 18 ♖f5 ♕b4 19 ♕f1 ♘xe4**

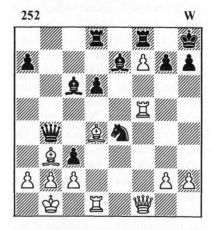

252               W

This position (Pos. 252) deserves our attention. Fischer has built a promising attacking position for the offered piece, and he perceives that ♕f4-h6 would be a winning manoeuvre now. It contains, though, one flaw: when the queen reaches h6, Black can play ... ♕xd4, and the queen at h6 remains hanging. Note that the

attempt to screen g7 by ... ♘f6, would fail under almost all circumstances in view of 1 ♖xf6 ♗xf6 2 ♕xf6 gxf6 3 ♗xf6 mate. Fischer plays the preliminary 20 a3, so as to drive the black queen back, and enable 21 ♕f4 to come in with full force. In retrospect it turned out that 20 a3 was a grave mistake which eventually lost the game, while both Fischer and Geller, seeing on this occasion eye to eye, agreed that 20 ♕f4 at once would have won for White, though in a problem-like manner. How did Geller manage to turn the tables? After **20 a3 ♕b7 21 ♕f4**, there came **21 ... ♗a4!!**. Fischer confessed: "I didn't see it!".[9]

This is probably a good opportunity to briefly dwell on his attitude to the commitment of a player of his class to divulging the complete truth of his deliberations during the game, through which we could gain some insight into his alleged chessic shortcomings.

Many other players would have used here a more sophisticated formula like: "I saw this move right after touching my queen, but, alas, it was too late!", and the good-humoured would probably add: "Why, for heavens' sake, don't they change this touch-move rule?". That Fischer dares to go on with: "Moreover, the strength of this resource didn't become fully apparent to me for another two moves", is simply outrageous.

With the exception of a couple of passages in Timman's *The Narrow Path* (in the Dutch language), I cannot recall seeing any similar statement by a top grandmaster. After all, what is one a grandmaster for if not to see *everything*? (see p.147). Occasional blunders and oversights are all right; one is entitled to some human faults even at that level! But "didn't become fully apparent"! – No, this goes too far, Bobby! One day they will strip a grandmaster of his title for confessing such delinquencies.

Geller, in comparison, is much more professional in this respect. We get no glimpse whatsoever from his comments, as to when he saw 21 ... ♗a4!!.[10] When we examine the diagrammed position, we realise that this move is hardly latent in the position, and that is two moves before playing it! Since there is no indication in the position that the move should be taken into any serious consideration, Geller must have busied himself with the one obvious theme in that position: White's mating attack versus the threat 1 ... ♘d2+, with all the ramifications of 2 ♖xd2 cxd2, etc.

Only after, and by virtue of, Fischer's mistaken 20 a3, did ... ♗a4 become an actual possibility,

and Geller's saving resource turns out to be a winning one.

For the speculative player this, however, is a point of no import. His main objective is the creation of positions pregnant with tactical possibilities, many of which are bound to be, by the very nature of this policy, ad hoc solutions. And this brings us closer to the crux of our matter. The tactical approach in chess almost always entails speculative thinking. Good examples nowadays are Ljubojević and Speelman. And when one reviews the annals of Russian and Soviet chess from Chigorin on, one realises that virutally almost all the great Russian and Soviet tactical players were speculative thinkers, too: Alekhine, Riumin, Tolush, Bronstein, Nezhmetdinov, Geller himself, Stein, Tal, Vaganian, to mention but few.

On this historical background it was probably quite impossible to develop a different conception; namely, that tactical gifts and clarity in chess might very well be compatible with each other, whereas clarity and speculative thinking are indeed mutually exclusive qualities. One definitely cannot be a clear thinker and a speculative one at the same time. Whereas this does not exclude the possibility that he be a clear thinker and an excellent tactician! With Fischer we encounter, probably for the first time, that remarkable combination of a first-class player of high tactical gifts and a distinctly clear chess vision. In practice this means that that clear vision would at times 'blind' him to certain options.

To unearth a power-move like 21 ... ♗a4!! is certainly something a player of a speculative bent would do with greater ease than a nonspeculative player. Not because the move itself is speculative – it led to a clear-cut win (**22 ♕g4 ♗f6 23 ♖xf6 ♗xb3, 0-1**) – but because it requires that turn of mind that is typical of the speculative player; a turn of mind in which coherency quite often gives way to on-the-spot improvisation.

This isn't yet equivalent to saying that Fischer played doubleedged positions badly. It implies one thing only: that a certain class of moves in double-edged positions lay less in his scope than in that of a typical speculative tactician. We shall see more of this in the next chapter (Pos. 258-261).

That he nonetheless was capable of playing excellently in doubleedged games, was borne out by many of his impeccable performances. Here is one of the most flawless modern masterpieces of double-edged chess.

The game is Minić-Fischer, Rovinj-Zagreb 1970. Raymond Keene expressed better than other writers the wonderful quality of this game, when he commented, after Black's 31 ... ♕a3!!: "What general principle is it which requires that Black's attack should be more successful than White's? It is clear now that White's situation is crucial (in spite of his extra rook) but on move 29 it was only the miracle of the sacrifice that turned the scales."[11] Can any game be considered more doubleedged than one that is thus described?

**1 e4 c5 2 ♘f3 d6 3 d4 cxd4 4 ♘xd4 ♘f6 5 ♘c3 a6 6 ♗g5 e6 7 f4 ♗e7 8 ♕f3 ♕c7 9 0-0-0 ♘bd7 10 g4 b5 11 ♗xf6 ♘xf6 12 g5 ♘d7 13 a3 ♖b8 14 h4 b4 15 axb4 ♖xb4 16 ♗h3 0-0 17 ♘f5 ♘c5 18 ♘xe7+ ♕xe7 19 h5!**. The only active try. Many commentators, among them Keres,[12] Gligorić,[13] Vuković,[14] and Levy,[15] believed White should do better to pile up on the d-file by 19 ♕e3, 20 ♖d4, 21 ♖hd1, etc. This fails quite simply to 19 ... ♕a7!, and Black has a won position. **19 ... ♗b7 20 h6 ♗xe4 21 ♘xe4 ♘xe4 22 hxg7 ♖c8! 23 ♖h2 ♖a4 24 ♔b1 d5 25 c4 ♖axc4 26 ♗f1 ♖b4 27 ♕h3 ♘c3+ 28 ♔c1 ♘a4+ 29 ♔b1 ♖xb2+! 30 ♖xb2 ♘c3+ 31 ♔c1 ♕a3!! 32 ♗d3 ♕a1+ 33 ♔d2 ♕xb2+ 34 ♔e1 ♘e4**, and White resigned.

Fischer's disagreement with speculative chess was not only a matter of playing style.

He was intellectually averse to it throughout his career.

At the 12th Olympiad, Moscow 1956, David Bronstein played the following sensational piece sacrifice against Rojahn from Finland: 1 e4 e5 2 ♘f3 ♘c6 3 ♗c4 ♘f6 4 ♘g5 d5 5 exd5 ♘a5 6 d3 h6 7 ♘f3 e4 8 dxe4 ♘xc4, scoring a crushing victory. In his analysis of the game, Bronstein tells: "As the game was over, my opponent asked me: "Did you forget your bishop when you played that move? – Definitely not!"[16]

Analysing his own game against Arthur Bisguier at the New York Open 1963, Fischer in *Chess Life* of December 1963, writes after playing the more common 6 ♗b5+: "Bronstein, one of the original Russian supermen, actually blundered away a piece in the 1956 World Team Tournament on the eighth move with 6 d3 h6 7 ♘f3 e4 8 dxe4??", and with the good-hearted irony that typified his writing at that time, he added between brackets: "David, the right move is 8 ♕e2".

For Fischer 8 dxe4 meant simply blundering away a piece. This kind of speculative chess was quite meaningless for him. As long as the outcome of a certain move couldn't be judged according to coherent positional criteria, it had to be avoided. This, for him, was a tenet of belief, a matter of

deep conviction.

At the Match of the Century, Belgrade 1970, Fischer faced Petrosian, and in their first encounter the following position was reached after Fischer's (White) 15th move (Pos. 253).

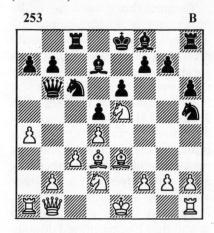

253                                    B

All the commentators who annotated the game, pointed out, without exclusion, the possibility 15 ... ♘xe5 16 dxe5 ♗c5 17 a5 ♕c7 18 g4!?. Among them were Petrosian himself,[17] Euwe,[18] Suetin,[19] Trifunović,[20] Neikirch,[21] and Flohr;[22] all but one – Fischer! How come? Why did he mention only "18 ♘f3 with a bind"?[23] What was there in 18 g4 that he found deserving no mention at all? After Black's 17th move the position is quite well organised, the pieces well deployed, and there are no structural weaknesses in White's camp. With 18 g4 White, though formally winning material, lets the coherent structure of the position drastically change, and the positional features which up to now have been very distinct are rendered obscure: 18 ... ♗xe3 19 fxe3 ♕xe5 20 gxh5 ♕xe3+ 21 ♗e2 ♗b5 22 ♕d1. Besides losing much of its aesthetic value, the game would have thus, for Fischer, deteriorated into an unpredictable 'catch-as-catch-can' match. It does not matter for him that White retains the better chances since, to begin with, he retains them by 18 ♘f3 as well, and, more importantly, the nature of White's advantage doesn't comply with his chess vision any longer – it doesn't offer a clear operative plan, and the position is indeed susceptible to 'irrational' developments. As far as Fischer was concerned this type of chess had to be avoided as long as there were more 'rational' alternatives at had. (For the complete game see p.118).

Players of the Benoni and the Semi-Benoni may temperamentally inclined to play wild and speculative chess. These openings easily lend themselves to such treatments – one sharp move can cause the game to flare up. Let's look at two examples from Fischer's games, and see how he approaches these positions. We follow, first, Larsen-Fischer, Santa Monica 1966 (Pos. 254), from Black's 13th move to move 34.

254               B

In the diagrammed position Fischer proceeded with **13 ... ♘d7**. R.Byrne gave this comment: "Fischer, chooses the simplest development in preference to the sharp but murky 13 ... f5 whose consequences are difficult to assess".[24]

No unclear consequences, no murkiness. The whole game stands under this sign. Fischer refrains from playing the standard ... a6 until late in the middle-game, takes no drastic steps such as 19 ... g4 (Larsen's suggestion),[25] and seems to be mainly concerned with enhancing the strategic value of his knight. The game is decided when Black's control of the e-file is no more challengable. **14 ♘c4 ♕e7 15 ♘e3 ♘f6 16 ♕c2 ♖e8 17 ♗b5 ♖d8 18 ♗e2 ♖e8 19 f3 ♘h7 20 g4 ♘f8 21 a4 ♘g6 22 ♔f1 ♖b8**

23 ♗b5 ♖d8 24 ♘f5 ♗xf5 25 exf5
♘e5 26 ♘e4 a6 27 ♗e2 ♘d7 28
♖e1 ♘f6 29 ♘c3 ♕d7 30 a5 ♖e8
31 ♔f2 ♕c7 32 ♖a1 c4 33 ♔g3
♖e3 34 ♕d2 ♖be8. (For the last
phase of this game see Pos. 270.)

255                                   B

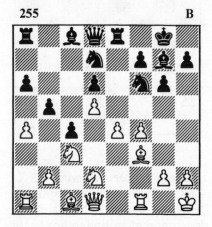

A couple of months after this
game, Fischer, at the Havana
Olympiad 1966 reached Pos. 255
in his game against Pomar. For
the speculative player 14 ... b4
would have been a most attractive
possibility to consider, and eventually play. It might lead to
enormous complications, and certainly to a most lively game. Let's
examine: 15 ♘a2 a5 (dubious and
very risky is 15 ... c3 16 bxc3 bxc3
17 ♘xc3 ♘xd5 18 ♘xd5 ♗xa1 19
♗a3 ♗g7 20 ♗xd6) 16 ♘xc4 ♘xe4
17 ♗xe4 ♖xe4 18 ♘xd6 ♖d4 19
♕f3 ♗a6. Black would regain his
pawn after either 20 ♖e1, 20 ♗e3!?
or 20 ♘b5.

A very interesting game develops
from 15 ... ♘c5!? (instead of 15 ...
a5) 16 e5 (16 ♘xb4 ♘fxe4 17
♘xc4 ♕h4, and Black has a
beautiful game) 16 ... dxe5 17 fxe5
(17 d6? e4) 17 ... ♘xd5 18 ♘xc4
♗e6, and if now 19 ♘d6?, then 19
... ♗xe5! 20 ♘xe8 (or 20 ♗xd5) 20
... ♕h4 21 g3 ♗xg3 22 ♕e2 ♖xe8,
and Black has little to complain
about; he has got more than
enough for his exchange.

This is, of course, no exhaustive
analysis of the position. It indicates
in broad outlines its main possibilities. Fischer doesn't wish to
delve into all this. What he plays
ensures Black the better prospects
without giving his opponent any
chance to start fishing in troubled
waters: 14 ... ♖b8. If he gets in ...
♘c5, White would be doomed to
complete passivity. Yet even after
Pomar's better choice – 15 axb5
axb5 16 e5!? – Fischer clearly had
the upper hand: 16 ... dxe5 17
♘de4 ♘xe4 18 ♘xe4 ♘f6 – see
further Pos. 293.

Piquant and revealing is our
last case. How deep Fischer's
aversion to speculative chess might
have been is shown by his reluctance to admit the correctness of a
certain speculative line, even when
retrospectively it turns out to be
completely sound.

Hans Berliner annotated his
game against Fischer from the
3rd round of the US Championship

**256** W

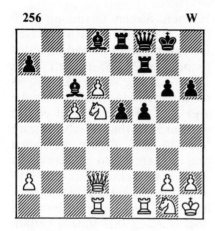

1962-63 for *The South African Chess Player* of February 1963. About Fischer's **27 ♕e2** in Pos. 256 he wrote: "Only now did I notice that the intended line 27 ♘b4 ♗a5 fails to 28 ♘xc6! ♗xd2 29 ♖xd2 ♖c8 30 ♘xe5 ♖xc5 31 ♘xf7 ♔xf7 32 d7 ♕d8 33 ♖fd1 and Black is helpless against the invasion of the white knight. In post-game analysis Bobby thought his move was better, a view which I do not share."[26]

After 27 ♕e2 White's advanced passed pawns do of course offer him some advantage, but Reshevsky's suggested defence 27 ... ♖e6![27] gives Black some reasonable hopes of survival: if 28 ♘f4 ♖e8, and 29 ♘xg6 doesn't work because of 29 ... ♕g7! and the knight has only e7 to go to, leaving Black with a won position. After other moves by White, Black consoli-

dates with 28 ... ♕e8!. "This seems to show the inferiority of White's ♕e2", Berliner concluded. And though the line he pointed out to Fischer was doubtless a winning one (there would follow ♖d6, ♘f3-d4-c6), Fischer persisted in disliking it nonetheless!

## MISSING TACTICAL TRICKS

When a player isn't constantly preoccupied with creating tactically-bevelled positions, he won't always pay heed to such combinative possibilities as happen to come by. In Fischer we find a player who, on the one hand, possessed great tactical gifts, yet not being a one-dimensional player, he occasionally missed tactical tricks.

**257** W

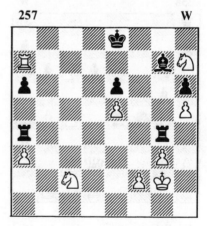

Thus, against Portisch at Santa

Monica 1966 (Pos. 257), the move 50 f4, aiming to net the black rook at g4, evidently fails in view of 50 ... ♖axf4. Fischer leaves it at that and doesn't try to probe deeper into this possibility. After his **50 f3** the rook found a safer haven at c4, and Portisch ultimately drew the game. However, as Portisch himself pointed out in the tournament book,[1] Fischer could weave a non-escapable net around the rook: 50 ♘e3 ♗xe5 51 ♘xg4 ♖xg4 52 f4!. Now the pawn is taboo – 52 ... ♗xf4 53 ♘f6+ – and after 52 ... ♗a1 the clasp shuts the rook in: 53 ♘g5!!. It seems that for Fischer the advance f2-f4 was connected solely with a possible ♔h3, and the preliminary imaginative interpolation of ♘g5 escaped his attention. (see also Pos. 188)

**258**                                     **W**

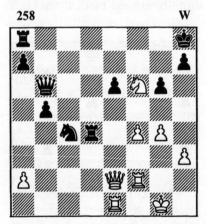

Well-known is the position after Black's 28th move in Spassky-

Fischer, Siegen Olympiad 1970 (Pos. 258). When Fischer played for this position he had intended to answer 29 ♕xe6 with 29 ... ♖d1, winning White's knight, as he threatens both 30 ... ♖xe1+ and 30 ... ♕xe6. It is of course unthinkable that Fischer didn't 'see' 30 ♕f7. Firstly, he had a prepared answer to it. Secondly, it is too elementary a move to overlook. As in the previous case, he didn't probe deeper into this line, missing this time a certain resource of his opponent's. After 30 ... ♖xe1+ 31 ♔g2, there are many potential threats on the h1-a8 diagonal, as well as a check by a knight at e3, all of which should apparently have sufficed to create insurmountable problems for White's king. It was only after Spassky played **29 ♕xe6!**, that Fischer realised that the white king escapes to safety via h4: 29 ... ♖d1 30 ♕f7!! ♖xe1+ 31 ♔g2 ♕c6+ 32 ♔g3 ♖e3+ 33 ♔h4 ♖xh3+ 34 ♔xh3 ♕h1+ 35 ♖h2 ♕f1+ 36 ♔h4 ♕e1+ 37 ♔g5. (see also Pos. 83, 165)

Less well known is a resource Fischer missed three rounds later, playing White against Hort (Pos. 259). Curiously, it was on a similar theme!

Fischer played **36 ♗a3**, which led after 36 ... ♘c8 37 ♕a8 ♕b6 38 ♗xb4 ♗xb4 39 ♕d5 ♕c5 40 ♕xe5 ♕xe5 41 ♘xe5 ♘d6, to a materially

259          W

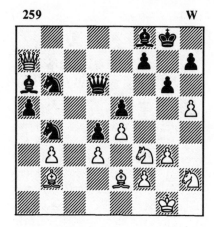

better endgame, but an unwinnable one. Again it is improbable he overlooked the quite elementary 36 ♘xe5. It must have been something else in the lines that proceeded from this. In *Chess Life* I gave an analysis of this position after 36 ... ♕xe5 37 ♕xb6.[2] Here it is (with some revisions):

I) 37 ... ♗c5 38 ♕d8+ ♔g7 39 h6+! ♔xh6 40 ♘g4+, winning Black's queen.

II) 37 ... ♗xd3 38 ♘g4 ♕d6 (38 ... ♕c5 39 ♘h6+! ♔g7 40 ♗xd4+, wins the same queen as above) 39 ♘f6+! ♔h8 40 ♕a7!!. This is the idea. As in Spassky-Fischer, so here, it is the combined efforts of a white queen at f7 and a knight at f6 which spell bad news for Black. Two pieces remain en prise, but they are both untouchable in view of this: 40 ... ♗xe2 41

♕xf7, and 40 ... ♕xf6 41 ♗xd4. Two other alternatives are: a) 40 ... ♗g7 41 ♘e8 ♕f8 42 ♘xg7 ♗xe2 43 ♕xd4 f6 (or 43 ... ♔g8 44 ♘e8!) when 44 ♕d7! is the most decisive. b) 40 ... ♗e7 41 ♘d5! ♘xd5 (41 ... ♗xe2 42 ♗xd4+ f6 43 ♘xe7 ♗xh5 44 ♕b8+!! ♕xb8 45 ♗xf6 mates elegantly, and 42 ... ♔g8 43 ♕a8+! ♗d8 44 ♘f6+ ♔h8 – 44 ... ♔f8 45 ♗c5! – 45 ♘d7+! ♕xd4 46 ♕xd8+ ♔g7 47 ♕f8 mates simply, but effectively enough) 42 ♕d4+ ♗f6 43 e5! ♗xe2 (or 43 ... ♗xe5 44 ♕xe5+ ♕xe5 45 ♗xe5+ f6 46 ♗xd3 fxe5 47 hxg6 hxg6 48 ♗xg6, winning the endgame) 44 exd6 ♗xd4 45 ♗xd4+ f6 46 d7, and the pawn promotes.

III) 37 ... ♘xd3 38 ♘g4 ♕c5 (or 38 ... ♕d6) 39 ♘f6+ ♔h8 (if 39 ... ♔g7 40 h6+! ♔xh6 41 ♘g8+! ♔g5 42 ♕f6 mate) 40 ♗xd4 ♕xb6 (40 ... ♕c1+ 41 ♔h2 ♘xf2 42 ♗xf2 ♗xe2 43 ♕d8 ♕a3 44 ♘d7, and White wins easily) 41 ♗xb6 ♗b4 (on 41 ... ♗g7 42 ♘e8 ♗e5 43 f4 ♗b8 44 ♗d4+ ♔g8 45 ♘f6+ wins) 42 ♗f1!. Simple, and much stronger than 42 ♗d4 expecting 42 ... ♔g7 43 h6+! ♔xh6 44 ♘g8+ ♔g5 45 ♗f6, mate, but failing against 42 ... ♘e5!!. After 42 ♗f1! Black would lose material in view of White's threat ♘d5-c7.

These three examples dealt with positions where the tactical nuance was covered by a small heap of moves. In the next two, the nuance was close to the surface.

**260**                                    **W**

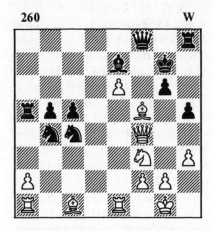

In Fischer-Stein, Sousse 1967 (Pos. 260) it was 30 ♘h4!! instead of Fischer's 30 ♗e4, which gave White only a slight endgame advantage after the queen exchange. In the *British Chess Magazine*, John Littlewood[3] indicated the following main variations after his suggested 30 ♘h4:

a) 30 ... gxf5 31 ♕g3+, and mates.

b) 30 ... ♗xh4 31 ♕xh4 gxf5 32 ♕g5+ ♔h7 33 e7!, winning.

c) 30 ... ♗xh4 31 ♕xh4 ♕xf5 32 ♕e7+ ♔g8 33 ♕d8+ ♔g7 (33 ... ♕f8 34 e7!) 34 ♕c7+ ♔g8 35 e7!, winning.

d) 30 ... g5 31 ♕g3 ♕f6 32 ♘g6! ♕xa1 33 ♘xe7 ♕f6 34 ♗xg5, again winning.

Against Reshevsky, US Championship 1963-64, Fischer as Black

**261**                                    **B**

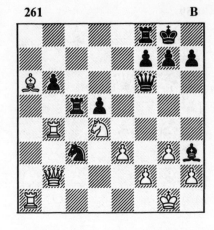

reached this position (Pos. 261, see also Pos. 192). Fischer's continuation led to a slightly inferior endgame for him: **28 ... b5 29 ♗xb5 ♘xb5 30 ♖xb5 ♖xb5 31 ♕xb5 ♕e5 32 ♖e1 h5 33 ♘c6**, etc. He could have turned it instead into a favourable endgame by playing 28 ... ♖a5!!. This move, as well as the key moves in the last two examples, belong to a class of moves which normally would be found in the arsenal of either the one-directional tactician, or of a player with a special knack of uncovering such 'power-moves' (of which Alekhine was, perhaps, the supreme example). The common denominator of these moves is that they change the course of the game drastically and unpredictably. In this position, for instance, moving the rook to a5 looks quite absurd indeed – the knight is left en prise, and Black attacks two well defended pieces. Very few players would have visualised the rook move in that direction, and fewer still would have gone on to calculating what happens after that – it all seems just a useless waste of time (and this explains how the author stumbled upon it . . .). The thing is, however, that the particular configuration of the pieces on the board makes it possible for this bizarre and off-beat move to be not only playable but, unexpectedly, Black's best. When a player has no knack for finding such sudden 'power-moves', they won't appear in his games, no matter how good a tactician he is otherwise.

Let's see what justifies this move here: 29 ♕xc3 (neither 29 ♗d3 ♖xa1+ 30 ♕xa1 ♖c8, nor 29 ♗b7 ♘e2+!, are better alternatives, while 29 ♖xa5 bxa5 30 ♖b6, is answered simply and effectively by 29 ... ♕d8) 29 ... ♖fa8! (This leads to an endgame in which Black runs no risk of losing, as was the problem in the actual game. His position remains superior, to one extent or another, in all variations.) 30 ♖ba4 (30 ♖b5 ♖5xa6 31 ♖xa6 ♖xa6 32 ♖xd5 ♖a2 33 ♕e1 ♕xf2+! 34 ♕xf2 ♖a1+ 35 ♕e1 ♖xe1+ 36 ♔f2 ♖f1+ 37 ♔e2 g6 38 ♖b5 ♖h1 39 ♖xb6 ♖xh2+ 40 ♔f3 h5 gives

Black excellent winning chances. Whereas 30 ♖xa5 bxa5 31 ♖b5 ♕xa6 32 ♖xd5?? ♕f1 is mate!) 30 ... ♖8xa6 31 ♖xa5 bxa5 32 ♖xa5 leads to 32 ... h5! (better than 32 ... ♕g6 33 ♕b2!, or 32 ... ♕b6 33 ♖b5 ♕c7 34 ♘e2! – but not 34 ♖xd5 h6! 35 ♕e1 ♕b7!, with enduring pressure for the pawn) 33 ♖xa6 (33 ♖xd5 ♖a2!) 33 ... ♕xa6 34 ♕e1 ♕a2 35 ♕c1 f6, followed by 36 ... g5, and White has a passive role to play in this endgame.

The difference between this and the next two examples is that in them the piece configuration more conspicuously points to an immediate tactical solution (either by Fischer or by his opponent).

These are some of those few odd cases in which Fischer's tactical orientation wasn't up to par.

262                                    W

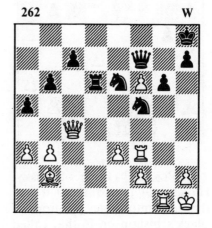

What should have triggered the imagination of the first player in Fischer-Andersson, Siegen 1970 (Pos. 262), is the pin on the a2-g8 diagonal, and a possible invasion of a rook to g7. Fischer's **34 ♗e5** ignored both these (winning the game, all the same, ten moves later). Had Fischer considered 34 ♖xf5! gxf5 35 ♖g7!, he couldn't have failed to see that after 35 ... ♕f8 (or 35 ... ♕h5 36 f7 ♕f3+ 37 ♖g2+) Black succumbs to 36 ♕xe6! (but not 36 ♖xc7 ♖d1+ 37 ♔g2 ♕g8+ 38 ♔f3 ♘d4+!! when Black wins!) and after 36 ... ♕a8+ 37 e4! ♖xe6 38 f7 ♕xe4+ 39 ♖g2+, Black gasps his last.[4] (see also Pos. 80)

**263**                                           **W**

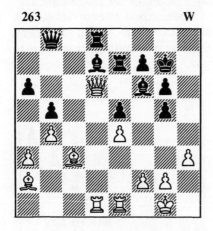

In Pos. 263 (Fischer-Spassky, Havana Olympiad 1966) it was the uncomfortable position of Black's bishop on f6 that called forth the need for a tactical treatment. Spassky suggested 36 ♖e3! without giving further analysis.[5] Before examining what this move implies, let's watch Fischer's choice: **36 ♕xa6?.** Driven by materialistic impulses this time, he not only fails to take advantage of his own chances, but also fails to see Black's tactical riposte – 36 ... ♖c8!, with the double threat 37 ... ♖xc3, and 37 ... ♖c6, putting the white queen in mortal danger. Fischer had to give up the exchange in order to save both these pieces – **37 ♖d6 ♖xc3 38 ♖xf6 ♗e6 39 ♖xe6 fxe6** – and had to be satisfied with a minor success, that of drawing the game eighteen moves later. Let's return now to 36 ♖e3!, a move, by the way, that would have been in concord with Fischer's traditional rook manoeuvring (see Pos. 116-122). So, after that move (better than the other tactical possibility: 36 ♗xe5!? ♖xe5 37 ♕xb8 ♖xb8 38 ♖xd7 ♖e7 39 ♖xe7 ♗xe7, with a drawish endgame) Black might do best to trade queens by 36 ... ♕xd6, since if he refrains from this and defends a6 by 36 ... ♕b7 or 36 ... ♕a7, White's 37 ♖f3 forces him to intercede on e6 with either a bishop or a rook. The results are either: a) 37 ... ♖e6 38 ♗xe6 ♗xe6 39 ♗xe5! ♖xd6 40 ♗xf6+ ♔h7 (he is free to choose another end with 40 ... ♔f8 41

♖xd6 ♗d7 42 ♖fd3 ♗e8 43 ♖d8)
41 ♖xd6 g4 42 ♖d8 g5 43 ♖f5!,
with a grip that would soon prove
fatal; or b) 37 ... ♗e6 38 ♕xd8
♗xa2 39 ♖xf6! ♔xf6 40 ♕h8+
♔e6 41 ♕xe5 mate. In *Chess Life*
I looked at the line 37 ♖xd6 ♖a8.[6]
On his last move, Black was left
with a choice of evils only. One is
37 ... ♖ee8, which leads to 38
♖xa6 (not 38 ♖ed3 ♗c6!!, drawing) 38 ... ♖a8 39 ♖b6! (the
routine 39 ♖xa8 ♖xa8 40 ♗b2
♖c8 41 ♗b3 ♔f8 might still be
tenable for Black, while 39 ♖xf6
♔xf6 40 ♖f3+ ♔e7 41 ♖xf7+
♔d8 is unclear) 39 ... ♖xa3 40
♗d5!. White is threatening both
41 ♗xe5 and 41 ♖f3, and this
means that Black would have to
part with his pawn on b5, after
which White's win remains solely
a matter of technique. Another

unsatisfactory try is 37 ... ♗e6 38
♖xd8 ♗xa2 39 ♖d6 ♖a7 40 ♖c6
♗c4 41 ♖f3 ♗e6 42 ♖d3, with
♖dd6 to follow. The main line
after 37 ... ♖a8 runs: 38 ♖ed3 (not
38 ♖f3 ♗e6 39 ♗d5 ♖a7 40 ♗d2
♖ed7!, equalising) 38 ... ♗e6 (38
... ♗e8? 39 ♖f3, or 38 ... ♗c8 39
♖b6 ♖d7 40 ♖f3, but even the
more stubborn 38 ... ♖a7 fails
against 39 ♗d2! ♗c8 40 ♖f3 ♗e6
41 ♗e3 ♖a8 42 ♗d5!) 39 ♗xe6
♖xe6 (if 39 ... fxe6 40 ♖c6!, and
the other rook soon joins forces
on the sixth rank) 40 ♖xe6 fxe6
41 ♖d7+ ♔f8 42 ♖c7!, and White's
endgame advantage is decisive. 42
... ♖d8 is met by 43 ♖c6 ♔e7!?
44 ♖xa6 ♖d1+ 45 ♔h2 ♖d3 46
♗b2 ♖d2 47 ♗c1 ♖xf2 48 ♗e3
♖e2 49 ♗c5+ ♔d7 50 ♖d6+, with
an easy White win, and passive
defence is just as hopeless.

# Technical Aspects

TECHNIQUE

264        W

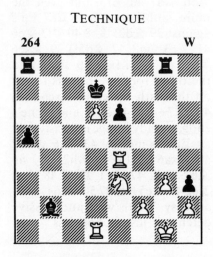

One of the very few private allusions found in *My 60 Memorable Games* is the one appearing after Black's 32nd move in Fischer's game against Najdorf from Santa Monica 1966. (Pos. 264 *MSMG p.336*) Najdorf has just played 32 ... a6-a5, to which Fischer remarks: "Different people feel differently about resigning". Actually, this very comment had originally been made by Robert Byrne in his analysis of the game in *Chess Life*, November 1966, yet with the

slight difference that he "let" Black play another nine moves (33 ♘c4 ♖gb8 34 ♖h4 ♔c6 35 ♖h7 ♗d4 36 ♖c7+ ♔d5 37 d7 a4 38 ♘b6+ ♖xb6 39 ♖c8 ♖d6 40 ♖xa8 ♖xd7 41 ♖xa4 e5), before making it. Fischer, by replacing this remark, meant to say, as it were: "Robert dear, you were certainly right, but didn't you realise Black's position was technically lost many moves earlier?" (see also Pos. 24). Like few other players, Fischer was keen on reducing the game to 'technicalities' at the earliest possible moment. This was more than a matter of convenience. It was with him a commitment of a professional player to his *metier*. He saw no reason to indulge in any kind of creative solutions once the game no longer demanded it. This he must have regarded as belonging to the realm of chess nonsense; and nonsense was the last thing he was interested in, as far as chess was concerned.

Rarely would he revel in the superfluous complexities of moves

214

265          B

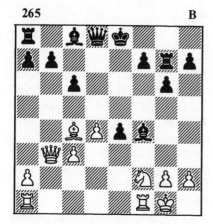

266          B

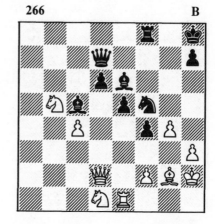

such as **21 ... b5** in his exhibition game against Larsen, Copenhagen 1962, (Pos. 265) allowing the game to flare up after **22 ♘xe4!? bxc4 23 ♕xc4 ♗e3+ 24 ♔h1 ♗f5 25 ♕xc6+ ♔f8 26 ♘d6**, etc. Normally, he would keep things under tight control in such circumstances with moves like 21 ... ♗e3, going for the technically winning position after **22 ♖ae1 ♗xf2+ 23 ♖xf2 f5**, as pointed out in *Chess Archives.*[1]

With the exception of examples like this and the following one (Pos. 266), Fischer made it a habit not to pursue creative solutions for their own sake.

Here, in Rossolimo-Fischer, US Championship 1966-67, both 37 ... ♘d4 (38 ♘xd4 ♗xd4 39 ♗d5 [39 ♕d3 ♕f7] 39 ... ♗xd5 40 cxd5 ♕b5 41 ♕a2 ♖c8), and 37 ... ♘h4 (38 ♗d5 h5!), would leave

Black with a solid winning advantage. Instead, Fischer courts complications with **37 ... ♗xc4 38 ♖xe5 ♘d4! 39 ♖e4 ♗xb5 40 ♖xd4! ♕g7! 41 ♖d5!? ♗c4 42 ♖h5 f3 43 ♗h1 ♗d4 44 ♘e3 ♗e2**, and only now, when it has become clear that White's last resource – **45 ♘f5** – leaves him high and dry after **45 ... ♗e5+ 46 ♔g1 ♖a8! 47 ♕e1 ♖a1! 48 ♕xa1 ♗h2+! 49 ♔xh2 ♕xa1**, did Black enjoy a really safe winning advantage.

It is much more common with Fischer simply to reject, and, at times, to be oblivious to such solutions, whenever a simple technical solution is at hand. In his game against Keres in the 1st cycle at Curaçao 1962 (Pos. 267), Fischer (White) could play on strangulation themes, having regard to the dire weakness of Black's back rank, starting with

**267**            **W**

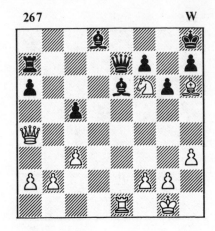

30 ♖e4 and 31 ♖h4, or even 30 ♗g5 ♕f8 (30 ... h5 31 ♖e5! ♕f8 32 ♖xc5!) 31 ♘xh7! ♔xh7 32 ♕h4+ etc. Fischer, however, sees that he can win a pawn, rather prosaically, by **30 ♘d5 ♕d7 31 ♕e4 ♕d6 32 ♘f4 ♖e7 33 ♗g5 ♖e8 34 ♗xd8 ♖xd8 35 ♘xe6**, and he is happy enough with this ample booty to forgo an even bigger one (33

♗f8!).[2]

Fischer (Black) won his game against Donald Byrne at the 1963-64 US Championship (Pos. 268), by the simple technical continuation **32 ... ♕xa7 33 ♖xa7 ♘d4 34 ♖d7 ♘xb3 35 ♖xd6 ♘c5 36 ♖b6 b3**, etc. Had he been interested in the pursuit of beauty for its own sake, he would certainly have opted for 32 ... ♗b7, with the following beautiful conclusive possibilities:

a) 33 ♕a5 ♕c8 34 ♖c1 ♖xe4! 35 ♗xe4 (35 ♘f3 ♖e2) 35 ... ♗xe4+ 36 ♘g2 (36 ♔g1 ♕g4+) 36 ... ♘e3 37 ♖g1 ♘xg2 38 ♖xg2 ♕a8!, and the pin leads to a winning pawn endgame.

b) 33 ♖c1 (33 ♖a4 ♖a8 34 ♕f2 ♖xa4 35 bxa4 b3, is another win) 33 ... ♖xe4! 34 ♕f2 ♕e7! 35 ♗xe4 ♗xe4+ (but not 35 ... ♕xe4+ 36 ♘g2 ♘e3 37 ♖e1!) 36 ♘g2 ♘e3!, or 36 ♘f3 ♘d4!.

**268**            **B**

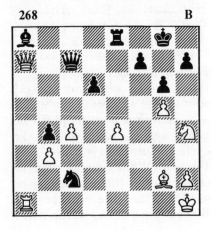

**269**            **B**

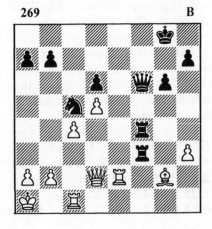

Very typical was the last phase of his game (as Black) against Suttles, at Palma de Mallorca 1970 (Pos. 269). The black rook at f3 is under attack, and there is a rich choice of squares on the third rank to go to: a3, b3, d3, and – probably best – g3. After 34 ... ♖g3 the threat of 35 ... ♘d3 is certainly annoying. For instance: 35 ♕e1 ♘d3 36 ♕xg3 ♘xc1 37 ♖e6 (37 ♖e4 ♖f2!, or 37 ♖c2 ♖f1!) 37 ... ♕d4 (threatening 38 ... ♖f2) 38 ♕e1 (38 ♕e3 ♕d1! 39 a3 ♘d3+ 40 ♔a2 ♕c2 41 ♕e2 ♘c1+) 38 ... ♘d3 39 ♖e8+ ♔g7 40 ♕e7+ ♔h6, and wins. A pretty conclusion also arises after 35 ♖ce1 ♘d3 36 ♖e8+ ♔f7 37 ♖1e7+ ♕xe7 38 ♖xe7+ ♔xe7 39 a3 (39 ♕e2+ ♔f8) 39 ... ♖e4!! (39 ... ♖f2 40 ♕c3!) 40 ♔a2 ♖e1 41 b4 ♘c1+ 42 ♔b1 ♖ge3!. Fischer rejects all these in favour of the simple technical continuation 34 ... ♖f2 35 ♖ce1 ♖xe2 36 ♖xe2. If 36 ♕xe2 ♖f2 37 ♕e8+ ♔g7 38 ♕e7+ (38 ♖e2 ♖xg2!) 38 ... ♕xe7 39 ♖xe7+ ♔f6, wins. 36 ... ♖xc4. So Black has a won pawn, and there remains only to convert this into a win, a task which Fischer, to be sure, performs immaculately: 37 ♕e3 ♕e5! 38 ♔b1 ♕xe3 39 ♖xe3 ♖f4 40 ♗f3 h5 41 ♔c2 ♔f7 42 ♔d2 ♖b4 43 ♔c3 ♖h4 44 b4 ♘d7 45 ♗e2 ♘f6 46 ♖f3 ♔g7 47 ♖d3 g5 48 a3 g4 49 ♗f1 ♘e4+ 50 ♔c2 ♘f2 51 ♖e3 gxh3 52 ♖e7+

♔f8, 0-1. (see also Pos. 68, 155)

A lot has been written about Fischer's wish to break his opponents' spirit. Yet it is important to make a distinction between the ends and the means. In the final analysis there was one fact only – emerging victorious – that was of importance for him, and the smoother this could be done, the better. He saw no reason whatever to impress his opponents by any spectacular displays. Beating them was enough. In the next two examples he faces two formidable opponents. In both cases he could conclude the struggle by having some fun at the expense of his rivals. Fun, of course, is one side in such affairs – humiliation the other. Typically, he restricts his search in both cases to one end only – the technically simplest way to win.

**270**                **B**

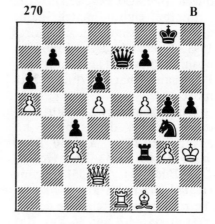

Against Larsen, at Santa Monica 1966, (Pos. 270), Fischer (Black) with two pawns ahead, wraps it up by forcing White into a hopeless endgame: **41 ... ♖e3 42 ♖xe3 ♕xe3 43 ♕xe3 ♘xe3**. The game was adjourned here, but Larsen resigned before resumption. Had Fischer wished to extract more than just a win from the position, he could have played 41 ... ♕f6, threatening the unpleasantries ensuing from 42 ... h4 or 42 ... ♖f2 or 42 ... ♕xf5. White's miserable king would soon be mated, or he would have to pay a high price to save himself. *Viz:* 42 ♖e8+ (42 ♕d4 ♘e5/♖xc3) 42 ... ♔h7 43 ♗g2 (43 ♕d4 h4! 44 ♔xg4 ♖xg3+ 45 ♔h5 ♕g6+!!? 46 fxg6+ fxg6 mate – certainly an imposing picture to imprint on an opponent's mind) 43 ... ♕xf5! 44 ♗xf3 ♘e3+ 45 ♔h2 ♘f1+, winning White's queen. (see also Pos. 254)

In the eighth match game against Petrosian, Buenos Aires 1971, Fischer had the following position (Pos. 271) in hand, after Petrosian's (that is, White's) 29th move.

With exemplary smooth technique Fischer drives home his advantage: **29 ... ♗e4 30 ♗xe4 ♖xe4 31 h3 d3 32 ♖b3 ♕c4 33 ♖b2 ♖dd4! 34 g3 ♖d5!**. Having created the necessary weakness, the rook is despatched to collect its fruit. **35 ♔h2 ♖b5 36 ♖a2 ♖b1**

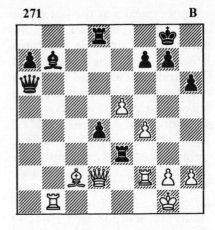

271          **B**

37 g4. Here was the moment to crack open White's position and Petrosian's spirit by 37 ... ♖be1, massacring him in style after either 38 ♔g3 ♖4e3+ 39 ♔h4 ♕xf4!! 40 ♖xf4 g5+ 41 ♔h5 ♖xh3 mate, or 38 ♕a5 ♖1e2 39 ♖axe2 dxe2 40 ♕e1 ♕d3 and ... ♕d1 next. Fischer found however, that **37 ... ♖e2 38 ♖xe2 dxe2 39 ♕xe2 ♕xf4+ 40 ♔f2 ♖b3** was sufficient to force Petrosian's resignation, which satisfied him completely. (see also Pos. 173)

One cannot fail to be impressed by the simple elegance of this approach. Kotov once wrote about Keres: "I have always been struck by one strange thing about his line of approach. Having found one way to win, the Estonian grandmaster straight away starts looking for another."[3] Fischer's approach is diametrically opposed to this. Having found one satisfactory way to win, he doesn't bother to look for another, provided the one found is technically simple and straightforward. (At times this verged on nonchalance – but that when he lost concentration altogether; see pp.237-40.)

As a matter of fact, when one speaks of technique in chess as the uncreative efficiency in exploiting one's positional or material advantages, one should bear in mind that this doesn't necessarily mean that technical virtuosity has no other values aside from that. With some players quite the contrary might be true. In Rubinstein's and Capablanca's games, for instance, technique and conceptual thinking were two sides of the same chess coin, complementing and sustaining each other. In a performance of a musical instrumentalist it is customary to make a distinction between 'musicality' and 'technique'. However, superb technique at the highest levels is as impressive and gratifying as any musicality, and one cannot tell them apart any longer. The same holds true in chess. The following illustrative examples are certainly as effective as they are elegant.

In Fischer-Mecking, Palma de Mallorca 1970 (Pos. 272), the realisation of the single pawn advantage (and a doubled pawn

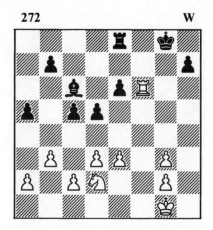

272      W

at that!) runs along the smoothest tracks. **22 g4 a4 23 ♘f3 axb3 24 axb3 ♔g7 25 g5 e5 26 ♘h4 ♗d7 27 ♖d6 ♗e6 28 ♔f2 ♔f7 29 ♖b6 ♖e7 30 e4 dxe4 31 dxe4 c4 32 b4 ♗g4 33 ♔e3 ♖d7 34 g6+!**. It looked as though the knight had been long prepared to jump to f5. 34 ♘f5 was quite good too, but not as quick, decisive and neat. **34 ... ♔f8 35 gxh7 ♖xh7 36 ♘g6+ ♔e8 37 ♘xe5 ♗c8 38 ♘xc4 ♔d8 39 ♘d6 ♖g7 40 ♔f2 ♔c7 41 ♘xc8 ♔xc8 42 ♖d6**, 1-0.

The knight manoeuvre first and the king manoeuvre later, in Bisguier-Fischer, US Championship 1966-67 (Pos. 273), make this endgame into a piece of sheer beauty. **43 ... ♘a4 44 ♘e2 ♘b2 45 ♘d4 ♘d1 46 ♘e2 ♘f2 47 ♔e3 ♘h3 48 ♘f4+ ♔xg5 49 ♘g2 f6 50 exf6 ♔xf6 51 ♘h4 e5 52 ♗c2 ♗d7 53 ♗b1 ♘g5 54 ♗c2 ♘f7 55 ♗b1**

273　　　　　　　　　　B

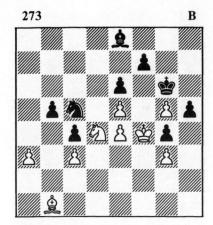

advantage is too slight to suffice for a win is irrelevant for our case. It is the almost magical way Fischer succeeds in accomplishing his intermediate task that is so exceptional.

274　　　　　　　　　　W

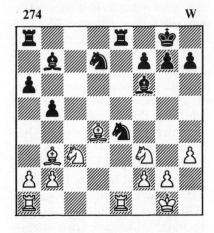

♘h8 56 ♗c2 ♘g6. The Moor has done his job. The Moor has to go. But what a remarkable job he has done! 57 ♘xg6 ♔xg6 58 ♔f2 ♔g5 59 ♔g2 h4 60 ♔h2 h3!. Considerably limiting the scope of the white king, and as a result of this Black's king gets a free hand to march to the other wing of the board. 61 ♔g1 ♔f6 62 ♔h2 ♔e7 63 ♔g1 ♔d6 64 ♔f2 ♔c5 65 ♔g1 ♔b6 66 ♔h1 ♔a5 67 ♔g1 ♗c6 68 ♔h1 ♗b7 69 ♔g1 ♗xe4!. Makes possible the decisive infiltration of his king. 70 ♗xe4 ♔a4 71 ♗f5 ♔b3 72 ♗xg4 e4 73 ♗xh3 ♔xc3 74 g4 ♔d2, 0-1.

Only a player of superb technique could convert Black's slightly weakened queenside in the otherwise totally even position in Fischer-Robatsch, Vinkovci 1968 (Pos. 274) into a concrete material advantage. The fact that this

21 ♗d5!. His sole aim at present is to weaken c6. 21 ... ♗xd5 21 ... ♘xc3? 22 ♗xb7 ♘e2+ 23 ♖xe2! 22 ♘xd5 ♗xd4 23 ♘xd4 ♘ef6 24 ♖xe8+ ♘xe8. If 24 ... ♖xe8 25 ♘c7 ♖e4 26 ♖d1 wins a pawn. 25 a4!. The reduction of material would eventually lead to a draw, yet Fischer manages to extract ever more juice out of this seemingly arid soil. 25 ... bxa4 26 ♖xa4. Now the advance of the b-pawn is imminent. 26 ... ♘c5 27 ♖c4 ♘d3 28 ♘c6!. He intends to 'mate' Black's rook with 29 ♘b6!. 28 ... a5 28 ... ♘d6 29 ♖d4, or 28 ... ♘xb2 29 ♖c2, cost dearly. 29 b3. Threat: 30 ♖a4 29 ... ♘b2 30

🗒c2 ♘d3 31 🗒a2!. Back to the a-file by circumnavigation! Now the advance of the b-pawn can't be stopped. **31 ... ♔f8 32 b4 🗒c8!**. The only saving chance. 32 ... a4 33 b5 is, of course, hopeless. **33 bxa5** 33 b5? fails to 33 ... ♘d6 34 ♘a7 🗒c5, and 33 ♘de7 to 33 ... ♘xb4! **33 ... 🗒xc6 34 a6 🗒c1+! 35 ♔h2 ♘c7 36 ♘xc7 🗒xc7 37 a7 🗒xa7 38 🗒xa7 ♘xf2**, and Robatsch succeeded in drawing this endgame.

**275**                  **W**

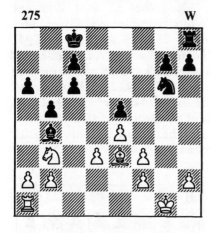

It is clear that in Pos. 275 (Fischer-Rubinetti, Buenos Aires 1970) any decisive result would come about through the exploitation of the weaknesses of either side's pawn formation. Roughly speaking d3, e4, f3, f2 are the equivalent of the a6, b5, c6, c7 pawns, and a2 and b2, have their counterparts on g7 and h7. It is the difference in the respective value of the pawns on h2 and e5

which gives White a slight edge – they are both weak, and should they be eliminated, White's central pawn mass is likely to be more dangerous than Black's passed h-pawn. However, when one compares White's central 'island' to Black's queenside's one, one realises that the latter is less vulnerable – Black's king is close to both a6 and c6, and his formation is frontally exposed only along the c-file as compared to White's d- and f-files, and there is no white pawn at b4 to emphasise the weaknesses at a5 and c5, as Black's e5 does nicely in respect of d4 and f4. Thus playing for an attack along the c-file by 17 🗒c1 is bound to be fruitless. True, a counterattack on the f-file is wrong: 17 ... 🗒f8? 18 a3! ♗d6 19 🗒xc6, and if 19 ... ♔b7? 20 ♘a5+. In the same way 17 ... ♔d7 fails to 18 a3 ♗d6 19 ♘a5. It is by attacking d3 that Black gets good counterplay: 17 ... 🗒d8! (17 ... ♘h4 18 f4 ♘f3+ 19 ♔h1!) 18 d4 (18 a3 🗒xd3!, or 18 🗒xc6 ♔b7, etc) 18 ... ♘h4!, etc. By simple technical play, Fischer resolves all the position's problems. He centralises his king first, then plays his rook to the other half-open file, the g-file, then dislodges the pawn on e5, and then ... there follows a mate! **17 ♔f1 🗒f8 18 ♔e2 ♘f4+** 18 ... ♘h4 19 🗒g1! ♘xf3 20 🗒g3! ♘xh2 21 f3, and 22 🗒h3 catches the stranded knight.

**19 ♗xf4 ♖xf4 20 ♖g1 ♖h4 21 ♖xg7 ♖xh2 22 a3 ♗d6 23 f4!**. A delay of just one move would have given Black the chance to consolidate with 23 ... c5. **23 ... exf4 24 d4 ♔d8 25 ♘a5 c5 26 e5 ♗f8 27 ♘c6+ ♔e8 28 ♖xc7.** The elegant touch. Black resigned in view of e6 followed by ♖c8+ mate, or the e-pawn's promotion.

Technique isn't, of course, a know-how confined to the very late stages of the game. It can play an important part in the late middle-game, as in the following example (Pos. 276), or even the early middlegame stage, as the last example (Pos. 277) shows.

**276**                                    **B**

Pos. 276 is Troianescu-Fischer, Netanya 1968. White has a weak pawn at e4. He has relinquished e5 to Black by pushing f5 – see Pos. 77. Moreover, f3 is accessible to Black's pieces. Let's watch how

Fischer makes use of all these elements: **25 ... ♘e5 26 ♘d3 ♘f3 27 ♖e2 ♗a6!**. He is in no hurry to play ... ♖c4, since 28 e5!? would give White some counterplay. **28 ♖g2 ♖c4 29 ♘e1 ♘e5!** keeps White cramped, and prevents ♗d3. **30 ♖gd2 ♖d8 31 f6+ ♔xf6 32 ♖xd6 ♖xd6 33 ♖xd6 ♖c6!**. Simple and very much to the point. His advantage could serve him best in an endgame. **34 ♖xc6** 34 ♖d1 ♘c4 35 ♘d4 ♖d6, and White crumbles ever faster. **34 ... ♘xc6 35 ♗d3 ♗b7! 36 ♘d2 g4!**. Taking f3 away from White, and fixing his kingside pawns on dark squares. **37 ♗e2 h5 38 ♘c4 ♗g1 39 ♘d3 ♘d4! 40 e5+ ♔e7 41 ♗f1**, and White resigned. After 41 ... ♗e4 he would lose his kingside pawns.

**277**                                    **W**

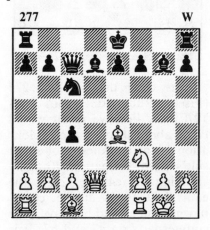

Fischer-Sherwin, US Championship 1962-63 (Pos. 277) proceeded

with **12 ♕e2!**. Without wasting time he starts pecking at Black's weaknesses. He is going to switch from one weakness to the other untill the (rather quick) end. More creative, for better or for worse, was 12 ♕g5 ♗f6 13 ♕c5, and if 13 ... ♗e6 14 ♘g5, or 13 ... c3!? 14 ♗g5! (14 bxc3 ♕a5!) 14 ... cxb2 15 ♖ab1 (or even 15 ♖ae1). This, for Fischer, is redundant. The technical targets at hand are well defined and easy to exploit. **12 ... c3 13 bxc3 ♗xc3 14 ♖b1 0-0-0 15 ♕c4!**. Less clear is 15 ♘g5 f5 (or 15 ... ♘d4 16 ♕d3, but not 16 ♕c4!!/?? ♘f3+!!, and Black wins) 16 ♗f3 (16 ♕c4 ♗e5!) 16 ... ♘d4 17 ♕xe7 ♖de8. There is a pawn there, see it? **15 ... f5 16 ♕xc3 fxe4**. The beautiful bishop goes, but a healthy pawn drops into White's pocket in return. **17 ♘g5 ♖hg8 18 ♘xe4 ♘d4!?**. An ingenious try. But Fischer keeps it as 'cool' as possible. **19 ♕xc7+ ♔xc7 20 ♘g3!**. A perfect move. He keeps an eye on f5 (bishop) and e2 (knight), while closing off the g-file. Moreover, c2 is untouchable. 20 c3, on the other hand would make 20 ... ♘e2+ 21 ♔h1 ♗c6 possible. and the game has just begun. **20 ... ♗c6** 20 ... ♘xc2? 21 ♗f4+ ♔c8 22 ♖fc1 ♗a4 23 ♖b4 wins. **21 ♖e1!**. Black wished to upset him with 21 ... ♘e2+!, but he is now facing a lost endgame

instead. **21 ... ♘xc2 22 ♖xe7+ ♖d7 23 ♗f4+ ♔c8 24 ♖xd7 ♔xd7 25 ♖d1+ ♔c8 26 ♘f5! ♖xg2+ 27 ♔f1 b6 28 ♘e7+ ♔b7 29 ♘xc6 ♖g4**, and he resigned. 30 ♘d8+, and White is a piece up.

## THE BISHOP PAIR

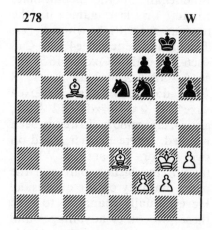

278    W

Fischer's predilection for keeping the bishop pair was well known. In Zürich 1959 he had this endgame (Pos. 278, Fischer White, after Black's 49th), featuring symmetrical racks of pawns on the same side of the board. His opponent was Larsen. His conviction in the superiority of the bishop pair made him play on for another forty moves before acquiescing in a draw.

We see Fischer striving to

maintain the bishop pair against the opponent's alternative configurations of minor pieces, in all phases of the game. In the same year as the above endgame was played, he showed his great confidence in the two bishops on another occasion. At Mar del Plata, where he was a contender for 1st place, he played Jacobo Bolbochan in the penultimate round, his last game in the tournament with the white pieces. The game opened: 1 e4 c5 2 ♘f3 ♘c6 3 d4 cxd4 4 ♘xd4 ♘f6 5 ♘c3 e6 6 ♘db5 ♗b4 7 a3 ♗xc3+ 8 ♘xc3 d5 9 ♗d3 dxe4 10 ♘xe4 ♘xe4 11 ♗xe4 ♕xd1+ 12 ♔xd1, and an endgame had already been reached, where Fischer relied on two factors to act in White's favour: the bishop pair and the pawn majority on the queenside. He eventually managed to turn these into other advantages and win convincingly – see Pos. 11-13. He employed the same opening variation, though with some modifications, a couple of years later against Addison, at the US Championship 1962-63. Quite similar structures ensued from other Sicilians Fischer played as White. On two occasions he took decisions that very much resembled each other: giving up the exchange for the bishop pair, a rook on the seventh rank and a 3-to-1 pawn majority on the queenside.

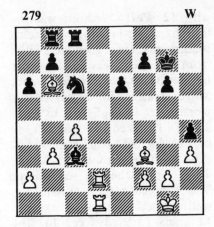

**279**                          **W**

Fischer-Bertok, Bled 1961 (Pos. 279) went: **30 ♖d7!**. The tame 30 ♖d3 would have allowed 30 ... ♗a5, and if 31 ♗xa5 ♘xa5 32 ♖d7 b5!?, with better chances than in the game.

**30 ... ♘e5 31 ♗xb7! ♘xd7 32 ♖xd7 ♖g8 33 c5 a5 34 c6 e5 35 ♗a7 ♖be8 36 c7 ♗d4 37 ♗xd4 exd4 38 ♖xd4 ♖c8 39 ♖c4**, and White won shortly.

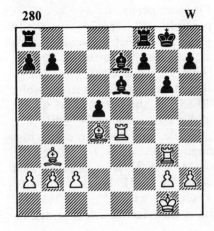

**280**                          **W**

Fischer-Larsen, 5th match game, Candidates 1971 (Pos. 280) proceeded with **20 ♗xd5 ♗d6?!** 20 ... ♗xd5 21 ♖xe7 came much closer to complete equality. **21 ♖xe6! ♗xg3 22 ♖e7 ♗d6 23 ♖xb7 ♖ac8 24 c4 a5 25 ♖a7 ♗c7 26 g3 ♖fe8 27 ♔f1 ♖e7 28 ♗f6 ♖e3 29 ♗c3 h5 30 ♖a6 ♗e5 31 ♗d2 ♖d3 32 ♔e2 ♖d4 33 ♗c3 ♖cxc4 34 ♗xc4 ♖xc4 35 ♔d3 ♖c5.** One of the bishops goes, and material is level again, but White has gained sufficient advantage in the shape of his active king to assure him of a technically won endgame. **36 ♖xa5 ♖xa5 37 ♗xa5 ♗xb2 38 a4 ♔f8 39 ♗c3 ♗xc3 40 ♔xc3 ♔e7 41 ♔d4 ♔d6 42 a5 f6 43 a6 ♔c6 44 a7 ♔b7 45 ♔d5 h4 46 ♔e6,** and Black resigned.

The endgame that occurred in Fischer-Schweber, Buenos Aires 1970 (see Pos. 121) also bears some resemblance to these two.

One can also find some similarity in the co-operation of the bishop pair and the rook in bringing about a gradual asphyxiation of the opponent's king in the following two endgames that Fischer played with the black pieces.

Souza Mendes-Fischer, Mar del Plata 1959 (Pos. 281) saw: **22 ... ♗h6+ 23 ♔d3 ♗d7 24 ♖g1+ ♔h8 25 ♘c3 b5 26 ♘e2 b4 27 ♔c2 ♖c8+ 28 ♔b3 a5 29 ♖g3 ♖f8 30 ♗h3 ♗b5 31 ♘g1 ♗f4 32 ♖g2 ♗f1!.** Winning through this move an important tempo on move 37. **33 ♖f2 ♗d3 34 ♗f5 ♖b8 35 ♘h3 a4+! 36 ♔xa4 b3! 37 axb3 ♗e3 38 ♖f3 ♖a8+.** White resigned. He is mated after 39 ♔b4 ♗d2.

**282**                                        **B**

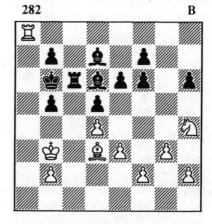

A year later, at Mar del Plata 1960 against Letelier, with the same pieces on the board and a white knight on the queenside, the process took the following

**281**                                        **B**

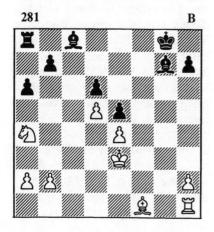

shape (Pos. 282): **27 ... 🛡c1! 28 🛡h8 b4 29 🛡xh6 ♚a5 30 ♚a2 b3+! 31 ♚xb3 ♗a4+ 32 ♚a2 ♚b4 33 b3 ♗xb3+ 34 ♚b2 🛡d1 35 ♗b1 🛡d2+ 36 ♚a1 ♚c3**, and White resigned in view of 37 ♘f3 ♗a3! 38 ♘xd2 ♗b2 mate.

Also very instructive, though this time less successful as far as the game's result was concerned, was Fischer's (Black's) late middlegame play in his encounter with Ciocaltea at the Varna Olympiad 1962 (Pos. 283). Again we witness the fruitful co-operation he creates between a rook and the two bishops, doing the almost impossible of reaching an endgame with fighting chances from a seemingly hopeless middle-game.

**283**                 **B**

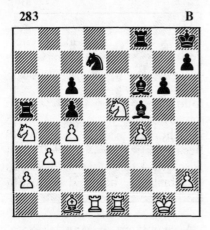

**37 ... ♘xe5.** Giving up the bishop pair at this juncture is simply suicidal: 37 ... ♗xe5? 38 fxe5 ♗g4 39 🛡d6 ♗h3 40 e6 ♘e5

41 e7, and White wins. **38 fxe5 ♗h4 39 🛡f1 ♚g7 40 🛡d6 🛡aa8 41 ♗e3 ♗h3.** Suddenly Black's position springs to life, with mating threats on the back rank looming large. **42 🛡xf8 🛡xf8 43 🛡d1 🛡f5!.** Not with the intention of capturing on e5, but to force White to capture on c5 with the knight, 44 ♗xc5?? being answered now by 44 ... 🛡g5+ and wins. **44 ♘xc5 🛡f3!.** Not in order to do any direct harm to White's bishop, but through the threat of doing so to acquire f4 for his rook. **45 ♗d4 🛡f4!.** The rook manoeuvre has yielded some nice threats on the g-file. **46 e6+ ♚f8 47 ♗e5 ♗f2+ 48 ♚h1 🛡g4 49 ♘d7+ ♚e7 50 ♗g3 ♚xe6!.** On the way to a well-nigh complete material recovery. 51 ♗xf2? will be answered by 51 ... ♗g2+ 52 ♚g1 ♗f3+, and wins. **51 🛡d6+ ♚e7 52 🛡d2.** Forced. If 52 🛡d3 🛡xg3 53 hxg3 ♗xd7, and the advantage is Black's. **52 ... ♗xg3.** His best practical chance. 52 ... 🛡d4 53 🛡xd4 ♗xd4 54 ♘b8! leaves very little to hope for. **53 hxg3 🛡xg3 54 ♘e5!.** Contriving to win the c-pawn, without which his prospects would have been inferior to Black's. **54 ... c5 55 ♚h2!.** Accurately played. 55 ♘d3 at once would permit 55 ... 🛡g5. **55 ... 🛡e3 55 ... 🛡g5? 56 ♘c6+** wins the bishop. **56 ♘d3 ♗f5 56 ...** ♚d6 57 ♘f4+ again wins the bishop. **57 ♘xc5.** It has taken the

very best play on White's part to stand up to Black's ingenious manoeuvring, thus retaining sufficient material advantage to have a won endgame in hand. This takes nothing away from Fischer's artistry. (see also Pos. 17 and comment in Pos. 236)

It is a mark of a great player that even when he does have a 'soft spot' for a certain piece or combination of pieces, he wouldn't normally misjudge its objective value. Here are two remarkable observations.

if we have to distance ourselves a bit from the assertion in the second sentence (as no player has ever managed to play exclusively the strongest moves), it still remains an interesting remark. (see also Pos. 73)

285                                    W

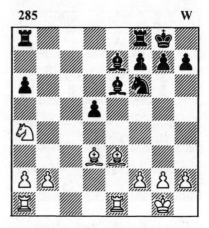

284                                    B

In Ivkov-Fischer, Santa Monica 1966 (Pos. 284) Fischer's **14 ... &xd3!** elicited the following remark from Ivkov: "I thought that Bobby would not give up one of his bishops, due to his known love for these pieces. But Bobby always plays the strongest moves regardless of his favourites."[1] And even

About **16 &c5** in Fischer-Petrosian, 7th match game, Candidates 1971 (Pos. 285), Botvinnik, among other things, had the following to say: [O]f the ... two logical moves 16 &c5 or 16 ♘c5 he chooses the former. Why? Because after 16 ♘c5 a5! 17 &d4 &xc5 18 &xc5, White, despite his two bishops, has had to lose a tempo and Black has got in ... a5. In the game White has time to get in b4 and so fix the weak a-pawn."[2] (That is, after **16 ... ♖fe8 17 &xe7 ♖xe7 18 b4!**). (see also Pos. 6, 158)

Even his decision in the next

game, which at first glance deserved criticism, was absolutely correct, and had no origination in Fischer's tastes or predilections. It is Jimenez-Fischer, Havana 1965 (Pos. 286), after Black's 39th move.

286　　　　　　　　　　W

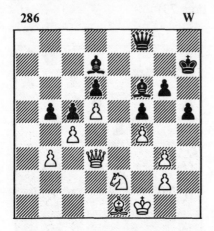

Jimenez's **40 ♗c3** offers the exchange of the dark-squared bishops for a very worthy return: taking complete control of g5. Fischer's **40 ... bxc4 41 bxc4 ♗d8!?** was not, as might be thought, a concession to his desires, but a sad yet necessary concession to the demands of the position. True, White gets a menacing battery on the a1-h8 diagonal (there followed: **42 ♗a1 ♗c8 43 ♕c3**), but forestalling it by letting White exchange those bishops, would have been even worse: 41 ... ♗c8 42 ♘g1 ♗a6 43 ♘f3 ♕e7 (threatening 44 ... ♕e4!) 44 ♗xf6 ♕xf6 45 ♔g1, and if 45 ...

♕a1+? 46 ♔h2 ♕c1 (or 46 ... h4 47 ♕e2!) 47 ♘g5+ ♔g8 48 ♕e2!, winning straightforwardly. The game was drawn after **43 ... ♗a6 44 ♔f2 ♗e7 45 ♘g1 g5 46 ♘f3 gxf4 47 gxf4 h4 48 ♕c2 ♔g6 49 ♕a2 ♕c8 50 ♕b2**, and that was certainly the utmost Black could have got out of the initial position.

## ROOK ENDGAMES WITH BISHOPS OF OPPOSITE COLOURS

Very few players would willingly play a rook ending with bishops of opposite colours, even with a slight material advantage in their favour, when entertaining winning intentions. None has made it a habit to enter this type of endgame deliberately. The reason is easy to fathom: it takes the finest technique to realise one's advantage in these endgames. And quite often this too wouldn't do. Fischer faced this type of endgame on nineteen occasions,[1] and if we can judge by this, and by his ability to cash in his advantage in many of these games, it seems he indeed had no objection in principle to playing this kind of endgame once he had acquired some slight advantages.

With the exception of Minić-Fischer, Skopje 1967, in all the cases Fischer entered this endgame, he reached it after first having two rooks versus two rooks plus opposite-coloured bishops. In this type of endgame the technical difficulties in converting one's advantage into a win are enormous. Fischer's primary objective after having gained sufficient advantage was, then, to exchange one pair of rooks.

♖a2+ 55 ♔f3 ♗d4 56 g4 ♖a3 57 ♔g2 ♗e3 58 ♔f3 ♗c5 59 ♔g3 e5 60 fxe5+ fxe5 61 ♔g2 hxg4 62 ♗xg6 ♖xa6 63 ♔g3 ♔e6 64 h5 ♗e3 65 ♔xg4 ♖a4+ 66 ♔f3 ♗h6 67 ♖b1 e4+ 68 ♔g3 ♖a3+ 69 ♔g4 ♔e5 70 ♖b8 ♖a1 71 ♖e8+ ♔d4 72 ♔f5 ♖f1+, and White resigned. (see also Pos. 69, 110)

**287**                                                    **W**

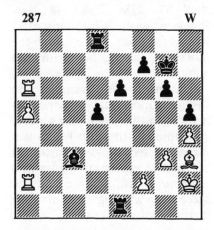

**288**                                                    **B**

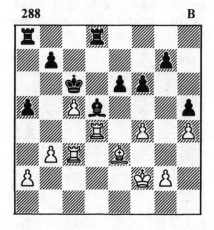

In the game Hort-Fischer, Palma de Mallorca 1970, (Pos. 287) this happened when White's passed a-pawn threatened to become too dangerous: **42 ♖c6 ♖a1!**, and the technical task that lay ahead after **43 ♖xa1 ♗xa1** was relatively uncomplicated. In the long run White couldn't prevent the creation of two passed pawns in the centre, nor stop their advance after that: **44 a6 ♗d4 45 ♖c2 ♔f6 46 f4 ♖b8 47 ♖a2 ♗a7 48 ♗f1 ♔e7 49 ♔g2 ♔d6 50 ♗d3 ♖b3 51 ♗e2 f6 52 ♖d2 ♖a3 53 ♗d3 ♗e3 54 ♖d1**

**31 ... a4!** in Pos. 288 (Pachman-Fischer, Havana Olympiad 1966) weakened White's pawns on the queenside, and induced the exchange of one pair of rooks: **32 ♖xa4 32 bxa4 ♗xa2 33 ♖xd8 ♖xd8** would lead to the game by transposition. Better, though, would have been to keep all four rooks on the board in this line by 33 ♖b4. Black would ultimately win the pawn on a4, but it would take more time to do so, and might have offered White some counterchances. In the sequence

... ♗d5, ... ♔c7, ... ♗c6, or ... ♖a5, ... ♖da8, White could unpleasantly advance c5-c6 in a number of variations. **32 ... ♖xa4 33 bxa4 ♗xa2.** Now White's isolated pawn at a4 is a handsome target, and Fischer went on to win it after a few moves: **34 ♖c2 ♗d5 35 ♖b2 ♖a8 36 ♖b4 ♖a5 37 g3 ♔c7 38 ♗d4 ♗c6 39 ♗e3 ♗xa4.** As for the end of the game, see Pos. 53, see also Pos. 31, 95.

**289**                                 **W**

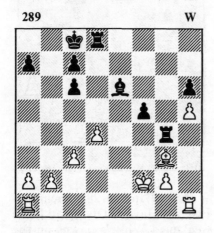

Exchanging one pair of rooks in Pos. 289 (Fischer-Wade, Vinkovci 1968) by **23 ♖h4**, is almost compulsory. Here a Black battery against g2 (... ♖dg8, ... ♗d5, ... f4) would of course be extremely undesirable for White. **23 ... ♖dg8 24 ♖xg4 ♖xg4.** White couldn't now prevent ... f4, shutting out his bishop from play (25 ♗e5? ♖h4). This, though, was far outweighed by his position's other advantages,

his superior pawn formation on the queenside in the first place: **25 ♖e1 ♔d7.** If 25 ... ♗d5, then 26 ♖e8+ ♔d7 27 ♖f8 ♗e4 28 ♖f6 ♔e7 29 ♖g6 ought to win. **26 ♖e5 f4 27 ♗h2 ♖h4 28 ♗g1 ♗d5 29 g3 ♖g4 30 ♗h2 f3 31 b3 a6 32 c4 ♖xd4 33 cxd5 ♖d2+ 34 ♔xf3 ♖xh2 35 dxc6+ ♔xc6 36 ♖e6+ ♔d7 37 ♖xh6 ♖xa2 38 ♖g6.** Black resigned. White ultimately won on the kingside through the pawns he had gathered on that wing.

The next two examples are Fischer's most impressive performances in this particular kind of endgame. In the first he gives a surpassing technical demonstration of gradual exploitation of a tiny advantage. In the second he succeeds in winning through subtle tactical endgame play.

**290**                                 **W**

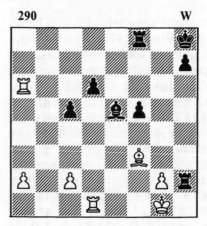

Parma-Fischer, Rovinj-Zagreb

1970 (Pos. 290) saw **29 ♖a8**. Here it is White who has to pursue the rook exchange. After **29 a4 ♖h4 30 a5 ♗d4+ 31 ♔f1 ♖e8 32 g3 ♖h2 33 ♗g2 ♖g8 34 ♖d3 f4**, Black's offensive meets no opposition. At the same time, Parma must have played his move with the strong conviction that Black's winning chances after exchanging rooks would be practically nil. Fischer's winning plan consisted of three stages a) Rook to a2, checking the advance of White's a-pawn and excercising great pressure on the second rank. b) The h-pawn to h4. The final objective of Black is to create a passed pawn by pushing, after due preparation, f4-f3. c) King to the queenside. It will attack the white bishop there, whose station at c6 is the only square from where it could both defend its own a-pawn and prevent Black's f4-f3. **29 ... ♖xa8 30 ♗xa8 ♖h4 31 ♗c6 ♖b4 32 a4 ♖b2 33 c4 ♔g7 34 ♖d3 ♖a2** otherwise 35 ♖a3! **35 ♔f1 ♔g6 36 ♖e3 h5 37 ♖e2 ♖a3 38 ♖d2 h4 39 ♔e2 ♗f4 40 ♖d3 ♖a2+ 41 ♔d1 ♔f6 42 ♖f3 ♗e5 43 ♖d3 ♔e7 44 ♖d2 ♖a3 45 ♔e2 ♗c3 46 ♖d3 ♖a2+ 47 ♔d1 ♗d4 48 ♖h3 ♗f6 49 ♖e3+ ♗e5 50 ♖d3 ♔d8 51 ♖d2 ♖a1+ 52 ♔e2 ♔c7 53 ♗b5 ♗f4 54 ♖c2 ♖a3 55 ♖b2 ♗e5 56 ♖d2 ♖g3 57 ♔d1 f4**, and White resigned. His bishop can't return to the long diagonal, and f4-f3 is imminent. In a sense,

White could disrupt Black's plan by playing 49 ♖f3 (instead of 49 ♖e3+). But after 49 ... ♔e6 50 ♗d5+ ♔e5 51 ♖e3+ ♔d4 52 ♖f3 ♖xa4 53 ♖xf5, a timely ... ♖xc4! would break down his defences. (see also Pos. 27)

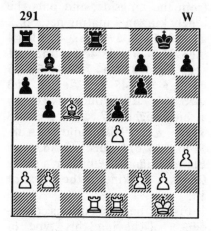

**291**    **W**

Black's compromised kingside pawn structure and exposed king in Pos. 291 (Fischer-Forintos, Monte Carlo 1967) stare us in the face. But how substantial can this be in this endgame? Fischer proves it is just critical! **27 ♖xd8+! ♖xd8 28 ♗e7 ♖d4 29 ♖e3!** 29 ♗xf6 ♖xe4, and White's rook can't penetrate the fourth rank's barrier: 30 ♖d1 ♖d4 31 ♖c1 ♖c4. But what a minimal advantage he's got here anyway! **29 ... ♗xe4** 29 ... ♖xe4?? 30 ♖g3+ **30 ♗xf6 ♔f8 31 a3 ♗c6 32 ♖xe5 ♖d5 33 ♖e3! ♖f5 34 ♗e5 h5 35 f3**. A delicate endgame requires delicate playing.

It could still have turned very unclear after the less cautious 35 f4. See: 35 ... h4 36 ♖c3 ♗d7 37 ♖c7 ♔e8 38 ♖a7 f6 39 ♗d6 ♖d5 40 ♖xa6 ♖d2,[2] threatening ♗f5-e4, with chances for both sides. Fischer now expels Black's forces from the kingside, and puts the lonely king in a mating net. **35 ... a5 36 ♔f2 a4 37 g4 hxg4 38 hxg4 ♖g5 39 ♗f6 ♖d5 40 f4 ♖d2+ 41 ♔g3 ♖g2+ 42 ♔h4 ♖d2 43 f5 ♗d5 44 ♔g5 ♖d1 45 ♖c3 ♖e1 46 ♖h3 ♔e8** 46 ... ♖h1 would have taken a bit longer: 47 ♖d3 ♗c6 48 ♖d8+ ♗e8 49 ♖b8 and 50 ♗d8, 51 f6, 52 ♗e7+ wins.[3] **47 ♖d3**, and Black resigned. A bishop's move forsakes his king to the worst of all.

Fischer had the curious coincidence of having this type of endgame three times at the US Championships against the same opponent: William Addison. The first encounter, from the 1962-63 Championship, was won by Fischer quite easily, due to the great material advantage he had in the endgame. Yet the other two, (from the 1965-66 and 1966-67 Championships) were both drawn, the first of them in a rather interesting way.

Pos. 292 shows the game after White's 32nd move, Fischer having the black pieces. **32 ... ♖g4 33 f3 ♖d4 34 ♔f2 ♖c8 35 ♖ac3 f6.** Well played. He covers h4 for the rook,

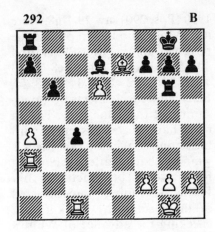

292                                    B

and clears f7 for the king. However, White's active pieces and advanced d-pawn compensate him for his pawn deficit. This happened to be one of the very few instances in which Fischer's material advantage in these endgames didn't suffice for a win. **36 ♔e3 ♖h4 37 g3 ♖xh2 38 ♖xc4 ♖xc4 39 ♖xc4 ♔f7 40 ♖c7 ♔e6 41 ♖xa7.** Now material has been levelled, yet still Fischer tries to exploit the last practical chances he has, to pose some problems for White. He comes close to achieving the improbable, but not close enough. **41 ... ♖b2 42 f4 ♖b3+ 43 ♔f2 f5 44 g4! g6 45 gxf5+ gxf5 46 a5 b5! 47 a6 ♖b4 48 ♔g3 ♖a4 49 ♗f8 h5 50 ♗e7 ♗c6 51 ♗f8 h4+ 52 ♔h3 ♗d7 53 ♗h6 ♔xd6 54 ♔xh4 ♗c8 55 ♔g5 ♗xa6 56 ♖a8 ♔c7 57 ♗g7 b4 58 ♗e5+ ♔d7 59 ♔f6**, and a draw was agreed.

# Superficiality

The by-product of the development of technical virtuosity in chess is a certain amount of superficiality. One tends to rely more and more on one's ability to handle efficiently many types of positions, and as a result the tendency to think afresh on each move and plan during the whole game might give way to mechanically played moves that look natural and good, and broadly conform to the overall structure of the position.

On the whole, one cannot expect a player of Fischer's stature, and, moreover, someone who made such rapid progress, to have developed a habit of falling back on routine solutions in his games. Yet he was not altogether free of it. Incidentally, it was he who made the following remark on Botvinnik when giving his list of chess history's 'greats' (the 1970 version): "He has become a real school of how to avoid superficiality".[1] Apparently, he was himself well aware that non-superficiality is unique even among players of the highest class.

I have chosen the following four examples to indicate how a certain superficial pattern might have found its place in Fischer's play. They all have to do with the same piece – Black's light-squared bishop.

293                     B

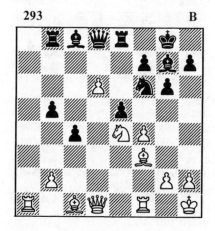

The first (Pos. 293) is Pomar-Fischer, Havana Olympiad 1966, after White's 19th move. **19 ... ♗e6?!**. It looks as though Fischer was concerned merely with developing his bishop 'somewhere'

233

along the h3-c8 diagonal. Why, actually, to e6? The main action on the e-file is around its two central squares: e4 and e5. Why block this file when his king's rook plays such an important role there? In fact he would have done better to have 'braced up' his control by 19 ... ♗f5!. A much more committal move, which, generally speaking, would perfectly agree with Fischer's style. Just compare this with his 10th move in the celebrated game against Letelier, Leipzig Olympiad 1960 (Pos. 294).

294                                    B

The two positions are, to be sure, quite different, but **10 ... ♗f5!** which Fischer played had the same aim – attacking the centralised knight, and deciding after that the shape of the pawn structure in the centre. After

Letelier's **11 ♘g3** Fischer considered 11 ... ♕c7, allowing White to compromise Black's pawn formation with 12 ♘xf5 gxf5.[2] (see also Pos. 66). While in the Pomar game 20 ♘g3 could have lead to the critical strengthening of Black's centre with 20 ... e4 (not 20 ... ♗d3? 21 fxe5 ♖xe5 22 ♗f4!), and other alternatives would have brought about the fall of the d6 pawn: 20 ♘xf6+ ♗xf6 21 ♗c6 ♖e6, or 20 ♖e1 ♗xe4! 21 ♗xe4 exf4. Even graver consequences follow the tactical 20 fxe5 ♘xe4 21 g4 ♗xe5! 22 gxf5 ♕h4, with a direct win. (see also Pos. 255)

In 1964 Fischer analysed a number of games from the match between Steinitz and Dubois, 1862, for the American magazine *Chess Life*. In the April issue of that year he took the opportunity to dwell at some length on a line of the King's Bishop's Gambit. It is noteworthy that that opening occupied a central place in Fischer's thoughts that year (otherwise a well-nigh complete sabbatical from chess activities). In the *American Chess Quarterly* he provided a "Bust to the King's Gambit" from the black side, whereas in the above article he took a reverse role, defending White's prospects after 1 e4 e5 2 f4 exf4 3 ♗c4 ♘f6 4 ♘c3 c6 5 ♗b3 d5 6 exd5 cxd5 7 d4 ♗d6 8 ♘ge2 0-0 9 ♗xf4 ♗xf4 10 ♘xf4 ♖e8+ 11 ♘fe2 ♘g4,

295 B

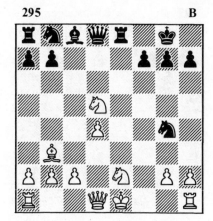

which was considered by the 'books' to give Black excellent attacking chances. Fischer disagrees and shows that "after 12 ♘xd5 [Pos. 295] ♗e6 (best) one line might run: 13 h3 ♗xd5 14 hxg4 ♗xg2 15 ♖h2 ♗f3 16 ♕d3 ♖xe2+ 17 ♖xe2 ♗xe2 18 ♕xe2 ♘c6 19 0-0-0 ♘xd4 20 ♗xf7+ ♔xf7 21 ♕c4+ ♔g6 22 ♖xd4 ♕g5+ 23 ♔b1 ♖f8 24 ♖d6+ ♖f6 25 ♕e4+ ♔h6 26 ♖d1 ♕f4 27 ♖h1+ ♔g5 28 ♕d5+ ♔xg4 – and White mates in four." He goes on further to show why 12 ... ♕h4+ is bad as well.

I find it hard to explain that Fischer should consider the almost mechanical 12 ... ♗e6 the best move in the diagrammed position. Again the bishop is doing a very bad job in blocking the e-file, even if temporarily. Black, it seems, could exert much greater pressure by playing 12 ... ♕d6! (preventing 13 h3, 13 0-0, and 13 ♘df4, while threatening 13 ... ♘xh2, and in some cases ... ♕h6) and follow it up with ... ♘c6 and ... ♗f5. Let's look at a couple of variations after 13 ♕d3 ♘c6:

I) 14 h3 ♗f5! 15 ♕xf5 ♖xe2+ wins the queen or the king's rook.

II) 14 c3 ♘e7! (if 14 ... ♗e6 15 ♕f3! ♖ad8 16 ♘df4 ♗xb3 17 axb3 ♘e3 18 ♔f2!, and Black is left empty-handed) 15 ♘xe7+ (bad is 15 ♘e3? ♘g6! – but not 15 ... ♘xe3 16 ♕xe3 ♗g4 17 0-0!! ♘f5 18 ♕f4, and White wins – 16 ♘c4 ♕e7, with a tremendous position for Black. Another possibility is 15 ♘df4 ♘f5 when 16 0-0-0 is met by 16 ... ♘fe3 followed by ... ♗f5, and 16 0-0 by 16 ... g5!? with sharp and lively play. Very unclear is 15 ♕g3 ♕xg3+ 16 hxg3 ♘f5!? 17 ♘c7 ♖e7 18 ♘xa8 ♘xg3) 15 ... ♖xe7, with ample compensation for the pawn. 16 ♕g3 is met by 16 ... ♕a6, 16 ♗c2 by 16 ... g6, and 16 0-0-0 by 16 ... ♘f2 or 16 ... ♘e3.

Where to develop the light-squared bishop to, was also the question in Fischer's 13th match game against Spassky, World Championship, Reykjavik, 1972 (Pos. 296). In contrast with his game against Pomar, and the above analysis, and in conformity with his general tendencies (see comment to Letelier-Fischer, Pos.

**296** B

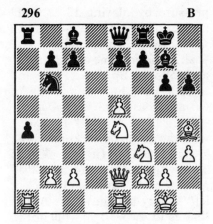

**297** B

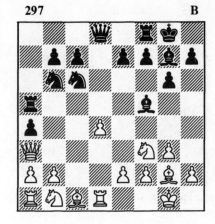

294), Fischer plays here **18 ... ♗f5**, insensitive to the fact that he allows Spassky to retort strongly with **19 g4!** to which he answered **19 ... ♗e6?**. Instead of these two facile moves (which proved to be quite otiose after **20 ♘d4! ♗c4 21 ♛d2!**), he could have posed serious problems for his opponent, as Gligorić pointed out in the match book,[3] with the modest yet much more effective **18 ... ♗d7**, or **19 ... ♗d7**, threatening ... **♗b5**, followed by ... **♘c4**.

These three examples dealt with the development of the bishop to an appropriate square on the h3-c8 diagonal. In the last it is already out and about there.

Black's developmental superiority in this position (Steinmeyer-Fischer, US Championship 1962-63, Pos. 297) needs no explanation.

With a move like 15 ... e5 he could increase it still further. 16 e3 is answered by 16 ... ♖e8, with the devastating threat 17 ... ♗f8; and after 16 ♗g5 ♛d7, White remains plagued by many problems. Fischer plays however: **15 ... ♗c2?** – a superficial move, associated with a superficial plan. **16 ♖e1 ♘xd4 17 ♘xd4 ♗xd4 18 ♛b4**. This simple move amounts to a refutation of Black's offhand treatment. **18 ... ♖a8 19 e3 ♗g7 20 ♘a3 ♗f5**. All the black pieces have been repulsed, and now is the time to claim back material: **21 ♗xb7**. Fischer has completely mishandled his opportunities, and as a result White succeeded in equalising the position.

As for other cases of superficiality, real or suspected, see Pos. 156, 157, and pp.249-53.

# Misplaying Won Positions

Somehow the fact that Fischer was prone to losing concentration once he reached a won position, went unnoticed throughout his career. A single exception was probably Larry Evans's comment on Fischer's play against Taimanov in their Candidates 1971 match: "The main weakness he displayed was a tendency to relax once he wrested the advantage"[1]

As the saying goes, there is nothing more difficult than winning a won position, and indeed some of Fischer's gravest mistakes were made in won positions through obvious lapses of concentration.

**298**                                    **W**

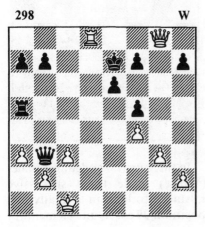

Against Sarapu, Sousse 1967, he had (as White) two(!) ways to force immediate mate (Pos. 298). The first was mate in three:

29 ♕g5+ f6 30 ♕g8, and 31 ♕e8/♕f8 is mate.

The other was mate in four:

29 ♕f8+ ♔f6 30 ♖d7 ♔g6 (30 ... e5 31 ♕h6 mate) 31 ♕xf7+ ♔h6 32 ♕xh7 mate.

Instead of these, he slid his rook one square to the right (**29 ♖e8+??**) and ... Sarapu resigned! (He did so probably because he couldn't force a mate himself . . . 29 ... ♔d6 30 ♕xf7 ♖d5?? – 30 ... ♖xa3 31 ♕e7+! – unfortunately weakens e6 too seriously). (see also Pos. 101)

Against Sherwin, at the US Championship 1958-59, he committed one of the gravest blunders in his entire career, and, typically, in a position which could hardly have been more winning (Pos. 299).

Fischer (Black), with nearly a queen(!) to the good, plays **51 ... ♖d8??**, most certainly overlooking that **52 ♖xd8** can't be answered by 52 ... ♕xd8 in view of 53 ♕xb3!

237

**299**                                    **B**

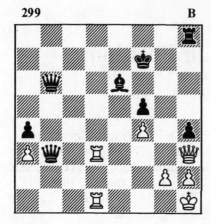

and White wins! . . . Having had such an excessive material plus, he could, luckily, maintain a winning advantage by **52 ... ♕xh3**. Naturally 51 ... ♕b1 (among other moves) would have won without the slightest effort. And if 'liquidate', then 51 ... ♕xd1+ 52 ♖xd1 ♕b3! did it better than other lines.

**300**                                    **W**

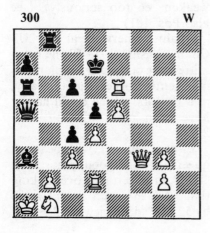

A year earlier, in the US Championship 1957-58, he unneccessarily dragged out a simple winning process in his game, with the white pieces, against Mednis (Pos. 300).

**33 ♘xa3?!** 33 ♕f7+! wins outright: 33 ... ♗e7+ 34 ♘a3 ♖e8 35 ♖d6+. **33 ... ♔xe6 34 ♕g4+ ♔e7 35 ♖f2?!**. Again slovenly played. 35 ♕g7+ ♔e6/♔e8 36 ♖f2 forces immediate resignation. It took a number of additional moves in the game: **35 ... ♖e8 36 ♕g5+ ♔d7 37 ♖f7+ ♔c8 38 ♕f5+ ♔b8 39 ♕d7**, 1-0.

In a number of cases this carelessness did cost points. For instance against Korchnoi at Curaçao 1962 (Pos. 301).

**301**                                    **W**

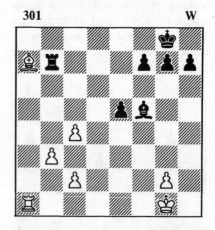

In this superior endgame Fischer (White) made three successive mistakes to land in a totally lost position: **29 c5?**. Quite elementary was 29 罩a2, and only then start marching with the c-pawn. **29 ... 奧xc2** loses then to both 30 奧e3 and 30 罩xc2. **29 ... 奧xc2 30 c6?**. Still on the same faulty track. **30 ... 罩xb3**. It might well be that Fischer considered now only 31 c7 罩c3? 32 奧c5! winning, and realised at the last moment that 30 ... 奧f5 forces an uneasy endgame: 31 罩d1 f6 32 罩d8+ 當f7 33 c8=豐 奧xc8 34 罩xc8, and a White win is no longer present. In order to prevent ... 奧f5 he played **31 g4??** overlooking this time **31 ... 罩g3+ 32 當f2 罩xg4** and he was faced with the insuperable task of holding four connected passed pawns after **33 c7 奧f5 34 奧e3 h5 35 罩a8+ 當h7 36 c8=豐 奧xc8 37 罩xc8**. He gave in a few moves later.

In Ivkov-Fischer, Mar del Plata 1959 (Pos. 302), Black is a piece up, and finding a way to win

**302**                         **B**

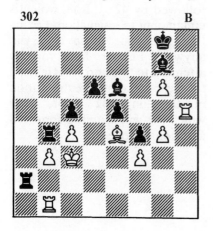

should be an easy task, it seems.

There are, as a matter of fact, no less than three ways to do it, all based on quite an obvious element in the position: White's bishop is pinned in view of lethal threats on the a1-h8 diagonal. The three winning methods are simply the three ways to dislodge it:

a) 42 ... d5! 43 cxd5 奧xg4 (Vuković, Trifunović)[2] with 44 ... 奧xf3! coming up next.

b) 42 ... 當f8! (Euwe)[3] with the devastating threat 43 ... d5 44 cxd5 奧xd5!.

c) 42 ... 奧xc4! 43 bxc4 (43 罩d1? 奧e6 etc) 43 ... 罩xb1 44 奧d5+ (44 奧xb1 e4+ 45 當b3 罩b2+ wins) 44 ... 當f8 45 罩f5+ 當e8 46 奧c6+ 當d8 47 罩f7 罩a3+ 48 當c2 罩g1 49 罩xg7 罩g2+ 50 當b1 罩e3, forcing mate (Kmoch).[4]

Strangely oblivious to all these, Fischer moves **42 ... 罩e2?**, straight away confronting a White counter-attack: **43 罩a1!**, with the aid of which Ivkov was able to force a draw ten moves later: **43 ... 罩e3+ 44 當c2 罩exb3 45 罩a8+ 罩b8 46 罩a7 罩b2+ 47 當c1 罩2b4 48 罩h7 奧f6 49 g7 罩xc4+ 50 當d1 罩d4+ 51 當c1 罩c4+ 52 當d1 罩d4+ 53 當c1, ½-½**.

The slips in the next two examples didn't affect the games' results, though it made Fischer work unnecessarily harder, and it flawed the elegance of his performances.

303          B          304          W

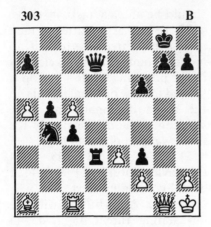
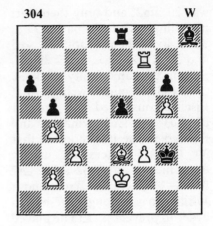

In Pos. 303 (Evans-Fischer US Championship 1965-66) 32 ... c3! wins swiftly. Black threatens 33 ... c2 and 34 ... ♖d1, so White is compelled to take the pawn: 33 ♗xc3 (33 ♖xc3 ♖d1) 33 ... ♘a2 34 ♗d4 (or 34 ♗xf6 ♘xc1 35 c6 ♕c7) 34 ... ♘xc1 35 ♕xc1 ♕h3 36 ♕g1 ♖d1, and he is mated next. Fischer's **32 ... ♔f7** gave Evans the opportunity to prolong the battle for another twenty moves, and is a move of a much more heavy-handed player than he.

Fischer's game against Reshevsky from the US Championship 1962-63 (Pos. 304), otherwise one of the best games he ever played, also deserved a more fitting finale.

After a superb performance up to this point, Fischer could conclude the game by catching his opponent's king in a neat mating web: 41 ♔f1! (as mentioned by Fischer in *MSMG*),[5] and now 42 ♗f2+ and 43 ♖h7 mate is quite a strong threat. It can be averted only by 41 ... ♗g7 (41 ... ♔h4 42 ♔g2, or 41 ... ♔h3 42 ♗f2), followed by 42 ... ♖h8, which is tantamount to resignation. Feeling that the game is an easy win anyway, Fischer fails to pay attention to this and plays instead for the more routine centralisation of the king: **42 ♔d3?**, after which the win required some ten additional moves.

# Typical Blunders and Oversights

Fischer, like any other player, was liable to blunders and oversights of diverse kinds. As late as 1970, a year in which his sportive and creative achievements reached one of their highest peaks, he could still blunder as elementary

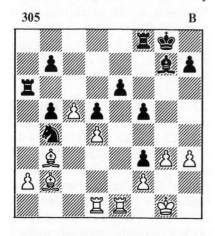

305            B

as pushing **28 ... f4??** in Pos. 305 (Browne-Fischer, Rovinj-Zagreb) dropping Black's lynchpin pawn on e6 after 29 a3 ♞c6 30 ♖xe6. Instead, 28 ... ♚f7 would have maintained all Black's advantages.[1] Such blunders are every player's lot, although they naturally occur less frequently in games of top

players. What kind of oversights were most common in Fischer's games? What typified them? In the chapter dealing with Fischer's alertness (pp.144-9) and in Pos. 1 we observed how great his attention was to what was going on in his opponent's mind. Yet possessing (as we already know) a tremendous will to win, he might have 'forgotten' his opponent at times, carrying his plans through as though no obstacle could be put up to counter them. We mark here, then, two contradictory tendencies which usually dwelt in peace with each other. Yet each could come to the fore at the expense of the other. As Bobby once confessed: "My opponents make good moves too – sometimes I don't take these things into consideration".[2] To paraphrase the utterance mentioned in 'Alertness' (p.144): Fischer plays worst when disregarding his opponent. This, to be sure, is true for many other players as well.

Against Uhlmann at Buenos Aires 1960, Fischer (White) reached a superior position (Pos. 306).

**306**                                    **W**

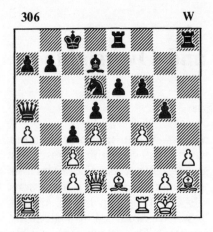

He must have thought that after **21 &f3**, taking e4 away from Black, Black's position offered no active resources. And indeed, Black's position collapses quickly after a pawn exchange either on f4 (Black) or g5 (White), in view of the tremendous threats on the h2-b8 diagonal. Uhlmann's response – **21 ... g4** – was regarded by virtually all the commentators [3] as a superb positional pawn offer. After both **22 hxg4 f5** (as played in the game), or **22 &xg4 f5**, White's dark-squared bishop is bound to stay hemmed-in for the rest of the game (and e4 does eventually fall into Black's hands). It is the lot of this bishop, which within two moves turned from the potential 'king of the board' into an actual pauper begging for some space, that brought about White's downfall. Yet 21 ... g4, for all its great

merits, was absolutely compulsory, and it is indeed ironic that the only move that saved Black's game was the one that eventually won it! Had Fischer been more attentive, he should not only have spotted the move, but would certainly have found the right way to face it and maintain a very favourable position: 21 fxg5 &e4 22 ₩f4! e5 23 ₩f3!, and now:

a) 23 ... fxg5 24 &xe5 g4!? (24 ... &d2 25 ₩f7 &xf1 26 &xf1 &hg8 27 &f5 &e6 28 &g4!!, or 24 ... &xe5 25 dxe5 ₩b6+ 26 &h2! g4 27 ₩f4 gxh3 28 g4 etc) 25 ₩e3! (but not 25 ₩f7? gxh3! 26 &xh8 h2+! 27 &xh2 &xh8+ 28 &g1 ₩xc3, and Black wins, or 25 hxg4? &xe5! 26 dxe5 ₩b6+, and again Black wins) 25 ... &hg8 (or 25 ... &xc3) 26 &xg4 &xg4 27 hxg4, with advantage to White.

b) 23 ... &d2 24 ₩xf6 &xf1 25 &xf1 ₩xc3 26 &xe5 ₩e3+ 27 ₩f2!, and White has too many pawns for the exchange. For instance: 27 ... ₩xf2+ 28 &xf2 &hg8 29 h4 &xa4 30 &f3 &c6 31 &f6, and the h-pawn advances.

c) 23 ... &xg5 24 ₩xf6 &hg8 25 &xe5 &xh3+ 26 &h1 ₩xc3 27 ₩f3!.

d) 23 ... &ef8 24 dxe5 &xg5 25 ₩e3 &hg8 26 &h1, with clear advantage.

e) 23 ... ₩xc3 24 gxf6 ₩xd4+ (or 24 ... ₩xf3 25 &xf3 exd4 26 f7 &ef8 27 &e5! etc) 25 &h1 &d2 26

♕a3 ♘xf1 27 ♖xf1, and the
threats of f7 and ♕d6 (or ♗g1)
would decide the issue. (see also
Pos. 233)

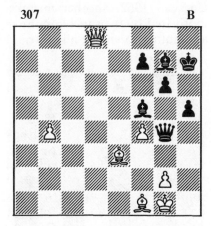

307 B

Against Geller at Havana 1965,
Fischer (Black) blundered in Pos.
307 with **37 ... ♗h6?**. It is most
likely that the cause for that was
Fischer's attempt to create winning
chances in case Geller misplayed
it. He apparently reckoned with
38 ♕c7, when White is more or
less forced to take a draw after 38
... ♗e6 39 b5 ♕g3 40 ♗f2 ♕g4! 41
♗e3 (or 41 b6 ♗xf4 42 ♕c5 h4 43
b7 h3, etc) 41 ... ♕g3, since it
might be more difficult for him to
achieve it after 42 ♗c1 ♗g7 43
♕c5 ♕e1 44 b6 ♗c8! (threatening
45 ... ♗a6) where, after 45 ♕xc8
♗d4+ 46 ♔h2 ♕xf1, he has to
find the only way to do so – 47
♕d7! – as 47 b7 ♗f2! wins, and
the same holds good for 47 ♕c7

♗g1+! 48 ♔h3 ♕d3+ 49 g3 ♕d5
50 ♔h4 ♕f5. What Fischer missed
was the rather simple **38 ♕f6!** and
all of a sudden Black has not only
the pawn on f7 vulnerable, but,
more importantly – the a1-h8
diagonal. White's threat 39 ♗d4
forced Black to retreat his bishop
to g7, thus parting straight away
with his f7 pawn. I analysed this
position in *Chess Life*,[4] and referred
to Geller's claim in *The Application
of Chess Theory*[5] that Black's
position was strategically lost
anyway. This doesn't stand up to
a thorough treatment, I believe.
After 37 ... ♗d7! – screening off
the white queen from the rest of
the d-file (37 ... h4? 38 ♕g5! –
Geller) – White has probably
nothing better than rush his
queen back to the lower ranks by
playing 38 ♕e7. Here is what
would happen as a consequence
of the more natural 38 b5: 38 ...
♕d1 39 b6 (it's too late to change
one's mind now. 39 ♕b6 ♗f5! 40
♔f2 ♗c3, and White is facing
some uneasy problems. Relatively
best is 39 ♔h2 ♕e1! 40 ♕xd7 –
but not 40 ♕e7?? ♗e6, and White
drops a bishop – 40 ... ♕xe3 41
♕xf7 h4 draw, as no side can
undertake anything without putting his own king in jeopardy) 39
... ♗d4! 40 ♗xd4 (White is risking
his skin with 40 ♗f2? ♗xf2+ 41
♔xf2 ♕d4+ 42 ♔e1? ♕e3+ 43
♗e2 ♗b5 44 ♕d2 ♕g1+, and

mate; or 40 ♔f2? ♛d2+; or 40
♛e7 ♝e6 41 ♛a3 ♛d2!) 40 ...
♛xd4+ 41 ♔h1 ♛xf4, and draw.
What else can White play instead
of 38 b5 –? If 38 ♝c4, then 38 ...
♝c6 39 ♛d2 ♝c3!, and White
loses any pride he has had in his
passed pawn, and on either 38
♔f2 or 38 ♔h2 comes the same 38
... ♝d4!. Just by way of illustrating
how easily White can go under in
this double-edged position, watch
the following plausible line: 38 ♔h2
♝d4! 39 ♝d2 ♔g7! 40 ♝b5!? h4!!
41 ♛xd7 ♛g3+ 42 ♔h1 ♛f2, and
Black cashes White's queen in
view of the mating threats. So
let's go back and see what happens
after 38 ♛e7. Black starts creating
annoying threats on White's first
rank by 38 ... ♛d1. White's 39
♛xf7? loses right away to 39 ...
♝b5; so 39 ♛c5 h4 40 b5 (40 ♛g5
is no longer effective: 40 ... ♛e1
41 ♝f2 ♛xb4 42 ♛xh4+ ♝h6,
draw, while exchanging queens
by means of 40 ♛c1 leads to
another draw after 40 ... ♛xc1 41
♝xc1 ♝d4+ 42 ♔h2 ♝f2!, and
the white king is detained in the
corner while the pawn on the
other wing can't be promoted.) 40
... h3 41 ♛c1 (now he is left with
no other choice, for if 41 b6 hxg2
42 ♔xg2 ♝e6 43 ♔f2 ♝f6, and
White's position is critical. And
41 gxh3 ♝xh3 42 ♛c4 ♛f3! is an
easy draw.) 41 ... ♛xc1 42 ♝xc1
♝d4+ 43 ♔h2 hxg2 44 ♔xg2 g5!

45 fxg5 f6 46 gxf6 ♝xb5! 47 ♝xb5
♝xf6, draw.

It was against the same opponent
that Fischer committed, back at
Curaçao 1962, another mistake
motivated by the same impulse –
attempting to win at all costs.

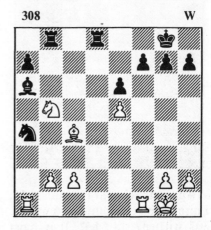

308                              W

White (Fischer) in Pos. 308 has
of course a draw with 19 ♖xa4
♝xb5 20 ♝xb5 ♖xb5 21 ♖xa7
♖xb2 22 ♖fxf7, etc. But Fischer
wants more, and this leads him to
play **19 ♘d6?**, probably overlooking this time that White gets
nowhere after **19 ... ♝xc4 20
♘xc4 ♘xb2 21 ♘d6 ♖d7 22 ♖fb1
♖c7!**. Now 23 c4 ♖b4 24 ♘b5
♖cxc4 25 ♖xa7 h6 26 ♘d6 ♖f4,
etc., leaves Black clearly better.
Fischer had to be satisfied with an
inferior ending: **23 h3 ♖b6 24 c4
h6 25 ♘b5 ♖c5 26 ♖xb2 a6 27 ♖f2
axb5 28 ♖a7 ♖xe5 29 ♖fxf7 ♖g5**,
losing it in the end.

309 B

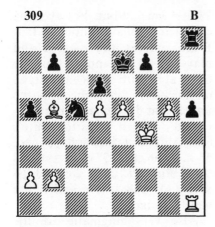

Good enough for a draw in Sanguinetti-Fischer, Santiago 1959 (Pos. 309) should be **34 ... h4**, which besides advancing the passed pawn, restricts the mobility of the white rook. Fischer, however, was still entertaining some ideas of winning after **34 ... ♘d7 35 ♗xd7 ♔xd7** – note that 35 ... dxe5+ loses to 36 ♔xe5 ♔xd7 37 ♔f6 ♖h7 38 ♖e1! h4 39 ♖e7+ ♔d6 40 g6! ♖h6 41 ♖xf7 h3 42 ♖h7. After Black's last White indeed might go under by 36 ♖h4 ♖h7 37 ♔f5 dxe5 38 ♔xe5 b5 39 ♔f6 ♔d6 40 ♖d4 (if 40 g6 fxg6 41 ♔xg6 ♖e7 42 ♖xh5 ♖e2, etc) 40 ... h4 41 g6 fxg6 42 ♔xg6 ♖e7 43 ♖d2 ♖e5, etc. Or 36 ♔f5 dxe5 37 ♔xe5 h4 38 ♔f6 ♖h7, leading to similar positions. What Fischer's will to win prevented him from seeing, was that White wins with **36 e6+! fxe6** 36 ... ♔e7 37 ♖c1!,

and it's lights out for Black. **37 g6!** **exd5 38 ♖xh5!**, which Sanguinetti carried out to its correct conclusion.

Another blunder with dramatic consequences was the one Fischer (Black) committed on his 41st move (just after resumption!) in this game against Eliskases at Buenos Aires 1960 (Pos. 310).

310 B

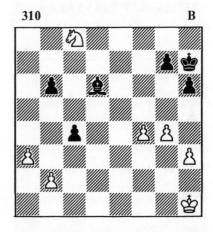

Black has the draw for the asking by 41 ... ♗xa3 42 ♘xb6 ♗xb2 43 ♘xc4 ♗c1, etc. Yet Fischer, a pawn down, looks for more! Under the impression that the above possibility won't run away, he plays **41 ... ♗c5**, to which White had only to answer with **42 a4** to get a winning endgame. It might well be that Fischer tried to put his opponent to the test: 42 ♔g2 b5 43 ♔f3 ♔g6 44 ♔e4 ♔f6 45 ♔d5 ♗xa3! 46 ♘a7 b4! 47 ♔xc4 ♗xb2 48 ♔xb4 ♗c1, when 49 ♔c4! is the only way to draw. Now, after 42 a4 this possibility is no longer present, and Black's overreaching cost him the game: **42 ... ♔g6 43 ♔g2 ♔f6 44 ♔f3 ♔e6 45 ♔e4 ♗f2 46 f5+ ♔d7 47 ♘a7 ♔d6 48 ♘b5+ ♔c5 49 ♘c7 ♗h4 50 ♘e8 ♔b4 51 ♔d5 ♗e7 52 ♘xg7 ♗f6 53 ♘e8! ♗xb2 54 f6 ♗xf6 55 ♘xf6 c3 56 ♘h5! ♔xa4 57 ♘f4 b5 58 ♘e2 c2, 1-0.**

**311**                                    **W**

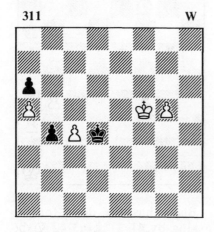

A strange and mysterious blunder was Fischer's **55 c5??** against Letelier at Mar del Plata 1959 (Pos. 311). It seems inevitable that he should have calculated the following line: **55 g6 b3 56 g7 b2 57 g8=♕ b1=♕+ 58 ♔f6 ♕f1+ 59 ♔e7 ♕xc4 60 ♕xc4+ ♔xc4 61 ♔d6 ♔b5 62 ♔d5 ♔xa5 63 ♔c4**, draw. Wishing to elicit from the position more than the position could possibly offer, Fischer hits upon **55 c5 ♔xc5 56 ♔e4!**, and

White wins. What, however, he completely fails to notice, is that Black ignores the c-pawn and plays **55 ... b3**, promoting the pawn at b1 with check – exactly as in the above line, but with the unpleasant difference that here, a tempo down, it leads to White's loss. And this is how it happened: **55 ... b3 56 c6 b2 57 c7 b1=♕+ 58 ♔e6 ♕b7 59 ♔d7 ♔d5 60 g6 ♕c6+ 61 ♔d8 ♕d6+.** and White had to resign.

Also very enigmatic are the next three cases, taken from earlier stages of the game, all of which have one thing in common: a blunder is committed in a position that must have been considered by Fischer previously, under slightly different circumstances.

**312**                                    **B**

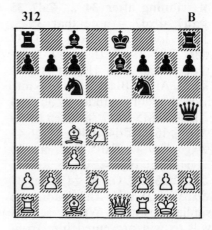

In Fischer-R.Byrne, US Championship 1965-66 (Pos. 312) Byrne

plays **10 ... 0-0!**, certainly not expecting Fischer to fall into 11 ♘xc6 ♗d6! 12 ♘f3 ♗g4 13 ♘e7+ ♔h8!, and Black wins. Fischer sees this too, of course, and plays **11 ♗e2**; Byrne answers **11 ... ♗g4**, and now, a single move later, Fischer plays the same **12 ♘xc6??**, calling for the same **12 ... ♗d6**, winning the exchange by force after **13 h3 ♗xe2**.

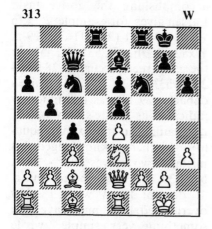

313                                    W

The scope of Fischer's blunder in this well-known (Fischer-Kholmov, Havana 1965) position (313), hasn't so far been fully fathomed. Fischer played here **19 b4?**, apparently overlooking **19 ... ♘d4! (20 cxd4 exd4 21 a3 d3!** with a clear advantage to Black). Bizzare as it might seem, Fischer had reached a very similar position in tournament play (Pos. 314). It was nine years earlier, when the far from mature Bobby took part in

the semi-finals of the Manhattan Club Championship, New York 1956.

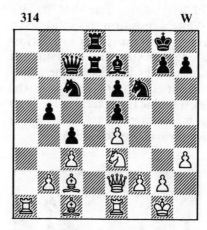

314                                    W

The game was Bobby Fischer-Samuel Baron. Here he played **21 b3!** anticipating **21 ... ♘d4** which his opponent played, and being ready with the line **22 cxd4 exd4 23 bxc4 dxe3 24 ♗xe3 bxc4 25 ♖a6** With White's slight advantage later leading to a win. Yet, as an experienced grandmaster he neither recalls the game nor plays the same good old move – 19 b3 – which should yield him the advantage after 19 ... ♘d4 20 cxd4 exd4 21 bxc4 dxe3 22 ♗xe3 ♕xc4 (or 22 ... bxc4 23 ♖ec1! with 24 ♗b3 to follow) 23 ♗b3! ♕xe4 24 ♗b6! (or even 24 ♗xh6!?, and if 24 ... ♕xe2 25 ♖xe2 gxh6 26 ♖xe6 ♔f7 27 ♖ae1!) 24 ... ♕xe2 25 ♖xe2 ♖de8 26 ♖xe6. Suetin-Nei, Vilnius 1967, went: 19 b3 ♗c5 20 ♖d1

♘d4! 21 cxd4 exd4 27 ♖xe3 ♖xc2, with equality. But White's 20th move was weak. Better was 20 ♖f1!!. (20 ... ♗xe3? 21 ♕xe3!). White's position is solid as a rock, whereas Black's deteriorated pawn structure is a source of concern for the rest of the game.

Last but not least was the inexplicable final phase of Fischer's game against Larsen at Santa Monica 1966 (Pos. 315).

**315**                 **W**

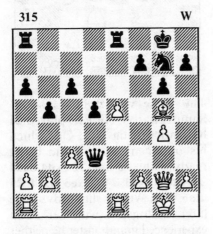

When Fischer (White) played **27 ♖e3** he clearly had in mind launching an attack along the h-file, where there were good possibilities of creating mating threats. After Larsen's **27 ... ♕d2** any process Fischer might have envisaged had to contain the following moves: ♕h3, ♗f6, ♕h6, g5, with a mate at h8 by either sacrificing the queen at h7 and then ♖h3-h8, or first ♖h3. This is quite a long process, and it can succeed only if Black plays exclusively passive moves. Whatever variations Fischer looked into in this position, he must have realised that White is at least one tempo short of accomplishing the above task. Larsen gives, for example: 28 ♗f6 ♕xb2 29 ♖d1 (29 ♖f1 d4!) 29 ... ♕xa2 30 ♕h3 ♕c2 31 ♖f1 g5!.[6] In the game there occurred: **28 b3 b4 29 ♕h3??**. The key to White's debacle. 29 f3 was unanimously indicated as White's only way of maintaining an approximate equality. Fischer acknowledged his mistake two moves later – **29 ... bxc3 30 ♕h6 ♘e6** – by resigning. "I do not know what Fischer overlooked, but it must have been something very simple" wrote Larsen. "Did [he] fail to see that the black queen can interpose after, for instance 31 ♗f6 d4 32 ♕xh7+ ♔xh7 33 ♖h3+? It looks like the only explanation".[7]

However these last three cases may be interpreted, they seem fated to remain enigmatic.

# Towards a Comprehensive Vision

## THE GRAND LINES

Every classical player, when his command of the game and his self-confidence have matured, evinces a growing tendency to negotiate lines that are less predictable and calculable yet manifest a grander vision of the game.

This transition from a concrete approach to a more detached one, might give, when viewed from a limited perspective, the impression of laxity and, at times, superficiality, leaving as it often does, many 'loose ends'.

**316**      **W**

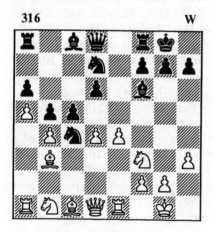

The tense situation in the cen-tre and queenside in Fischer-Matanović, Vinkovci 1968 (Pos. 316), called for a quick and definite resolution. A move like 17 ♘a3!? would have done just that. White has somewhat the better of it after either 17 ... ♘xa3 18 ♗xa3, or 17 ... cxd4 18 ♘xd4 ♘de5 (if 18 ... ♘xa3 19 ♖xa3! ♗b7 20 ♘f5, or 19 ... ♘e5 20 ♗d5) 19 f4. Fischer instead embarked on a very imaginative plan, which was at the same time highly unpredictable. Calculations wouldn't have helped here. It is a player's vision which dictates such decisions, and his abilities that prove whether it was justifiably put into practice. After **17 ♗f4! cxb4 18 ♘bd2! d5! 19 exd5 ♘xa5** the question was whether the greater mobility of the white pieces, and his central doubled pawn, would outweigh Black's pawn mass on the queenside. Fischer proved it would: **20 ♗d6 ♘xb3 21 ♕xb3 ♖e8 22 ♗c7!** **♖xe1+ 23 ♖xe1 ♕xc7.** Chandler-Nikolić, Linares 1988, deviated with 23 ... ♕f8 24 ♘e4 a5 25 ♕d3 a4 26 ♗d6 ♕d8 27 ♗xb4 ♗a6 28 ♘d6 ♕c7 29 ♕f5 g6 30 ♕f4 ♖f8

249

31 ♘e5 ♘b6 32 ♘g4 ♗d8 33 ♘h6+ ♔g7 34 ♘df5+, 1-0[1] **24 ♖e8+ ♘f8 25 ♕xb4 ♗e7 26 ♖xe7 ♕d8 27 ♘e5 ♘g6 28 ♘c6 ♕f8 29 ♕c5 a5 30 ♖c7**, after which White's advantage was unambiguous.

**317**                  **W**

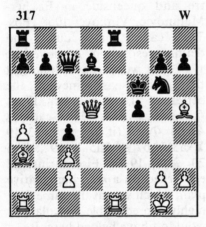

The magnificent battle that was waged between Fischer (White) and Larsen (Black) in their 1st match game, Candidates 1971, saw in Pos. 317 **21 ♗f3!**. Again a decision in the spirit of the grand lines, with a number of loose ends. A much tighter treatment was offered by 21 ♗d6!. Black's three main alternatives are 21 ... ♕b6+, 21 ... ♕d8, and 21 ... ♕c8. Let's examine them one by one.

I) 21 ... ♕b6+ 22 ♗c5 ♕c6 23 ♕d4+ ♔g5. Pachman concludes that White has no decisive attacking continuation.[2] This seems questionable after 24 ♗f3 ♕c7 25 a5! ♖xe1+ (25 ... ♘e5 is answered simply by 26 ♗d6! ♘xf3+ 27 gxf3 and wins, which the more spectacular 26 ♕f4+ fails to achieve after 26 ... ♔g6! 27 ♕g3+ ♔f6! 28 ♗d4 g5!. 25 ... ♔h6 is rebutted by 26 ♕d2+ f4 27 ♗d6) 26 ♖xe1 ♕xa5 27 ♗e7+ ♘xe7 28 ♖xe7, with a quick mate in sight.

II) 21 ... ♕d8. Kholmov recommends now 22 ♖ab1 or 22 g4.[3] Yet even better might be 22 ♕d4+, which has two sub-variations: a) 22 ... ♔g5 23 ♗f3 ♗c6 24 h4+! ♘xh4 (24 ... ♔h6? 25 ♕d2+) 25 ♕xg7+ ♘g6 26 ♗f4+!! ♔xf4 27 ♕h6+ ♕g5 (27 ... ♔g3 28 ♕h2 mate) 28 g3+ ♔xg3 29 ♕xg5+ ♔xf3 30 ♖f1+, and mates; b) 22 ... ♔f7 23 ♖e8! ♗xe8 (23 ... ♕xe8 24 ♗e5!) 24 ♕d5+ (24 g4 ♔g8!) 24 ... ♔f6 25 ♖e1!, and Black is beset with insoluble problems.

III) 21 ... ♕c8 22 ♗c5 ♗e6 23 ♕d4+ ♔g5 (on 23 ... ♔f7, 24 ♗xa7 is good enough) 24 ♗f3, with obvious advantage. Black's king is likely to get executed around his 30th birthmove.

Fischer's 21 ♗f3 should be understood in a different perspective. It comes from the hand of a master draughtsman, who even in such a sharp position, allows himself to 'sketch' his moves, as it were, quite freely, matching them with the broad contours of the position. For all the good the bishop has done on h5 Fischer switched it to f3 probably for two principle reasons: a) believing that in this open position the bishop would, if placed on the long diagonal, contribute to a more harmonious co-operation of the white pieces; b) preventing Black from playing ... ♔g5 with tempo gain. It is quite possible that he started calculating variations only after **21 ... ♘e5 22 ♕d4 ♔g6**. He was quite right in his policy in as much as White had little to fear. He could maintain some advantage by 23 ♔h1, a move pointed out by Timman.[4] One variation might run: 23 ... ♘xf3 24 gxf3 ♔f7 25 ♖g1 (23 ♗e7!? ♔g8!) 25 ... g6 26 ♖g3, and Black remains dangerously exposed to threats on the g- and h-files, as well as on the open diagonals. 23 ... ♘g4 leads to some further interesting variations: 24 ♗d6 ♕b6 25 ♖eb1! – Timman probably underestimated the strength of this move when indicating 25 ♗c5, drawing – 25 ... ♕xd4 26 cxd4: a) 26 ... ♘f2+ (26 ... ♖e6 27 ♗g3) 27 ♔g1 ♘e4 28 ♖xb7 ♘xd6 (28 ... ♗c6 29 ♖c7 ♗d5 30 ♗e5 ♖g8 31 ♖b1) 29 ♖xd7 ♘e4 30 ♖b1 ♖ab8 31 ♖bb7! ♖xb7 32 ♖xb7 ♘c3 33 ♖xa7 ♖e1+ 34 ♔f2 ♖c1 35 ♔e3 ♖xc2 36 d5, and White's advantage can't be challenged; b) 26 ... ♘e3 27 ♖xb7 ♘xc2 28 ♖c1 ♗xa4 29 ♗e5 ♖g8, and both 30 ♗d5 and 30 ♗d1

♗c6 31 ♖c7 ♘b4 32 ♖xc4 win. Yet, in the same spirit of the grand lines, Fischer opted for something quite different: **23 ♖xe5 ♕xe5 24 ♕xd7 ♖ad8 25 ♕xb7**. We all know what he had up his sleeve after **25 ... ♕e3+ 26 ♔f1 ♖d2 27 ♕c6+ ♖e6**, namely, the fantastic retort **28 ♗c5!!**. But ever since the game was played, it has been a moot point what he might have had in mind in response to 25 ... ♕xc3. Igor Zaitsev,[5] and later Timman,[6] developed the following line: 26 ♕c6+ ♔g5 27 ♗c1+ f4 28 h4+ ♔f5 29 g4+! fxg3 *e.p.* 30 ♔g2 ♕xa1 (30 ... ♕d4 31 ♔xg3 is better for White – Timman) 31 ♗g4+ ♔e5 32 ♕c5+ ♖d5 33 ♕e3+ ♔d6 34 ♗a3+ ♔c7 35 ♕xa7+ ♔c6 36 ♕a6+ ♔c7 37 ♕xc4+ ♔b8/♔b6 38 ♕xd5 ♕xa3 39 ♕b5+, and, according to Timman, White stands better. Quite convincing as it is, Fischer wouldn't have looked in advance into such an ultra-speculative line. Imaginative yet dubious is 27 h4+ ♔xh4 28 ♕c7(!) ♕xa1+ 29 ♔h2 ♕e5+! 30 ♕xe5 ♖xe5 31 ♗c1 f4 32 ♗xf4 ♖g5 33 g3+ ♖xg3 34 ♗xg3+ ♔g5, and White has a tough endgame to hold. Worth mentioning is that after 26 ♕c6+ ♔g5 27 ♗c1+ f4 28 ♗xf4+ ♔xf4 29 ♖f1, Black extricates himself by 29 ... ♔g5 30 ♕c7 ♕d4+ 31 ♔h1 ♔h6!, and if 29 g3+? (instead of 29 ♖f1), then 29 ... ♔e3(!) 30

♕c5+ (30 ♖f1 ♔d2!! wins) 30 ...
♕d4! 31 ♖e1+ ♔xf3+ 32 ♕xd4
♖xe1 mate! If one rejects these
continuations, then what is left is
the timid retreat 26 ♕b1, when,
according to Zaitsev, after 26 ...
♖e5 Black could more than hold
his own.

We are thus driven to the
conclusion that whatever Fischer
might have prepared as answer
to 25 ... ♕xc3 hadn't been worked
out by him in great detail, and
had remained in a rather sketchy
state. As shown in the Zaitsev-
Timman line, he wasn't wrong in
his assessment that White should
somehow get the upper hand in
the complications which might
eventually have ensued, but he
would have played that line, I
guess, only with great reluctance.
(see also Pos. 170)

**318**                          **W**

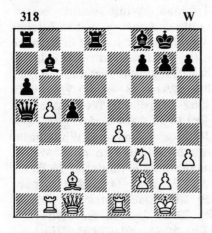

Another grand conception was

Fischer's attacking plan in his
10th match game against Spassky,
World Championship, Reykjavik
1972 (Pos. 318). With 26 ♗b3!
Fischer gave his opponent the
opportunity to create two connected passed pawns on the queenside
for a fierce attack on the kingside,
which liquidated to a materially
superior endgame: **26 ... axb5 27
♕f4 ♖d7 28 ♘e5 ♕c7 29 ♖bd1!
♖e7 30 ♗xf7+! ♖xf7 31 ♕xf7+
♕xf7 32 ♘xf7 ♗xe4 33 ♖xe4
♔xf7**. Fischer, absorbed in calculating and evaluating the ins and
outs of his profound and imposing
plan, remains this time oblivious
of a certain nuance. A more
accurate move order was first 26
♕f4, and only then 27 ♗b3. The
reason is simple: this would have
made Spassky face problems Fischer denied him by playing 26
♗b3 first. Calculating the ramifications of 26 ♕f4 axb5 27 ♘g5,
should have taken Black several
long minutes, as White gets threats
all over the place: 27 ... f6 (27 ...
♖d7?? 28 ♕f5 wins the rook) 28
♘xh7!? (on 28 ♘e6 Black succeeds
in warding off all White's threats
by 28 ... ♕d2! 29 ♕g3 ♖e8! [after
29 ... ♕xc2 30 ♘xd8 ♖xd8 31
♕c7, Black is forced to enter the
hazards of 31 ... ♗xe4, since 31 ...
♖d2 loses elegantly to 32 ♕xb7
♖xf2 33 e5 fxe5 34 ♖f1!] 30 ♗b3
c4 31 ♖ed1 ♕b4!, and Black is
out of any danger after 32 ♘xg7

or other moves) 28 ... ♕d2! (Black's only resource. The knight is taboo: 28 ... ♔xh7 29 e5+ ♔g8 30 e6 ♗d6 [or 30 ... ♖d2 31 ♗g6! ♗d6 32 ♕h4, with a winning attack] 31 ♕f5 ♔f8 32 ♕h5, and Black wouldn't survive for long) 29 ♕xd2. Unfortunately, White can't carry out his attack: 29 ... ♘xf6+ gxf6 30 ♗b3+ c4 31 ♕g4+ ♕g5 32 ♗xc4+ bxc4 33 ♕e6+ ♔h8 34 ♖xb7 c3, and Black wins. Now after 29 ... ♖xd2 30 ♘xf8 ♖xc2 31 ♖xb5!, a drawn endgame is reached after a few moves. All this had to be calculated by Black at the board. (see also Pos. 48)

What typified the way Fischer handled the 'grand lines', then, is some nonchalance towards details. It seems that as far as he was concerned, creating a bold conception and drawing its main outlines was a factor at least as important as calculating the variations associated with it. Yet this might well be a common feature of every classical player, or indeed any player who ever conceived grand plans.

## THE UNIFIED VISION

The greatest artistry a chess player can strive to attain is that of combining the game's elements into a homogeneous whole. Their perception on the one hand, and balanced application on the other, is what distinguishes a player of a comprehensive vision from a player of fragmentary vision. This, of course, is very much so with regard to the two most general consituents of the game – the positional and the tactical.

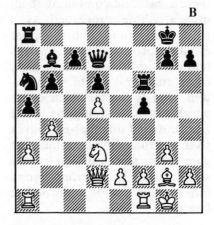

B

While analysing a game between Lilienthal (White) and Botvinnik (Black), from the 12th USSR Championship 1940, Petrosian had the following to say about the position after White's 19 ♘e1-d3: "Even when the game takes on a quiet course, one is not exempted from calculating sharp variations, notwithstanding the fact that they aren't always likely to materialise in the game. On 19 ... axb4 20 axb4 ♕b5, Lilienthal had prepared the following beautiful variation: 21 ♘f4 ♕xb4 22 ♕xb4 ♘xb4 23

Ixa8+ ♗xa8 24 Ial If8 25 Ia4
c5 26 dxc6 ♘xc6 27 ♗d5+ ♔h8 28
♘g6+! hxg6 29 Ih4 mate!".[1]
This is a splendid illustration of a
perfect coalescence of tactical and
positional elements.

In Fischer's case, we can (by
now) rightly speak of a player
who was a great master in both
these areas; and combining them
into a whole proceeded as a
matter of course in a great
number of his games. Such a
unified vision implies in most
cases another kind of vision as
well, that is the technical one –
which is to say: seeing the whole
board. As in Lilienthal-Botvinnik
so in the following examples, the
game takes place not in a limited
section (that is, a certain wing),
but spreads out over the whole
board.

**319**                                    **W**

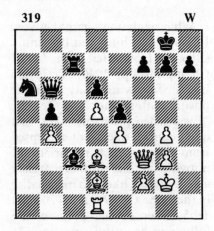

The main issue in Pos. 319

(Fischer-Unzicker, Leipzig Olympiad 1960), seems to be the fate of
White's pawn on b4. It is attacked
and isn't easily defendable. Black
is saddled with a similar problem
with regard to his pawn at b5,
although this is merely under
veiled threats. For the time being,
suffice it to point out these two
positional weaknesses. Other positional factors will soon come to
the fore.

**14 ♗e3**

Ther was no way to defend b4
straightforwardly. 41 ♗xc3? Ixc3
42 Ibl ♛d4, leads to heavy
material losses.

**41 ... ♛b8 42 Ih1!**

Indirectly attacking ... b5!.
This pawn turns out to be no less
vulnerable than White's b4. The
threat is now 43 ♛f5. If 42 ... g6?
43 ♛f6, and the mate after 44
♗h6 is to be averted only at the
cost of a queen (... ♛f8). Black is
forced to play his next move.

**42 ... ♛c8 43 ♗xb5 ♘xb4 44
♛d1!**

Switching from one wing to the
other. White prevents 44 ... ♘c2,
and threatens 45 ♛a4 followed by
46 Icl or 46 Ibl.[2] Was he, then,
concealing his true intentions –
playing, actually, for a decision
on the queenside?

**44 ... ♗d4 45 ♗xd4 exd4 46 g5!!**

Not quite! His options range
over the whole board, and he
decides for the most forceful one.

I) Queenside-wards: 46 ♕a4 ♘c2 (if 46 ... ♕xg4 47 ♕xb4 ♕xe4+ 48 ♔h2 ♖c2 49 ♖e1, offers a complete defence) 47 ♗c6 d3 48 ♖b1, isn't bad, but it might well be considerably slower (48 ... ♕xg4? 49 e5!, but not 49 ♗d7 ♘e1+!).

II) Centre-wards: 46 ♕xd4 ♘c2 47 ♕d1 isn't bad either, but is certainly *much* slower. Black gets some counterplay after 47 ... ♕b8 48 ♗c6 ♘b4.

46 g5!! has two sides to it: a) making way for a kingside assault in one variation (the game continuation); b) creating an ideal post for the white queen on f6 in another variation (see next note).

**46 ... ♕b8**

After 46 ... g6, White wins due to the weak black pawn at d6 – another positional factor which so far hasn't played a role: 47 ♕xd4 ♘c2 48 ♕f6! ♕f8 (or 48 ... ♖c5 49 ♗c6 ♕c7 50 ♖b1 etc) 49 e5!, and wins.

**47 ♕h5!**

The game is now decided tactically on the kingside.

**47 ... ♕xb5 48 ♕xh7+ ♔f8 49 ♕h8+ ♔e7 50 ♕xg7 ♘xd5 51 ♕xd4!**. To chase the knight away from defending f6. **51 ... ♘c3 52 ♕f6+ ♔d7 53 g6!** ♘xe4 53 ... fxg6 54 ♖h7+ ♔c8 55 ♖xc7+ ♔xc7 56 ♕xc3+ ♔b6 57 ♕f6, is just as hopeless. **54 ♕xf7+ ♔c8 55 g7!**, Black resigns.

Against the Yugoslav Kiril Danov, at Skopje 1967, Fischer (Black) made another impressive demonstration of this vision. We shall follow the game (Pos. 320) for some fifteen moves, in order to watch the unfolding of the various motifs to their end.

320                B

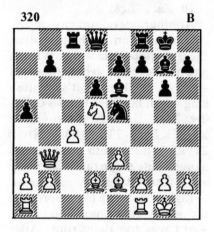

**16 ... b5!**

A positional sacrifice of a pawn, the objective of which is to establish a rook on White's second rank.

**17 ♕xb5**

17 cxb5 a4 18 ♘xe7+ ♕xe7 19 ♕xa4 ♗c4 is certainly a bad bargain for White.

**17 ... ♖b8 18 ♕xa5 ♖xb2 19 ♗f3**

19 ♕xd8 ♖xd8 20 ♖fd1 ♔f8 21 a4 ♖c8, with advantage to Black.

**19 ... ♕d7**

By this simple developing move, Fischer diverts the attention from the queenside to the kingside.

Black will be able to create threats against the white king by a double exchange on f3 and d5, thus freeing the queen's route to h3. At the same time, he maintains his positional threats on the queenside. An immediate threat is 20 ... ♘xc4.

**20 ♖ac1 ♖c8!**

Another development move, that entails an exchange offer. Clearly enough he wants White's pawn at c4. But what about 21 ♘b6 – ? Well, then it's White's king which becomes Black's bull's-eye: 21 ... ♖xb6 22 ♕xb6 ♘xf3+ 23 gxf3 ♗xc4 (23 ... ♗h3 24 ♕b5!) 24 ♖fe1 ♖c5!, with grim threats along White's fifth rank ( ♖b5/g5).

**21 ♗c3 ♘xf3+!**

Rightly deciding to compromise the white king's position. 21 ... ♘xc4 was too dangerous. After 22 ♕a6! both rooks are under attack; note the threat 23 ♕xc8+!.

**22 gxf3 ♗xd5 23 ♕xd5**

He would certainly be happy to get rid of his pawn weakness on c4, but again that would have been fatal to his king's integrity: 23 cxd5 ♖b5 24 ♕a3 ♖xd5 25 ♗xg7 ♖g5+ 26 ♔h1 ♖xc1 27 ♖xc1 ♕h3! with mate. To an even quicker end would lead 23 ♗xg7? ♗xf3!.

**23 ... ♗xc3 24 ♖xc3**

All the light pieces have been traded, yet White's basic predicament remains as valid.

**24 ... ♖c5 25 ♕a8+ ♔g7 26 f4 ♖b7!.** Blocking the h1-a8 diagonal from the white queen 27 ♖fc1 ♕g4+ 28 ♔f1 ♖b2! 29 ♕g2 ♕e2+ 30 ♔g1 ♖xa2. At long last Black has equalised materially, and has managed to gain a complete positional sway, with the better pawn structure, and the more active rooks. He has made the utmost of all the nuances of the positions which arose from move 16 up till the present move. The game was won by Fischer seven moves later.

The last example is the most fascinating of the three. It epitomises our present subject at its highest artistic level. The fugue is a musical form in which two or more musical 'voices' (i.e. themes), are played or sung at the same time, crossing and complementing each other. In chess we are limited to playing one move at a time. It is all the more amazing that one could create "chess-fugues" in which, by constantly playing single notes – moves, that is – one could nonetheless produce different 'voices', which, moreover, co-mingle in perfect harmony. Our musical piece is taken from the encounter between Bertok (White) and Fischer (Black), played at Vinkovci 1968 (Pos. 321).

**13 ... ♕g5!**

"How crude!", you might say. "And what has this to do with

321
B

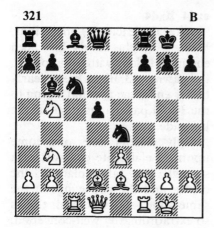

chess-fugues, or whatever you call it? It is just as straightforward as any beginner would have played."

Please, let me explain, then. He evidently has some evil schemes against White's king, or, more specifically – g2. But it is far from being that single-themed 'melody'! The other 'voice', a more subtle one, has to do with the domination of d4. From now on we shall witness a fierce struggle being fought out as to who would be the ultimate boss of this strategic outpost. As long as White can't set a firm foot there, the activity of Black's bishop along the g1-a7 diagonal would be very annoyingly felt by him. For the moment 14 ♘3d4 is unplayable: 14 ... ♘xd4 15 ♘xd4 ♗xd4 16 exd4 ♕xd2, while 14 ♘5d4 loses a pawn after 14 ... ♗xd4!.

**14 ♗c3 ♖e8!**
'Voice A' is the manoeuvre ... ♖e6-g6, playing 'for mate'. 'Voice B' is the pressure along the e-file, reinforcing sacrificial themes on f2 and e3. This implies that White has to act quickly to block Black's dark-squared bishop.

**15 ♗d4**
The first concession. He trades off this bishop for Black's relatively less-active knight at c6. Yet 15 ♘(either)d4, would allow 15 ... ♗h3 16 ♗f3 ♘e5, with a beautiful position.

**15 ... ♘xd4 16 ♘5xd4**
Why not 16 ♘3xd4, keeping the threat of 17 ♘c7 on? – because after 16 ... ♕e5! White has to reckon with the threat of 17 ... a6 followed by 18 ... ♘xf2! winning material – another aspect of the 'battle for d4'.

**16 ... a5!**
Clearly doing everything to undermine the support of White's knight on d4. The tactical justification is quite impressive: 17 a4 ♗h3 18 ♗f3 ♗d7! 19 ♘b5 (19 ♗xe4 dxe4, with the two threats 20 ... ♗xa4 and 20 ... ♗h3) 19 ... ♗xb5 20 axb5 ♘xf2!! 21 ♖xf2 ♕xe3, and White can't defend both the rook on f2 and the knight on b3, for if 17 ♕c2 then 17 ... ♕e1+!.

**17 ♗b5 ♗h3**
In this case 'Voice A' is clearer than ever! 'Voice B' however is to

force a queen exchange on *f4*, again undermining White's stronghold on d4.

**18 ♕f3 ♝g4 19 h4!**

Putting up some fight. After 19 ♕f4 ♕xf4 20 exf4 a4! 21 ♝xe8 ♖xe8 or 21 ... axb3, White is lost.

**19 ... ♕xh4 20 ♕f4 g5! 21 ♕h2 ♕xh2+ 22 ♔xh2 ♖ed8 23 f3**

Black keeps his extra pawn and some positional advantage after 23 a4 ♞d6 24 ♝d3 ♝d7 25 ♖a1 ♖ac8, but this would have offered White better practical chances than in the game.

**23 ... a4 24 fxe4 axb3 25 axb3 ♖a5.** Playable, too, was 25 ... dxe4.

**26 ♝d3 dxe4 27 ♝xe4 ♝xd4 28**

exd4 ♖xd4

After these lengthy operations, White's knight on d4 has been eliminated along with its supporter, the pawn at e3. Black has a clearly better endgame at hand owing to the 3-to-1 pawn advantage on the kingside.

Only seldom does one come upon an elaborate example of a struggle that takes place in the centre and the two wings at the same time, and where all this is so extraordinarily well-concerted, one action perfectly bearing upon the other to create the desired strategic outcome.

A classical representation of a marvellous classical player.

# Epilogue

Being a universal player has always been one of chess's highest ideals. We imagine by that a player who can handle successfully many types of position, who is good in both attack and defence, and whose positional and tactical insights match each other.

We have to bear in mind, at the same time, that the ideal of universality is a very wide substratum which encompasses players of great individual differences. Kasparov, Spassky, Timman and Belyavsky are all universal players; yet what a huge difference there is in the personal chess outlook of each of them!

I hope that this book has given a fairly complete and authentic picture of one of the greatest universal players of chess's short history. But beyond his universality we could mark the personal properties of Fischer's chess approach. Would it be unjust of me to sum it up, for the sake of brevity, in one word – 'coherency'? And yet, one cannot truly be considered a universal player unless one's play manifests one important quality: it has to be, to one extent or another, paradoxical!

The elements of chess are varied and, like those of life itself – which every all-embracing activity largely reflects – are contradictory. If a player truly succeeds in combining them into a whole, it implies that it would be impossible to predict when he would turn from one set of considerations to another, and when he would decide to make use of one element or another: when he would give preference to, say, dynamic positional considerations over material ones, or when taking risks would be considered by him more appropriate than reducing his opponent's options, or when exactly he would liquidate to a technical endgame, and not play for an elegant tactical solution.

Botvinnik once said about Fischer that he was born with the gift for chess – when he played one never knew what he was going to undertake a little bit later. As far as unpredictability is concerned, this is true for any universal player.

And this calls to mind one of the hottest current issues: the future of artificial intelligence in chess.

Much has been written lately about the computer's prospects of taking man's place on the highest chess throne within a few years. Being pre-programmed, the computer would ever fall short of equalling man in one respect: its programs would not be paradoxical enough to make its play unpredictable. Given that its technical capacities would ultimately outmatch human countergifts, it is inconceivable that a computer would make it to the top and stay an absolute chess monarch there. That one weakness – its predictability – would constantly enable human players to devise new methods to oppose it successfully.

And although we could, at times, find fault with a universal player like Fischer for not being true to himself in some of his decisions, a playing machine's greatest weakness, even at the outmost limits of universality possible for AI, would dwell in its being too true to itself.

# References

**What's in a Style?**
1) In his article 'von Stockholm nach Curaçao', *Schweizerische Schachzeitung*, April 1962, p.65.
2) *Shahmat* (Israel), April 1964, p.17.

**Pawn Structure**
1) *Chess Life*, June 1964, p.142.
2) Bobby Fischer, *My 60 Memorable Games*, New York: Simon & Schuster, 1969, p.298.
3) *Chess Life*, November 1966, p.261.
4) Bobby Fischer, *My 60 Memorable Games*, New York: Simon & Schuster, 1969, p.298.
5) 'Shakhmatny Obozrenye', *64*, 1971/21, translated by Peter Avery in *Chess Canada*, June-July 1971, p.3.
6) Bernard Cafferty, Candidates Matches 1971, Nottingham: *The Chess Player*, 1972, p.76.
7) *Fischer versus Spassky*, New York: Simon & Schuster, 1972, p.49.
8) See Karpov-Miles, Skara 1980, which opened 1 e4 a6. Incidentally, the game was won by Miles!
9) *Chess Life & Review*, September 1970, p.491.
10) Aleksei Suetin, *Schachstrategie der Weltmeister*, Sportverlag Berlin, 1983, p.231.
11) Edmar Mednis, *How to Beat Bobby Fischer*, Quadrangle/The New York Times Book Co., p.27.
12) The development of this game up to White's 14th move is identical with four previous games: Gligorić-Sanguinetti, Gligorić-Neikirch and Panno-Benko, all from the 1958 Portorož Interzonal, as well as Kupper-Neikirch from Munich 1958.
13) Vladas Mikenas in: Max Euwe, *From Steinitz to Fischer*, Belgrade: Chess Informant, 1976, p.66.
14) David Bronstein, *The Chess Struggle in Practice*, New York: David McKay Co., 1978, p.470.
15) Bobby Fischer, *My 60 Memorable Games*, New York: Simon & Schuster, 1969, p.293.
16) Idem, p.108.
17) Edmar Mednis, *How to Beat Bobby Fischer*, Quadrangle/The New York Times Book Co., p.27.
18) See for instance:
   Bondarevsky-Petrosian, Moscow 1951
   Petrosian-Szabo, Zürich 1953
   Nezhmetdinov-Petrosian, Kiev 1954

Czerniak-Petrosian, Belgrade 1954
Donner-Petrosian, Gothenburg 1955
Petrosian-Guimard, Gothenburg 1955
Petrosian-Bannik, Riga 1958
Petrosian-Barendregt, Beverwijk 1960
Petrosian-Unzicker, Hamburg 1960
Gurgenidze-Petrosian, Moscow 1961
Bonch Osmolovsky-Petrosian, Moscow 1961
Korchnoi-Petrosian, Candidates (3rd cycle) 1962
Petrosian-Botvinnik, match (7) 1963
Spassky-Petrosian, match (3) 1966
Petrosian-Donner, Santa Monica 1966
Petrosian-Spassky, match (20) 1969
Petrosian-Portisch, match (13) 1974
Petrosian-R.Byrne, Moscow 1975
Petrosian-Portisch, Varese 1976.

19) Tigran Petrosian and Alexander Matanović, eds., *Soviet Union vs. World*, Belgrade: Chess Informant, 1970, p.74.
20) Idem. These moves were mentioned by Fischer.
21) *Chess Life & Review*, August 1970, p.424.
22) Robert G. Wade, *Sousse 1967*, Nottingham: The Chess Player, 1968, p.20.
23) *Schach-Echo* 1972/6, p.89.
24) I am referring to Levy, Chernev, Kmoch, Bisguier & Soltis, Purdy, Paoli, Chistyakov, Reinfeld and Vuković, in various publications. They all mention either 38 ♗g5 followed by ♗xg6 and ♔xh5, or 38 ♖e1 ♔d8 39 ♖e6, as White's methods of maintaining an endgame advantage.
25) Bucharest: Editura Sport-Turism, 1978, p.33.
26) Florin Gheorghiu, *Partide Alese*, Bucharest: Editura Sport-Turism, 1980, p.217.
27) Bobby Fischer, *My 60 Memorable Games*, New York: Simon & Schuster, 1969, p.25.
28) Bernard Cafferty, *Candidates Matches 1971*, Nottingham: The Chess Player, 1972, p.113.
29) Bobby Fischer, *My 60 Memorable Games*, New York: Simon & Schuster, 1969, p.34.
30) Idem, p.176.
31) Idem, p.188.
32) Idem.
33) *New In Chess* magazine 1989/4, p.30.

**Piece Placement**

1) In: Arnold Denker, *My Best Games of Chess*, New York: Dover, 1981, p.194.
2) Related by Zuckerman in an article on the game in *Chess Life*, February 1967, p.39.
3) Isaac Kashdan, ed., *Second Piatigorsky Cup*, Los Angeles: The Ward Ritchie Press, 1968, p.34.
4) *Chess World* (Australia), September-October 1967.
5) November 1970, p.278.
6) *Chess Review*, November 1968, p.329.
7) *Suplemento* No. 29, 1970, p.18.

## Material Considerations

1) Yakov Estrin, *Weltmeister Lehren Schach*, Hollfeld: Joachim Berger Verlag, 1979, p.151.
2) Efim Geller, *The King's Indian Defence*, London: Batsford, 1980, p.93.
3) Mikhail Tal, *The Life and Games of Mikhail Tal*, New York: R.H.M. Press, 1976, p.160.
4) Bobby Fischer, *My 60 Memorable Games*, New York: Simon & Schuster, 1969, p.107, remark to Black's 5th move.
5) *Chess Life*, December 1963, p.302.
6) Alexander Matanović, ed., *Encyclopedia of Chess Openings*, Belgrade: Chess Informant, 1975, Volume B, p.316/65.
7) *Schweizerische Schachzeitung*, June 1960, p.118.
8) Max Euwe, *Bobby Fischer and His Predecessors*, London: Bell & Sons, 1976, p.169. Euwe mentions only 21 ... ♗xf4 and 21 ... ♕d4+.

## Timing

1) Bobby Fischer, *My 60 Memorable Games*, New York: Simon & Schuster, 1969, p.293, remark to White's 19th move.
2) Idem, p.124.
3) *Ajedrez*, December 1966, p.400.
4) Bernard Cafferty, *Candidates Matches 1971*, Nottingham: The Chess Player, 1972, p.177.
5) Idem.
6) Idem.
7) Bobby Fischer, *My 60 Memorable Games*, New York: Simon & Schuster, 1969, p.177.
8) *Deutsche Schachblätter*, January 1971, p.3.
9) Robert G. Wade and Kevin J. O'Connell, eds., *The Games of Robert J. Fischer*, London: Batsford, 1973, p.392.
10) January 1988, pp.22-23.
11) June 1988, p.7.

## Strategy

### Strategic Plans

1) Gideon Barcza, Läszlo Alföldy, Jenö Kapu, *Die Weltmeister des Schachspiels*, Vol. 2, Hungary: Corvina Verlag, 1975, p.320.
2) Max Euwe, *Veldheerschap op 64 Velden*, Amsterdam: Elsevier, p.143. Raymond Keene & David Levy, *Siegen Chess Olympiad*, Sutton Coldfield: Chess, p.127.

### Seizing the Initiative

1) *Deutsche Schachzeitung*, October 1968, game 5368.
2) Robert G. Wade and Les S. Blackstock, eds., *Interzonal Chess Tournament, Palma de Mallorca 1970*, Nottingham: The Chess Player, 1970, p.52. Wade pointed out that after 16 ♖ac1 ♕b7 "Black should have the opportunity to play ... d3 keeping the file on to the weak d-pawn closed".

### Typical Manoeuvres

1) Max Euwe, *Bobby Fischer and His Predecessors*, London: Bell & Sons, 1976, p.99.
2) *Chess Canada*, September 1971, p.8.

3)  Aleksei Suetin, *Schachstrategie der Weltmeister*, Sportverlag Berlin, 1983, p.233.
4)  Chief amongst them Suetin in the above.
5)  Idem.

*The Art and Craft of Liquidation*

1)  *Suplemento* No 29, 1970, p.28.
2)  Idem.
3)  Fischer won by: **40 ♗c6 ♔e7 41 h4 h6 42 ♔e3 ♘c8 43 ♔d3 ♘d6 44 ♔e3 ♔d8 45 ♔d3 ♔c7 46 ♗a4 ♔b6 47 ♔e3 ♔c5 48 ♗d7 ♔b6 49 ♗a4 ♔c7 50 ♔d3 ♔d8 51 ♗c6 ♔e7 52 ♔e3 ♔e6 53 ♔f3 ♔f6 54 g4 g5 55 h5 ♔e7 56 ♔e3 ♔d8 57 ♔d3 ♔c7 58 ♗a4 ♔b6 59 ♗d7 ♔c5 60 ♗a4 ♘c8 61 ♗e8 ♘e7 62 ♔e3 ♘g8 63 ♗d7 ♘f6 64 ♗f5 ♔b5 65 ♔d3 a4 66 bxa4+ ♔xa4 67 ♔c4 ♔a3 68 ♔c5 ♔xa2 69 ♔xb4 ♔b2 70 ♔c5 ♔c3 71 ♔d6 ♔d4 72 ♔e6 ♘xe4 73 ♔f7 ♘f2 74 ♔g6 e4 75 ♔xh6 e3 76 ♔g7 e2 77 h6 e1=♕ 78 h7 ♕e7+ 79 ♔g8 ♘e4, 0-1.** Damjanović maintained that his 66th move was a grave error (??), and that **66 ♔e3 a3 67 ♔d3** was the right way to draw. However, in *The Best Endings of Capablanca and Fischer*, published by Chess Informant, Belgrade 1978, Matanović, on p.129, Pos. 190, shows that Black wins by **67 ... ♔c5 68 ♔e3 ♘e8 69 ♔d3 ♘d6 70 ♗d7 ♘c4! 71 ♗e8 ♘b2+ 72 ♔c2 ♔d4,** or **72 ♔e3 ♘d1+** followed by ... ♘c3.
4)  Bernard Cafferty, *Candidates Matches 1971*, Nottingham: The Chess Player, 1972, p.176, remark to Black's (Fischer's) 13th move in the 6th match game against Petrosian, Candidates, Buenos Aires 1971.
5)  Isaac Kashdan, ed., *Second Piatigorsky Cup*, Los Angeles: The Ward Ritchie Press, 1968, p.26.
6)  *Chess Review*, September 1959, p.269.
7)  *Shakhmatny Moskva*, 30 June 1962, p.2.
8)  *Shakhmatny Ezhegodnik 1962*, Moscow: Fizkultura i Sport, 1964, p.49.
9)  *Turnir Pretendentov*, Central Chess Club, Moscow, 16th June 1962.
10) *Petrosian's Best Games of Chess*, London: Bell & Sons, 1964, p.180.
11) 1962/8, p.123.
12) *Shakhmatny Ezhegodnik 1962*, Moscow: Fizkultura i Sport, 1964, p.180.
13) Bobby Fischer, *My 60 Memorable Games*, New York: Simon & Schuster, 1969, p.227.
14) April 1989, p.14.

*Maintaining the Positional Tension*

1)  *Shakhmatny Ezhegodnik 1960*, Moscow: Fizkultura i Sport, 1962, p.359.
2)  Robert G. Wade and Kevin J. O'Connell, eds., *The Games of Robert J. Fischer*, London: Batsford, 1973, p.211.
3)  The details of this incident were related by Andy Soltis in *Chess Life*, June 1986, p.10.
4)  Aleksandr S. Nikitin, *Sitsilianskaya Zashchita*, Moscow: Fizkultura i Sport, 1969, p.50.
5)  R.Byrne, Moiseyev, Tal and Balashov, among others.
6)  *Chess Life & Review*, August 1971, p.421.

*Switching Advantages*

1)  Boris S. Vainstein, *David Bronstein – Chess Improviser*, Oxford: Pergamon Press, 1983, p.121.
2)  Bernard Cafferty, *Candidates Matches 1971*, Nottingham: The Chess Player, 1972, p.177.

3) Idem.
4) Idem.
5) April 1972, p.54.
6) *Chess Canada*, December 1971, p.3.
7) Reuben Fine, *The World's Great Chess Games*, New York: Dover, 1976, p.376.
8) *British Chess Magazine*, December 1971, p.431.
9) *Chess Life & Review*, February 1972, p.85.
10) José Maria González, ed., *Match Final de Candidatos Fischer-Petrosian Buenos Aires 1971*, San Sebastián: Jaque, 1971, p.65.
11) *Three Steps to Chess Mastery*, Oxford: Pergamon Press, 1982, p.156.

*Playing for Space*
1) Hans Kmoch, *Chess Review* May 1969, p.152.
2) *Partide Alese*, Bucharest: Editura Sport-Turism, 1980, p.217.

*The Role of Aesthetics*
1) *New in Chess* magazine 1989/2, p.97.
2) Anatoly Karpov, *Chess at the Top*, Oxford: Pergamon Press, 1984, p.190.
3) *Chess Praxis*, New York: Dover Publications Inc., 1962, p.329.
4) Uldis Roze, *The Living Earth, An Introduction to Biology*, New York: Thomas J. Crowell Company, 1976, p.87.
5) *Scientific American*, November 1989, p.19.
6) Yakov Estrin, *Weltmeister Lehren Schach*, Hollfeld: Joachim Berger Verlag, 1979, p.152.
*Weltgeschichte des Schachs, Lieferung 27 – Boris Spassky*, Hamburg: Verlag Dr E. Wildhagen, 1972, last page.
7) *Sahovski Glasnik* (Yugoslavia) 1970/7, p.213.

*The Poetry of Empty Squares*
1) Yakov Estrin & Isaac Romanov, *The World Champions Teach Chess*, London: A & C Black, 1988, p.145.
2) *Chess Review*, April 1962, p.106.
3) Bobby Fischer, *My 60 Memorable Games*, New York: Simon & Schuster, 1969, p.146.
4) *Schach*, December 1960, p.358.
5) Mikhail Tal, *The Life and Games of Mikhail Tal*, New York: R.H.M. Press, 1976, p.213.
6) Fischer-Darga, West Berlin 1960; Fischer-Mednis, US Championship 1962-63.
7) Jan Timman, *The Art of Chess Analysis*, New York: R.H.M. Press, 1980, p.241.
8) May 1964, p.145.
9) January 1964, p.9.
10) Bobby Fischer, *My 60 Memorable Games*, New York: Simon & Schuster, 1969, p.289.
11) Explained in his book *Think Like a Grandmaster*, London: Batsford, 1971, pp.56-58.
12) *Boys' Life*, June 1968, p.22.
13) Bernard Cafferty, *Candidates Matches 1971*, Nottingham: The Chess Player, 1972, p.188.
14) *Chess Review*, March 1963, p.72.
15) *How to Beat Bobby Fischer*, Quadrangle/The New York Times Book Co., p.182.

**Clarity**
1) The liquidation to an active queen + rooks endgame, which might be the con-

sequence of this move, was quite typical of Capablanca, and occurred in a great number of his games. See for instance:

Janowski-Capablanca, New York 1918
Capablanca-Marshall, New York 1924
Yates-Capablanca, Moscow 1925
Dus Khotimirsky-Capablanca, Moscow 1925
Maroczy-Capablanca, Lake Hopatcong 1926
Capablanca-Vidmar, New York 1927
Nimzowitsch-Capablanca, New York, March 1927
Capablanca-Alekhine, match (1) 1927
Capablanca-Alekhine, match (5) 1927
Capablanca-Alekhine, match (25) 1927
Capablanca-Alekhine, match (27) 1927
Rubinstein-Capablanca, Berlin 1928
Capablanca-Michell, Ramsgate 1929
Winter-Capablanca, Ramsgate 1929
Yates-Capablanca, Ramsgate 1929
Colle-Capablanca, Carlsbad 1929
van den Bosch-Capablanca, Budapest 1929
Prokeš-Capablanca, Budapest 1929
Ribera-Capablanca, Barcelona 1929
Euwe-Capablanca, match (6) 1931
Alatortsev-Capablanca, Moscow 1935
Capablanca-Eliskases, Moscow 1936
Capablanca-Stahlberg, Buenos Aires 1939

Of interest are also:

Watson-Capablanca, London 1922
Bogoljubow-Capablanca, New York 1924
Nimzowitsch-Capablanca, New York, February 1927

2) Bobby Fischer, *My 60 Memorable Games*, New York: Simon & Schuster, 1969, p.256.
3) *Europe Echecs*, November 1962, p.237.
4) *Deutsche Schachblätter*, October-November 1962, p.241.
5) New York: David McKay Co., 1978, p.139.
6) 'Bronstein on his match for the World Championship', in Boris S. Vainstein, *David Bronstein – Chess Improviser*, Oxford: Pergamon Press, 1983, pp.118-9.

**Straightforwardness**
1) 'Shakhmatny Obozrenye', *64*, 1971/21, p.4, translated by Peter Avery, *Chess Canada*, June-July 1971, p.3.
2) *Chess Life & Review*, August 1971, p.20.
3) *Chess Informant* 9/356.
4) Irving Chernev, *The Most Instructive Games of Chess Ever Played*, London: Faber & Faber, 1966, p.125.
5) Tigran Petrosian, *Strategiya Nadezhnosti*, Moscow: Fizkultura i Sport, 1985, p.271, translated in David Levy, *How Fischer Plays Chess*, Glasgow and London: Collins 1975, p.135.

6) Tigran Petrosian and Alexander Matanović, eds., *Soviet Union vs. World*, Belgrade: Chess Informant, 1970, p.72.
7) Anatoly Karpov: 'After the match that did not take place', in: Kevin J. O'Connell and David Levy, *Anatoly Karpov's Games as World Champion 1975-77*, London: Batsford 1978, p.14.
8) Mikhail Tal, V.Chepizhny & Aleksandr Roshal, *Montreal 1979, Tournament of Stars*, Oxford: Pergamon Press, 1980, p.114, notes to the game Ljubojević-Larsen from the 10th round.
9) *Chess Life*, December 1962, p.275.
10) Isaac Kashdan, ed., *Second Piatigorsky Cup*, Los Angeles: The Ward Ritchie Press, 1968, p.63.
11) *Grandmaster Preparation*, Oxford: Pergamon Press, 1981, p.230.

**Alertness**

1) *Chess Review*, September 1959, p.267.
2) Ničevski's birthplace was taken from: Jeremy Gaige, *Chess Personalia: A Biobibliography*, Jefferson: McFarland & Co. Inc., 1987, p.302.
3) Bobby Fischer, *My 60 Memorable Games*, New York: Simon & Schuster, 1969, p.28.
4) Mentioned by Fischer in the above, p.29.

**Reducing the Opponent's Options**

1) David Levy, *Karpov's Collected Games*, London: Robert Hale Company, 1975. Karpov's notes to game 461, p.239.
2) *Fischer versus Spassky*, New York: Simon & Schuster, 1972, p.104.
3) *Bobby Fischer's Conquest of the World Chess Championship*, London: Bell & Sons, 1973, p.251.
4) December 1972, p.747.
5) Mikhail Tal, *The Life and Games of Mikhail Tal*, New York: R.H.M. Press, 1976, p.241.

**Playing to Win**

*The Will to Win*

1) 7/407.
2) Idem.

*Active Defence and Counterplay*

1) Related by Tal in *The Life and Games of Mikhail Tal*, New York: R.H.M. Press, 1976, p.106.
2) Pointed out by Ludek Pachman in *Schach-Echo*, January 1967, p.8.
3) *XVII Schacholympiade 1966*, Sportverlag Berlin 1967, p.171.
4) This line was partly mentioned by Hans Kmoch in *Chess Review*, September 1968, p.281.
5) 'The chance I missed', September 1971, p.9.
6) Mr Joop Piket, father of GM Jeroen Piket.

*Taking Risks*

1) October 1965, p.317.

2) Wade (in *Chess*, 22nd October 1965), *Ajedrez* (*Suplemento* No. 13, 1965, p.4) besides Kmoch and Najdorf.
3) Kmoch in *Chess Review* (October 1965, p.317) writes: "Najdorf, who happened to be in New York, was shown this game and recalled that 16 ♗g5 was once played with devastating effect".
4) *Fischer's Chess Games*, Oxford University Press, 1980, p.43.
5) Y.Averbakh, M.A.Beyline, *Voyage au royaume des échecs*, Paris: Payot, 1980, p.280.
6) *Fischer's Chess Games*, Oxford University Press, 1980, p.20.
7) Vol. 7 No. 9, September 1968, pp.241-2.
8) August 1968, pp.183-4.
9) *Chess Review*, May 1966, p.157.

## Practical Chances

### Exploiting Practical Chances

1) *Weltschachturnier, Zürich 1959*, Zürich: Edition Olms, 1959, p.199.
2) *Chess Life & Review*, January 1971, p.66.
3) Bronstein (in *64*), O'Kelly (in *Europe Echecs*), Wade (in the tournament book), Medina (in *Jaque Mate*), the magazines *Revista de Sah* and the Latvian *Sahs*.

### Traps

1) Item 1696 in The Russell Collection, taken from *Chess Notes* No. 45, Edward Winter, ed., Geneva, May-June 1989, p.75.
2) *Sahovski Glasnik* (Yugoslavia), July 1970, pp.203-4.
4) Svetozar Gligorić and Vladimir Ragozin, *Kandidatenturnier Für Schachweltmeisterschaft, Bled, Zagreb, Beograd 1959*, Belgrade: Yugoslav Chess Federation, 1960, p.79.
5) *Chess Review*, November 1961, p.332.
6) *Editor's note.* Obviously the author refers to the first game of the 1972 World Championship match, in which the following position was reached:

      White: ♔d3 ♗c1  ♙a3, b5, e3, f2, g2, h2
      Black: ♔f8 ♗d6  ♙a7, b7, e6, f6, g7, h7.

    Fischer played 29 ... ♗xh2, and after 30 g3 followed by king to the kingside Black was soon a piece for two pawns down.

    At one level, a 'primary school blunder' certainly, but on reading the chapters on 'Taking Risks' and 'Exploiting Practical Chances', one suspects that this was a deliberate effort by Fischer to *win*, or at least to create residual winning chances. In which case, one wonders whether Spassky was not so much setting a shallow chess trap but rather a very deep psychological one. In his preparation for the match he would doubtless have taken note of games in which Fischer had gone very close to the brink in attempting to win a drawish position, and might well have reasoned that if presented with highly simplified positions early in the match, before he had had time to settle down, there was a fair chance that Fischer would present an easy point by going berserk trying to win. Plausible?

## Tactics

### Tactical Insight

1) Keres, Euwe, Sosonko, Wade, Gheorghiu, Stefaniu, Trifunović, in various publi-

cations, mentioned only the unplayability of 28 ... dxe4 29 ♘3xe4.
2)  Mednis, Gligorić, Cirić, Boleslavsky, in various publications.
3)  April 1967, pp.88-89.

*Double-Edged and Speculative Chess*
1)  *Chess Review*, July 1962, p.220.
2)  *Chess Review*, April 1962, p.108.
3)  José María González, ed., *Match Final de Candidatos Fischer-Petrosian Buenos Aires 1971*, San Sebastián: Jaque 1971, p.35. Remark to move 11 in the 3rd game.
4)  Paul Keres: 'Bobby Fischer — from the opposite side of the board', in: Robert G. Wade and Kevin J. O'Connell, eds., *The Games of Robert J. Fischer*, London: Batsford, 1979, p.323.
5)  p.364.
6)  *Schach-Echo* 1968/4, pp.56-7.
7)  Oxford: Pergamon Press, 1984, p.246.
8)  May 1967, p.87.
9)  Bobby Fischer, *My 60 Memorable Games*, New York: Simon & Schuster, 1969, p.365. What Fischer missed was the fact that after 22 ♕g4 ♗f6 23 ♖xf6 ♗xb3 24 ♖f4 Black had 24 ... ♗a2+!, forcing mate.
10)  *The Application of Chess Theory*, Oxford: Pergamon Press, 1984, pp.251-2.
11)  Raymond Keene, *The Chess Combination from Philidor to Karpov*, Oxford: Pergamon Press, 1977, p.139.
12)  Paul Keres and Ivo Nei, *4 x 25*, Tallinn: Eesti Raamat, 1975, p.60.
13)  *Shakhmaty v SSSR*, November 1970, p.19.
14)  *Sahovski Glasnik* (Yugoslavia), July 1970, p.185.
15)  *How Fischer Plays Chess*, Glasgow and London: Collins 1975, p.138.
16)  Román Torán, *David Bronstein*, Amsterdam: W. Ten Have Verlag, 1962, p.22.
17)  Tigran Petrosian and Alexander Matanović, eds., *Soviet Union vs World*, Belgrade: Chess Informant, 1970, p.40.
18)  *Bobby Fischer and His Predecessors*, London: Bell & Sons, 1976, p.109.
19)  David Levy, *How Fischer Plays Chess*, Glasgow and London: Collins, 1975, p.132.
20)  *Chess Life & Review*, July 1971, p.369.
21)  *Sachmatna Mis'l* (Bulgaria), 1970/6, p.64.
22)  *Chess*, April 20th 1970, p.255.
23)  Tigran Petrosian and Alexander Matanović, eds., *Soviet Union vs World*, Belgrade: Chess Informant, 1970, p.40.
24)  *Chess Life*, October 1966, p.247.
25)  Isaac Kashdan, ed., *Second Piatigorsky Cup*, Los Angeles: The Ward Ritchie Press, 1968, p.181.
26)  p.18.
27)  Idem

*Missing Tactical Tricks*
1)  Isaac Kashdan, ed., *Second Piatigorsky Cup*, Los Angeles: The Ward Ritchie Press, 1968, p.27.
2)  October 1989, p.22.
3)  *Chess*, December 11th 1967, p.102.

4) The main line of this continuation was mentioned in Robert G. Wade and Kevin J. O'Connell, eds., *The Games of Robert J. Fischer*, London: Batsford, 1973, p.279.
5) *XVII Schacholympiade Havana 1966*, Sportverlag Berlin, 1967, p.26.
6) July 1988, pp.28-9.

**Technical Aspects**

*Technique*
1) Robert G. Wade and Kevin J. O'Connell, eds., *The Games of Robert J. Fischer*, London: Batsford, 1973, p.207.
2) Pointed out by Fischer in *My 60 Memorable Games*, New York: Simon & Schuster, 1969, p.239.
3) *Think Like a Grandmaster*, London: Batsford, 1974, p.63.

*The Bishop Pair*
1) Isaac Kashdan, ed., *Second Piatigorsky Cup*, Los Angeles: The Ward Ritchie Press, 1968, p.34.
2) Bernard Cafferty, *Candidates Matches 1971*, Nottingham: The Chess Player, 1972, pp.183-4.

*Rook Endgames with Bishops of Opposite Colours*
1) Feurstein-Fischer, Log Cabin 1957 (½-½),
   Fischer-Sandrin, North Central Open 1957 (1-0),
   Walther-Fischer, Zürich 1959 (½-½),
   Benko-Fischer, 1st cycle, Candidates 1959 (½-½),
   Fischer-Reshevsky, match (4) 1961 (½-½),
   Fischer-Benko, 2nd cycle, Candidates 1962 (1-0),
   Fischer-Korchnoi, 3rd cycle, Candidates 1962 (0-1, Pos. 301),
   Fischer-Addison, US Championship 1962-63 (1-0),
   Greenwald-Fischer, New York Open 1963 (0-1),
   Fischer-Addison, US Championship 1966-67 (½-½),
   Minić-Fischer, Rovinj-Zagreb 1970 (½-½),
   Korchnoi-Fischer, Rovinj-Zagreb 1970 (½-½),
   Fischer-Polugayevsky, Palma de Mallorca 1970 (½-½),
   plus the six games from which the positions in this section are taken.
2) Alexander Matanović, ed., *The Best Endings of Capablanca and Fischer*, Belgrade: Chess Informant, 1978, p.100, Position 106.
3) Idem.

**Superficiality**
1) Yakov Estrin and Isaac Romanov, *The World Champions Teach Chess*, London: A & C Black, 1988, p.148.
2) See his remark in *My 60 Memorable Games*, p.139.
3) *Fischer versus Spassky*, New York: Simon & Schuster, 1972, p.83.

**Misplaying Won Positions**
1) *Chess Life & Review*, August 1971, p.421.
2) Vuković in *Sahovski Glasnik*, June 1959, p.124. Trifunović in *Yugoslav Chess*

*Triumphs*, Belgrade: Chess Informant, 1976, game 708, pp.277-8.
3) *Losbladige Schaakberichten* (Chess Archives), 5 September 1959.
4) Chess Review, June 1959, p.179.
5) p.275.

**Typical Blunders and Oversights**
1) Fischer's comment in *Chess Informant* 10/155.
2) *Chess Life*, October 1963, p.238, with reference to White's 12th move in Greenwald-Fischer, New York State Open 1963.
3) Kmoch, Euwe, Unzicker, Milić, Mednis, in various publications.
4) May 1988, p.18.
5) Oxford: Pergamon Press, 1984, p.242.
6) Bent Larsen, *Larsen's Selected Games of Chess 1948-69*, London: Bell & Sons, 1970, p.123.
7) Idem, p.124.

**Towards a Comprehensive Vision**

*The Grand Lines*
1) Jaan Eslon pointed out the relationship of these two games in an article in *New In Chess* magazine 1988/4, pp.43-7.
2) Ludek Pachman, *Decisive Games in Chess History*, New York: Dover, 1972, p.243.
3) Svetozar Gligorić, *The French Defence*, New York: R.H.M. Press, 1975, p.85.
4) *Het Groot Analyseboek*, Amsterdam: Andriessen, 1979, p.32.
5) Idem, pp.32-3.
6) Idem.

*The Unified Vision*
1) *Shahmat* (Israel), April 1966, p.96.
2) These moves were pointed out by David Levy in his book *How Fischer Plays Chess*, Glasgow and London: Collins, 1975, p.61.

# Index

*Numbers refer to diagrams and neighbouring text*

Addison   3, 108, 178, 292
Ader   102
Agdestein   41
Alekhine   74, 102, 167, 252, 261
Alvarez   75
Andersson   80, 102, 204, 262
Averbakh   98, 157, 225

Balashov   25
Barcza   4, 104, 167, 179
Baron   314
Bazan   208
Belyavsky   epilogue
Benko   42, 171, 207
Berliner   1, 256
Bertok   166, 279, 321
Bhend   92
Bijl   introduction
Bisguier   2, 25, 37, 89, 105, 153, 196, 253, 273
Blau   139
Bogdanović   251
Bolbochan, Jacopo   11, 12, 13, 278
Boleslavsky   90, 144, 217
Botvinnik   1, 52, 102, 137, 155, 167, 190, 217, 231, 285, 293, 319, epilogue
Bronstein   41, 52, 155, 180, 252, 253
Browne   305
Bukić   90
Burger   228
Byrne, Donald   65, 268
Byrne, Robert   18, 150, 154, 158, 181, 200, 254, 264, 312

Capablanca   157, 162, 175, 272
Cardoso   85

Chandler 316
Chigorin 252
Ciocaltea 17, 151, 236, 283
Clarke 144
Coudari 230
Czerniak 218

Damjanović 132
Danov 320
Doda 249
Donner 19, 214, 248
Durao 58, 118, 149, 246
Dubois 295

Eliskases 41, 310
Elo 213
Emma 21
Euwe 20, 92, 104, 121, 253, 302
Evans 234, 298, 303

Filip 112, 212
Fine 158, 200
Flohr 253
Foguelman 241
Forintoš 291
Frost, Robert 167

Geller 84, 114, 169, 181, 202, 205, 250, 251, 252, 307, 308
German 38
Gheorghiu 57, 64, 111, 120, 130
Gligorić 30, 47, 71, 78, 81, 142, 164, 175, 187, 199, 200, 204, 237, 238, 244, 252, 296
Gufeld 186

Hort 69, 93, 110, 259, 287
Hübner 100, 234

Ibrahimoglu 74
Ilievski 152
Ivanchuk 65
Ivkov 36, 40, 73, 245, 284, 302

Jacob, François 162
Jimenez 247, 286
Johannessen 176, 217
Johansson 106

Kagan 51
Kalme 210, 211
Kan 144
Karpov 162, 170, 175, 184, 185, 197, 217
Kashdan 184
Kasparov 41, 102, 145, 167, 184, epilogue
Keene 104, 252
Keller 43
Keres 39, 96, 114, 145, 231, 250, 252, 267, 271
Kholmov 313, 317
Kmoch 167, 171, 174, 222, 228, 239, 251, 302
Korchnoi 35, 98, 173, 181, 182, 206, 215, 220, 301
Kotov 4, 171, 271
Kuprejanov 230
Kurajica 131

Larsen 61, 127, 128, 129, 131, 156, 157, 162, 170, 204, 219, 220, 254, 265, 270, 278, 280, 315, 317
Lasker 220, 226
Lehmann 222
Letelier 66, 68, 282, 294, 296, 311
Levy 104, 252
Lilienthal 251, 319
Littlewood 260
Ljubojević 252
Lombardy 50

Matanović 101, 316
Matulović 78, 86, 197, 205
Mecking 272
Mednis 8, 36, 43, 76, 91, 174, 227, 300
Mendes 281
Miagmarsuren 52, 168, 172
Miles 31
Minev 94
Minić 70, 252, 287
Monod, Jacques 162
Moss 226
Muñoz 127, 128, 131

Najdorf 16, 19, 24, 60, 67, 124, 157, 158, 163, 179, 183, 223, 250, 264
Naranja 127, 129
Nei 314
Neikirch 253

Nezhmetdinov 252
Ničevski 22, 191
Nikitin 41, 154
Nikolić, Predrag 316
Nimzowitsch 162, 218

Olafsson, Fridrik 10, 44, 45, 49, 146, 147
O'Kelly 179, 251

Pachman 31, 53, 95, 235, 242, 288, 317
Panno 97, 243
Parma 27, 290
Penrose, Roger 162, 166
Petrosian 5, 6, 23, 46, 59, 70, 88, 98, 102, 144, 157, 158, 166, 173, 184, 185, 194, 217, 250, 253, 271, 285, 319
Perez 221
Pilnik 62
Polugayevsky 158, 189, 248
Pomar 141, 255, 293
Popel 117
Popov 229
Porat 109
Portisch 26, 97, 125, 136, 166, 188, 244, 257

Reshevsky 29, 41, 63, 64, 99, 107, 151, 192, 193, 239, 256, 261, 271, 304
Riumin 252
Robatsch 70, 274
Rogers 162
Rojan 253
Romanishin 170
Rossetto 14
Rossolimo 266
Roze, Uldis 162
Rubinetti 275
Rubinstein 272
Rustaveli, Shota 167

Saidy 32, 116, 160, 195, 204
Sanguinetti 309
Sarapu 101, 298
Schoene 138
Schweber 121, 244, 280
Seirawan 204
Shamkovich 98, 134, 157, 180

Sherwin 113, 240, 277, 299
Smyslov 34, 115, 119, 123, 148, 162, 175, 203
Soruco 79
Spassky 27, 28, 30, 48, 72, 83, 96, 147, 165, 185, 200, 204, 250, 258, 263, 296, 318, epilogue
Speelman 252
Stefaniu 57
Stein 252, 260
Steiner, Herman 184
Steinitz 295
Steinmeyer 297
Suarez 157
Suetin 33, 61, 131, 144, 158, 253, 315
Sultanbeieff 91
Suttles 68, 155, 269
Szabo 103, 135, 209, 225

Taimanov 7, 13, 25, 55, 56, 122, 154, 156, 181, 205, 224
Tal 1, 25, 42, 54, 84, 102, 137, 162, 169, 175, 181, 190, 201, 216, 230, 231, 250, 251, 252
Tarrasch 162
Tatai 74
Timman 65, 162, 170, 252, 317, epilogue
Tolush 252
Trifunović 9, 33, 47, 237, 253, 302
Troianescu 77, 276
Tukmakov 82

Udovčić 33
Uhlmann 87, 143, 198, 230, 232, 233, 306
Uitumen 159
Unzicker 104, 134, 319

Vaganian 204, 252
Verhoeven introduction
Vitolins 157
Vuković 237, 252, 302

Wade 52, 112, 168, 289

Yanofsky, Daniel 140, 226

Zagoriansky 225
Zaitsev, Igor 317
Zuckerman 72, 236